PIMLICO

271

# PERSONAL IMPRESSIONS

Sir Isaiah Berlin, OM, who died in 1997, was born in Riga, capital of Latvia, in 1909. When he was six, his family moved to Russia: there in 1917, in Petrograd, he witnessed both the Social-Democratic and the Bolshevik Revolutions.

In 1921 his family came to England, and he was educated at St Paul's School and Corpus Christi College, Oxford. At Oxford he was a Fellow of All Souls, a Fellow of New College, Professor of Social and Political Theory, and founding President of Wolfson College. He also held the Presidency of the British Academy. His published work includes *Karl Marx*, *Four Essays on Liberty*, *Vico and Herder*, *Russian Thinkers*, *Concepts and Categories*, *Against the Current*, *The Crooked Timber of Humanity*, *The Sense of Reality* and *The Proper Study of Mankind*. As an exponent of the history of ideas he was awarded the Erasmus, Lippincott and Agnelli Prizes: he also received the Jerusalem Prize for his lifelong defence of civil liberties.

Dr Henry Hardy, a Supernumerary Fellow of Wolfson College, Oxford, has edited several other collections of Isaiah Berlin's work, and is currently preparing his letters and his unpublished writings for publication.

Lord Annan's career reflects a lifelong dedication to education and the arts. He has been Provost of King's College, Cambridge, Provost of University College London, and Vice-Chancellor of the University of London. He has also been Chairman of the Trustees of the National Gallery, a Trustee of the British Museum, and a Director of the Royal Opera House, Covent Garden. His books include *Leslie Stephen* and *Our Age*.

*Also by Isaiah Berlin*

✻

KARL MARX
THE AGE OF ENLIGHTENMENT
FOUR ESSAYS ON LIBERTY
VICO AND HERDER

*Edited by Henry Hardy and Aileen Kelly*

RUSSIAN THINKERS

*Edited by Henry Hardy*

CONCEPTS AND CATEGORIES
AGAINST THE CURRENT
THE CROOKED TIMBER OF HUMANITY
THE MAGUS OF THE NORTH
THE SENSE OF REALITY

*Edited by Henry Hardy and Roger Hausheer*

THE PROPER STUDY OF MANKIND

# PERSONAL IMPRESSIONS

## ISAIAH BERLIN

Edited by Henry Hardy
With an introduction by Noel Annan

*Second Edition*

PIMLICO

Published by Pimlico 1998

2 4 6 8 10 9 7 5 3 1

Copyright Isaiah Berlin 1949, 1951, 1955
© Isaiah Berlin 1958, 1964, 1965, 1966, 1971, 1972, 1973,
1975, 1976, 1979, 1980, 1986, 1987, 1989, 1993
This selection and editorial matter © Henry Hardy 1980, 1998
Introduction © Noel Annan 1980, 1998

Isaiah Berlin asserts the moral right to be identified as the
author of this work and Henry Hardy as its editor in
accordance with the Copyright, Designs and Patents Act, 1988

First edition first published by
The Hogarth Press in 1980

Pimlico
Random House, 20 Vauxhall Bridge Road,
London SW1V 2SA

Random House Australia (Pty) Limited
20 Alfred Street, Milsons Point, Sydney,
New South Wales 2061, Australia

Random House New Zealand Limited
18 Poland Road, Glenfield,
Auckland 10, New Zealand

Random House South Africa (Pty) Limited
Endulini, 5A Jubilee Road, Parktown 2193, South Africa

Random House UK Limited Reg. No 954009

A CIP catalogue record for this book
is available from the British Library

ISBN 0 7126 6601 X

Papers used by Random House UK Limited are natural,
recyclable products made from wood grown in sustainable forests.
The manufacturing processes conform to the environmental
regulations of the country of origin

Typeset by Deltatype Limited, Birkenhead, Merseyside
Printed and bound in Great Britain by
Mackays of Chatham PLC

To the memory of
Geoffrey Wilkinson
1921–1996

# CONTENTS

# ILLUSTRATIONS

*between pages 96 and 97*

1 Winston Churchill on his way to 10 Downing Street, 1940
2 Franklin D. Roosevelt
3 Chaim Weizmann in 1945
4 Albert Einstein in Christ Church Meadow, Oxford, 1932
5 Yitzhak Sadeh
6 L. B. Namier
7 Felix Frankfurter in his office in the Supreme Court
8 Richard Pares
9 Hubert Henderson
10 J. L. Austin in 1952
11 John Plamenatz
12 Maurice Bowra in Oxford, 1950
13 Lord David Cecil and the author in the cloisters, New College, Oxford, 1950
14 Virginia Woolf
15 Edmund Wilson, c.1953
16 Auberon Herbert in the garden at Pixton, his home in Somerset
17 Aldous Huxley
18 Anna Akhmatova and Boris Pasternak at a public reading in Moscow, 1946

Photo credits: 1, 2, 4, 6, 10, 12, The Hulton Getty Collection; 3, Bernard Hoffmann/*Life* © Time Inc. 1945 (print supplied by the Weizmann Archives); 5, Yoram Sadeh; 7, *New York Times*; 8, 9, The Warden and Fellows of All Souls College, Oxford; 11, The Warden and Fellows of Nuffield College, Oxford; 13, 18, author's collection; 14, Ian Parsons; 15, Sylvia Salmi (print supplied by Farrar, Straus and Giroux); 16, Mrs E. Grant; 17, Chatto and Windus

# AUTHOR'S PREFACE
# TO THE FIRST EDITION

THIS VOLUME consists of writings that resemble what in the eighteenth century were called *éloges* – addresses commemorating the illustrious dead. All but two of these were composed in response to specific requests: the exceptions, those on Franklin Roosevelt and Lewis Namier, as well as 'Meetings with Russian Writers', were not commissioned, and were written because I believed that I had something to say which had not, so far as I knew, been said elsewhere.

The form, and to some extent the content, of these tributes was largely determined by the purposes for which they were intended. Thus the memoirs of Maurice Bowra and John Plamenatz were obituary addresses read at memorial services in Oxford; the article on Chaim Weizmann was delivered as a public lecture in London on a somewhat similar occasion; those on Richard Pares, Hubert Henderson, J. L. Austin, Aldous Huxley, Felix Frankfurter and Auberon Herbert were requested by editors of academic journals or commemorative volumes. The essay on Albert Einstein was the inaugural address read at a centenary symposium in his honour: my intention was to bring out his sharp awareness of social reality and of the importance of truths unwelcome to some of those who paid him homage as a saintly and withdrawn thinker who saw the world through a haze of vague-minded idealism. The essay on Churchill was originally a review of the second volume of his war memoirs; it was written at a time when he was Leader of the Opposition in the House of Commons and had begun to be widely and fiercely criticised, sometimes with good reason, on both sides of the Atlantic. I thought, and still think, that his part in 1940 in saving England (and, indeed, the vast majority of mankind) from Hitler had been insufficiently remembered and that the balance needed to be restored. So, too, in the case of President Franklin

Roosevelt, I wished to remind readers of the fact that for my generation – those who were young in the 1930s – the political skies of Europe, dominated by Hitler, Mussolini, Stalin, Franco, Salazar and various dictators in Eastern Europe and the Balkans, were very dark indeed; the policies of Chamberlain and Daladier held out no hope; for those who had not despaired of the possibility of a socially and morally tolerable world the only point of light seemed to many of us to come from President Roosevelt and the New Deal. This article, too, was written largely during the recriminations of the immediate post-war years.

The last essay is new and written for this volume. It deals with my visits to Russia in 1945 and 1956. I wanted to give an account principally of the views and personalities of two writers of genius whom I had met and come to know, which I had not found elsewhere, not even in the memoirs of Nadezhda Mandel'shtam and Lydia Chukovskaya, the most detailed and moving accounts that we have of the lives of writers and artists at a terrible time, to which my narrative (a part of which was delivered as a Bowra Lecture under the auspices of Wadham College, Oxford) can claim to be no more than a marginal supplement.

I wish to record my deep gratitude to my friend Noel Annan for writing the Introduction to this miscellany, and to tell him, and his readers, that I am only too well aware of what reserves of sensibility, conscience, time, sheer labour, capacity for resolving the conflicting claims of truth and friendship, knowledge and moral tact, such a task unavoidably draws upon; and to thank him for his great goodwill in agreeing to perform it. Finally, I should like to take this opportunity of once again acknowledging my deep and ever-growing debt to the Editor of this edition of my essays. No author could ask for a better, more disinterested, scrupulous or energetic editor; and I should like to offer Dr Henry Hardy my thanks for exhuming, and putting together, this collection, composed over a long period, against what must, at times, have seemed not inconsiderable odds – some of them due to the idiosyncrasies of the author.

ISAIAH BERLIN

June 1980

# EDITOR'S PREFACE

THIS is the second edition of one of five volumes in which I have brought together, and prepared for reissue, most of the published essays by Isaiah Berlin which had not hitherto been made available in a collected form.[1] His many writings were previously scattered, often in obscure places; most were out of print; and only half a dozen essays had been collected and reissued.[2] These five volumes, together with the complete list of his publications which one of them (*Against the Current*) contains,[3] and subsequent volumes in which I have published much of his previously unpublished work,[4] have made much more of his *oeuvre* readily accessible than before.

The essays in the present volume are tributes to or memoirs of twentieth-century figures whom, with the exception of Roosevelt

---

[1] The first edition of this volume was originally published in London in 1980, and in New York in 1981; it was the last of four volumes published, in the first instance, under the collective title *Selected Writings*, which explains the author's reference on page x to 'this edition of my essays'. The other three volumes were *Russian Thinkers* (London and New York, 1978), co-edited with Aileen Kelly; *Concepts and Categories: Philosophical Essays* (London, 1978; New York, 1979); and *Against the Current: Essays in the History of Ideas* (London, 1979; New York, 1980). The fifth volume followed a decade later: *The Crooked Timber of Humanity: Chapters in the History of Ideas* (London, 1990; New York, 1991). There is also a selection of essays drawn from these volumes and their predecessors: *The Proper Study of Mankind: An Anthology of Essays*, ed. Henry Hardy and Roger Hausheer (London, 1997; New York, 1998).

[2] *Four Essays on Liberty* (Oxford, 1969; New York, 1970) and *Vico and Herder: Two Studies in the History of Ideas* (London and New York, 1976). Other collections had appeared only in translation.

[3] The currently most up-to-date version of this bibliography appears in the Pimlico paperback edition (London, 1997).

[4] *The Magus of the North: J. G. Hamann and the Origins of Modern Irrationalism* (London, 1993; New York, 1994) and *The Sense of Reality: Studies in Ideas and their History* (London, 1996; New York, 1997).

and Einstein, the author knew personally, together with a chapter on his meetings in 1945 and 1956 with Boris Pasternak, Anna Akhmatova and other Russian writers in Moscow, where he was working in 1945 for the British Embassy, and in Leningrad. Original publication details of the pieces included in the first edition are as follows. 'Winston Churchill in 1940' (with 'Felix Frankfurter at Oxford', one of only two pieces published in the lifetimes of their subjects) first appeared in 1949 in *Atlantic Monthly* 184 No 3 (as 'Mr Churchill') and *Cornhill Magazine* 981 (as 'Mr Churchill and F.D.R.'), and was reissued in book form as *Mr Churchill in 1940* by John Murray of London in 1964. 'President Franklin Delano Roosevelt' appeared in 1955 in *Political Quarterly* 26 and, as 'Roosevelt Through European Eyes', in *Atlantic Monthly* 196 No 1. 'Chaim Weizmann', the second Herbert Samuel Lecture, was published by Weidenfeld and Nicolson of London in 1958. 'Einstein and Israel', which appeared in the *New York Review of Books*, 8 November 1979, is the major part of an address given on 14 March 1979 at the opening of a symposium held to mark the centenary of Einstein's birth – the full address appeared in Gerald Holton and Yehuda Elkana (eds), *Albert Einstein: Historical and Cultural Perspectives*, the Centennial Symposium in Jerusalem (Princeton, 1982: Princeton University Press). 'L. B. Namier' was published in 1966 in Martin Gilbert (ed.), *A Century of Conflict* (London: Hamish Hamilton), and in *Encounter* 17 No 5 (November 1966). 'Felix Frankfurter at Oxford' was a contribution to Wallace Mendelson (ed.), *Felix Frankfurter: A Tribute* (New York, 1964: Reynal). 'Richard Pares' appeared in the 1958 *Balliol College Record*. 'Hubert Henderson at All Souls' was part of a supplement, devoted to Henderson, to *Oxford Economic Papers* 5 (1953). 'J. L. Austin and the Early Beginnings of Oxford Philosophy' was a contribution to Sir Isaiah Berlin and others, *Essays on J. L. Austin* (Oxford, 1973: Clarendon Press). 'John Petrov Plamenatz' was the address at Plamenatz's memorial service in the University Church of St Mary the Virgin, Oxford, in 1975, and was published privately in that year by All Souls College. 'Maurice Bowra' was the address at Bowra's memorial service, also in St Mary's, in 1971, and was published privately in that year by Wadham College. 'Auberon Herbert' was a contribution to John Jolliffe (ed.), *Auberon Herbert: A Composite Portrait* (Tisbury, 1976: Compton Russell), 'Aldous Huxley' to Julian Huxley (ed.), *Aldous Huxley* (London, 1965: Chatto and

Windus). 'Meetings with Russian Writers in 1945 and 1956', an abbreviated version of which was given as a Bowra Lecture on 13 May 1980, was first published in this volume, for which, as the author says, it was specially written.

Four essays published since 1980 have been added in this second edition. 'Yitzhak Sadeh', which appeared in *Midstream* 39 No 4 (May 1993), I constructed at the author's request from two shorter pieces he had written on Sadeh, one previously unpublished, the other, 'On Yitzhak Sadeh' (a short talk broadcast on the English-language service of Israeli radio), published in Hebrew translation in *Davar*, 5 September 1986. 'Edmund Wilson at Oxford' appeared in the *Yale Review* 76 (1987). 'Memories of Virginia Woolf' was published as 'Writers Remembered: Virginia Woolf' in *The Author* 100 (1989). 'David Cecil' appeared in *Reports for 1985–86 and 1986–87; List of Fellows and Members for 1987* (London, [1987]: Royal Society of Literature).

Apart from necessary corrections and the addition of a few references, the reprinted essays appear here essentially in their original form. I have made a few further corrections and added a few further references in this new edition.

Not included here are several other pieces in the same genre, mostly shorter than or overlapping with the pieces in this volume. Their principal subjects are Chaim Weizmann, Meyer Weisgal, Michael Tippett, Randolph Churchill, Jacob Herzog, Arthur Lehning, Jacob Talmon, Teddy Kollek, Yishayahu Leibowitz, Nahum Goldmann, Martin Cooper, David Ben-Gurion, Adam von Trott, John Plamenatz, Yehudi Menuhin, Alexander and Salome Halpern, and H. L. A. Hart; full details can be found in the bibliography already mentioned.[1]

I remain grateful for all the help I received in preparing the first edition seventeen years ago. Then, as always, Isaiah Berlin patiently answered my queries and Pat Utechin, his secretary, gave indispensable aid. Virginia Llewellyn Smith assisted me with 'Meetings with Russian Writers in 1945 and 1956'. I should also like to thank Zvi Dror, Henry Near and Yoram Sadeh for help with 'Yitzhak

[1] See p. xi above, note 3. Of the people I have listed, Chaim Weizmann is the subject of items 49 and 84, and the others of items 91, 97, 123, 129, 140, 171a, 173a, 181a, 188a, 191, 192, 192a, 193, 203, 203a and 215 respectively.

Sadeh', and Helen McCurdy, Rowena Skelton-Wallace and Will Sulkin for help with the second edition.

HENRY HARDY

Wolfson College, Oxford
July 1997


## Postscript

Isaiah Berlin died on 5 November 1997. This new edition of *Personal Impressions* had by then been passed for press, but not actually printed. No changes have been made to the body of the book, but the opportunity has been taken to add, as an epilogue, a slightly shortened version of the address Berlin gave in Jerusalem in May 1979 when he received the Jerusalem Prize for his contribution to the idea of freedom. This moving and perceptive piece – which was printed in *Jewish Quarterly* 27 Nos 2–3 (Summer/Autumn 1979) and in *Conservative Judaism* 33 No 2 (Winter 1980) – has always seemed to me, and to others whom I have consulted, to belong in the book, since it is in effect an autobiographical personal impression. I suggested to Berlin more than once that it should be reprinted in this natural context, but he always gave the characteristic reply that it seemed to him too personal, perhaps too self-regarding, to reappear in a collection in his lifetime; thereafter, however, I should do what I thought best. To my bitter regret, I am now free to add this finishing touch to the volume.

H.H.

November 1997

# INTRODUCTION

*Noel Annan*

THE *éloge* is not much favoured as a literary form in England today: it is hauled out of the cupboard only for use at memorial services, decently to extol the dead man's virtues. The profile and the interview, the literary forms now much in use, are designed not to praise but to cut people down to size. This was the vogue which delighted Beaverbrook: he called it 'lopping off the heads of the tall poppies'. The journalist probes for the weak spot, inserts the *banderilla*, and so goads the wretched bull that he plunges to the doom of self-exposure. Professional interviewers regard this special skill with grave self-satisfaction. They are unanimous in declaring that it does the victim a positive service: he may not appear admirable but he is at least credible.

Intellectuals disparage journalists, but the course they have been following runs alongside the journalists' trail. Social scientists have depersonalised acres of human experience so that history resembles a ranch on which herds move, driven they know not why by impersonal forces, munching their way across the prairie. Critics, like crabs in a rock-pool, scuttle sideways into the recesses of post-modernism and avoid considering how people actually speak and write; or they replace the living artist by an artificial persona composed from his works. No wonder the public buys biographies. Yet how many of the two-volume lives, arid with documentation, fill the throat with dust? Those biographers who are not frightened to paint portraits in the primary colours of virtue and vice seem often to be enslaved by the principle which the harsh-tongued father of the novelist Henry Green characterised years ago as *de mortuis nil nisi bunkum*; and those who preserve certain reticences prudently let it be known that they did so to avoid damages for libel.

Isaiah Berlin ignores these current fashions. His thought, his theories, always refer to people: the very life he leads pullulates with people. His essays on those who intrigue him are studies in praise. Like the son of Shirach he wants us to praise famous men. But it is not their fame which attracts him, it is their genius. He is not ashamed to worship heroes. He has no wish to pose as God and see with equal eye a hero perish or a sparrow fall. Heroes enhance life, the world expands and becomes less menacing and more hopeful by their very existence. To know a great man is to change one's notions of what a human being can do or be. To see Shelley plain, to meet as Berlin has done men and women such as Pasternak or Stravinsky, Virginia Woolf or Picasso, Russell or Einstein, he finds exciting. But he does not consider only geniuses. Someone whose prejudices are outrageous and whose behaviour disturbs the *bien-pensants* may exhibit reckless vitality; and that challenges Berlin to find the precise words which best convey his quality and quiddity. Nor need such people be lions or stars. An obscure scholar with an unusual combination of gifts will make him feel the world well won. He likes people to show attractive qualities: austerity is praiseworthy, but so is gaiety. His austere friend John Austin found few pleasures in life equal to that of being able to praise someone unreservedly, and Berlin, no less than Keynes, who was a devastating critic of people, revels in celebrating men and women whom he admires.

But it would be an error to dismiss these studies in praise as conventional tributes. Like all his writing, they are deceptively entertaining and conceal his true originality of mind. Newspapers picture great scientists making a breakthrough which alters the course of physics or biology, or economists are praised for producing a theory which relates both logically and paradoxically all the variables within their branch of knowledge. These are the means, so it is said, by which knowledge is advanced. But Berlin does not enlarge our understanding in this way. To have done so – to have written an abstract treatise on the history of ideas, a subject which has been distorted and misunderstood precisely because it has so often been reduced to abstractions – would have been to contradict the very message he wants us to receive. He has, of course, written on theories of freedom and on historiography; but these critiques are inadequate in themselves to convey what he has added to his own interpretation of life.

That interpretation is pluralism. How the imagination droops at the mention of that dingy word! 'We live in a pluralist age' is the castrating cliché of our times. Most people when they use the term mean that society is formed of numbers of minorities who are moved each by their own interests and values. But since the interests of all these groups conflict they have to learn to tolerate each other's existence. Indeed the institution which needs to exercise the greatest tolerance is the State itself: although it has to express politically the highest common factor of agreement in society it must be especially sensitive in accommodating those whose views are opposed to the consensus. Not only the State. Every controlling body, every institution, management in its various disguises, should respond to minority feelings. But there is a difficulty in sustaining this theory in practice. When government in all its forms is weakened and drained of blood by giving transfusions to enable minorities to flourish, it becomes incapable of resisting determined and ruthless interest-groups or parties. Having benefited by the application of pluralism, they kick over the theory and elbow the government out by taking over its most important functions; they then blandly declare the interests of all other minorities to be subordinate to their own. Must not a government so hesitant about its legitimacy collapse when its power to give orders is challenged?

Isaiah Berlin's interpretation of pluralism is far more profound. He does not spend time conjecturing how far the State should or should not yield to pressure groups. What fascinates him is not the political consequences of pluralism but its justification. It needs to be justified not only against its enemies but against many of those who preen themselves on being pluralists but would be indignant if they became aware of the implications of what Berlin is saying. For those who pay lip-service to pluralism fail to understand just how disturbing he is. He believes that you cannot always pursue one good end without setting another on one side. You cannot always exercise mercy without cheating justice. Equality and freedom are both good ends but you rarely can have more of one without surrendering some part of the other. This is dispiriting for progressives who like to believe that the particular goal which at present they are pursuing is not incompatible with all the other goals which they like to think they value as much. But Berlin, disbelieving in panaceas or total solutions, is sceptical of many remedies which purport to cure social ills and to reintegrate those said to be alienated from their society. Masterful men and implacable women, planners, moving their fellow citizens about and disposing of the future of their children, determining how and where they should live in the name of efficiency or equality, justifying the brutality of their decisions by declaring how inescapable these decisions are, do not rejoice his heart. Bureaucrats who take pleasure in defining the rules and regulations which govern everyone else's jobs awaken in him the suspicion that so far from fulfilling what people want they are more interested in manipulating them. But if for him the ideals of the powerful civil servant insult too wantonly the nature of man, he does not display much enthusiasm for the political movements which grew up to oppose the gospel of efficiency. He has reservations about populism or syndicalism. He wonders how much they care for the liberty of minorities.

But these reservations give no comfort to conservatives. Unlike Michael Oakeshott, Berlin is not sceptical of reason in politics or of theories as such. He may have no views about monetarism or deficit budgeting or on other statistical or sociological analyses: but he does not regard such efforts to apply reason to politics as valueless. Such theories, the product of abstract reason and analysis, may, if put into practice, diminish the bruising and dispiriting conflicts between good ends. Life is not one long struggle against impaling oneself on the horns of a dilemma: peaceful trade-offs are possible, nor are they always agonising. Sometimes equality and liberty may be reconciled; sometimes not; but Berlin disagrees with those who deny that tangles of this sort can be combed out. Again, participatory populism is not a form of political organisation likely to make the blood surge through his veins; but if it could be shown that it led to a clear advance towards greater equality he would not reject it. Unlike even moderate conservatives he regards equality as one of the ultimate goals for men, a sacred value, obliged no doubt to yield when other sacred values would have to suffer if they were to collide with it, but to be realised so long as it cannot be shown to be doing irreparable damage. If many people are starving and can be fed if the liberty of the few is curtailed, then the few must lose their liberty. If that gives pain, well, pain must be given. All Berlin asks is that there should be no equivocation and it should be frankly admitted that liberty was curtailed – in a good cause. Nor has he sympathy with the conservative notion that all culture is founded on inequality, nor with a view dear to some intellectuals that art is the supreme value in life which must be protected and fostered at whatever cost.

If the agonising choice had to be made between the destruction of, say, Rome, glistening with the treasures of the ages, and the loss of the independence of a nation and the subjugation of its citizens to a tyranny, Berlin would throw his lot for scorched earth and resistance. Some might guess that in his sympathy for Turgenev he would follow him in loathing the right and fearing the left; and if he were faced with the alternatives which confronted Turgenev in nineteenth-century Russia the guess would be right. Berlin finds reactionary regimes odious, and terrorist revolutionaries insupportable. But within the range of Western democratic politics he follows his fancy.

To want to maximise a particular virtue is common enough: to admit that it is not always possible to do this without fatally diminishing others is not. Unfortunately people, Berlin argues, want to be assured that in fact they can always follow simultaneously all good ends. They therefore listen respectfully to political thinkers who declare that this can be done. Such sages declare that they have discovered a better kind of freedom, positive freedom, which will reconcile the desire for justice, equality, opportunity for self-fulfilment with their wish to be as free and live under as few prohibitions as possible. Positive freedom is the benign name given to the theory which maintains that not merely wise philosophers but the State, indeed governments themselves, can identify what people would *really* want were they enlightened, if they understood fully what was needed to promote a good, just and satisfying society. For if it is true that this can be identified then surely the State is justified in ignoring what ordinary people say they desire or detest. What people say is the mere rumbling of their lower self, a pathetic underdeveloped persona insufficiently aware of all the possibilities of life, often the slave of evil passions. Who in his senses would want to be a slave to the bottle? Who would not agree that art is vital to anyone who wants to lead a full life? But since all too many people are alcoholics and vast numbers of people care not at all for art, the State is compelled to enforce sobriety and propagate art so long as it is healthy and opens men's eyes to a better future.

People are often convinced by this vision of freedom because they want to believe in a common-sense view of goodness. Surely goodness must be indivisible, surely truth is beauty and beauty truth, surely the different aspects of truth and goodness can always be reconciled. But Berlin declares that sometimes they cannot.

Ideology answers the questions 'How should I behave?' and 'How should I live?' People want to believe that there is one irrefutable answer to these questions. But there is not.

There is not, because life is more than a series of solutions to problems. Berlin's pluralism has far deeper roots than politics. It is grounded in his understanding of linguistic philosophy and of history. Other philosophers grew weary of John Austin's devastating ability to dissect a proposition and expose error in their own arguments. 'You are like a greyhound', Berlin remembers Ayer saying to Austin, 'who doesn't want to run himself, and bites the other greyhounds, so that they cannot run either.' But Berlin found Austin sympathetic, not so much for the ferocity with which he argued, but because Austin, like the later Wittgenstein, rejected the doctrine that one could assemble a logically perfect language capable of reflecting the structure of reality. Unlike Ayer, who started with the verification principle and rejected an argument if it appeared to conflict with that principle, Austin believed that the only way to analyse knowledge, belief and experience was to study how people actually use words; and he rejected distinctions between empirical and logical truths – between those terms necessary to what Berlin calls 'all or nothing' philosophies.

Austin too was a theorist. He invented the theory of the illocutionary use of language (performatory, ascriptive and prescriptive expressions), and he believed in systems and in teamwork for cracking philosophical conundrums, which Berlin did not – much. But Austin did not take problems and force them into a Procrustean bed of a single all-embracing system. Whereas some logical postivists faced with a problem reformulated it in their own terms so that it ceased to be the problem it was, or else rejected it as a pseudo-problem, Austin took every problem as it came. Like Dr Johnson, Austin had a fine scorn for determinism as a doctrine which flew in the face of all experience; and this too Berlin found sympathetic. He does not see human beings as flies struggling vainly in the cobweb of historical causation, incapable of acting as free agents.

But sympathetic as Austin was to him personally and encouraging as his precept was to consider language as an act, something people do in a particular situation, Berlin's pluralism stands independent from Oxford philosophy; and it is arguable that it is never more palpable and convincing than when he writes about people. Nobody else in our time has invested ideas with such personality; no one has given them corporeal shape and breathed life into them more than Berlin; and he succeeds in doing so because ideas for him are not mere abstractions. They live – how else could they live? – in the minds of men and women, inspiring them, shaping their lives, influencing their actions and changing the course of history. But it is men and women who create these ideas and embody them. Some are scholars enclosed in their hermetic world, despising histrionics, intrigue, ambition – the game of getting on and cashing in. They recoil when confronted with brutal discourtesy, or mere counter-assertion in argument, intended to bludgeon an opponent to the ground, because they find such behaviour intensely distasteful. And yet, wholly admirable as such men are and impressive as their standard of value is, theirs is not the only way of reflecting upon life, nor are their values the one sure guide for mankind. Isaiah Berlin has compared the murmur of Bloomsbury to chamber music: and chamber music certainly resembles that exchange of views, voice answering voice, between intellectuals, like a never-ending series of telephone calls, which so delighted him as a young don in the 1930s. But this is not the only kind of existence to be regarded as admirable or profitable. Chamber music is indeed an austere and demanding musical form: neither Beethoven nor Bach wrote more profound works than the posthumous quartets or the partitas. But symphonies, great choral works and operas demanding a huge orchestra and more than half a dozen soloists also delight and astonish us, and we would think it absurd if some pedant declared that they were all vulgar or grandiose.

Why then should we not recognise that the world of affairs has its own validity and is governed by its own rules? Why should we not admit that statesmen cannot be scholars or scholars statesmen, just as long ago the Church divided mankind into the laity, the secular clergy and 'religious'? 'Life', writes Berlin, 'may be seen through many windows, none of them necessarily clear or opaque, less or more distorting than any of the others.' Bloomsbury had a right to their own scale of values: but they were in error when they assumed that all sensible and intelligent individuals should conform to it. It is all very well to believe that you have discovered the truth about ethics, history, painting and personal relations; but to declare that anyone in the vast world who does not accept these conclusions is either a fool or a knave is grotesque. Statesmen must, therefore, display very different qualities and live by ideals far removed from those of the scholars who later interpret them. Pluralism means the acceptance of a multitude of ideals appropriate in different circumstances and for men of different callings. Indeed there are different kinds of statesmen and it would be foolish to judge that one type inspired by one set of ideas is necessarily worse than another type acting under the influence of a different set of ideas. At one point, in describing Roosevelt, Berlin contrasts two types of statesmen, the first consisting of men of single principle and fanatical vision, ignoring men and events and bending them to their powerful will, the second consisting of men who possess delicate antennae which enable them to sense how events are moving and how their fellow citizens feel, to divine where the means lie for effecting what they desire; 'the distinction I am drawing', writes Berlin, 'is not a moral one, not one of value but one of type'. In each category some are noble or attractive, some dubious or deplorable. On the one hand there stand Garibaldi, Trotsky, Parnell, de Gaulle, Woodrow Wilson and Hitler; on the other Bismarck, Lincoln, Lloyd George, Masaryk, Gladstone and Roosevelt.

Immediately we begin to see that many of the moral judgements commonly made about politics are simply untrue. It is not true that good men alone bring dignity and prosperity to their people. But neither is it true, as so-called realists like to argue, that desirable ends in politics are nearly always achieved by employing undesirable means. Honourable and conscientious men have all too often failed ignominiously to govern well, while ruffians and fanatics have imposed law and order upon chaotic conditions and replaced enfeebled popular governments by vigorous despotic regimes. But it is also true that tyrants such as Hitler have died seeing the empire they created crumbling before their eyes, while indomitable leaders such as Ben-Gurion, pursuing justice and independence, lead their compatriots out of the wilderness and die lapped by the waves of their gratitude. Berlin is no Mosca or Michels, the kind of political realist who relishes telling his readers that, if the State is to defy its enemies, society to be stable and the masses happy, the ticket you buy for such a performance will cost you dear in lost liberties, the deaths of innocent creatures and the execution of opponents of the regime. Too high a price and Berlin, like Ivan Karamazov, would return his ticket.[1] He is not a party man. He joins no camp and

---

[1] Karamazov says: 'too high a price has been placed on harmony. We cannot

excludes as few visionaries as possible. Both Tolstoy and Marx he considers mistaken but far fuller of truth than of error, and worthy of the deepest respect. Belinsky, a fierce believer in one ideology after another, dedicated to propagating the truth as he saw it, intolerant of anyone whom he considered to be wilfully living a life of error, is most unlike Weizmann, the politician whom Berlin so admires; but the human race would be impoverished without men such as Belinsky. That is why he chooses the *éloge* as his paradigm. It is a way of expressing the variety of life, or reminding us how in someone who at first sight seems antipathetic or perverse good qualities abound: how the person in question lives by standards entirely appropriate to his calling. For unless society acknowledges that men both do and should live according to different ideals, the men and women within it will not be free.

Like all thinkers of importance Isaiah Berlin writes in a style which is entirely his and his alone and without which he could not express his meaning. In recent years it has become even more personal as he records what he has to say on tape and amends the transcript to produce the final draft. Such a method would be ruinous for most writers; but Berlin's mind is of such distinction that he thinks and speaks, whether in a room among friends or on the rostrum delivering a lecture, in long periods, clause upon clause, the predicate lengthening out into a profusion of participles, a manner which in the hands of other men would have become a cumbersome imitation of Cicero. He is not a Henry Moore shaping a great mass of stone which relates human beings to the elemental forces of nature. Rather he resembles a Seurat, a *pointilliste* who peppers his canvas with a fusillade of adjectives, epithets, phrases, analogies, elucidations and explanations so that at last a particular idea, a principle of action, a vision of life emerges before our eyes in all its complexity; and no sooner have we comprehended it than he begins using the same methods to create a conflicting or, it may be, a complementary vision of life, so that by contrast we may understand the first conception better. He will always use two words where one will not do. He has no fear that his reader will get lost in the labyrinth of his sentences because they have the rhythm and the spring of the spoken word. He

afford to pay so much for admission. And therefore I hasten to return my ticket of admission.' *The Brothers Karamazov*, book 5, chapter 4, trans. David Magarshack (Harmondsworth, 1958), vol. 1, p. 287.

defends what he calls Churchill's Johnsonian prose. The self-conscious revival of the style of a bygone age, such as the Gothic Revival, need not be fake; it can be genuine. And Churchill's prose is a projection of himself and his vision of history, highly coloured, vivid, big, bright, unsubtle, addressed to the world at large, not a vehicle for introspection or the private life, but suffused with deep sentiment for his own country and its place in the hierarchy of nations. Berlin's style reflects his own sense of values no less faithfully.

For, of course, he is a man with a sharp sense of right and wrong. No one should suppose that a pluralist is a relativist. He is as much entitled to his vision of life as the Catholic or the Marxist. Berlin reminds us that a vision should not be expected to be as precise as an equation.

> Nor do we complain of 'escapism' or perversion of the facts [he writes] until the categories adopted are thought to do too much violence to the 'facts'. To interpret, to relate, to classify, to symbolise are those natural and unavoidable human activities which we loosely and conveniently describe as thinking. We complain, if we do, only when the result is too widely at variance with the common outlook of our own society and age and tradition.

That is, not the conventional wisdom or even the accepted beliefs of a culture, but the very concepts and categories in which we can hardly help thinking, being who we are and when and where we exist. What, then, is Isaiah Berlin's own vision of life and what are the virtues he particularly esteems?

His heart has always been given to the life of the mind and to Oxford. Oxford has sustained him as a scholar and he has tried to repay the debt by helping to found a graduate college and assuming other duties he would not otherwise have willingly performed. He has deliberately chosen to praise men very different in temperament from himself, austere or withdrawn figures, not perhaps noted for their ebullient humour, scholars who thought a day lost if fourteen hours had not been spent in the Bodleian, college men whose minds sucked up like a sponge details in the accounts such as the singular low rate of interest earned by the reserve building fund. He practised pluralism in life: he genuinely admired those who were, like himself, indisputably intellectuals but more severe and dry. Yet even among such he cannot help making us aware that it is useless to expect them all to exhibit the same good qualities. Hubert Henderson and Richard Pares were good college men, but would it not be ludicrous to blame the shy Plamenatz for detesting committees and the noise of repartee in the common room after a feast? And would it not be equally ludicrous to condemn those who liked noise, such as Maurice Bowra, who preferred vehemence to reticence, pleasure to austerity, exuberance to melancholy, intellectual gaiety and the deflating of the establishment, the self-important and the pompous, to *pietas* and *gravitas*? High spirits are also part of what a university should prize. Professors such as Felix Frankfurter, effervescent, dispelling the prim self-consciousness that is the bane of academic communities, preferring the company of his younger colleagues to the right-thinking conventional men who consider themselves to be the arbiters of academic life – they too are essential to a great university.

Nowhere does Isaiah Berlin better reveal his commitment to Oxford and the life of the mind than in his incomparable essay on John Austin, worthy to rank with Keynes's memories of his early beliefs, in which he describes Austin pursuing truth without regard for friend or foe or for the consequences, and with a single-mindedness which Berlin found later only when he got to know Keynes's mentor G. E. Moore. There will be some who will regard his description of what was actually discussed in that seminar as final proof that British philosophy loses itself in a wilderness of pedantry. They will be wrong. Philosophers of every age, Plato's disciples, the Schoolmen, Cartesians, Hegelians, have always worked on minute points, or upon sharply defined problems such as perception and epistemology. Berlin is not complacent. Looking back, he thinks those young dons such as himself who took part in Austin's seminar were too self-centred to publish much. They were gratified enough if one of their points won acceptance from the rest of the group. But, as he says, those who have never believed that they and their colleagues were discovering for the first time new truths which would have profound consequences for their subject, 'those who have never been under the spell of this kind of illusion, even for a short while, have not known true intellectual happiness'.

Scholars are often bores – even the greatest among them. One day when Berlin was a young man a scholar called on him who was regarded by some people as a genius and by others as a champion among bores. This was Namier and, as Berlin says, 'He was, in fact, both.' Not that Berlin was bored. Not even when Namier explained to him slowly and at length, not once but several times, that he was wasting his life because Marx was someone unworthy to occupy his attention and because ideas were merely the product of men's sub-conscious drives for power, glory, wealth and pleasure, was he cast down. When Namier explained that the reason why England was a Great Power, at once humane and civilised, was precisely that the English recognised how unimportant ideas were and kept intellectuals firmly in their place, he became even more interested and over the years treasured with amusement examples of Namier's more terrifying insults. For this mounting interest there were two reasons. Unlike other scholars who when told that their subject is worthless write off their persecutor as a maniac, Berlin asked himself why it was that Namier thought as he did and what sort of a man he was. Namier seemed to him to be both the most anti-metaphysical of rationalists, at one with the analyses of Mach and Freud or later of the Vienna circle, yet at the same time a Jew and, like Disraeli, a nationalist and a romantic. What was more he was an East European Jew. What was best he was a Zionist.

From the time that he was a boy at St Paul's Isaiah Berlin has been a Zionist. This loyalty has inspired some of his finest writing. Some Zionists despise and hate Jews who assimilate successfully to the culture of the country in which they live: but not Berlin. He has no quarrel with the children or grandchildren of those whom Namier called 'trembling Israelites', men and women of Jewish descent who have long ceased to tremble, and live happily among their neighbours, accepted for what they are, who are free from envy, anxiety and apprehension and who do not observe Jewish rituals or festivals and indeed may be hostile to religion as such. He may, it is true, regard as faintly odious the contortions of those Jews who attract attention to their origins by their efforts to suppress them, who wince at hearing the name of Zion mentioned and would prefer to be strolling in the Long Room at Lord's wearing the tie of the Marylebone Cricket Club. Similarly, although he does not seek out their company, he would not decline to talk to those Foreign Office officials whose whole training has been devoted to fostering sound pro-Arab policies and distrust of Israel. He knows well that some of those whom he fascinates harbour in their secret heart mild anti-Semitic views, upper-class people who almost forget he is a Jew because, devoid of anxiety or resentment about the matter, he is as secure in his Jewishness as they are in their cocoon. Indeed he has a keen eye for those snubs, insults, pin-pricks and acts of exclusion to which even now Jews are subjected in ordinary life. Others, smooth as Jacob's hands, may make light of such things or ignore them; but for him such humiliations convince him of the necessity of the State of Israel. He did not become a Zionist because the Jews should inhabit their natural land promised them by Jehovah. He became a Zionist because he wanted there to be somewhere on earth where Jews are not always in a minority, fearful that, if they did not behave well and ape an alien culture, the Gentiles would despise them – or even murder or expel them. You feel that he speaks for himself when, writing about Weizmann, he notes how 'martyrs, failures, casualties, victims of circumstance or of their own absurdities – the stock subjects of the mocking, sceptical Jewish humour – filled him with distress and disgust'. The mordant, sophisticated jokes of central European Jews ('I have bad luck: every time I buy a dwarf it grows') – jokes full of avant-garde sophistication, cynicism, and vulgarity masking a desperate political fanaticism – are not for him. Again, when he speaks of Weizmann's love of England, the respect which as an East European Jew he had for its humane democracy, its civil liberty, legal equality, toleration, moderation, dislike of extremes and lack of cruelty, even its taste for the odd and the eccentric, Berlin is saying something about his own love for the country in which his parents settled.

For a few years during the War Berlin worked on the staff of the British Embassy in Washington, and he has measured all the imponderables, the might-have-beens, the swing of the pendulum of fate which led to the collapse of his hopes and those of Weizmann that Britain might have been the willing midwife at the birth of Israel. He never excuses his own misapprehensions but nor does he admit error when in fact despite events he was at the time right.

Some may have wondered whether he suffered from divided loyalties. Such doubts used long ago to be entertained about Catholics and there were plenty of worldly-wise establishmentarians such as Harold Nicolson who considered that it was unwise to employ Jews in the Foreign Office because they were 'not one of us' and could hardly be expected to recognise that British oil interests in Arab States were paramount. Dual allegiance can create tensions and strain loyalty; it is untrue to deny that the problem exists. But it did not exist for Berlin. He had no doubt that he was a servant in Washington of the British Government, of his own country, a country which had not conscripted him or compelled him to hold views and pursue policies deeply repugnant to him. He was under no constraint. As a civilian he was free, even in wartime, to resign. And being free he had no right to disobey or cavil. He took for granted the supremacy of total loyalty to England, which at one time had stood alone against Hitler. The clarity and purity of his moral perception relieved him of those fearful upheavals and soul-searchings which lesser men suffered over such issues as the atom bomb. Occasionally, of course, in discussing the Middle East with his colleagues in the embassy, most of whom were anti-Zionist, he found himself in disagreement and hence in some discomfort. Again, it was painful for him when some fanatical Zionists considered him tainted by his British allegiance. But discomfort or pain are different from moral contortion and strain. For had he suffered in that way then indeed the contention held by the Nicolsons of this world that no one can loyally serve two ideals would gain credence and provide tinder for xenophobia in general and anti-Semitism in particular. Nor does he stop at dual loyalties. As a pluralist he sees no contradiction in observing quadruple or quintuple loyalties.

Nevertheless it was perhaps the experiences of those years which determined him, except for a short sojourn in Moscow, never to work again for any government. Nor was he dazzled by the powerful, and if they sought him out he did not necessarily respond. After the War Beaverbrook, who had heard of Berlin's renowned weekly telegram to the Foreign Office, a commentary on the Washington political scene, summoned him and used all his repertoire of blandishments to inveigle Berlin to write for his papers. Beaverbrook was incredulous when his overtures were not immediately accepted. 'Why, Arnold Bennett wrote for me until the last breath he drew' – why should not Mr Berlin accept? There could be luxurious living which he, Beaverbrook, knew well how to arrange. There could be – and it was an offer, he declared, which was not made to many – there could be a discreet flat where Berlin could entertain – a lady; indeed ladies, if need be, could even materialise. The offer was not taken up. Shortly after, Berlin was denounced by one of Beaverbrook's minions in a leading article. Berlin enormously enjoyed the episode.

'The Jews are a peculiar and difficult people in many ways,' he has written, 'not least because their history has contradicted most of the best-known and most admired theories of historical causation.' In the history of the Jews and in the creation of the State of Israel Berlin finds his most telling argument against those who maintain that history is the study of classes and social movements, impersonal forces such as demography and climatic changes, of technological development and terms of trade. In Braudel's great work, *The Mediterranean and the Mediterranean World in the Age of Philip II*, the Spanish King makes his appearance only well on into the second volume, and for the most part, along with other princes and geniuses of that time, does not cut much of a figure. That is not how Berlin sees history. The foundation of the State of Israel was inherently improbable. That it came about was principally due, in Berlin's view, to a great statesman, Chaim Weizmann. No explanation of how it came about which eliminated Weizmann would hold water. And so little is history inevitable or determined that Weizmann's own reasonable assumptions and policies for bringing about the birth of the State were blown away by incalculable and fortuitous events.

The foundation of the State of Israel is not the only example in our times of the actions of individuals confounding determinism in history. The resistance by the British in 1940, or Hitler's invasion of Russia a year later, are as telling. If Weizmann was a great man because by his intervention in history he made the improbable happen, so were Churchill and Roosevelt. But the question immediately bursts in the sky like a shower of fireworks: how are we to regard great men? Berlin would vehemently deny that great men are beyond moral scrutiny, as Hegel declared they were. In praise of Weizmann he declares: '[He] committed none of those enormities for which men of action, and later their biographers, claim justification, on the ground of what is called *raison d'état* ... Weizmann, despite his reputation as a master of *realpolitik*, forged no telegrams, massacred no minorities, executed and incarcerated no political opponents.' Politicians should not sacrifice, even when trapped in a crisis, the accepted standards of private morality to the alleged claims of the State or some interest group. Yet at the same time, while you may, if you choose, ask questions about a great man which would be perfectly appropriate if you were considering the life of one of your friends – whether he was kind, sensitive, good company – you should recognise that these are not the most important questions. It is more appropriate to ask what this statesman achieved, what was his vision of life and how it affected his policies. Just as Matthew Arnold declared that any translation of Homer should recognise that Homer was noble and sublime and wrote in the grand manner, so Berlin suggests that Roosevelt's critics should recognise that it was due to his personality that America was regarded on his death as the natural champion of democracy and of humane social policies. It was Roosevelt who gave Americans a status both inside and outside their country which they had never had before; and in achieving this he never sacrificed any fundamental political principle to retain power nor whipped up wicked passions to crush his enemies. And similarly Churchill was recognised all over the world as the man who had saved his country and prevented Europe from falling under an evil power. Both men had, and will always have, their critics, and part of what these critics say will be true. But their criticisms pale beside the qualities, the style and the achievements which these men displayed; and they displayed them because they were animated each by a vision of life – Churchill ruling his days and controlling his passions by his sense of the past and of his place in history, Roosevelt understanding the future and shaping his policies so as to give Americans the maximum scope to deal with its problems. Devoted though he is to the virtues of the private life, Berlin has a just estimate of public virtue.

Few of us have the imagination or the integrity to see life as a whole, but you do not have to be a statesman or an artist to have a vision of life. There are people in every class in society who do so and Berlin records how in 1946, when staying at the embassy in Paris, he met such a person. This was Auberon Herbert, who having held him not in conversation but in monologue long after everyone else had retired, when Berlin was hoping for a few hours' sleep before departing at five the next morning, followed him to his bedroom and stayed talking. Berlin says he did not find this strange; he could hardly have done so, since in those days he was capable of doing exactly that himself if, as was always so, plenty was still left to say. Berlin came to realise then and in the subsequent years of friendship that Herbert did not merely hold strong, quixotic, eccentric and sometimes deplorable views, but that he lived under the spell of a code, in part that of the landed aristocracy, but made all the more piquant by a singular fastidiousness and generosity of spirit. It was a limited vision; it was a prejudiced vision; but it was not an ignoble vision. As Berlin puts it, Herbert disliked philistines, cowards and hypocrites more than he disliked liars, barbarians or cunning adventurers. Bizarre as some of the ends were which he pursued without regard to whether the means existed to attain them, Herbert's contempt for utilitarian principles was admirable precisely because his religion checked his natural lack of moderation.

It is more difficult for an intellectual to see the point of eccentricity in another intellectual – eccentricity not in his habits but in his rational and dispassionate analysis of phenomena. That Berlin was charmed by Aldous Huxley, a man of singular sweetness of nature, humility and range of mind, is not surprising. What is unusual is the way Berlin rejects the assumption common among intellectuals that Huxley wasted his maturity investigating paranormal psychology. On the contrary: perhaps no one since Spinoza has believed as unswervingly as Huxley that knowledge liberates; and Berlin praises Huxley for extending the panorama of knowledge to include occult as well as open knowledge. He believes that Huxley had an insight into what may prove to be the field in which the greatest advances will be made in the next century: in the relation of body to mind and of myth and ritual to empirical investigation.

No one should suppose that these *éloges* emerge from a vapid disposition. Dear people exist who have never been heard to say a harsh word about anyone: for the good reason that they have taught themselves to live in a world of their own imagining where none hear, see or speak evil. Berlin is not one of them. He is not blind to human failings and is quick to spot the feet of clay of those he likes or esteems as well as of those whom he thinks of little account. As Jack Gallagher at Cambridge used to say, each of us has awful friends; and we are all somebody's awful friend. But if Isaiah Berlin cannot help regarding some awful people with sympathy and affection, even if they embarrass him, there are others who seem to him not merely awful but unattractive because they are insensitive or inhuman. He distinguishes between the awful and the bad. It is bad to be the kind of careerist who begins life as an oily opportunist only too willing to betray his friends in a crisis and ends it by gratuitously harming others in order to feed his unappeasable appetite for power and position. Others are worse than bad: downright evil or sinister or both. The sinister and evil are quite different from certain able and successful men and women whom he would rather not meet but, if he did, would make the best of it. They are different again from certain types of celebrities or snobs or complacent *bien-pensants* or proud and corrupt European aristocrats who lie on the other side of his frontier of tolerance. The sinister and evil give him the horrors and, if faced by them, he melts from the room like a displeased ghost vanishing.

Unlike some who have such a sharp eye he is not interested – none less so – in doing others down. He may be censorious but, unlike many moralists, censoriousness is not a state of mind in which he finds pleasure. In the act of observing a crook or a charlatan, a dullard or a devious fellow, he enjoys discovering redeeming features. Redemption not condemnation, merits not failings, stimulate him to write; and when he writes he chooses those he wants to praise and particularises only their good qualities. He hardly ever attributes defects: defects he generalises. For instance, if he saw fit to praise a man for the style, even the abandon, with which he dressed, he would contrast him with those who are natty or trendy – and leave his reader to guess who they were. Like Hamlet he stands amazed at what a piece of work is a man; unlike Hamlet he delights in man.

Human beings delight him because he possesses a special gift which some of those who make sapient judgements upon people singularly lack. That is an irrepressible sense of humour. Its special qualities are spontaneity, playfulness, delight in absurdity. It is not entirely English: it owes something to his Russian origins. It is like the humour which bubbles up like a spring in Dostoevsky and is at the heart of Chekhov. Not for nothing did he regard the composer, Nicolas Nabokov, whose sense of comedy was highly developed, with special affection: he loves jokes and lightheartedness even when they spring from the facetious schoolboy humour with which Churchill used to discomfit his enemies, entertain his friends and hearten his countrymen.

These tributes, then, are not sketches thrown on one side, the refuse of the artist's studio. They are as much part of Isaiah Berlin's *oeuvre* as are his essays on liberty and on the intellectuals of the Enlightenment and the nineteenth century. No one can understand ideas unless he sees them as the expression of the passions, desires, longings and frustrations of human beings; and the word 'life' itself has no meaning unless it calls to mind men and women – past, present and to come.

# WINSTON CHURCHILL IN 1940

I

IN THE now remote year 1928, an eminent English poet and critic published a book dealing with the art of writing English prose.[1] Writing at a time of bitter disillusion with the false splendours of the Edwardian era, and still more with the propaganda and phrasemaking occasioned by the First World War, the critic praised the virtues of simplicity. If simple prose was often dry and flat, it was at least honest. If it was at times awkward, shapeless and bleak, it did at least convey a feeling of truthfulness. Above all, it avoided the worst of all temptations – inflation, self-dramatisation, the construction of flimsy stucco façades, either deceptively smooth or covered with elaborate baroque detail which concealed a dreadful inner emptiness.

The time and mood are familiar enough: it was not long after Lytton Strachey had set a new fashion by his method of exposing the cant or muddleheadedness of eminent Victorians, after Bertrand Russell had unmasked the great nineteenth-century metaphysicians as authors of a monstrous hoax played upon generations eager to be deceived, after Keynes had successfully pilloried the follies and vices of the Allied statesmen at Versailles. This was the time when rhetoric and, indeed, eloquence were held up to obloquy as camouflage for literary and moral Pecksniffs, unscrupulous charlatans who corrupted artistic taste and discredited the cause of truth and reason, and at their worst incited to evil and led a credulous world to disaster. It was in this literary climate that the critic in question, with much skill and discrimination, explained why he admired the last recorded words spoken to Judge Thayer by the poor fish-pedlar Vanzetti[2] – moving, ungrammatical fragments uttered by a simple man about to die – more than he did

---

[1] Herbert Read, *English Prose Style* (London, 1928).
[2] ibid., p. 165.

the rolling periods of celebrated masters of fine writing widely read by the public at that time.

He selected as an example of the latter a man who in particular was regarded as the sworn enemy of all that the author prized most highly – humility, integrity, humanity, scrupulous regard for sensibility, individual freedom, personal affection – the celebrated but distrusted paladin of imperialism and the romantic conception of life, the swashbuckling militarist, the vehement orator and journalist, the most public of public personalities in a world dedicated to the cultivation of private virtues, the Chancellor of the Exchequer of the Conservative Government then in power, Winston Churchill.

After observing that 'These three conditions are necessary to Eloquence – firstly, an adequate theme; then a sincere and impassioned mind; and lastly a power of sustainment or pertinacity', the writer drove his thesis home with a quotation from the first part of Churchill's *World Crisis*, which had appeared some four years previously, and added: 'Such eloquence is false because it is artificial . . . the images are stale, the metaphors violent. The whole passage exhales a false dramatic atmosphere . . . a volley of rhetorical imperatives.' He went on to describe Churchill's prose as being high-sounding, redundant, falsely eloquent, declamatory, derived from undue 'aggrandisation of the self' instead of 'aggrandisation of the theme'; and condemned it root and branch.[1]

This view was well received by the young men who were painfully reacting against anything which appeared to go beyond the naked skeleton of the truth, at a time when not only rhetoric but even noble eloquence seemed outrageous hypocrisy. Churchill's critic spoke, and knew that he spoke, for a post-war generation; the psychological symptoms of the vast and rapid social transformation then in progress, from which the government in power so resolutely averted its gaze, were visible to the least discerning critics of literature and the arts; the mood was dissatisfied, hostile and insecure; the sequel to so much magnificence was too bitter, and left behind it a heritage of hatred for the grand style as such. The victims and casualties of the disaster thought they had earned the right to be rid of the trappings of an age which had heartlessly betrayed them.

Nevertheless the stern critic and his audience were profoundly

[1] ibid., pp. 191–2.

mistaken. What he and they denounced as so much tinsel and hollow pasteboard was in reality solid: it was this author's natural means for the expression of his heroic, highly coloured, sometimes over-simple and even naïve, but always genuine, vision of life. The critic saw only an unconvincing, sordidly transparent pastiche, but this was an illusion. The reality was something very different: an inspired, if unconscious, attempt at a revival. It went against the stream of contemporary thought and feeling only because it was a deliberate return to a formal mode of English utterance which extends from Gibbon and Dr Johnson to Peacock and Macaulay, a composite weapon created by Churchill in order to convey his particular vision. In the bleak and deflationary 1920s it was too bright, too big, too vivid, too unstable for the sensitive and sophisticated epigoni of the age of imperialism, who, living an inner life of absorbing complexity and delicacy, became unable and certainly unwilling to admire the light of a day which had destroyed so much of what they had trusted and loved. From this the critic and his supporters recoiled; but their analysis of their reasons was not convincing.

They had, of course, a right to their own scale of values, but it was a blunder to dismiss Churchill's prose as a false front, a hollow sham. Revivals are not false as such: the Gothic Revival, for example, represented a passionate, if nostalgic, attitude towards life, and while some examples of it may appear bizarre, it sprang from a deeper sentiment and had a good deal more to say than some of the thin and 'realistic' styles which followed; the fact that the creators of the Gothic Revival found their liberation in going back into a largely imaginary past in no way discredits them or their achievement. There are those who, inhibited by the furniture of the ordinary world, come to life only when they feel themselves actors upon a stage, and, thus emancipated, speak out for the first time, and are then found to have much to say. There are those who can function freely only in uniform or armour or court dress, see only through certain kinds of spectacles, act fearlessly only in situations which in some way are formalised for them, see life as a kind of play in which they and others are assigned certain lines which they must speak. So it happens – the last war afforded plenty of instances of this – that people of a shrinking disposition perform miracles of courage when life has been dramatised for them, when they are on the battlefield; and might continue to do so if they were constantly in uniform and life were always a battlefield.

This need for a framework is not 'escapism', not artificial or abnormal or a sign of maladjustment. Often it is a vision of experience in terms of the strongest single psychological ingredient in one's nature: not infrequently in the form of a simple struggle between conflicting forces or principles, between truth and falsehood, good and evil, right and wrong, between personal integrity and various forms of temptation and corruption (as in the case of the critic in question), or between what is conceived as permanent and what is ephemeral, or between the material and the immaterial, or between the forces of life and the forces of death, or between the religion of art and its supposed enemies – politicians or priests or philistines. Life may be seen through many windows, none of them necessarily clear or opaque, less or more distorting than any of the others. And since we think largely in words, they necessarily take on the property of serving as an armour. The style of Dr Johnson, which echoes so frequently in the prose of *Their Finest Hour*, particularly when the author indulges in a solemn facetiousness, was itself in its own day a weapon offensive and defensive; it requires no deep psychological subtlety to perceive why a man so vulnerable as Johnson – who belonged mentally to the previous century – had constant need of it.

## II

Churchill's dominant category, the single, central, organising principle of his moral and intellectual universe, is a historical imagination so strong, so comprehensive, as to encase the whole of the present and the whole of the future in a framework of a rich and multicoloured past. Such an approach is dominated by a desire – and a capacity – to find fixed moral and intellectual bearings, to give shape and character, colour and direction and coherence, to the stream of events.

This kind of systematic 'historicism' is, of course, not confined to men of action or political theorists: Roman Catholic thinkers see life in terms of a firm and lucid historical structure, and so, of course, do Marxists, and so did the romantic historians and philosophers from whom the Marxists are directly descended. Nor do we complain of 'escapism' or perversion of the facts until the categories adopted are thought to do too much violence to the 'facts'. To interpret, to relate, to classify, to symbolise are those natural and unavoidable human activities which we loosely and conveniently describe as thinking. We complain, if we do, only when the result is too widely at variance with the common outlook of our own society and age and tradition.

Churchill sees history – and life – as a great Renaissance pageant: when he thinks of France or Italy, Germany or the Low Countries, Russia, India, Africa, the Arab lands, he sees vivid historical images – something between Victorian illustrations in a child's book of history and the great procession painted by Benozzo Gozzoli in the Riccardi Palace. His eye is never that of the neatly classifying sociologist, the careful psychological analyst, the plodding antiquary, the patient historical scholar. His poetry has not that anatomical vision which sees the naked bone beneath the flesh, skulls and skeletons and the omnipresence of decay and death beneath the flow of life. The units out of which his world is constructed are simpler and larger than life, the patterns vivid and repetitive like those of an epic poet, or at times like those of a dramatist who sees persons and situations as timeless symbols and embodiments of eternal, shining principles. The whole is a series of symmetrically formed and somewhat stylised compositions, either suffused with bright light or cast in darkest shadow, like a legend by Carpaccio, with scarcely any nuance, painted in primary colours, with no half-tones, nothing intangible, nothing impalpable, nothing half spoken or hinted or whispered: the voice does not alter in pitch or timbre.

The archaisms of style to which Churchill's wartime speeches accustomed us are indispensable ingredients of the heightened tone, the formal chronicler's attire, for which the solemnity of the occasion called. Churchill is fully conscious of this: the style should adequately respond to the demands which history makes upon the actors from moment to moment. 'The ideas set forth', he wrote in 1940 about a Foreign Office draft, 'appeared to me to err in trying to be too clever, to enter into refinements of policy unsuited to the tragic simplicity and grandeur of the times and the issues at stake.'

His own narrative consciously mounts and swells until it reaches the great climax of the Battle of Britain. The texture and the tension are those of a tragic opera, where the very artificiality of the medium, both in the recitative and in the arias, serves to eliminate the irrelevant dead level of normal existence and to set off in high relief the deeds and sufferings of the principal characters. The moments of comedy in such a work must necessarily conform to the style of the whole and be parodies of it; and this is Churchill's practice. When he says that he viewed this or that 'with stern and tranquil gaze', or informs his officials that any 'chortling' by them over the failure of a chosen scheme 'will be viewed with great disfavour by me', or describes the 'celestial grins' of his collaborators over the development of a well-concealed conspiracy, he does precisely this; the mock-heroic tone – reminiscent of *Stalky & Co.* – does not break the operatic conventions. But conventions though they be, they are not donned and doffed by the author at will: by now they are his second nature, and have completely fused with the first; art and nature are no longer distinguishable. The very rigid pattern of his prose is the normal medium of his ideas not merely when he sets himself to compose, but in the life of the imagination which permeates his daily existence.

Churchill's language is a medium which he invented because he needed it. It has a bold, ponderous, fairly uniform, easily recognisable rhythm which lends itself to parody (including his own) like all strongly individual styles. A language is individual when its user is endowed with sharply marked characteristics and succeeds in creating a medium for their expression. The origins, the constituents, the classical echoes which can be found in Churchill's prose are obvious enough; the product is, however, unique. Whatever the attitude that may be taken towards it, it must be recognised as a large-scale phenomenon of our time. To ignore or deny this would be blind or frivolous or dishonest. The utterance is always, and not merely on special occasions, formal (though it alters in intensity and colour with the situation), always public, Ciceronian, addressed to the world, remote from the hesitancies and stresses of introspection and private life.

## III

The quality of Churchill's volumes on the Second World War is that of his whole life. His world is built upon the primacy of public over private relationships, upon the supreme value of action, of the battle between simple good and simple evil, between life and death; but, above all, battle. He has always fought. 'Whatever you may do,' he declared to the demoralised French ministers in the bleakest hour of 1940, 'we shall fight on for ever and ever and ever', and under this sign his own whole life has been lived.

What has he fought for? The answer is a good deal clearer than in the case of other equally passionate but less consistent men of action. Churchill's principles and beliefs on fundamental issues have never faltered. He has often been accused by his critics of inconstancy, of veering and even erratic judgement, as when he changed his allegiance from the Conservative to the Liberal Party, to and fro. But with the exception of the issue of protection, when he supported the tariff as Chancellor of the Exchequer in Baldwin's cabinet in the 1920s, this charge, which at first seems so plausible, is spectacularly false. Far from changing his opinions too often, Churchill has scarcely, during a long and stormy career, altered them at all. If anyone wishes to discover his views on the large and lasting issues of our time, he need only set himself to discover what Churchill has said or written on the subject at any period of his long and exceptionally articulate public life, in particular during the years before the First World War: the number of instances in which his views have in later years undergone any appreciable degree of change will be found astonishingly small.

The apparently solid and dependable Baldwin adjusted his attitudes with wonderful dexterity as and when circumstances required it. Chamberlain, long regarded as a grim and immovable rock of Tory opinion, altered his policies – more serious than Baldwin, he pursued policies, not being content with mere attitudes – when the Party or the situation seemed to him to require it. Churchill remained inflexibly attached to first principles.

It is the strength and coherence of his central, lifelong beliefs that have provoked greater uneasiness, more disfavour and suspicion, in the central office of the Conservative Party than his vehemence or passion for power, or what was considered his wayward, unreliable brilliance. No strongly centralised political organisation feels altogether happy with individuals who combine independence, a free imagination and a formidable strength of character with stubborn faith and a single-minded, unchanging view of the public and private good. Churchill, who believes that 'ambition, not so much for vulgar ends but for fame, glints in every mind', believes in and seeks to attain – as an artist his vision – personal greatness and personal glory. As much as any king conceived by a Renaissance dramatist or by a nineteenth-century historian or moralist, he thinks it a brave thing to ride in triumph through Persepolis; he knows with an unshakeable certainty what he considers to be big, handsome, noble and worthy of pursuit by someone in high station, and what, on the contrary, he abhors as being dim, grey, thin, likely to lower or destroy the play of colour and movement in the universe. Tacking and bending and timid compromise may commend themselves to those sound men of sense whose hopes of preserving the world they defend are shot through with an often unconscious pessimism; but if the policy they pursue is likely to slow the tempo, to diminish the forces of life, to lower the 'vital and vibrant energy' which he admires, say, in Lord Beaverbrook, Churchill is ready for attack.

Churchill is one of the diminishing number of those who genuinely believe in a specific world order: the desire to give it life and strength is the most powerful single influence upon everything which he thinks and imagines, does and is. When biographers and historians come to describe and analyse his views on Europe or America, on the British Empire or Russia, on India or Palestine, or even on social or economic policy, they will find that his opinions on all these topics are set in fixed patterns, set early in life and later only reinforced. Thus he has always believed in great States and civilisations in an almost hierarchical order, and has never, for instance, hated Germany as such: Germany is a great, historically hallowed State; the Germans are a great historic race and as such occupy a proportionate amount of space in Churchill's world picture. He denounced the Prussians in the First World War and the Nazis in the Second; the Germans scarcely at all. He has always entertained a glowing vision of France and her culture, and has unalterably advocated the necessity of Anglo-French collaboration. He has always looked on the Russians as a formless, quasi-Asiatic mass beyond the walls of European civilisation. His belief in and predilection for the American democracy are the foundation of his political outlook.

His vision in foreign affairs has always been consistently romantic. The struggle of the Jews for self-determination in Palestine engaged his imagination in precisely the way in which the Italian Risorgimento captured the sympathies of his Liberal forebears. Similarly his views on social policy conform to those Liberal principles which he received at the hands of the men he most admired in the great Liberal administration of the first decade of this century – Asquith, Haldane, Grey, Morley, above all Lloyd George before 1914 – and he has seen no reason to change them, whatever the world might do; and if these views, progressive in 1910, seem less convincing today, and indeed reveal an obstinate blindness to social and economic – as opposed to political –

injustice, of which Haldane or Lloyd George can scarcely be accused, that flows from Churchill's unalterable faith in the firmly conceived scheme of human relationships which he established within himself long ago, once and for all.

IV

It is an error to regard the imagination as a mainly revolutionary force – if it destroys and alters, it also fuses hitherto isolated beliefs, insights, mental habits, into strongly unified systems. These, if they are filled with sufficient energy and force of will – and, it may be added, fantasy, which is less frightened by the facts and creates ideal models in terms of which the facts are ordered in the mind – sometimes transform the outlook of an entire people and generation.

The British statesman most richly endowed with these gifts was Disraeli, who in effect conceived that imperialist mystique, that splendid but most un-English vision which, romantic to the point of exoticism, full of metaphysical emotion, to all appearances utterly opposed to everything most soberly empirical, utilitarian, anti-systematic in the British tradition, bound its spell on the mind of England for two generations.

Churchill's political imagination has something of the same magical power to transform. It is a magic which belongs equally to demagogues and great democratic leaders: Franklin Roosevelt, who as much as any man altered his country's inner image of itself and of its character and its history, possessed it in a high degree. But the differences between him and Churchill are greater than the similarities, and to some degree epitomise the differences of continents and civilisations. The contrast is brought out vividly by the respective parts which they played in the war which drew them so closely together.

The Second World War in some ways gave birth to less novelty and genius than the First. It was, of course, a greater cataclysm, fought over a wider area, and altered the social and political contours of the world at least as radically as its predecessor, perhaps more so. But the break in continuity in 1914 was far more violent. The years before 1914 look to us now, and looked even in the 1920s, as the end of a long period of largely peaceful development, broken suddenly and catastrophically. In Europe, at

least, the years before 1914 were viewed with understandable
nostalgia by those who after them knew no real peace.

The period between the Wars marks a decline in the development
of human culture if it is compared with that sustained and fruitful
period which makes the nineteenth century seem a unique human
achievement, so powerful that it persisted, even during the war
which broke it, to a degree which seems astonishing to us now.
The quality of literature, for example, which is surely one of the
most reliable criteria of intellectual and moral vitality, was incom-
parably higher during the War of 1914–18 than it has been after
1939. In Western Europe alone these four years of slaughter and
destruction were also years in which works of genius and talent
continued to be produced by such established writers as Shaw and
Wells and Kipling, Hauptmann and Gide, Chesterton and Arnold
Bennett, Beerbohm and Yeats, as well as such younger writers as
Proust and Joyce, Virginia Woolf and E. M. Forster, T. S. Eliot and
Alexander Blok, Rilke, Stefan George and Valéry. Nor did natural
science, philosophy and history cease to develop fruitfully. What
has the more recent war to offer by comparison?

Yet perhaps there is one respect in which the Second World War
did outshine its predecessor: the leaders of the nations involved in
it were, with the significant exception of France, men of greater
stature, psychologically more interesting, than their prototypes. It
would hardly be disputed that Stalin is a more fascinating figure
than Tsar Nicholas II; Hitler more arresting than the Kaiser;
Mussolini than Victor Emmanuel; and, memorable as they were,
President Wilson and Lloyd George yield in the attribute of sheer
historical magnitude to Franklin Roosevelt and Winston Churchill.

History, we are told by Aristotle, is 'what Alcibiades did and
suffered'.[1] This notion, despite all the efforts of the social sciences
to overthrow it, remains a good deal more valid than rival
hypotheses, provided that history is defined as that which historians actually do. At any rate Churchill accepts it wholeheartedly,
and takes full advantage of his opportunities. And because his
narrative deals largely in personalities and gives individual genius
its full and sometimes more than its full due, the appearance of the
great wartime protagonists in his pages gives his narrative some of
the quality of an epic, whose heroes and villains acquire their
stature not merely – or indeed at all – from the importance of the

[1] *Poetics* 1451$^b$11.

events in which they are involved, but from their own intrinsic human size upon the stage of human history; their characteristics, involved as they are in perpetual juxtaposition and occasional collision with one another, set each other off in vast relief.

Comparisons and contrasts are bound to arise in the mind of the reader which sometimes take him beyond Churchill's pages. Thus Roosevelt stands out principally by his astonishing appetite for life and by his apparently complete freedom from fear of the future; as a man who welcomed the future eagerly as such, and conveyed the feeling that whatever the times might bring, all would be grist to his mill, nothing would be too formidable or crushing to be subdued and used and moulded into the pattern of the new and unpredictable forms of life into the building of which he, Roosevelt, and his allies and devoted subordinates would throw themselves with unheard-of energy and gusto. This avid anticipation of the future, the lack of nervous fear that the wave might prove too big or violent to navigate, contrasts most sharply with the uneasy longing to insulate themselves so clear in Stalin or Chamberlain. Hitler, too, in a sense, showed no fear, but his assurance sprang from a lunatic's violent and cunning vision, which distorted the facts too easily in his favour.

So passionate a faith in the future, so untroubled a confidence in one's power to mould it, when it is allied to a capacity for realistic appraisal of its true contours, implies an exceptionally sensitive awareness, conscious or half-conscious, of the tendencies of one's milieu, of the desires, hopes, fears, loves, hatreds of the human beings who compose it, of what are impersonally described as social and individual 'trends'. Roosevelt had this sensibility developed to the point of genius. He acquired the symbolic significance which he retained throughout his presidency largely because he sensed the tendencies of his time and their projections into the future to a most uncommon degree. His sense, not only of the movement of American public opinion but of the general direction in which the larger human society of his time was moving, was what is called uncanny. The inner currents, the tremors and complicated convolutions of this movement seemed to register themselves within his nervous system with a kind of seismographical accuracy. The majority of his fellow citizens recognised this – some with enthusiasm, others with gloom or bitter indignation. Peoples far beyond the frontiers of the United States rightly looked to him as the most genuine and unswerving spokesman of democracy of his time, the most contemporary, the most outward-looking, the boldest, most imaginative, most large-spirited, free from the obsessions of an inner life, with an unparalleled capacity for creating confidence in the power of his insight, his foresight, and his capacity genuinely to identify himself with the ideals of humble people.

This feeling of being at home not merely in the present but in the future, of knowing where he was going and by what means and why, made him, until his health was finally undermined, buoyant and gay: made him delight in the company of the most varied and opposed individuals, provided that they embodied some specific aspect of the turbulent stream of life, stood actively for the forward movement in their particular world, whatever it might be. And this inner *élan* made up, and more than made up, for faults of intellect or character, which his enemies – and his victims – never ceased to point out. He seemed genuinely unaffected by their taunts: what he could not abide was, before all, passivity, stillness, melancholy, fear of life or preoccupation with eternity or death, however great the insight or delicate the sensibility by which they were accompanied.

Churchill stands at almost the opposite pole. He too does not fear the future, and no man has ever loved life more vehemently and infused so much of it into everyone and everything that he has touched. But whereas Roosevelt, like all great innovators, had a half-conscious premonitory awareness of the coming shape of society, not wholly unlike that of an artist, Churchill, for all his extrovert air, looks within, and his strongest sense is the sense of the past.

The clear, brightly coloured vision of history in terms of which he conceives both the present and the future is the inexhaustible source from which he draws the primary stuff out of which his universe is so solidly built, so richly and elaborately ornamented. So firm and so embracing an edifice could not be constructed by anyone liable to react and respond like a sensitive instrument to the perpetually changing moods and directions of other persons or institutions or peoples. And, indeed, Churchill's strength (and what is most frightening in him) lies precisely in this: that, unlike Roosevelt, he is not equipped with numberless sensitive antennae which communicate the smallest oscillations of the outer world in all its unstable variety. Unlike Roosevelt (and unlike Gladstone and Lloyd George for that matter) he does not reflect a contemporary social or moral world in an intense and concentrated fashion; rather he creates one of such power and coherence that it becomes a reality and alters the external world by being imposed upon it with irresistible force. As his history of the War shows, he has an immense capacity for absorbing facts, but they emerge transformed by the categories which he powerfully imposes on the raw material into something which he can use to build his own massive, simple, impregnably fortified inner world.

Roosevelt, as a public personality, was a spontaneous, optimistic, pleasure-loving ruler who dismayed his assistants by the gay and apparently heedless abandon with which he seemed to delight in pursuing two or more totally incompatible policies, and astonished them even more by the swiftness and ease with which he managed to throw off the cares of office during the darkest and most dangerous moments. Churchill too loves pleasure, and he too lacks neither gaiety nor a capacity for exuberant self-expression, together with the habit of blithely cutting Gordian knots in a manner which often upset his experts; but he is not a frivolous man. His nature possesses a dimension of depth – and a corresponding sense of tragic possibilities – which Roosevelt's light-hearted genius instinctively passed by.

Roosevelt played the game of politics with virtuosity, and both his successes and his failures were carried off in splendid style; his performance seemed to flow with effortless skill. Churchill is acquainted with darkness as well as light. Like all inhabitants of inner worlds, and even transient visitors to them, he gives evidence of seasons of agonised brooding and slow recovery. Roosevelt might have spoken of sweat and blood, but when Churchill offered his people tears, he spoke a word which might have been uttered by Lincoln or Mazzini or Cromwell, but not by Roosevelt, great-hearted, generous and perceptive as he was.

## V

Not the herald of the bright and cloudless civilisation of the future, Churchill is preoccupied by his own vivid world, and it is doubtful how far he has ever been aware of what actually goes on in the heads and hearts of others. He does not react, he acts; he does not mirror, he affects others and alters them to his own powerful measure. Writing of Dunkirk he says:

> There is no doubt that had I at this juncture faltered at all in the
> leading of the nation I should have been hurled out of office. I was

sure that every Minister was ready to be killed quite soon, and have all his family and possessions destroyed, rather than give in. In this they represented the House of Commons and almost all the people. It fell to me in these coming days and months to express their sentiments on suitable occasions. This I was able to do because they were mine also. There was a white glow, overpowering, sublime, which ran through our Island from end to end.[1]

And on 28 June of that year he told Lord Lothian, then ambassador in Washington, 'Your mood should be bland and phlegmatic. No one is down-hearted here.'[2]

These splendid sentences hardly do justice to his own part in creating the feeling which he describes. For Churchill is not a sensitive lens which absorbs and concentrates and reflects and amplifies the sentiments of others; unlike the European dictators, he does not play on public opinion like an instrument. In 1940 he assumed an indomitable stoutness, an unsurrendering quality on the part of his people, and carried on. If he did not represent the quintessence and epitome of what some, at any rate, of his fellow citizens feared and hoped in their hour of danger, this was because he idealised them with such intensity that in the end they approached his ideal and began to see themselves as he saw them: 'the buoyant and imperturbable temper of Britain which I had the honour to express' – it was indeed, but he had a lion's share in creating it. So hypnotic was the force of his words, so strong his faith, that by the sheer intensity of his eloquence he bound his spell upon them until it seemed to them that he was indeed speaking what was in their hearts and minds. Doubtless it was there; but largely dormant until he had awoken it within them.

After he had spoken to them in the summer of 1940 as no one has ever before or since, they conceived a new idea of themselves which their own prowess and the admiration of the world has since established as a heroic image in the history of mankind, like Thermopylae or the defeat of the Spanish Armada. They went forward into battle transformed by his words. The spirit which they found within them he had created within himself from his inner resources, and poured it into his nation, and took their vivid reaction for an original impulse on their part, which he merely had the honour to clothe in suitable words. He created a heroic mood

[1] *Their Finest Hour* [*The Second World War*, vol. 2] (London, 1949), p. 88.
[2] ibid., p. 201.

and turned the fortunes of the Battle of Britain not by catching the mood of his surroundings (which was not indeed, at any time, one of craven panic or bewilderment or apathy, but somewhat confused; stout-hearted but unorganised) but by being stubbornly impervious to it, as he has been to so many of the passing shades and tones of which the life around him has been composed.

The peculiar quality of heroic pride and a sense of the sublimity of the occasion arises in him not, as in Roosevelt, from delight in being alive and in control at a critical moment of history, in the very change and instability of things, in the infinite possibilities of the future whose very unpredictability offers endless possibilities of spontaneous moment-to-moment improvisation and large imaginative moves in harmony with the restless spirit of the time. On the contrary, it springs from a capacity for sustained introspective brooding, great depth and constancy of feeling – in particular, feeling for and fidelity to the great tradition for which he assumes a personal responsibility, a tradition which he bears upon his shoulders and must deliver, not only sound and undamaged but strengthened and embellished, to successors worthy of accepting the sacred burden.

Bismarck once said that there was no such thing as political intuition: political genius consisted in the ability to hear the distant hoofbeat of the horse of history – and then by superhuman effort to leap and catch the horseman by the coat-tails. No man has ever listened for this fateful sound more eagerly than Winston Churchill, and in 1940 he made the heroic leap. 'It is impossible', he writes of this time, 'to quell the inward excitement which comes from a prolonged balancing of terrible things', and when the crisis finally bursts he is ready, because after a lifetime of effort he has reached his goal.

The position of the Prime Minister is unique: 'If he trips he must be sustained: if he makes mistakes they must be covered; if he sleeps he must not be wantonly disturbed; if he is no good he must be pole-axed', and this because he is at that moment the guardian of the 'life of Britain, her message and her glory'. He trusted Roosevelt utterly, 'convinced that he would give up life itself, to say nothing about office, for the cause of world freedom now in such awful peril'. His prose records the tension which rises and swells to the culminating moment, the Battle of Britain – 'a time when it was equally good to live or die'. This bright, heroic vision of the mortal danger and the will to conquer, born in the hour when defeat seemed not merely possible but probable, is the product of a burning historical imagination, feeding upon the data not of the outer but of the inner eye: the picture has a shape and simplicity which future historians will find it hard to reproduce when they seek to assess and interpret the facts soberly in the grey light of common day.

## VI

The Prime Minister was able to impose his imagination and his will upon his countrymen, and enjoy a Periclean reign, precisely because he appeared to them larger and nobler than life and lifted them to an abnormal height in a moment of crisis. It was a climate in which men do not usually like – nor ought they to like – living; it demands a violent tension which, if it lasts, destroys all sense of normal perspective, overdramatises personal relationships, and falsifies normal values to an intolerable extent. But, in the event, it did turn a large number of inhabitants of the British Isles out of their normal selves and, by dramatising their lives and making them seem to themselves and to each other clad in the fabulous garments appropriate to a great historic moment, transformed cowards into brave men, and so fulfilled the purpose of shining armour.

This is the kind of means by which dictators and demagogues transform peaceful populations into marching armies; it was Churchill's unique and unforgettable achievement that he created this necessary illusion within the framework of a free system without destroying or even twisting it; that he called forth spirits which did not stay to oppress and enslave the population after the hour of need had passed; that he saved the future by interpreting the present in terms of a vision of the past which did not distort or inhibit the historical development of the British people by attempting to make them realise some impossible and unattainable splendour in the name of an imaginary tradition or of an infallible, supernatural leader. Churchill was saved from this frightening nemesis of romanticism by a sufficiency of that libertarian feeling which, if it sometimes fell short of understanding the tragic aspects of modern despotisms, remained sharply perceptive – sometimes too tolerantly, but still perceptive – of what is false, grotesque, contemptible in the great frauds upon the people practised by totalitarian regimes. Some of the sharpest and most characteristic epithets are reserved for the dictators: Hitler is 'this evil man, this monstrous abortion of hatred and defeat'. Franco is a 'narrow-minded tyrant' of 'evil qualities' holding down a 'blood-drained people'. No quarter is given to the Pétain regime, and its appeal to tradition and the eternal France is treated as a repellent travesty of national feeling. Stalin in 1940-1 is 'at once a callous, a crafty, and an ill-informed giant'.

This very genuine hostility to usurpers, which is stronger in him than even his passion for authority and order, springs from a quality which Churchill conspicuously shared with President Roosevelt – uncommon love of life, aversion for the imposition of rigid disciplines upon the teeming variety of human relations, the instinctive sense of what promotes and what retards or distorts growth and vitality. But because the life which Churchill so loves presents itself to him in a historical guise as part of the pageant of tradition, his method of constructing historical narrative, the distribution of emphasis, the assignment of relative importance to persons and events, the theory of history, the architecture of the narrative, the structure of the sentences, the words themselves, are elements in an historical revival as fresh, as original and as idiosyncratic as the neo-classicism of the Renaissance or the Regency. To complain that this omits altogether too much by assuming that the impersonal, the dull, the undramatic are necessarily also unimportant may well be just; but to lament that this is not contemporary, and therefore in some way less true, less responsive to modern needs, than the noncommittal, neutral glass and plastic of those objective historians who regard facts and only facts as interesting and, worse still, all facts as equally interesting – what is this but craven pedantry and blindness?

VII

The differences between the President and the Prime Minister were at least in one respect something more than the obvious differences of national character, education, and even temperament. For all his sense of history, his large, untroubled, easygoing style of life, his unshakeable feeling of personal security, his natural assumption of being at home in the great world far beyond the confines of his own country, Roosevelt was a typical child of the twentieth century and of the New World; while Churchill for all his love of the present hour, his unquenchable appetite for new knowledge, his sense of the technological possibilities of our time, and the restless roaming of his fancy in considering how they might be most imaginatively applied, despite his enthusiasm for Basic English, or the siren suit which so upset his hosts in Moscow – despite all this, Churchill remains a European of the nineteenth century.

The difference is deep, and accounts for a great deal in the incompatibility of outlook between him and the President of the United States, whom he admired so much and whose great office he held in awe. Something of the fundamental unlikeness between America and Europe, and perhaps between the twentieth century and the nineteenth, seemed to be crystallised in this remarkable interplay. It may perhaps be that the twentieth century is to the nineteenth as the nineteenth was to the eighteenth. Talleyrand once made the well-known observation that those who had not lived under the *ancien régime* did not know what true *plaisir de vivre* had been. And indeed, from our distant vantage-point, this is clear: the earnest, romantic young men of the early part of the nineteenth century seemed systematically unable to understand or to like the attitude to life of the most civilised representatives of the pre-revolutionary world, particularly in France, where the break was sharpest; the irony, the sharpness, the minute vision, the perception of and concentration upon fine differences in character, in style, the preoccupation with barely perceptible dissimilarities of hue, the extreme sensibility which makes the life of even so 'progressive' and forward-looking a man as Diderot so unbridgeably different from the larger and simpler vision of the romantics – this is something which the nineteenth century lacked the historical perspective to understand.

Suppose that Shelley had met and talked with Voltaire, what would he have felt? He would most probably have been profoundly shocked – shocked by the seemingly limited vision, the smallness of the field of awareness, the apparent triviality and finickiness, the almost spinsterish elaboration of Voltaire's malice, the preoccupation with tiny units, the subatomic texture of experience; he would have felt horror or pity before such wanton blindness to the large moral and spiritual issues of his own day – causes whose universal scope and significance painfully agitated the best and most awakened minds; he might have thought him wicked, but even more he would have thought him contemptible, too sharp, too small, too mean, grotesquely and unworthily obscene, prone to titter on the most sacred occasions, in the holiest places.

And Voltaire, in his turn, would very probably have been dreadfully bored, unable to see good cause for so much ethical eloquence; he would have looked with a cold and hostile eye on all this moral excitement: the magnificent Saint-Simonian vision of one world (which so stirred the left-wing young men half a century later), altering in shape and becoming integrated into a neatly organised man-made whole by the application of powerfully concentrated scientific, technical and spiritual resources, would to him have seemed a dreary and monotonous desert, too homogeneous, too flavourless, too unreal, apparently unconscious of those small, half-concealed but crucial distinctions and incongruities which give individuality and savour to experience, without which there could be no civilised vision, no wit, no conversation, certainly no art deriving from a refined and fastidious culture. The moral vision of the nineteenth century would have seemed to him a dull, blurred, coarse instrument unable to focus those pin-points of concentrated light, those short-lived patterns of sound and colour, whose infinite variety as they linger or flash past are comedy and tragedy – are the substance of personal relations and of worldly wisdom, of politics, of history, and of art.

The reason for this failure of communication was not a mere change in the point of view, but the kind of vision which divided the two centuries. The microscopic vision of the eighteenth century was succeeded by the macroscopic eye of the nineteenth. The latter saw much more widely, saw in universal or at least in European terms; it saw the contours of great mountain ranges where the eighteenth century discerned, however sharply and perceptively, only the veins and cracks and different shades of but a portion of the mountainside. The object of vision of the eighteenth century was smaller and its eye was closer to the object. The enormous moral issues of the nineteenth century were not within the field of its acutely discriminating gaze: that was the devastating difference which the great French Revolution had made, and it led to something not necessarily better or worse, uglier or more beautiful, profounder or more shallow, but to a situation which above all was different in kind.

Something not unlike this same chasm divides America from Europe (and the twentieth century from the nineteenth). The

American vision is larger and more generous; its thought transcends, despite the parochialism of its means of expression, the barriers of nationality and race and differences of outlook, in a big, sweeping, single view. It notices things rather than persons, and sees the world (those who saw it in this fashion in the nineteenth century were considered Utopian eccentrics) in terms of rich, infinitely mouldable raw material, waiting to be constructed and planned in order to satisfy a world-wide human craving for happiness or goodness or wisdom. And therefore to it the differences and conflicts which divide Europeans in so violent a fashion must seem petty, irrational and sordid, not worthy of self-respecting, morally conscious individuals and nations; ready, in fact, to be swept away in favour of a simpler and grander view of the powers and tasks of modern man.

To Europeans this American attitude, the large vista possible only for those who live on mountain heights or vast and level plains affording an unbroken view, seems curiously flat, without subtlety or colour, at times appearing to lack the entire dimension of depth, certainly without that immediate reaction to fine distinctions with which perhaps only those who live in valleys are endowed, and so America, which knows so much, to them seems to understand too little, to miss the central point. This does not, of course, apply to every American or European – there are natural Americans among the natives of Europe and vice versa – but it seems to characterise the most typical representatives of these disparate cultures.

## VIII

In some respects Roosevelt half-consciously understood and did not wholly condemn this attitude on the part of Europeans; and even more clearly Churchill is in many respects in instinctive sympathy with the American way of life. But by and large they do represent different outlooks, and the very high degree to which they were able to understand and admire each other's quality is a tribute to the extraordinary power of imagination and delight in the variety of life on the part of both. Each was to the other not merely an ally, the admired leader of a great people, but a symbol of a tradition and a civilisation; from the unity of their differences they hoped for a regeneration of the Western world.

Roosevelt was intrigued by the Russian sphinx; Churchill

instinctively recoiled from its alien and to him unattractive attributes. Roosevelt, on the whole, thought that he could cajole Russia
and even induce her to be assimilated into the great society which
would embrace mankind; Churchill, on the whole, remained
sceptical.

Roosevelt was imaginative, optimistic, episcopalian, self-confident, cheerful, empirical, fearless, and steeped in the ideas of social
progress; he believed that with enough energy and spirit anything
could be achieved by man; he shrank as much as any English
schoolboy from probing underneath the surface, and saw vast
affinities between the peoples in the world, out of which a new,
freer and richer order could somehow be built. Churchill was
imaginative and steeped in history, more serious, more intent, more
concentrated, more preoccupied, and felt very deeply the eternal
differences which could make such a structure difficult of attain-
ment. He believed in institutions and the permanent characters of
races and classes and types of individuals. His government was
organised on clear principles; his personal private office was run in
a sharply disciplined manner. His habits, though unusual, were
regular. He believed in a natural, a social, almost a metaphysical
order – a sacred hierarchy which it was neither possible nor
desirable to upset.

Roosevelt believed in flexibility, improvisation, the fruitfulness
of using persons and resources in an infinite variety of new and
unexpected ways; his bureaucracy was somewhat chaotic, perhaps
deliberately so. His own office was not tidily organised, he
practised a highly personal form of government. He maddened the
advocates of institutional authority, but it is doubtful whether he
could have achieved his ends in any other way.

These dissimilarities of outlook went deep, but both were large
enough in scope and both were genuine visions, not narrowed and
distorted by personal idiosyncrasies and those disparities of moral
standard which so fatally divided Wilson, Lloyd George and
Clemenceau. The President and the Prime Minister often disagreed;
their ideals and their methods were widely different; in some of the
memoirs and gossip of Roosevelt's entourage much has been made
of this; but the discussion, at all times, was conducted on a level of
which both heads of government were conscious. They may have
opposed but they never wished to wound each other; they may
have issued contrary instructions but they never bickered; when
they compromised, as they so often did, they did so without a

sense of bitterness or defeat, but in response to the demands of history or one another's traditions and personality.

Each appeared to the other in a romantic light high above the battles of allies or subordinates: their meetings and correspondence were occasions to which both consciously rose; they were royal cousins and felt pride in this relationship, tempered by a sharp and sometimes amused, but never ironical, perception of the other's peculiar qualities. The relationship born during the great historical upheaval, somewhat aggrandised by its solemnity, never flagged or degenerated, but retained a combination of formal dignity and exuberant high spirits which can scarcely ever before have bound the heads of States. Each was personally fascinated not so much by the other as by the idea of the other, and infected him by his own peculiar brand of high spirits.

The relationship was made genuine by something more than even the solid community of interest or personal and official respect or admiration – namely, by the peculiar degree to which they liked each other's delight in the oddities and humours of life and their own active part in it. This was a unique personal bond, which Harry Hopkins understood and encouraged to the fullest degree. Roosevelt's sense of fun was perhaps the lighter, Churchill's a trifle grimmer. But it was something which they shared with each other and with few, if any, statesmen outside the Anglo-American orbit; their staffs sometimes ignored or misunderstood it, and it gave a most singular quality to their association.

Roosevelt's public utterances differ by a whole world from the dramatic masterpieces of Churchill, but they are not incompatible with them in spirit or in substance. Roosevelt has not left us his own account of his world as he saw it; and perhaps he lived too much from day to day to be temperamentally attracted to the performance of such a task. But both were thoroughly aware of their commanding position in the history of the modern world, and Churchill's account of his stewardship is written in full consciousness of this responsibility.

It is a great occasion, and he treats it with corresponding solemnity. Like a great actor – perhaps the last of his kind – upon the stage of history, he speaks his memorable lines with a large, unhurried and stately utterance in a blaze of light, as is appropriate to a man who knows that his work and his person will remain the object of scrutiny and judgement to many generations. His narrative is a great public performance and has the attribute of formal magnificence. The words, the splendid phrases, the sustained quality of feeling, are a unique medium which conveys his vision of himself and of his world, and will inevitably, like all that he has said and done, reinforce the famous public image, which is no longer distinguishable from the inner essence and the true nature of the author: of a man larger than life, composed of bigger and simpler elements than ordinary men, a gigantic historical figure during his own lifetime, superhumanly bold, strong and imaginative, one of the two greatest men of action his nation has produced, an orator of prodigious powers, the saviour of his country, a mythical hero who belongs to legend as much as to reality, the largest human being of our time.

# PRESIDENT
## FRANKLIN DELANO ROOSEVELT

I NEVER met Roosevelt, and although I spent more than three years in Washington during the War, I never even saw him. I regret this, for it seems to me that to see and, in particular, to hear the voice of someone who has occupied one's imagination for many years must modify one's impression in some profound way, and make it somehow more concrete and three-dimensional. However, I never did see him, and I heard him only over the wireless. Consequently I must try to convey my impression without the benefit of personal acquaintance, and without, I ought to add, any expert knowledge of American history or of international relations. Nor am I competent to speak of Roosevelt's domestic or foreign policies: or their larger political or economic effect. I shall try to give only a personal impression of the general impact of his personality on my generation in Europe.

When I say that some men occupy one's imagination for many years, this is literally true of Roosevelt and the young men of my own generation in England, and probably in many parts of Europe, and indeed the entire world. If one was young in the 1930s, and lived in a democracy, then, whatever one's politics, if one had human feelings at all, the faintest spark of social idealism, or any love of life whatever, one must have felt very much as young men in Continental Europe probably felt after the defeat of Napoleon during the years of the Restoration, that all was dark and quiet, a great reaction was abroad: and little stirred, and nothing resisted.

It all began with the great slump of 1931, which undermined the feeling, perhaps quite baseless, of economic security which a good many young people of the middle classes then had. There followed the iron '30s, of which the English poets of the time – Auden, Spender, Day Lewis – left a very vivid testament: the dark and leaden '30s, to which, alone of all periods, no one in Europe wishes to return, unless indeed they lament the passing of Fascism. There came Manchuria, Hitler, the Hunger Marchers, the Abyssinian War, the Peace Ballot, the Left Book Club, Malraux's political novels, even the article by Virginia Woolf in the *Daily Worker*, the Soviet trials and purges, the conversions of idealistic young liberals and radicals to Communism, or strong sympathy with it, often for no better reason than that it seemed the only force firm enough and strong enough to resist the Fascist enemy effectively; such conversions were sometimes followed by visits to Moscow or by fighting in Spain, and death on the battlefield, or else bitter and angry disillusionment with Communist practice, or some desperate and unconvinced choice between two evils of that which seemed the lesser.

The most insistent propaganda in those days declared that humanitarianism and liberalism and democratic forces were played out, and that the choice now lay between two bleak extremes, Communism and Fascism – the red or the black. To those who were not carried away by this patter the only light that was left in the darkness was the administration of Roosevelt and the New Deal in the United States. At a time of weakness and mounting despair in the democratic world Roosevelt radiated confidence and strength. He was the leader of the democratic world, and upon him alone, of all the statesmen of the '30s, no cloud rested – neither on him nor on the New Deal, which to European eyes still looks a bright chapter in the history of mankind. It is true that his great social experiment was conducted with an isolationist disregard of the outside world, but then it was psychologically intelligible that America, which had come into being in the reaction against the follies and evils of a Europe perpetually distraught by religious or national struggles, should try to seek salvation undisturbed by the currents of European life, particularly at a moment when Europe seemed about to collapse into a totalitarian nightmare. Roosevelt was therefore forgiven, by those who found the European situation tragic, for pursuing no particular foreign policy, indeed for trying to do, if not without any foreign policy at all, at any rate with a minimum of relationship with the outside world, which was indeed to some degree part of the American political tradition.

His internal policy was plainly animated by a humanitarian purpose. After the unbridled individualism of the 1920s, which had led to economic collapse and widespread misery, he was seeking to establish new rules of social justice. He was trying to do this without forcing his country into some doctrinaire strait-jacket, whether of socialism or State capitalism, or the kind of new social organisation which the Fascist regimes flaunted as the New Order. Social discontent was high in the United States, faith in businessmen as saviours of society had evaporated overnight after the famous Wall Street Crash, and Roosevelt was providing a vast safety-valve for pent-up bitterness and indignation, and trying to prevent revolution and construct a regime which should provide for greater economic equality and social justice – ideals which were the best part of the tradition of American life – without altering the basis of freedom and democracy in his country. This was being done by what to unsympathetic critics seemed a haphazard collection of amateurs, college professors, journalists, personal friends, freelances of one kind or another, intellectuals, ideologists, what are nowadays called eggheads, whose very appearance and methods of conducting business or constructing policies irritated the servants of old-established government institutions in Washington and tidy-minded conservatives of every type. Yet it was clear that the very amateurishness of these men, the fact that they were allowed to talk to their hearts' content, to experiment, to indulge in a vast amount of trial and error, that relations were personal and not institutional, bred its own vitality and enthusiasm. Washington was doubtless full of quarrels, resignations, palace intrigues, perpetual warfare between individuals and groups of individuals, parties, cliques, personal supporters of this or that great captain, which must have maddened sober and responsible officials used to the slower tempo and more normal patterns of administration; as for bankers and businessmen, their feelings were past describing, but at this period they were little regarded, since they were considered to have discredited themselves too deeply, and indeed for ever.

Over this vast, seething chaos presided a handsome, charming, gay, very intelligent, very delightful, very audacious man, Franklin Delano Roosevelt. He was accused of many weaknesses. He had betrayed his class; he was ignorant, unscrupulous, irresponsible. He was ruthless in playing with the lives and careers of individuals. He was surrounded by adventurers, slick opportunists, intriguers. He made conflicting promises, cynically and brazenly, to individuals and groups and representatives of foreign nations. He made up, with his vast and irresistible public charm, and his astonishing high spirits, for lack of other virtues considered as more important in the leader of the most powerful democracy in the world – the virtues of application, industry, responsibility. All this was said and some of it may indeed have been just. What attracted his followers were countervailing qualities of a rare and inspiring order: he was large-hearted and possessed wide political horizons, imaginative sweep, understanding of the time in which he lived and of the direction of the great new forces at work in the twentieth century – technological, racial, imperialist, anti-imperialist; he was in favour of life and movement, the promotion of the most generous possible fulfilment of the largest possible number of human wishes, and not in favour of caution and retrenchment and sitting still. Above all, he was absolutely fearless.

He was one of the few statesmen in the twentieth or any other century who seemed to have no fear at all of the future. He believed in his own strength and ability to manage, and succeed, whatever happened. He believed in the capacity and loyalty of his lieutenants, so that he looked upon the future with a calm eye, as if to say 'Let it come, whatever it may be, it will all be grist to our great mill. We shall turn it all to benefit.' It was this, perhaps, more than any other quality, which drew men of very different outlooks to him. In a despondent world which appeared divided between wicked and fatally efficient fanatics marching to destroy, and bewildered populations on the run, unenthusiastic martyrs in a cause they could not define, he believed in his own ability, so long as he was at the controls, to stem this terrible tide. He had all the character and energy and skill of the dictators, and he was on our side. He was, in his opinions and public action, every inch a democrat. All the political and personal and public criticism of him might be true; all the personal defects which his enemies and some of his friends attributed to him might be real; yet as a public figure he was unique. As the skies of Europe grew darker, in particular after war broke out, he seemed to the poor and the unhappy in Europe a kind of benevolent demigod who alone could and would save them in the end. His moral authority – the degree of confidence which he inspired outside his own country, and far more beyond America's frontiers than within them at all times – has no parallel. Perhaps President Wilson, in the early days, after the end of the First World War, when he drove triumphantly through Paris and London, may have inspired some such feeling; but it disappeared quickly and left a terrible feeling of disenchantment behind it. It was plain even to his enemies that President Roosevelt would not be broken as President Wilson was. But to his

prestige and to his personality he added a degree of political skill –
indeed virtuosity – which no American before him had ever
possessed. His chance of realising his wishes was plainly greater;
his followers would be less likely to reap bitter disappointment.

Indeed he was very different from Wilson. For they represent
two contrasting types of statesman, in each of which occasionally
men of compelling stature appear. The first kind of statesman is
essentially a man of single principle and fanatical vision. Possessed
by his own bright, coherent dream, he usually understands neither
people nor events. He has no doubts or hesitations and by
concentration of will-power, directness and strength he is able to
ignore a great deal of what goes on outside him. This very
blindness and stubborn self-absorption occasionally, in certain
situations, enable him to bend events and men to his own fixed
pattern. His strength lies in the fact that weak and vacillating
human beings, themselves too insecure or incapable of deciding
between alternatives, find relief and peace and strength in submit-
ting to the leadership of a single leader of superhuman size, to
whom all issues are clear, whose universe consists entirely of
primary colours, mostly black and white, and who marches
towards his goal looking neither to right nor to left, buoyed up by
the violent vision within him. Such men differ widely in moral and
intellectual quality, and, like forces of nature, do both good and
harm in the world. To this type belong Garibaldi, Trotsky, Parnell,
de Gaulle, perhaps Lenin too – the distinction I am drawing is not
a moral one, not one of value but one of type. There are great
benefactors, like Wilson, as well as fearful evil-doers, like Hitler,
within this category.

The other kind of effective statesman is a naturally political
being, as the simple hero is often explicitly anti-political and comes
to rescue men, at least ostensibly, from the subtleties and frauds of
political life. Politicians of this second type possess antennae of the
greatest possible delicacy, which convey to them, in ways difficult
or impossible to analyse, the perpetually changing contours of
events and feelings and human activities round them – they are
gifted with a peculiar, political sense fed on a capacity to take in
minute impressions, to integrate a vast multitude of small evanes-
cent unseizable detail, such as artists possess in relation to their
material. Statesmen of this type know what to do and when to do
it, if they are to achieve their ends, which themselves are usually

not born within some private world of inner thought, or intro-
verted feeling, but are the crystallisation, the raising to great
intensity and clarity, of what a large number of their fellow citizens
are thinking and feeling in some dim, inarticulate, but nevertheless
persistent fashion. In virtue of this capacity to judge their material,
very much as a sculptor knows what can be moulded out of wood
and what out of marble, and how and when, they resemble doctors
who have a natural gift for curing, which does not directly depend
upon that knowledge of scientific anatomy which can be learned
only by observation or experiment, or from the experiences of
others, though it could not exist without it. This instinctive, or at
any rate incommunicable, knowledge of where to look for what
one needs, the power of divining where the treasure lies, is
something common to many types of genius, to scientists and
mathematicians no less than to businessmen and administrators and
politicians. Such men, when they are statesmen, are acutely aware
of which way the thoughts and feelings of human beings are
flowing, and where life presses on them most heavily, and they
convey to these human beings a sense of understanding their inner
needs, of responding to their own deepest impulses, above all of
being alone capable of organising the world along lines which the
masses are instinctively groping for. To this type of statesman
belonged Bismarck and Abraham Lincoln, Lloyd George and
Thomas Masaryk, perhaps to some extent Gladstone, and to a
minor degree Walpole. Roosevelt was a magnificent virtuoso of
this type, and he was the most benevolent as well as the greatest
master of his craft in modern times. He really did desire a better life
for mankind. The great majorities which he obtained in the
elections in the United States during his four terms of office,
despite mounting hostility by the press, and perpetual prophecies
on their part that he had gone too far, and would fail to be re-
elected, were ultimately due to an obscure feeling on the part of the
majority of the citizens of the United States that he was on their
side, that he wished them well, and that he would do something for
them. And this feeling gradually spread over the entire civilised
world. He became a legendary hero – they themselves did not
know quite why – to the indigent and the oppressed, far beyond
the confines of the English-speaking world.

   As I said before, he was, by some of his opponents, accused of
betraying his class, and so he had. When a man who retains the
manners, the style of life, the emotional texture and the charm of

the old order of some free aristocratic upbringing revolts against
his milieu and adopts the ideas and aspirations of the new, socially
revolted class, and adopts them not out of expediency but out of
genuine moral conviction, or from love of life, inability to remain
on the side of what seems to him narrow, mean, restrictive – the
result is fascinating and attractive. This is what makes the figures of
such men as Condorcet or Charles James Fox, or some of the
Russian, Italian and Polish revolutionaries in the nineteenth century, so attractive; for all we know this may have been the secret
also of Moses or Pericles or Julius Caesar. It was this gentlemanly
quality together with the fact that they felt him to be deeply
committed to their side in the struggle and in favour of their way
of life, as well as his open and fearless lack of neutrality in the war
against the Nazis and the Fascists, that endeared him so deeply to
the British people during the war years. I remember well how
excited most people were in London, in November 1940, about the
result of the Presidential election in the United States. In theory
they should not have worried. Willkie, the Republican candidate,
had expressed himself forcibly and sincerely as a supporter of the
democracies. Yet it was absurd to say that the people of Britain
were neutral in their feelings *vis-à-vis* the two candidates. They felt
in their bones that Roosevelt was their lifelong friend, that he hated
the Nazis as deeply as they did, that he wanted democracy and
civilisation, in the sense in which they believed in it, to prevail, and
that he knew what he wanted, and that his goal resembled their
own ideals more than it did those of all his opponents. They felt
that his heart was in the right place, and they did not, therefore, if
they gave it a thought, care whether his political appointments
were made under the influence of bosses or for personal reasons, or
thoughtlessly; or whether his economic doctrines were heretical or
whether he had a sufficiently scrupulous regard for the opinion of
the Senate or the House of Representatives, or the prescriptions of
the United States Constitution, or for the opinions of the Supreme
Court. These matters were very remote from them. They knew
that he would, to the extent of his enormous energy and ability, see
them through. There is no such thing as long-lived mass hypno-
tism; the masses know what it is that they like, what genuinely
appeals to them. What the Germans thought Hitler to be, Hitler, in
fact, largely was, and what free men in Europe and in America and
in Asia and in Africa and in Australia, and wherever else the
rudiments of political thought stirred at all – what all these felt

Roosevelt to be, he in fact was. He was the greatest leader of democracy, the greatest champion of social progress in the twentieth century.

His enemies accused him of plotting to get America into the War. I do not wish to discuss this controversial issue, but it seems to me that the evidence for it is lacking. I think that when he promised to keep America at peace he meant to try as hard as he could to do so, compatibly with helping to promote the victory of the democracies. He must at one period have thought that he could win the War without entering it, and so, at the end of it, be in the unique position, hitherto achieved by no one, of being the arbiter of the world's fate without needing to placate those bitter forces which involvement in a war inevitably brings about, and which are an obstacle to reason and humanity in the making of the peace. He no doubt too often trusted in his own magical power of improvisation. Doubtless he made many political mistakes, some of them difficult to remedy: some would say about Stalin and his intentions, and the nature of the Soviet State; others might justly point to his coolness to the Free French movement, his cavalier intentions with regard to the Supreme Court of Justice in the United States, his errors about a good many other issues. He irritated his staunchest supporters and faithful servants because he did not tell them what he was doing; his government was highly personal and it maddened tidy-minded officials and humiliated those who thought the policy should be conducted in consultation with and through them. He sometimes exasperated his allies, but when these last bethought them of who his ill-wishers were in the USA and in the world outside, and what *their* motives were, their respect, affection and loyalty tended to return. No man made more public enemies, yet no man had a right to take greater pride in the quality and the motives of some of those enemies. He could justly call himself the friend of the people, and although his opponents accused him of being a demagogue, this charge seems to me unjust. He did not sacrifice fundamental political principles to a desire to retain power; he did not whip up evil passions merely in order to avenge himself upon those whom he disliked or wished to crush, or because it was an atmosphere in which he found it convenient to operate; he saw to it that his administration was in the van of public opinion and drew it on instead of being dragged by it; he made the majority of his fellow citizens prouder to be Americans than they had been before. He raised their status in their own eyes – immensely in those of the rest of the world.

It was an extraordinary transformation of an individual. Perhaps it was largely brought about by the collapse of his health in the early 1920s and his marvellous triumph over his disabilities. For he began life as a well-born, polite, not particularly gifted young man, something of a prig, liked but not greatly admired by his contemporaries at Groton and at Harvard, a competent Assistant Secretary of the Navy in the First World War; in short, he seemed embarked on the routine career of an American patrician with moderate political ambitions. His illness and the support and encouragement and political qualities of his wife – whose greatness of character and goodness of heart history will duly record – seemed to transform his public personality into that strong and beneficent champion who became the father of his people, in an altogether unique fashion. He did more than this: it is not too much to say that he altered the fundamental concept of government and its obligations to the governed. The Welfare State, so much denounced, has obviously come to stay: the direct moral responsibility for minimum standards of living and social services, which it took for granted, are today accepted almost without a murmur by the most conservative politicians in the Western democracies; the Republican Party victorious in 1952 made no effort to upset the basic principles – which seemed Utopian in the 1920s – of Roosevelt's social legislation.

But Roosevelt's greatest service to mankind (after ensuring the victory against the enemies of freedom) consists in the fact that he showed that it is possible to be politically effective and yet benevolent and human: that the fierce left- and right-wing propaganda of the 1930s, according to which the conquest and retention of political power is not compatible with human qualities, but necessarily demands from those who pursue it seriously the sacrifice of their lives upon the altar of some ruthless ideology, or the practice of despotism – this propaganda, which filled the art and talk of the day, was simply untrue. Roosevelt's example strengthened democracy everywhere, that is to say the view that the promotion of social justice and individual liberty does not necessarily mean the end of all efficient government; that power and order are not identical with a strait-jacket of doctrine, whether economic or political; that it is possible to reconcile individual liberty – a loose texture of society – with the indispensable minimum of organising and authority; and in this belief lies what Roosevelt's greatest predecessor once described as 'the last best hope of earth'.[1]

---

[1] Abraham Lincoln, Annual Message to Congress, 1 December 1862: p. 537 in *The Collected Works of Abraham Lincoln*, ed. R. P. Basler (New Brunswick, 1953), vol. 5.

# CHAIM WEIZMANN

## I

CHAIM WEIZMANN'S achievement – and the details of his public life – are too well documented to need description or analysis from me. His personal characteristics are less well known. He was the only statesman of genius whom I have ever had the good fortune of knowing intimately, and I would like to try to convey something of the quality of that genius. Something: no more than a small part of a character and a life unique in our time.

To know – to enjoy the friendship of – a great man must permanently transform one's ideas of what human beings can be or do. Social theorists of various schools sometimes try to convince us that the concept of greatness is a romantic illusion – a vulgar notion exploited by politicians or propagandists, and one which a deeper study of the facts will always dispel. There is no way of finally refuting this deflationary theory save by coming face to face with an authentic instance of greatness and its works. Greatness is not a specifically moral attribute. It is not one of the private virtues. It does not belong to the realm of personal relations. A great man need not be morally good, or upright, or kind, or sensitive, or delightful, or possess artistic or scientific talent. To call someone a great man is to claim that he has intentionally taken (or perhaps could have taken) a large step, one far beyond the normal capacities of men, in satisfying, or materially affecting, central human interests. A great thinker or artist (and by this I do not necessarily mean a man of genius) must, to deserve this title, advance a society, to an exceptional degree, towards some intellectual or aesthetic goal, for which it is already, in some sense, groping; or else alter its ways of thinking or feeling to a degree that would not, until he had performed his task, have been conceived as being within the powers of a single individual. Sometimes such an achievement is felt as a great act of liberation by those upon whom such a man binds his spell, sometimes as an enslavement, sometimes as a peculiar mixture or succession of both. Similarly, in the realm of action, the great man seems able, almost alone and single-handed, to transform one form of life into another; or – what in the end comes to the same – permanently and radically alters the outlook and values of a significant body of human beings. The transformation he effects, if he is truly to deserve his title, must be such as those best qualified to judge consider to be antecedently improbable – something unlikely to be brought about by the mere force of events, by the 'trends' or 'tendencies' already working at the time – that is to say, something unlikely to occur without the intervention, difficult or impossible to discount in advance, of the man who for this very reason deserves to be described as great. At any rate that is how the situation will look in retrospect. Whether this is a vast mistake – whether, in fact, human beings (as Marx, or Tolstoy, for instance, believed) overestimate the importance of some of their own number – whether some more impersonal view of history that does not admit the possibility of heroes is in fact correct, cannot be discussed here. If the notion of the hero who makes or breaks a nation's life springs from an illusion, it is, despite all the weighty arguments produced against it, a very persistent, obsessive and universal illusion, to which the experience of our own time has given powerful support. At any rate, I propose, for my present purpose, to assume that it is not delusive, but a true view of society and history. And thence I should like to embark only on the comparatively modest proposition that if great men – heroes – have ever existed, and more particularly if individuals can in any sense be said to be the authors of revolutions that permanently and deeply alter many human lives – then Chaim Weizmann was, in the sense which I have tried to explain, a man of this order.

I have said that one of the distinguishing characteristics of a great man is that his active intervention makes what seemed highly improbable in fact happen. It is surely difficult to deny that the actions which culminated in the creation of the State of Israel were of this improbable or surprising kind. When Theodor Herzl began to preach that it was both desirable and possible to set up a sovereign Jewish State of a modern type by means of a formal, public act of recognition by the great powers, most sane, sensible, reasonable people, both Jews and Gentiles, who heard of this plan regarded it as quite insane. Indeed, it is difficult to see how they could have thought otherwise.

In the nineteenth century the Jews presented an exceedingly

anomalous spectacle. Scattered among the nations of the world, they constituted something which it was hard or perhaps impossible to define in terms of such concepts as nation, race, association, religion or the other terms in which coherent groups of a hereditary or traditional type were commonly described. The Jews were clearly not a nation in any normal sense of the word: they occupied no fixed territory of which they constituted the majority of the population; they could not even be described as a minority in the sense in which the ethnic or national minorities of multi-national empires – the Austro-Hungarian, or Russian, or British Empires – were so denoted; they occupied no stretch of country which could be called their native territory in the sense in which Welshmen, or Slovaks, or Ruthenians, or Zulus, or Tartars, or even Red Indians or Australian aborigines – compact continuous groups living on their ancestral soil – patently did so. The Jews certainly had a religion of their own, although a good many of them did not appear to profess it in any clearly recognisable sense; but they could not be defined as a solely religious body; when in modern times Jews were discriminated against or persecuted, it was, for the most part, not their religious observances that were in the first place abhorred; when Jews who had left their faith and had become converted to Christianity – like Disraeli or Karl Marx or Heine – were thought of, the fact that they were still looked upon as Jews, or as being of Jewish origin, certainly did not imply merely that their ancestors had practised a religion different from that of the surrounding populations. Nobody, after all, spoke of persons of Presbyterian, or Roman Catholic, or even Muslim origin or descent; a man might be of Turkish or Indian origin – but hardly of Muslim descent or of Muslim race.

What, then, were the Jews? Were they a race? The word 'race' was, and is still, felt to carry somewhat disreputable associations. Vague historical notions such as those of Indo-European or Mongol race were at times used by ethnologists. Groups of languages were occasionally classified as Aryan or Hamitic or Semitic, but these were at most technical terms for defining the culture of those who spoke them. The idea of race as a political description was not, towards the end of the last century, one which intellectually respectable persons held with; it was felt to be connected with the undesirable attitudes of national or cultural chauvinism. Indeed it was its lurid propagandist colour that made the word itself, whatever its context, seem a strong appeal to prejudice. Competent ethnologists, anthropologists and sociologists vied with each other in proving that there were no 'pure' races, that the notion was hopelessly vague and confused.

But if the Jews were not a race, what were they? A culture, or 'way of life'? Apart from the fact that they participated, at any rate in the countries of the West, in the civilisation of their surroundings, this seemed a very thin notion in terms of which to define something so immediately recognisable, a group of persons towards whom feelings were as strong and definite as they quite clearly were in respect of the Jews. For there undoubtedly existed certain cardinal differences in outlook and behaviour, and to a large degree in outward physical characteristics, that appeared to be persistent, hereditary and easily recognisable both by the Jews themselves and by non-Jews. So much seemed clear to any honest man who was not either too embarrassed or too polite to face the obvious facts. The martyrdom of the Jews in the Christian world was so painful and notorious, the wounds which it had inflicted on both persecutors and persecuted were so deep, that there was a natural temptation on the part of enlightened and civilised people to try to ignore the problem altogether, or to insist that it had been much exaggerated, and might, if only it was not so frequently discussed and mentioned, with luck perhaps soon vanish altogether.

This was an attitude which a good many Jews themselves were only too anxious to adopt. The more optimistic 'assimilationists' among them fondly supposed that with the general spread of education and liberal culture the Jews would peacefully melt into their surroundings so that, if the Jewish religion continued to exist, those who practised it would come to be thought of by their Christian fellow citizens as being neither less nor more different than, let us say, Presbyterians or Anglicans or, at the most, Unitarians or Quakers in countries with Roman Catholic majorities. To some degree this process was, in fact, already taking place in the countries of the West; not, to be sure, to a great degree as yet, but from small beginnings great consequences sometimes issued. At any rate, the notion that the Jews were in some sense a nation, as the Italians or, at least, the Armenians were a nation, and had just claims – could, indeed, be conceived as having any claims at all – to a territorial existence as a nation organised in the form of a State, seemed a wild absurdity to the vast majority of those who gave the matter any thought. It was very well for isolated romantics with strong imaginations – Napoleon or Fichte, for example, or the Russian Decembrist revolutionary Pestel' – to suggest that the Jews were in fact a nation, though certainly a very odd, scattered one, and should be returned to Palestine, there to create some sort of State of their own. These remained idle fancies which no one, not even their authors, took very seriously. So also later in the century, when benevolent Christians like Laurence Oliphant in England or Ernest Laharanne in France, or Jewish publicists like Salvador or Moses Hess, or the rabbi Hirsch Kalischer, advocated a return to the Holy Land, this was regarded as mere eccentricity, sometimes dangerous perversity. When novelists – Disraeli or George Eliot – played with romantic nostalgia of this kind, this could be written off as a sophisticated version of the visions of an idealised past that Chateaubriand and Scott and the German romantics had made fashionable – exotic fruit of the new historical imagination, of possible religious or aesthetic or psychological significance, but with no possible relevance to political practice. As for the fact that pious Jews everywhere thrice daily prayed to be returned to Zion, that was, again quite naturally, regarded as an expression of the longing for the coming of the Messiah, for the end of the world of evil and pain, and for the coming of the reign of God on earth, and wholly remote from secular ideas about political self-determination. Even when the growth among the Jews of Eastern Europe of secular education, with the nationalist and socialist ideas which it brought with it, had caused a sufficient ferment among the poorer Russian Jews to cause some of them (especially after the wave of pogroms in Russia that followed the assassination of the Emperor Alexander II) to found small, idealistic, agricultural settlements in Palestine; even after Baron Edmond de Rothschild in Paris had, by a unique act of imaginative generosity, saved these colonies from extinction and made possible a considerable degree of agricultural develop-ment; all this still seemed nothing more than a Utopian experiment, queer, noble, moving, but a sentimental gesture rather than real life.

When finally the idea of a Jewish State began to be seriously bruited, and reached Western countries, and caught the imagina-tion of such serious and effective statesmen as Joseph Chamberlain and Milner, and when it stirred the enthusiasm of so temperate, sagacious and deeply responsible a man as Herbert Samuel, need we be surprised that some solid and respectable Western Jews could scarcely credit this? The most characteristic reaction was that of Samuel's political colleague and kinsman Edwin Montagu, at that time himself a member of Asquith's (and subsequently Lloyd George's) Cabinet, who felt personally traduced. The late Lord Norwich once told me that Montagu used to address his colleagues with anger and indignation, declaring that the Jews did not wish – and did not think they deserved – to be sent back to the ghetto; and buttonholed his friends in various drawing-rooms in London, and asked them vehemently whether they regarded him as an oriental alien and wanted to see him 'repatriated' to the eastern Mediterranean. Other sober and public-spirited British Jews felt no less upset and bitter; similar feelings were expressed in corresponding circles in Paris and Berlin.[1]

All this is perfectly intelligible in terms of the life led by the Jews of the Western world, even of the great twentieth-century Jewish settlement in the United States. Whatever the truth about the status of the Jews in these countries – whether one was to call them a race, a religion, a community, a national minority, or invent some unique term to cover their anomalous attributes – a new nation and State could not be constructed out of them; neither they nor their leaders conceived this as a real possibility; and this remains true of them still. For, despite all the social friction, discomfort, even humiliation and, in bad times, persecution that they have had to suffer, they were and are, by and large, too deeply involved in the life of the societies of which they form a part, and have in the process lost too great a part of their original, undiluted national personality to have retained the will to build a totally new life on new foundations. Even Hitler's onslaught did not seem to stir within the majority of the German Jews a feeling of specific Jewish nationalism, but mainly bewilderment, indignation, horror, individual heroism or despair. Jewish nationalism was given reality almost entirely by the Jews of the Russian Empire and to some degree of the Muslim East.[2]

Assimilation, integration, Russification, Polonisation had, of course, to some degree also occurred among the Jews of Russia and Poland. Nevertheless the bulk of them lived under their own dispensation. Herded by the Russian government into the so-called

---

[1] 'To be a Zionist it is not perhaps absolutely necessary to be slightly mad,' Weizmann is reported to have said, 'but it helps.'

[2] This was predicted over a hundred years ago with unparalleled prescience by Moses Hess in his most remarkable book, *Rome and Jerusalem* (Leipzig, 1862), to this day the most telling analysis and indictment of 'emancipated' Jewish society.

Pale of Settlement, bound by their own traditional religious and social organisation, they constituted a kind of survival of medieval society, in which the secular and the sacred were not divided, as they had been (at any rate since the Renaissance) among the middle and upper classes in Western Europe. Speaking their own language, largely isolated from the surrounding peasant population, trading with them, but confined within their own world by a wall of reciprocal distrust and suspicion, this vast Jewish community formed a geographically continuous enclave that inevitably developed its own institutions, and thereby, as time went on, came to resemble more and more an authentic national minority settled upon its own ancestral soil.

There are times when imagination is stronger than so-called objective reality. Subjective feeling plays a great part in communal development, and the Yiddish-speaking Jews of the Russian Empire came to feel themselves a coherent ethnic group: anomalous indeed, subject to unheard-of persecution, remote from the alien world in which their lives were cast, but, simply in virtue of the fact that they were densely congregated within the same relatively small territory, tending to resemble, say, the Armenians in Turkey: a recognisably separate, semi-national community. In their involuntary confinement they developed a certain independence of outlook, and the problems which affected and sometimes tormented many of their co-religionists in the West – in particular the central question of their status – were not crucial for them. The Jews of Germany, Austria, Hungary, France, America, England tended to ask themselves whether they were Jews, and if so, in what sense, and what this entailed; whether the view of them held by the surrounding population was true or false, just or unjust, and, if distorted, whether any steps could be taken to correct it without too much damage to their own self-esteem; whether they should 'appease' and assimilate at the risk of losing their identity, and perhaps of the guilt that comes of the feeling of having 'betrayed' their ancestral values; or, on the contrary, resist at the risk of incurring unpopularity and even persecution. These problems affected the Russian Jews to a far smaller degree, relatively secure as they were – morally and psychologically – within their own vast, insulated ghetto. Their imprisonment, for all the economic, cultural and social injustice and poverty that it entailed, brought with it one immense advantage – namely that the spirit of the inmates remained unbroken, and that they were not as powerfully tempted to seek escape by adopting false positions as their socially more exposed and precariously established brethren without. The majority of the Jews of Russia and Poland lived in conditions of squalor and oppression, but they did not feel outcast or rootless; their relations with each other and with the outside world suffered from no systematic ambivalence. They were what they were; they might dislike their condition, they might seek to escape from it, or revolt against it, but they did not deceive themselves or others, nor did they make efforts to conceal from themselves their own most characteristic attributes that were patent to all – particularly their neighbours – to see. Their moral and spiritual integrity was greater than that of their more prosperous and civilised and altogether grander brothers in the West; their lives were bound up with religious observance, and their minds and hearts were filled with the images and symbolism of Jewish history and religion to a degree scarcely intelligible in Western Europe since the waning of the Middle Ages.

When Herzl with his magnificent appearance and visionary gaze appeared like a prophet from a distant land, many of them were dazzled by the very strangeness and distance which divided them from this Messianic messenger from another world, who could not speak to them in their own language – a remoteness which made him and his message all the more magical and magnetic. But when their leader seemed prepared to accept the compromise solution, offered by the British Colonial Secretary, Joseph Chamberlain, of a settlement in Uganda in place of the unattainable Palestine, many of them were shocked and alienated. Herzl's talent for heroic over-simplification is one that fanatics, possessed by a single idea, often exhibit – indeed it is one of the qualities that make them exceptionally, dangerously effective – and Herzl ignored difficulties, cut Gordian knots, electrified the Jewish masses in Eastern Europe, developed his ideas before politicians and important personages in the Western world with logic, simplicity, imagination and great fire. The Jewish masses followed him uncomprehending, but aware that here at last was a path towards the light. Like many visionaries Herzl understood issues but not human beings: least of all the culture and feelings of his devoted Eastern European followers. Paris was surely worth a mass; the Jewish problem was urgent and desperate; he was prepared, for the sake of a concrete territory waiting for immigration, to disregard, at least for the time being, the saturation of Jewish thought and feeling

with the image and symbol of Zion and Palestine, its preoccupation, its obsession by the actual words of the Prayer Book and the
Bible. Never has any people lived so much by the written word:
not to have realised the crucial importance of this was a measure of
the distance of the West from the East. The Russian Zionist leaders
did not require to be taught this truth: they grew up with it, and
took it for granted. The prospect of nationhood without the land
which was the oldest root, the only goal of all their faith, was
virtually meaningless for most of them; it could be accepted only
by the more rational, but more exhausted – the thinner-blooded –
Jews of the West, who in any case were not the stuff from which a
new society could be moulded overnight. If the Jews of Russia had
not existed, neither the case for, nor the possibility of realising,
Zionism could have arisen in any serious form.

There is a sense in which no social problem arose for the Jews so
long as rigid religious orthodoxy insulated them from the external
world. Until then, poor, downtrodden and oppressed as they
might be, and clinging to each other for warmth and shelter, the
Jews of Eastern Europe put all their faith in God and concentrated
all their hope either upon individual salvation – immortality in the
sight of God – or upon the coming of the Messiah whose approach
no worldly force could accelerate or retard. It was when this great
frozen mass began to melt that the social and political problem
arose. Once the Enlightenment – secular learning and the possibility of a freer mode of life – began at first to seep, and then to flood,
into the Jewish townlets and villages of the Pale, a generation grew
up no longer content to sit by the waters of Babylon and sing the
songs of Zion in exile. Some, in search of a wider life, renounced
the religion of their fathers and became baptised and earned
positions of eminence and distinction in Russian society. Some did
so in Western Europe. Some believed that the injustice done to
their people was only a part of the larger injustice constituted by
tsarist despotism, or by the capitalist system, and became radicals,
or socialists, or members of other social movements which claimed
that the peculiar anomalies of the Jewish situation would disappear
as part of the general solution of all political and economic
problems. Some among these radicals and socialists and believers in
'Russification' or 'Europeanisation' desired the total dissolution of
the Jews as a closely knit group among their neighbours. Others,
infected by the 'populism' of that time (an idealistic movement of
the 'conscience-stricken' sons and daughters of the Russian gentry,

seeking to improve the lot of the peasants), conceived in vague and sentimental terms of semi-autonomous Jewish communities, speaking their own Yiddish language and creating in it works of art and science, as one among a family of free communities, constituting, between them, some kind of decentralised, semi-socialist, free federation of peoples within the Russian Empire. Again there were those who, still faithful to the ancient religion, were resolved to keep out the menace of secularism by raising the walls of the ghetto still higher, and devoted themselves with an even more rigid and fanatical faith to the preservation of every jot and tittle of Jewish law and tradition, viewing all Western movements – whether nationalist or socialist, conservative or radical – with equal detestation or horror. But the vast majority of the younger generation of the Russian Jews in the 1880s and '90s joined none of these movements. Affected and, indeed, fascinated by the general ideas then afloat they might be; but they remained bourgeois Jews, semi-emancipated from the shackles of their fathers, aware of – discontented by, but not ashamed of – their anomalous status, with a mild but uninhibited devotion to the traditional ways of life in which they were brought up, neither conscious heretics, nor in the least degree renegades, neither zealots nor reformers but normal human beings, irked by their legal and social inferiority, seeking to lead the most natural and unbroken lives that they could, without worrying overmuch about ultimate ends or fundamental principles. They were devoted to their families, to their traditional culture, their professional pursuits. Faced with persecution, they preserved their closely knit social texture (often by means of bizarre subterfuges and stratagems) with astonishing optimism, tenacity, skill and even gaiety, in circumstances of unexampled difficulty.

To this generation, and to this solid milieu, Weizmann belonged, and he became its fullest, most gifted, and most effective representative. When he spoke, it was to these people, whom he knew best, that his words were addressed; to the end of his days he was happiest among them. When he thought of the Jews, he thought of them; his language was theirs, and their view of life was his. Out of them he created the foundations of the new State, and it is their character, ideals, habits, way of life that have, more than any other single set of factors, imposed themselves on the State of Israel. For this reason, it is perhaps the most faithful nineteenth-century democracy at present extant in the modern world.

II

Chaim Weizmann was born and bred in a completely Jewish milieu near the city of Pinsk, in western Russia. His father was a timber-merchant of small means, a typical member of a lively and devout community, and developed in his many children his own energetic and hopeful attitude to life; in particular, respect for education, for fully formed personality, for solid achievement in every sphere, together with a clear-eyed, concrete – and, at times, irreverent – approach to all issues, combined with a belief that with effort, honesty, faith and a critical faculty a good life can be lived on earth. Realism, optimism, self-confidence, admiration for human achievement, and above all an insatiable appetite for life as such, whatever it might bring, accompanied by the conviction that all that comes (or nearly all) can, late or soon, be turned to positive advantage – a vigorously extroverted attitude, rooted in a sense of belonging to the unbroken historical continuity of Jewish tradition, as something too strong to be dissolved or abolished by either man or circumstance – these are the characteristics most prominent, it seems to me, in the outlook of this most constructive man. He was, moreover, of a monolithic solidity of character, incapable of self-pity and self-deception, and absolutely fearless. There is no evidence that he was ever prey to agonising doubts about moral or political issues. The traditional framework in which he was born was too secure.

Early in life he accepted the proposition that the ills of the Jews were caused principally by the abnormality of their social situation; and that so long as they remained everywhere a semi-helot population, relegated to an inferior and dependent status, which produced in them the virtues and vices of slaves, their neuroses, both individual and collective, were not curable. Some might bear this fate with dignity, others were broken by it, or betrayed by their principles and played false roles because they found the burden too heavy. Personal integrity and strength were not enough: unless their social and political position was somehow altered – made normal – brought into line with that of other peoples, the vast majority of Jews would remain permanently liable to become morally and socially crippled, objects of compassion to the kindly, and of deep distaste to the fastidious. For this there was no remedy save a revolution – a total social transformation, a mass emancipation.

Others had reached this conclusion before him: indeed it formed the substance of the most celebrated of all the pre-Zionist pamphlets – Leo Pinsker's *Auto-Emancipation* – and animated the colonising efforts of the early pioneers of the settlement in Palestine. Herzl translated it into Western terms and gave it coherent and eloquent political shape. Weizmann was not an intellectual innovator: his originality lay in the exceptionally convincing, wholly concrete content which he poured into ideas he received from others. His political, no less than his scientific, genius lay in applied, not in pure, theory. Like his contemporary Lenin, he translated doctrine into reality, and like him he transformed both. But unlike Lenin he had a harmonious nature, free from that streak of bigoted rationalism which breeds belief in final solutions for which no price – in terms of human suffering and death – can be too high. He was above all things an empiricist, who looked on ideas primarily as tools of practical judgement, and he was endowed with a very strong and vivid sense of reality and the allied faculty of historical imagination – that is to say, with an almost infallible sense of what cannot be true, of what cannot be done.

Weizmann and his generation assumed without question that if Jews were to be emancipated, they must live in freedom in their own land, that there alone they would no longer be compelled to extort elementary human rights by that repellent mixture of constant cunning, obsequiousness and occasional arrogance which is forced on all dependants and clients and slaves; and finally that this land must – could only – be Palestine. In his milieu scarcely anyone who was convinced of the main thesis seriously conceived of other possibilities. Spiritual ties rightly seemed to them more real than any other; economic and political factors appeared less decisive by comparison. If a people has lived and survived against unbelievable odds by purely ideal resources, material considerations will not, for good or ill, divert it from its vision. At the centre of this vision was the Holy Land. Herzl, Israel Zangwill, others who were born or bred in the West might need convincing of this: in Russia it was taken for granted by most of those who accepted the fundamental promise – that the Jews could neither assimilate and melt away, nor remain segregated. If this was sound, the rest followed.

Weizmann shared other unspoken assumptions with his milieu: he was not troubled by the problem of what the government of the future State would or should be: whether, for example, it should be religious or secular, socialist or bourgeois. His notions of justice, equality, communal organisation, were non-sectarian and pre-Marxist; he was no more concerned to graft on to his simple, moderate, instinctive, democratic nationalism this or that precisely formulated political or social doctrine than were Garibaldi or Kossuth or other great nineteenth-century nationalist leaders, who believed in, and promoted, the renaissance of their peoples not as a policy founded on a particular doctrine, but as a movement which they accepted naturally and without question. Such men – from Moses to Nehru – create or lead movements primarily because, finding themselves naturally bound up with the aspirations of their society, and passionately convinced of the injustice of the order by which they are kept down, they know themselves to be stronger, more imaginative, more effective fighters against it than the majority of their fellow victims. Such men are not, as a rule, theorists: they are sometimes doctrinaire, but more often adapt current ideas to their needs. Little that Weizmann believed throughout his life came to him from books, from the beliefs of this or that social or political teacher, or from any other source than the community that he knew best, from its common stock of ideas, from the very air that he breathed. In this sense, if in no other, he was a very true representative of his people. All his life he instinctively recoiled from *outré* or extremist tendencies within his own movement. He was one of those human beings who (as someone once said of an eminent Russian critic)[1] stood near the centre of the consciousness of his people, and not on its periphery; his ideas and his feelings were, as it were, naturally attuned to the often unspoken, but always central, hopes, fears, modes of feeling of the vast majority of the Jewish masses, with which he felt himself, all his life, in deep and complete natural sympathy. His genius largely consisted in making articulate, and finding avenues for the realisation of, these aspirations and longings; and he did this without exaggerating them in any direction, or forcing them into a preconceived social or political scheme, or driving them towards some privately conceived goal of his own, but always along the grain.

For this reason, although he was not a great popular orator, practised no false humility, often behaved in a detached, ironical

[1] Vissarion Belinsky.

and contemptuous fashion, was proud, imperious, impatient, and an utterly independent commander of his troops, without the least inclination to demagogy, or talent for it, he never, despite all this, lost the confidence of the vast majority of his people. He was not sentimental, said biting and unpopular things, and addressed himself always to the reason and never to the passions. In spite of this, the masses instinctively felt that he understood them, knew what was in their hearts, and wanted this himself. They trusted and, therefore, followed him. They trusted him because he seemed to them an exceptionally powerful, self-confident, solid champion of their deepest interests. Moreover he was both fearless and understanding. He understood their past and their present, but above all was not frightened of the future.

This last quality is rare enough anywhere; but is, for obvious reasons, particularly seldom found among the crushed and the oppressed. Like the other great leaders of democracies in our time, like Lloyd George and the two Roosevelts, Weizmann had an unconquerable belief that whatever the future brought could be made grist to his, and his people's, mill. He never abandoned hope, he remained balanced, confident, representative. He never disappeared from the view of his followers into private fantasies or egomaniacal dreams. He was a man of immense natural authority, dignity and strength. He was calm, paternal, imperturbable, certain of himself. He never drifted with the current. He was always in control. He accepted full responsibility. He was indifferent to praise and blame. He possessed tact and charm to a degree exceeded by no statesman of modern days. But what held the Jewish masses to him until the very last phase of his long life was not possession of these qualities alone, dazzling as they were, but the fact that although outwardly he had become an eminent Western scientist (which made him financially and therefore politically independent), and mingled easily with the remote and unapproachable masters of the Western world, his fundamental personality and outlook remained unchanged. His language, his images, his turns of phrase were rooted in Jewish tradition and piety and learning. His tastes, his physical movements, the manner in which he walked and stood, got up and sat down, his gestures, the features of his exceedingly expressive face, and above all his tone of voice, the accent, the inflexion, the extraordinary variety of his humour, were identical with theirs – were their own. In this sense he was flesh of their flesh, a man of the people. He knew this.

But in his dealings with his own people he behaved without any self-consciousness. He did not exaggerate or play up even his own characteristics. He was not an actor. He dramatised neither himself nor his interlocutors. He cultivated no idiosyncrasies. His unshakeable authority derived from his natural qualities, from his combination of creative and critical power, his self-control, his calm, from the fact that he was a man of wide horizons, obsessed by nothing, not even his own ideals, and therefore never blinded by passion or prejudice to any relevant factor in his own Jewish world.

The failures of the Zionist movement – and they were many – did not embitter him; its successes did not drive him into unrealistic assessments. He combined an acute and highly ironical awareness of the shortcomings and absurdities of the Jewish character – it was a subject on which he was seldom silent – with a devoted affection for it, and a determination at all costs to rescue his people from the humiliating or perilous predicaments in which it landed them. To this end he directed all his extraordinary resources. He believed in long-term strategy; he distrusted improvisation; he was a master of manoeuvre, but despite all that his critics have alleged, he was not in the least machiavellian. He was not prepared to justify wrongdoing by appeals to historical or political necessity. He did not attempt to save his people by violence or cunning – to beat them into shape, if need be with the utmost brutality, like Lenin, or to deceive them for their own good, like Bismarck, or to turn their heads with promises of blessings awaiting them in some remote future which could be shaped to anyone's fantasy. He never called upon the Jews to make terrible sacrifices, or offer their lives, or commit crimes, or condone the crimes of others, for the sake of some felicity to be realised at some unspecified date, as the Marxists did; nor did he play upon their feelings unscrupulously, or try deliberately to exacerbate them against this or that real, or imaginary, enemy, as extremists in his own movement have frequently tried to do. He wished to make his nation free and happy,[1] but not at the price of sinning against any human value in which he and they believed. He wished to lead

---

[1] Hermann Cohen, the philosopher, is said to have remarked, with the scorn of an old Stoic sage, to Franz Rosenzweig, who tried to convince him of the merits of Zionism, 'Oho! So the gang now wants to be happy, does it?' Weizmann wanted exactly that; he could not see why this was thought a shameful act of surrender.

them out of exile into a land where they could live a life worthy of human beings, without betraying their own ideals or trampling on those of others.

Like Cavour, whom politically he much resembled in his hatred of violence and his reliance on words as his sole political weapons, he was prepared to use every possible stratagem, to expend his immense charm upon cajoling this or that British or American statesman, or cardinal, or millionaire, into providing the means he needed for his ends. He was prepared to conceal facts, to work in secret, to fascinate, and enslave, individuals, to use his personal followers, or anyone who appeared to him to be useful, as a means for limited ends – only to lose all interest in them, to their bewildered indignation (which was at times exceeding articulate and bitter), once the need for them was at an end. But he was not prepared to compromise with his own central moral and political principles, and never did so. He was not afraid of making enemies, nor of public or private opinion, nor, in the least degree, of the judgement of posterity. He understood human beings and took an interest in them; he enjoyed his power of casting his spell over them; he liked political flirtation; he was, indeed, in addition to his gifts as a statesman, a political virtuoso of the highest, most inspired order.

These qualities carried their defects with them. They entailed a certain disregard for the wills and attitudes – perhaps rights – of others. He was at times too little concerned with the purposes and characters of those with whom he did not sympathise, and they complained of neglect or heartless exploitation or despotism. He was, in a sense, too fearless, he was too confident that his cause and his friends must triumph, and often underestimated the violence and sincerity of the convictions held by his opponents, both in his own party and in the world at large. This was both a strength and a weakness; it added immeasurably to his feeling of inner security and his optimism, and it liberated his creative energies; but it blinded him to the effects of the fears and the implacable hostility he was bound to encounter among those men outside his own community whom Zionism offended or upset – anti-Semites open and concealed, Arabs and their champions, British Government officials, churchmen of many faiths, the respectable and established in general. It seemed a necessary element in his positive, unswerving, vigorous, almost too uncompromising constructive temper to ignore individual human weaknesses – envy, fear, prejudice, vanity, small acts of cowardice or spite or treachery, in particular obstructive tactics on the part of the feeble, or stupid, or timid, or ill-disposed officials, which more, perhaps, than major decisions cumulatively blocked his path, and, in the end, as everyone knows, led to bloodshed.

Similarly he tended to ignore his opponents and enemies, personal and ideological. These he had in plenty, not least in his own nation. The fanatically religious Jews saw him as an impious would-be usurper of the position of the divine Messiah. Tremulous Jews in important positions in Western countries, especially those prosperous or prominent figures who had at last attained to what they conceived as secure positions in modern society, achieved after much wandering and at great expense, regarded him as a dangerous troublemaker likely to open wounds that they had taken much trouble to bandage and conceal; at best they treated him with nervous respect, as a highly compromising ally. Socialists, radicals, internationalists of many hues – but especially of course the Marxists – regarded him as a reactionary nineteenth-century nationalist, seeking to lead the Jews back from the broad and sunlit uplands of the world-wide society of their dreams to the stifling confines of a petty little nationality exiled to a backward region of the eastern Mediterranean – a grotesque anachronism destined to be swept aside by the inexorable impersonal forces of history. Then there were the Jewish populists in Russia or America who believed in a kind of local or regional Jewish popular culture – a kind of quasi-nationality in exile – Yiddish-speaking, plebeian, unpolitical, a parody of the Russian populism of the time. These looked on Weizmann as a snob, a calculating politician, an enemy to their programmes of warm-hearted social welfare, embellished by amiable and unpretentious arts and crafts and the preservation of carefully protected centres of old-fashioned Jewish life in an unsympathetic and unsentimental Gentile world. And finally there were sceptics and scoffers, sane and ironical, or bitter and cynical, who looked on Zionism as nothing but a foolish dream. He paid little attention to his opponents; but he felt sure that he knew what was strong and what was weak in them – as they did not – and felt sufficiently superior to them morally and intellectually to be determined to save them from themselves (humility, as I said before, was not one of his characteristics). He did not hate them as they hated him – save only the Communists, whom all his life he genuinely feared and detested as swarms of political locusts who, whatever their professions, always destroyed far more than they created. So far as he took notice of them at all, he looked on his opponents as so many sheep that he must attempt to rescue from the inevitable slaughter towards which they seemed to be moving with such fatal eagerness. Consequently he regarded the Russian socialist leaders, with whom he used to argue (and with whom, at least once, before the First World War, he formally debated in a public hall in Switzerland), simply as so many rival fishers of souls, likely to detach from the movement of Jewish liberation and drive to their doom some of the ablest and most constructively minded sons of his people. It is a pity that these debates[1] are not extant. Never can two movements have come into sharper or more articulate collision than in these acrimonious and uniquely interesting controversies between the leaders of the two conceptions of life destined to divide the modern world – communism and nationalism. It is a historical irony that this crucial debate was conducted on the small and obscure platform of the specifically Jewish needs and issues of the time.

Weizmann believed that he would win – he never doubted this – not because of any overwhelming faith in his own powers, great though these were; not from *naïveté* – although, in some respects, he did possess the deep simplicity and trustfulness of a certain type of great man, especially in his dealings with Englishmen – but because he was convinced that the tendencies in Jewish life which he represented were central and indestructible, while the case of his opponents was built on the shifting sands of history, rested on smaller areas of experience, and arose out of issues more personal and factional, and therefore ephemeral, than the great, overmastering human desire for individual liberty, national equality and a tolerable life that he felt that he himself represented. He derived great moral strength from his belief in the central ends, the deepest interests, of mankind, that could not for ever be thwarted, that alone justified and guaranteed the ultimate success of great and revolutionary undertakings. He did not, I am sure, distinguish his personal sentiments from the values for which he stood, the historical position that he felt himself to occupy.

When biographers come to consider his disagreements with the

[1] Plekhanov, Lenin, Trotsky, Radek are the names that, to the best of my recollection, he mentioned to me as being among those who debated against him in Berne and elsewhere at this time. I do not know whether any record of this has been found.

founder of the movement, Theodor Herzl, his duels with Justice
Louis Brandeis, and with the leader of the extreme right-wing
Zionists, Vladimir Jabotinsky; or, for that matter, his differences
with such genuine supporters of his own moderate policies as
Sokolow, or Ben-Gurion, and many a lesser figure, they will[1] –
they inevitably must – ask how much of this was due to personal
ambition, love of power, underestimation of opponents, impatient
autocracy of temper; and how much was principle, devotion to
ideas, rational conviction of what was right or expedient. When
this question is posed, I do not believe that it will find any very
clear answer: perhaps no answer at all. For in this case, as in that of
virtually every statesman, personal motives were inextricably
connected with, at the lowest, conceptions of political expediency
and, at the highest, a pure and disinterested public ideal. Weizmann
committed none of those enormities for which men of action, and
later their biographers, claim justification, on the ground of what is
called *raison d'état* – the notorious reasons of State which permit
politicians caught in some major crisis to sacrifice the accepted
standards and principles of private morality to the superior claims
of State, or society, or Church, or party. Weizmann, despite his
reputation as a master of *realpolitik*, forged no telegrams, massacred no minorities, executed and incarcerated no political opponents. When Jewish terrorism broke out in Palestine he felt and
behaved much as Russian liberals did when reactionary tsarist
ministers were assassinated by idealistic revolutionaries. He did not
support it; in private he condemned it very vehemently. But he did
not think it morally decent to denounce either the acts or their
perpetrators in public. He genuinely detested violence: and he was
too civilised and too humane to believe in its efficacy, mistakenly
perhaps. But he did not propose to speak out against acts, criminal
as he thought them, which sprang from the tormented minds of
men driven to desperation, and ready to give up their lives to save
their brothers from what, he and they were equally convinced, was
a betrayal and a destruction cynically prepared for them by the
foreign offices of the Western powers.

Bevin's Palestine policy had finally caused Weizmann to wonder
whether his own lifelong admiration for, and loyalty to, England
and British governments had perhaps cost his people too dear. His
devotion to his cause was deeper than to any personal issue. And

[1] This was written in 1958.

since he was neither vain, nor constitutionally obstinate, he was not blinded to the possibility of error on his own part. He did not literally give up hope; he believed that it would take more than ministers and civil servants to defeat the Jewish settlement fighting for its very survival. He kept saying about the Foreign and Colonial Offices, as he paced up and down his hotel room in London, and listened to reports about this or that post-war anti-Zionist move by Whitehall, 'It is too late. It will not help them.' But he wondered whether his own earlier trust in England had not gratuitously lengthened the birth-pangs of the new Jewish State. He was not convinced that a Jewish State might not be premature; he would have preferred dominion status. The Peel Commission's partition scheme of 1936 had marked the highest point of fruitful collaboration between the British Government and himself, and he regarded those who had wrecked this scheme, especially in the Foreign Office, as responsible for the calamities that followed. He knew that hc had himself been removed from his office because he trusted these men too much. But his own lifelong reputation as an Anglophile, as a moderate, as a statesman, was now to him as nothing in the face of the struggle for life of the Jewish settlement in Palestine. He had moments of black pessimism; but he believed that men fighting in a just cause must, when the worst came to the worst, sell their lives as dearly as possible – if need be – like Samson in the temple of the Philistines. And he held this to be no less true for nations than individuals.

When the Arab–Jewish war broke out his conscience was clear. He was not a pacifist, and the war was – no Jew doubted this – one of self-defence. All his life he believed in, and practised, a policy of accommodation; he had politically suffered for it, and the war was not one of his making.

Like the late Justice Holmes, Weizmann had all his life believed that when great public issues are joined one must above all take sides; whatever one did, one must not remain neutral or uncommitted, one must always – as an absolute duty – identify oneself with some living force in the world, and take part in the world's affairs with all the risk of blame and misrepresentation and misunderstanding of one's motives and character which this almost invariably entails. Consequently, in the Jewish war of independence he called for no compromise, and he denounced those who did. He regarded with contempt the withdrawal from life on the part of those to whom their personal integrity, or peace of mind, or purity of ideal, mattered more than the work upon which they were engaged and to which they were committed, the artistic, or scientific, or social, or political, or purely personal enterprises in which all men are willy-nilly involved. He did not condone the abandonment of ultimate principles before the claims of expediency or of anything else; but political monasticism – a search for some private cave of Adullam to avoid being disappointed or tarnished, the taking up of consciously Utopian or politically impossible positions in order to remain true to some inner voice, or some unbreakable principle too pure for the wicked public world – that seemed to him a mixture of weakness and self-conceit, foolish and despicable. He did not disguise his lack of respect for purists of this type. He did not always treat them fairly; and his point of view is one which has, of course, been opposed, and indeed detested, by men of the greatest courage and integrity; but I should be less than candid if I did not confess that it is a point of view that seems to me superior to its opposite. However that may be, it was of a piece with all that he believed and was.

Weizmann lived a rich inner life, but he did not escape into it to avoid the second-best realities of the outside universe. He loved the external world. He loved whatever seemed to him likely to contribute to a broad, full, generous tide of life in which the full resources of individuals could be developed to their richest and most diversified extent. Best of all he liked positive human gifts: intelligence, imagination, beauty, strength, generosity, steadfastness, integrity of character, and especially nobility of style, that inner elegance and natural breadth and sweep and confidence which only old and stable cultures, free from calculation, narrowness and neurotic self-preoccupation, seemed to him to possess. England seemed to him to display these qualities most richly, and he remained devoted to her until the end of his days. This fidelity, which was not unreciprocated, at first sustained, and then broke, his political life. He loved her independence, freedom, dignity, style. These were free men's virtues, and them, above all, he desired the Jews to acquire and develop and possess.

The connection of England with the Zionist experiment, and in particular with Weizmann's part in the securing of the Balfour declaration and the mandate over Palestine, is usually regarded as a somewhat fortuitous one. It is sometimes asserted that, had he not happened to obtain a post in the University of Manchester, he might never have settled in England, and would then scarcely have

met Arthur Balfour in the early years of the century, and, in that
case, would certainly have been in no position to influence either
him or Lloyd George or any of the other British statesmen whose
voice was decisive in the establishment of the Jewish settlement.
This is true, and is, perhaps, a characteristic case of the influence of
accident in history. But then one may begin to wonder if it is
altogether an accident that it was to England that Weizmann
migrated from the continent of Europe. For to him, as to so many
Jews of his background and upbringing in Eastern Europe,
England, above all other lands, stood for settled democracy,
humane and peaceful civilisation, civil liberty, legal equality,
stability, toleration, respect for individual rights, and a religious
tradition founded as much on the Old Testament as on the New.
She embodied all those free middle-class virtues that made for
Anglomania in France in the last century of the *ancien régime*, and
in Eastern Europe, for much the same reasons, in the nineteenth
century. She was, above all, a country in which the Jews enjoyed a
secure and peaceful and progressive existence, in full possession of
the rights of men and citizens – everything, in short, that the more
educated among them craved for most of all, and lacked most
deeply in their own midst. This was the atmosphere in which
Weizmann was brought up, and he therefore arrived in England
with a preconceived respect bred in him by the attitude of his
entire milieu.[1] His long and fascinated flirtation with Lord
Balfour, from which so much in his life and that of the Zionist
movement sprang, is not intelligible unless it is realised that in
Balfour he met what, at all times, he found most attractive:
aristocratic attributes in their finest and most fastidious form.

Weizmann was a celebrated and, indeed, when he set himself to
it, an irresistible political seducer, but he did not offer himself
except to those whom he truly admired, and he was not prepared
to enter into a personal relationship for the sake of mere political
expediency with those who morally or politically – and, at times
indeed, aesthetically – repelled him. Perhaps he would have been
wiser not to quarrel with Justice Brandeis, not to despair of
'building a bridge between Pinsk and Washington'; not to ignore

[1] It is a significant fact that in a letter written in Hebrew before he was twelve
to his former schoolmaster, he speaks of England as the good and free country
which will help the Jews to establish their own State. I owe this fascinating piece
of information to Boris Guriel, who did so much to preserve the record of
Weizmann's life and activity.

Arab leaders, or dignitaries of the Roman Church; not to react so
strongly to the brutal ill-humour of Ernest Bevin; but he could not
break his own temperament. He liked only large, imaginative and
generous natures, and he believed that the future of his people was
bound up with what they alone could give, that agreement could
be reached only with such men, and that marriages of pure political
convenience were bound to fail. His opponents condemned this as
mere romanticism, mistakenly as I believe. He believed that lasting
agreement required a large measure of genuine harmony of
interests, principles and outlook between negotiators, and came to
believe that this affinity obtained between the Jews and the English
to a unique degree. This last, like most generalisations of this type,
may have been a sentimental error, and one for which both sides
have paid dearly, but it was an interesting and attractive error, and
one that deeply influenced the character of the new State.

Perhaps Weizmann was carried away too far by his personal
tastes. He liked the English almost too well: he liked the
concreteness of English life, language, ideals; the moderation, the
civilised disdain of extremes, the whole tone of public life, the lack
of cruelty, of excitement, of shoddiness. He liked still more the
wayward imagination, the love of the odd and the idiosyncratic,
the taste for eccentricity, the quality of independence. He was a
great charmer, as Disraeli had been before him; and the English like
to be charmed. They might be conscious, as Queen Victoria
perhaps knew when Disraeli wrote or spoke to her, that they were
being enticed; but they were not – until their bad days – suspicious
of it; they did not think that the power to delight, the play of
fancy, gay and often mordant humour, bold ideas moderately
expressed, political romanticism conveyed in a mixture of vivid
similes, sober, temperate language and perpetual reference to
intelligible material achievement were necessarily insincere or
wicked, or constituted a danger to themselves. They were secure
themselves and, therefore, they were courteous; they listened, and
they welcomed opportunities of being fascinated. No French
statesman, no American (not to speak of the Germans whom Herzl
tried to address) would have let himself be as deeply and, above all,
as willingly influenced by Weizmann's political imagination and
historical memories as Balfour or Lloyd George or Churchill, and
many a soldier, many a politician and professor and journalist,
gladly allowed themselves to be. They were not merely beguiled by
a clever and delightful talker; the values of the foreign chemist and

his English hosts did in fact largely coincide. They did not find it difficult to think of the world in the terms in which he spoke, or at any rate were quite ready to see it so, and were grateful to anyone who lifted them to that level. And in fact they were right, and those who dismissed his talk as full of cunning or deliberate exoticism were morally and politically unperceptive. For it turned out that history conformed to Weizmann's vision, compounded of hard-headed common sense and deep historical emotion, and not to the normal categories of the 'realists' in the government departments of Britain, France and the United States. What he advocated was nearly always practicable. What his opponents urged was for the most part falsified by events.

I have said that his words were addressed to reason rather than feeling. His method of argument was, as a rule, neither a demonstration founded on statistical or other carefully docu-mented evidence, nor emotional rhetoric, nor a sermon addressed to the passions; it consisted in painting a very vivid, detailed, coherent, concrete picture of a given situation or course of events; and his interlocutors, as a rule, felt that this picture, in fact, coincided with reality and conformed to their own experience of what men and events were like, of what had happened, or might happen, or, on the contrary, could not happen; of what could and what could not be done. The moral, historical, economic, social and personal factors were blended in Weizmann's remarkable, unrecorded expositions much as they combine in life (thus he spoke most effectively face to face, in private, and not before an audience). He was not an analytic but a synthetic thinker, and presented a pattern or amalgam of elements, not the essence of each separate component isolated, taken apart and looked at by itself. There was no country in which such concreteness was a more habitual form of thought than in England, and the natural sympathy which his mode of thought and action found here caused him to invest – invest irretrievably – far more of his emotional capital in his friendship for England than, I think, he realised. And an element in the opposition to him and to his ideas, whether by his own followers or from outside his movement, derived from the instinctive revulsion from English values on the part of those who found themselves in greater sympathy with other outlooks or forms of life.

I must be forgiven for reverting again to the theme of his passion for England; it was very central in him, and in his ideal, for he wanted the new Jewish society – the new State – to be a political child of English – almost exclusively English – experience. He valued especially the tendency toward instinctive compromise, whereby sharp edges are not indeed planed away, but largely ignored by both sides in a dispute if they threaten to disrupt the social texture too widely, and break down the minimum conditions for common life. Moreover he believed profoundly in the application of scientific method to human life, in which England once led the world; his interest in pure science was very limited; but he was a magnificent inventor, and wanted invention to respond to basic human needs and create new, more civilised ones – he believed in the unlimited transforming powers of natural science. This was at the heart of his optimism, of his hope and faith in the future; and he liked to think of this view as characteristically British. It was therefore one of the bitterest disappointments of his life when, in the later 1930s, and during the Second World War, his services as a scientist were virtually ignored by the British government departments.

When war broke out in 1939, he offered to lay aside some of his political preoccupations, in order once more to try to be of service to his adopted country, as he had been with his celebrated invention in the First World War. He met with lack of response. He complained of dullness, timidity, pettiness, conservatism, fear of the future on the part of most of the British officials with whom he discussed these matters, of their total inability to grasp the economic position of their country, still less the dangers and opportunities in the world that was bound to come. Throughout the War he reverted to this fact with melancholy incredulity; he found it difficult to accept that as a scientist he had, in fact, met with a far readier response in America. He wondered whether British imagination and appetite for life were dying. It seemed to him that one and the same negative attitude – a symptom of exhaustion and defeat – was palpably present in the fears of the new world and the desperate attempts to cling to an outworn conception of the world political order that he found in Whitehall, and in the squalid efforts to back out of British commitments to the Jews in Palestine. It all seemed to him part and parcel of the general retreat from moral and political principles, beginning with the condoning of Arab violence in Palestine, of Japanese aggression in Manchuria, of Mussolini in Abyssinia, of Franco in Spain, and, above all, of course, of Hitler. And when, speaking of anti-

Zionists, he said to the Prime Minister, Winston Churchill, in 1940 or 1941, with characteristic boldness, 'Remember, sir, our enemies are also yours', this is certainly part of what he meant. Political appeasement, weakness, nervous fears, blindness to distasteful facts, seemed to him merely an aspect of one and the same gloomy condition of decline, which blinded the eyes of British economic planners to the possibility – to the necessity, indeed – of recouping the slipping British position by one of the main devices which, he felt sure, could still help to save it – the imaginative application of the resources of the African empire to the creation of a great new synthetic materials industry; it was a field about which he himself, as a chemist, knew a great deal, and one he had done much to develop. Since he thought in vast, synoptic terms, he saw the Jewish establishment in Palestine in these same scientific terms. As he reflected on the poverty of the land and its lack of natural resources, he placed his hope upon turning the one kind of capital that the Jews did seem to possess – technical skills, ingenuity, energy, desperation – to the production of miracles in scientific technology that would contribute to the building of the new world, and especially the new, post-Chamberlain Britain. He believed that the British would understand this, and was depressed by finding that this seemed no longer so. He felt rebuffed, he no longer recognised the nation he had loved so steadfastly and disinterestedly.

He felt he had a right to complain. On the two principal occasions when he suffered public defeat at the hands of his own followers, the principal cause of it lay in what seemed to them his fanatical reliance on the good faith of British governments. He was compelled to resign in 1931 as a protest against the policy of concessions to Arab violence at the expense of its victims, begun by the Labour Government with the Passfield White Paper, and continued by its successors. In 1946 a very similar situation once again arose; and it could plausibly be argued that Weizmann's policy of accommodation with Britain, which had led to a total betrayal of the Jewish position in 1938–9, must, if persisted in (he was then advocating acceptance of what was called the Morrison Plan), lead to a further series of promises broken and hopes destroyed. In the end he began, with painful reluctance, to think that this might be true. He could not bring himself to admit this publicly; but in private he spoke with bitter scorn about what seemed to him the complacent stupidity of post-Churchillian statesmanship. When some of his English friends (Lord Keynes for example) tried to say to him that England was too tired and too poor to carry the burden of its incompatible promises to the Jews and the Arabs any longer, and consequently must abandon both parties to their own devices, he rejected this doctrine with scorn and fury, as craven, unworthy of the men who urged it, and above all a false analysis and a suicidal policy for any great power.

His own position became increasingly unenviable. His followers in Palestine and elsewhere looked on his Anglophile policy as bankrupt, and on him as too deeply committed to it – and with it to a world that had vanished – to be anything but a dignified but obsolete mammoth of an earlier age. No member of the government in England or America was anxious to see him. He was a tragic, formidable and politically embarrassing figure. It had always been a somewhat daunting, not to say punishing, experience both for ministers and their officials to meet the full impact of Weizmann's terrifying indignation. This was now no longer necessary. The relief was almost audible. The Colonial Office treated him with icy politeness. He was systematically snubbed by the Foreign Office, as often as not by junior officials, who took their cue from their superiors, or perhaps felt that they could with impunity allow their own solidly pro-Arab sentiments free expression. He was treated with brutal rudeness by Bevin, who conceived for him, and for the entire Zionist movement, a notorious personal hostility which nothing staunched. And yet he could not give up his oldest political love. England meant more to him than all other countries put together.

When I stayed with him in Palestine, as it still was, in 1947, during the height of Jewish military and terrorist activity against the British forces stationed in that country, his fondness for, and delight in seeing, the British commander of his district and other British officers continued unabated, to the mounting scandal of his followers. He felt betrayed, and he could not, despite all his realism and his tough-minded approach to politics, understand what had happened. The romantic, somewhat Churchillian, image of England as moved, in the last resort, by her moral imagination, and not by a short view of her self-interest or passing emotion, would not leave him. The England which had stood alone against barbarism and evil, the England for which his son had lost his life, was scarcely less real to him than his vision of the Jewish past and future. He tried to close his eyes. He fell back on his scientific work. He often said that nothing had a morally more purifying effect, after the unavoidable contaminations of public life, than the impersonal work of a researcher in his laboratory, where the truth could not be cheated, and the vices and follies of men played little part. He busied himself in his work in the Institute at Rehovot that bears his name.[1] But the remedy was not wholly effective. He had put his faith in British statesmen and had rendered his followers into their hands; every shipload of immigrants turned away by Bevin and Sir Harold McMichael brought his part in the betrayal home to him. From it he never fully recovered.

The British Government – in particular the Labour Government – had wounded him as no one else ever could; least of all the Jews. He did not ask, and did not expect, gratitude from his own people. The fate of Moses seemed to him natural and perhaps deserved. To his own close followers he seemed, if anything, altogether too invulnerable: especially when he behaved toward them (as he often did) with casual offhandedness, or ill-concealed contempt, or, from time to time, the sudden ruthlessness of a great man of action. Yet their personal loyalty survived most of the shocks which he administered. For his personal magnetism was quite unique. Men crossed great distances to visit him, knowing or suspecting that he had completely forgotten why he had sent for them, and that when they arrived he would be genuinely puzzled by their appearance, at best agreeably surprised, and would dismiss them with a few careless, gay and friendly sentences. His relationship to his immediate followers was, in some ways, not unlike that of Parnell to the Irish party in the House of Commons. And they treated him with much the same mixture of adoration, nervous respect, resentment, worship, envy, pride, irritation, and almost always, in the end, the overwhelming realisation that before them stood someone of more than human size, a powerful, sometimes terrifying, leader of newly liberated prisoners in terms of whose thoughts and activities their own history was largely made. They might revolt, but in the end they always – most of them – submitted to the force of his intellect and personality.

---

[1] The Institute was the deepest love of his old age. He always spoke of it, and of all his colleagues and, indeed, everyone connected with its work, with immense personal pride and affection, and derived from it a feeling of satisfaction that nothing else gave him to an equal degree. The flourishing state of this great establishment is evidence of the lasting vitality that he communicated to all that he truly believed in.

It was otherwise with England. His preoccupation – it grew at times to an obsession (perhaps his only *idée fixe*) – with Anglo-Zionist relations blinded him to too many other factors in the situation: the attitude of other powers, especially in Europe, of the Arab rulers, of social and political forces within the Palestine settlement itself. The collapse of the Anglo-Zionist connection was not only intertwined for him with his own personal failure to retain real power in the movement that was his life; it also seemed to support the claims of those who said that against Britain only violence paid – that nothing would save the Jewish settlement but methods of terrorism – a view that he abhorred and rejected passionately with his whole being, then and all his life. But there was something far greater at stake even than that. He could not bear the thought that the State that he had desired to establish, and which he desired to place under the protection of Great Britain, would now perhaps never acquire those moral and political attributes which he had so long and steadfastly admired as peculiarly English and which, he now gloomily began to wonder, were disappearing everywhere – even from this island where he had spent his happiest years.

He was in due course elected President of the State of Israel, a position of splendid symbolic value, but little power. He accepted it, fully realising what it meant and what it did not mean, amid the acclamation of Jews and their well-wishers everywhere. He understood the extent of his own achievement and never spoke of it; he was one of those rare human beings who estimate themselves at their true worth, and see themselves in the true perspective in which they see others. His autobiography, particularly in its earlier chapters, is an astonishingly objective and lifelike narrative, without a trace of dramatisation, exaggeration, vanity, self-pity, self-justification; it conveys his authentic, richly and evenly developed, autonomous, proud, firmly built, somewhat ironical nature, free from inner conflict, in deep, instinctive harmony with the forces of nature and society, and therefore possessed of natural wisdom, dignity and authority.

His unhappiness came from without, hardly ever from within; he remained inwardly tranquil to the end of his days. He knew well that his achievement was without parallel. He knew that, unlike any man in modern history, he had created a nation and a State out of the flotsam and jetsam of the Diaspora, and had lived to see it develop an independent, unpredictable life of its own. This worried him. Freedom and independence were not enough. Like the ancient prophet that Western statesmen sometimes saw in him, he craved for virtue. He disliked certain elements in Jewish life, and wondered uneasily whether they would emerge uppermost. Obsessed and lop-sided natures repelled him; he was contemptuous of addiction to doctrine and theory without constant concrete contact with empirical reality. He did not value the achievements of the unaided intellect for their own sake, and admired them only when they made some contribution to human life. He liked solidity, practical judgement, vitality, gaiety, understanding of life, dependability, courage, stoutness of heart, practical achievement. Martyrs, failures, casualties, victims of circumstance or of their own absurdities – the stock subjects of the mocking, sceptical Jewish sense of humour – filled him with distress and disgust. The central purpose of the entire Zionist experiment, the settlement in Palestine, was designed to cure the Jews of precisely these wounds and neuroses that only their enforced rootlessness had bred in them. He therefore particularly disliked the mixture of avant-garde sophistication, political fanaticism, cynicism, vulgarity, cleverness, *humeur noire*, knowingness and occasional bitter insight with which able, typically Central European, Jewish journalists were filling the pages of the world's Press. Even more he hated stupidity, and he did not trouble to conceal this. In his last years, when he was living in peace and great honour in his home in Rehovot, a figure respected by the entire world, he was occasionally haunted by nightmare visions of the future of the State of Israel. He saw it jeopardised by just such a combination of stupidity – innocent, fearless, but blind – with the corrupt and destructive cleverness of slaves, the aimless, feckless, nihilistic restlessness inherited from too long a sojourn in the ghetto. Yet he also saw that this might not happen; and then the thought that the dream had come true against all the overwhelming odds of his youth and manhood, that he was actually living among Jews, a free nation in their own country, would fill him with incredible happiness.

He was not a religiously orthodox Jew, but he lived the full life of a Jew. He had no love for clericalism, but he possessed an affectionate familiarity with every detail of the rich, traditional life of the devout and observant Jewish communities, as it was lived in his childhood, in the villages and small towns of Eastern Europe. I cannot speak of his religious beliefs; I can only testify to his profound natural piety. I was present on more than one occasion, towards the end of his life, when he celebrated the Seder service of the Passover with a moving dignity and nobility, like the Jewish patriarch that he had become. In this sense he had always lived in close contact with the life of the Jewish masses, and his optimism had its source in the belief which they shared – that their cause was just, their sufferings could not last for ever, that somewhere on earth a corner must exist in which their claim to human rights – their deepest desires and hopes – would find satisfaction at last. Neither he nor they would accept the proposition that the mass of mankind could remain for ever indifferent to the cry for justice and equality even on the part of the weakest and most wretched minority on earth. Men must themselves work and fight to secure their basic rights. This was the first prerequisite. Then, if these claims were recognised as valid in the great court of justice that was the public conscience of mankind, they would, soon or late, obtain their due. Neither force nor cunning could help. Only faith and work, founded on real needs. 'Miracles do happen,' he said to me once, 'but one has to work very hard for them.'

He believed that he would succeed – he never doubted it – because he felt the pressure of millions behind him. He believed that what so many desired so passionately and so justifiably could not for ever be denied; that moral force, if it was competently organised, always defeated mere material power. It was this serene and absolute conviction that made it possible for him to create the strange illusion among the statesmen of the world that he was himself a world statesman, representing a government in exile, behind which stood a large, coherent, powerful, articulate community. Nothing was – in the literal sense – less true, and both sides knew it well. And yet both sides behaved – negotiated – as if it were true, as if they were equals. If he did not cause the embarrassment that suppliants so often engender, it was because he was very dignified, and quite free. He could be very intimidating; he uttered, in his day, some very memorable insults. Ministers were known to shrink nervously from the mere prospect of an approaching visit from this formidable emissary of a non-existent power, because they feared that the interview might prove altogether too much of a moral experience: and that, no matter how well briefed by their officials, they would end, for reasons which they themselves could not subsequently explain or understand, by making some crucial concession to their inexorable guest. But whatever the nature of the extraordinary magic that he exercised, the one element signally absent from it was pathos. Chaim Weizmann was the first totally free Jew of the modern world, and the State of Israel was constructed, whether or not it knows it, in his image. No man has ever had a comparable monument built to him in his own lifetime.

# EINSTEIN AND ISRAEL

ALBERT EINSTEIN'S chief title to immortal fame is his transcendent scientific genius, about which, like the vast majority of mankind, I am totally incompetent to speak. Einstein was universally revered as the most revolutionary innovator in the field of physics since Newton. The exceptional respect and attention that were everywhere paid to his person and to his opinions on other topics sprang from this fact. He knew this himself: and although he was a genuinely modest man, embarrassed by the adulation which he excited, and disliked publicity, he expressed pleasure at the thought that, if homage was to be paid to individuals at all, it should go to those who could claim achievement in fields of intellect and culture rather than of power and conquest. Indeed, that a mathematical physicist should have become a great world figure is a remarkable fact and a credit to mankind.

If the impact of Einstein's ideas outside the realms of theoretical physics and, perhaps, of the philosophy of physics is compared to that made by the ideas of other great scientific pioneers, an odd conclusion seems to emerge. Galileo's method, to go no further back, and his naturalism, played a crucial role in the development of seventeenth-century thought, and extended far beyond technical philosophy. The impact of Newton's ideas was immense: whether they were correctly understood or not, the entire programme of the Enlightenment, especially in France, was consciously founded on Newton's principles and methods, and derived its confidence and its vast influence from his spectacular achievements. And this, in due course, transformed – indeed, largely created – some of the central concepts and directions of modern culture in the West, moral, political, technological, historical, social. No sphere of thought or life escaped the consequences of this cultural mutation. This is true to a lesser extent of Darwin – the concept of evolution affected many fields of thought outside biology: it upset the theologians, it influenced the historical sciences, ethics, politics, sociology, anthropology. Social Darwinism, founded on a misapplication of Darwin's and Huxley's views, with its eugenic and sometimes racist implications, did social and political harm. I should perhaps hesitate to refer to Freud as a natural scientist; but there is no doubt that his teaching, too, affected fields far outside psychology – history, biography, aesthetics, sociology, education.

But Einstein? His scientific achievement touched on the philosophy of science; his own views – his early acceptance of Mach's phenomenalism, and his subsequent abandonment of that view – show that he possessed the gifts of a philosopher, and so, indeed, did his views of the central doctrines of Spinoza, Hume, Kant, Russell. In this respect, Einstein and Planck were virtually unique among the outstanding physicists of our century. But his influence on the general ideas of his time? On educated opinion? Certainly he presented a heroic image of a man of pure heart, noble mind, unusual moral and political courage, engaged in unswerving pursuit of the truth, who believed in individual liberty and social equality, a man sympathetic to socialism, who hated nationalism, militarism, oppression, violence, the materialistic view of life. But apart from embodying a combination of human goodness with a passion for social justice and unique intellectual power, in a society in which many seemed to live by the opposite values – apart, that is, from his exemplary life, from being, and being seen to be, one of the most civilised, honourable and humane men of his time – what impact did Einstein have?

It is true that the word 'relativity' has been, to this day, widely misinterpreted as meaning relativism, the denial of, or doubt about, the objectivity of truth or of moral and other values. But this is a very old and familiar heresy. Relativism in the sense in which Greek Sophists, Roman Sceptics, French and British subjectivists, German romantics and nationalists professed it, and in which theologians and historians and ordinary men have, in modern times, been tormented by it – this was the opposite of what Einstein believed. He was a man of simple and absolute moral convictions, which were expressed in all he was and did. His conception of external nature was that of a scientifically analysable, rational order or system; the goal of the sciences was objective knowledge of an independently existent reality, even though the concepts in which it was to be analysed and described were free, arbitrary human creations.

What general impact did his doctrines have? Modern theoretical physics cannot, has not, even in its most general outlines, thus far been successfully rendered in popular language as Newton's central doctrines were, for example, by Voltaire. High-minded public men in England like Haldane and Herbert Samuel tried to derive general metaphysical or theological truths, usually somewhat trite ones, from the general theory of relativity, but this only showed that their gifts lay in other spheres.

But if the impact of Einstein's scientific thought on the general ideas of his time is in some doubt, there can be none about the relevance of his non-scientific views to one of the most positive political phenomena of our time. Einstein lent the *prestige mondial* of his great name, and in fact gave his heart, to the movement which created the State of Israel. Men and nations owe a debt to those who help to transform their realistic self-image for the better. No Zionist with the least degree of self-esteem can refuse to pay him homage if the opportunity of doing so is offered to him. Einstein's support of the Zionist movement and his interest in the Hebrew University were lifelong. He quarrelled with Weizmann more than once; he was highly critical of the Hebrew University and, in particular, of its first President; he deplored the shortcomings of Zionist policy towards the Arabs; but he never abandoned his belief in the central principles of Zionism. If young people (or others) today, whether Jews or Gentiles, who, like the young Einstein, abhor nationalism and sectarianism and seek social justice and believe in universal human values – if such people wish to know why he, a child of assimilated German Jews, supported the return of the Jews to Palestine, Zionism and the Jewish State, not uncritically nor without the anguish which any decent and sensitive man cannot but feel about acts done in the name of his people which seem to him wrong or unwise, but nevertheless steadily, to the end of his life – if they wish to understand this, then they should read his writings on the subject. With his customary lucidity and gift for penetrating to the central core of any issue, whether in science or in life, Einstein said what had to be said with simplicity and truth. Let me recall some of the things he said and did, and in particular the path which led toward them.

He was born in Ulm, the child of irreligious parents. He was educated in Munich, where he seems to have encountered no discrimination; if he reacted strongly against his school and suffered something approaching a nervous breakdown, this does not seem to have been due to anti-Jewish feeling. What he reacted against was, perhaps, the quasi-military discipline and nationalist fervour of German education in the 1890s. He studied intermittently in Milan and Zurich, taught in Zurich, obtained a post in the Patent Office in Bern, then held university chairs in Prague and Zurich, and in 1913 was persuaded by Nernst and Haber, as well as Planck, whose reputations were then at their peak, to accept a research post in Berlin.

I do not need to describe the atmosphere of Prussia on the eve of the First World War. In a letter written in 1929 to a German Minister of State, Einstein said, 'When I came to Germany fifteen years ago [that is, in 1914] I discovered for the first time that I was a Jew. I owe this discovery more to Gentiles than Jews.'[1] Nevertheless, the influence of some early German Zionists, in particular Kurt Blumenfeld, the apostle to the German Jews, played a significant part in this – and Einstein remained on terms of warm friendship with him for the rest of his life. But, as in the case of Herzl, the decisive factor in his awakening as a Jew was not so much encounter with an unfamiliar doctrine (he had met adherents of it in Prague but apparently took no interest in it then) as the chauvinism and xenophobia of leading circles, in this case in Berlin, which led him to a realisation of the precarious predicament of the Jewish community even in the civilised West. 'The best in man can only flourish', he declared, 'when he loses himself in a community. Hence the moral danger of the Jew who has lost touch with his own people and is regarded as a foreigner by the people of his adoption.'[2] 'The tragedy of the Jews is ... that they lack the support of a community to keep them together. The result is a want of solid foundations in the individual which in its extreme form amounts to moral instability.'[3]

The only remedy, he argued, is to develop a close connection with a living society which would enable individual Jews to bear the hatred and humiliation to which they are often exposed by the rest of mankind. Herzl is to be admired, Einstein tells us, for saying

[1] Albert Einstein, *Ideas and Opinions* (based on *Mein Weltbild*, ed. Carl Seeling, and other sources), new translations and revisions by Sonja Bargmann (London and New York, 1954), p. 171. All subsequent references for quotations from Einstein are to this volume, by page number alone.
[2] p. 184.     [3] p. 171.

'at the top of his voice' that only the establishment of a national home in Palestine can cure this evil. It cannot be removed by assimilation. The Jews of the old German ghettos were poor, deprived of civic and political rights, insulated from European progress. Yet

> these obscure, humble people had one great advantage over us: each of them belonged in every fibre of his being to a community in which he was completely absorbed, in which he felt himself a fully privileged member, and which demanded nothing of him that was contrary to his natural habit of thought. Our forefathers in those days were pretty poor specimens intellectually and physically, but socially speaking they enjoyed an enviable spiritual equilibrium.[1]

Then came emancipation; rapid adaptation to the new open world; eager efforts to don clothes made to fit others, involving loss of identity, the prospect of disappearance as a group. But this was not to be:

> However much the Jews adapted themselves, in language, manners, and to a great extent even in the forms of religion, to the European peoples among whom they lived, the feeling of strangeness between the Jews and their hosts never disappeared. This spontaneous feeling is the ultimate cause of anti-Semitism, which is, therefore, not to be got rid of by well-meaning propaganda. Nationalities want to pursue their own path, not to blend.[2]

To ignore, or argue against, emotional prejudice or open hostility, Einstein declared, is wholly futile; the baptised Jewish *Geheimrat* was to him merely pathetic. National frontiers, armies he regarded as evil, but not national existence as such: the life of peaceful nations, with reciprocal respect for one another and toleration of each other's differences, was civilised and just. There follows a statement of Zionism not unlike the reaction to a similar predicament of another internationalist and socialist, Moses Hess, in the 1860s. Let me quote Einstein's words in 1933: 'It is not enough for us to play a part as individuals in the cultural development of the human race, we must also tackle tasks which only nations as a whole can perform. Only so can the Jews regain social health.'[3] Consequently: 'Palestine is not primarily a place of

---

[1] p. 181.    [2] p. 182.    [3] p. ibid.

refuge for the Jews of Eastern Europe but the embodiment of the re-awakening corporate spirit of the whole Jewish nation.'[1]

This seems to me a classical formulation of the Zionist creed, with an affinity to the unpolitical cultural nationalism of Ahad Ha'am: what Einstein was advocating was, in essence, the creation of a social and spiritual centre. But when British policy and Arab resistance, in his judgement, made the State inevitable, he accepted it, and the use of force to avoid annihilation, as being, perhaps, something of a necessary evil, but nevertheless as a burden and a duty to be borne with dignity and tact, without arrogance. Like all decent Zionists he was increasingly worried about the relationship with the Arabs of Palestine. He wished for a State in which Jews and Arabs could fully co-operate. But he realised, sadly, that events made this unlikely for the time being. He remained a consistent supporter of the Jewish State of Israel; here Jewish ideals must be pursued, especially three of them: 'the pursuit of knowledge for its own sake, an almost fanatical love of justice, and the desire for personal independence'.[2]

I need hardly say how sharply this differed from the general attitude of the educated German Jews of his milieu, not to speak of men of similar origin and social and intellectual formation elsewhere in Western Europe. When one remembers Einstein's earlier life, remote from Jewish affairs, his lifelong idealistic internationalism, his hatred of all that divided men, it seems to me to argue a remarkable degree of insight, realism and moral courage, of which his fellow Jews today have good reason to feel proud. After all, other eminent German-Jewish scientists, honourable men of unimpeachable personal integrity, Fritz Haber, Max Born, James Franck, reacted very differently. So did writers and artists like Schnitzler, Stefan Zweig, Mahler, Karl Kraus or Werfel, who were all too familiar with anti-Semitism in Vienna.

I do not wish to imply that Einstein necessarily condemned assimilation to the culture of the majority as always ignoble or doomed to failure. It was plainly possible for children of Jewish parents to find themselves so remote from their community and its traditions that, even if they considered it, they were unable psychologically to re-establish genuine links with it. He was clear that in a civilised society every man must be free to pursue his own path in the manner that seemed to him best, provided that this did

[1] p. 181.  [2] p. 183.

not do positive harm to others. He did not accuse these scientists and writers and artists of dishonourable or craven motives; their human dignity was not, for him, in question, only their degree of self-understanding.

It was his incapacity for self-deception or evasion, his readiness to face the truth, and – if the facts demanded it – to go against the current of received ideas, that marked Einstein's bold rejection of the central elements in the Newtonian system, and it was this independence that characterised his behaviour in other spheres. He rejected conventional wisdom: 'Common sense', he once said, 'is the deposit of prejudice laid down in the mind before the age of eighteen.' If something did not seem to him to fit, morally or politically, no less than mathematically, he would not ignore, escape, forget it; adjust, arrange, add a patch or two in the hope that it would last his time; he would not wait for the Messiah – the world revolution – the universal reign of reason and justice – to dissolve the difficulty. If the shoe does not fit, it is no use saying that time and wear will make it less uncomfortable, or that the shape of the foot should be altered, or that the pain is an illusion – that reality is harmonious, and that therefore conflict, injustice, barbarism belong to the order of appearances, which superior spirits should rise above. If his philosophical mentors, Hume and Mach, were right, there was only one world, the world of human experience; it alone was real; beyond it there might be mystery; indeed, he regarded the fact, of which he was totally convinced, that the universe was comprehensible as the greatest of mysteries; yet no theory was valid which ignored any part of direct human experience, in which he included imaginative insight, arrived at by paths often far from conscious.

It was this sense of reality that saved him, despite his deep convictions, from being doctrinaire. When what he knew, understood directly, was in conflict with doctrinal orthodoxy, he did not ignore the immediate evidence of his moral, social or political sense. He was a convinced pacifist; during the First World War he made himself unpopular in Germany by denouncing it. But in 1933 he accepted the necessity of resisting Hitler and the Nazis, if need be by force, which horrified his pacifist allies. He was an egalitarian, a democrat, with an inclination towards socialism. Yet his sense of the need to protect individuals from the State was so strong that he believed that Bills of Rights would be trampled on unless an élite of educated and experienced persons in authority at times effectively resisted the wishes of majorities. He praised the American Constitution, and in particular the balance of power between the President, Congress and public opinion (his early political mentor, the Austrian socialist Fritz Adler, would scarcely have approved). He hated walls between human beings, exclusiveness. But when Jewish students were being hounded by nationalist students in German or Polish universities, he declared that Weizmann was right; liberal and socialist resolutions were useless; the Jews must act, and create their own university in Jerusalem.

He hated nationalism all his life. But he recognised the acute need of the Jews for some form of national existence; above all, he did not regard a sense of national identity and nationalism as being one and the same thing. It is clear that he took political allegiance seriously. He renounced his German nationality twice. He would not, as a young man, have chosen to adopt Swiss or, after Hitler, American citizenship, had he not felt that he could give his full allegiance to these democratic countries when, for obvious reasons, he found it unbearable to retain his German passport. It was this combination of social sensitiveness and concrete insight into what it is that men live by that saved him from doctrinaire fanaticism; it was this that made him morally convincing.

He was an innocent man, and sometimes, I should think, taken in by fools and knaves. But innocence has its own modes of perception: it sometimes sees through its own eyes, not those of the spectacles provided by conventional wisdom or some uncriticised dogma. The very same independence which caused him to reject the accepted notions of physical space-time, and boldly offer the hypothesis of gravitational waves and light quanta against the resistance of physicists and philosophers, also liberated him morally and politically.

Consequently this man who sought privacy, who remained wholly uncorrupted by adulation and unparalleled fame in five continents, who believed in salvation by work and more work to unravel the secrets of nature – secrets miraculously amenable to analysis and solution by human reason – this gentle, shy and modest man displeased many establishments: German nationalists, Germanophobe Frenchmen, absolute pacifists, Jewish assimilationists, Orthodox rabbis, Soviet Marxists, as well as defenders of absolute moral values in which, in fact, he firmly believed.

He was neither a subjectivist nor a sceptic. He believed that the concepts and theories of science are free creations of the human imagination, not, as Bacon or Mill or Mach thought, themselves abstracted from the data of experience; but what the scientist seeks to analyse or describe by means of these theories and concepts is itself an objective structure of which men, viewed scientifically, are themselves a part. Moral and aesthetic values, rules, standards, principles cannot be derived from the sciences, which deal with what is, not with what should be; but neither are they, for Einstein, generated or conditioned by differences of class or culture or race. No less than the laws of nature, from which they cannot be derived, they are universal, true for all men at all times, discovered by moral or aesthetic insight common to all men, and embodied in the basic principles (not the mythology) of the great world religions.

Like Spinoza, he thought that those who deny this are merely blinded by the passions; indeed, he felt Spinoza to be a kindred spirit. Like Spinoza, he conceived God as reason embodied in nature, as being, in a literal sense, a divine harmony, *deus sive natura*; and, again like Spinoza, he showed no bitterness towards his detractors, nor did he compromise with them – he remained serene and reasonable, humane, tolerant, undogmatic. He did not wish to dominate, and did not demand blind fidelity from his followers. He supported any movement – say, the League of Nations or left-wing groups in America – if he thought that on the whole it did good, or at least more good than harm.

So with Jewish Palestine. He hated the chauvinists; he was critical, at times to an unrealistic degree, of the attitude of the Zionist leadership towards the Arabs, but this did not make him lean over backward occasionally as it did others; he denounced the Eisenhower Administration for seeking to please the Arab States at the expense of Israel, a policy which he attributed to American imperialism. He was critical of some of the Hebrew University's policies: for instance, he thought that, among the academic refugees from Fascist Europe, young scholars, not the old and famous, should be offered appointments. But his loyalties remained unimpaired. He was not prepared to abandon the Zionist movement because of the deficiencies of some of its leaders. His Zionism was grounded in the belief that basic human needs create a right to their satisfaction: men have an inalienable right to freedom from hunger, nakedness, insecurity, injustice, and from homelessness too.

He was somewhat homeless himself. In a letter to his friend Max Born he wrote that he had no roots; that he was a stranger everywhere. He was, on his own admission, a lonely man who instinctively avoided intimacy. He was a solitary thinker, not easy to know as a human being. His deep humanity and sympathy with the victims of political oppression, social discrimination, economic exploitation, were central to his outlook and need no special explanation; they were in part, perhaps, a compensation for his difficulty in forming close personal relationships.

Like many physicists connected in some way with the production of the atom bomb, he was, in his later years, oppressed by a sense of the responsibility of scientists for introducing a terrible new means of destruction into the world; and he condemned the use of it made by his adopted country, which seemed to him bent on a dangerously imperialist course. His hatred of the cruelty and barbarity of reactionaries and Fascists at times led him to believe that there were no enemies on the left – an illusion of many decent and generous people, some of whom have paid for it with their lives.

Perhaps his very gifts as a scientist led him to schematise, to oversimplify practical problems, including complex political and cultural ones, which allow of no clear-cut solutions, to be too sweeping and to ignore the wrinkles and unevennesses of daily life, insusceptible as they are to exact quantitative analysis. For it seems to me that there may exist a certain difference between the gifts of scientists and humanists. It has often been pointed out that major discoveries and inventions – as opposed to demonstrations of their validity – require great imaginative power and an intuitive sense, not rationally analysable, of where the right solution must lie, and that this is not dissimilar from the vision of artists or the sympathetic insight into the past of gifted historians or scholars. This may well be true. Yet those who deal with human beings and their affairs need some awareness of the essential nature of all human experience and activity, a sense of the limits of what it is possible for men and women to be or to do; without some such awareness of the limits imposed by nature there is no criterion for dismissing an infinity of logically possible but wildly improbable or absurd historical or psychological hypotheses.

About what makes men rational Aristotle and Kant and Voltaire and Hume may well be right: on this sense of what can, and what clearly cannot, be the case in human affairs, on the normal association of ideas, on such basic concepts as those of past, future, things, persons, causal sequence, logical relations – a closely woven network of categories and concepts – human rationality, perhaps even sanity, in practice, depends. Departure from these, as attempted, for example, by surrealist painters or poets, or aleatory composers, may be interesting, but it is deliberately counter-rational.

But in mathematics or theoretical physics this sense of reality does not necessarily seem to be required. Indeed, something close to the opposite may, at times, be needed. In the case of seminal discoveries – say, of imaginary numbers, or non-Euclidean geometry, or the quantum theory – it is precisely dissociation of commonly associated ideas, that is, departure from some categories indispensable to normal human experience, that seems to be required, namely a gift for conceiving what cannot in principle be imagined, nor expressed in ordinary language, which is concerned with day-to-day communication, with the facts and needs of human life. It is this detachment from, even flouting of, everyday reality that leads to the popular image of the abstract thinker – Thales who falls into a well, the absent-minded professor who boils his watch in place of an egg.

This kind of escape into abstractions – an ideal world of pure forms expressed in a specially invented symbolism free from the irregularities and untidiness, or even the basic assumptions, of ordinary experience – may possibly, at times, be connected with a psychic disturbance, some kind of displacement in early life. Einstein's breakdown as a schoolboy in Munich is paralleled by similar childhood experiences of Newton and Darwin, who also remained somewhat inaccessible emotionally. These thinkers, too, spoke of a type of experience which Einstein described as a deeply religious feeling before a vision of the divinity revealed in the all-embracing unity and rational harmony of the rigorously causal structure of nature. This was a vision of reality which nothing could shake: consequently Einstein remained an unyielding determinist, and never accepted the uncertainty principle as an ultimate category of natural knowledge, or as an attribute of objective nature – only as part of our provisional and incomplete analysis of it.

Such addiction to pure abstraction and generalisation may, at times, be connected with an incapacity for close personal relationships with others, a full social life; this appears to me to be a plausible hypothesis. It may well have been so with Albert Einstein. What he withheld from private life he gave to the world. Not only the fame of his achievement, but his figure, his face, are known to millions of men and women. His appearance became a visible symbol, a stereotype, of what people supposed a scientist of genius should look like, much as an idealised Beethoven became a commercialised image of the inspired artist. How many people know what other scientists of genius – Planck, Bohr, Rutherford – looked like? Or, for that matter, Newton or Galileo, or even Darwin? Einstein's features, with their simple, kindly, bemused, melancholy expression, moved men's hearts everywhere. He was very famous, virtually a folk hero, and his appearance was as familiar and as widely loved as Charlie Chaplin's, long before he was portrayed on American stamps or Israeli banknotes.

Let me return briefly, in conclusion, to the State of Israel. The Zionist movement, like the State of Israel, has often been attacked, today more than ever, both by countries outside its borders and from within; sometimes with, more often without, reason or justice. That Einstein, who tolerated no deviation from human decency, above all on the part of his own people – that he believed in this movement and this State and stood by it through thick and thin, to the end of his life, however critical he was at times of particular men or policies – this fact is perhaps among the highest moral testimonials on which any State or any movement in this century can pride itself. Unswerving public support by an utterly good (and reasonably well-informed) man, against a virtually complete lack of sympathy for it on the part of the members of his social and intellectual milieu (whose general moral and political views he largely shared), may not by itself be enough to justify a doctrine or a policy, but neither can it be dismissed; it counts for something; in this case for a great deal.

# YITZHAK SADEH

YITZHAK SADEH is today chiefly known as one of the heroes of the Israeli War of Independence. This is doubtless his chief claim to immortality, but his earlier life was so unusual and filled with such peculiar contrasts that its claim on our interest is scarcely smaller.

His father, Jacob Landoberg, was a rich merchant, a man of considerable charm, vitality and sense of pleasure, and a deeply sensual nature, which made the confines of an orthodox Jewish marriage intolerable to him, with the result that he left his wife Rebecca, the handsome, opulent-looking daughter of one of the most celebrated and saintly rabbis of his time, idolised by his community in the city of Lublin in Russian Poland, and led a feckless, unhappy but not uninteresting life, in the course of which he scattered his originally considerable fortune, and, it is said, died in poverty and illness.

His son was somewhat spoilt in childhood, grew up as a rich, good-looking, physically well-developed, precocious boy, adored by his mother, and determined, as soon as he reached maturity, to break away from the suffocating atmosphere of philistine respectability and conventional religion in which prosperous middle-class Jewish families then lived, and their deeply provincial outlook: against these restrictions he spoke with vehemence for the rest of his life.

Isaac was a wayward, obstinate, strikingly handsome young man. He obtained a normal Russian school education, but refused to go to university, which appeared to him to be a waste of his talents.[1] In sharp reaction against what was in effect the vast ghetto in which the Jews of Russia were then confined, he

---

[1] He did have a thirst for knowledge – he liked reading and study – and indeed became a student during his army days in the civil war: in 1918–20, at the University of Simferopol in the Crimea, he studied philosophy and linguistics, of all subjects.

developed a fanatical passion for physical self-improvement. He became a boxer, a wrestler and, what was very rare indeed in Russia at the turn of the century, a passionate footballer, who played the game as often as he could, taught it to others, and became a notable sporting figure in his (and my) native city of Riga.

Riga at this time was a city largely dominated by German culture, which derived both from the Baltic barons, who owned vast estates and formed a solid and fanatical caste of servants of the Russian monarchy, and the solid German middle class, which in Riga created an outpost of German nineteenth-century culture, a German opera, a German theatre, and a nationalist outlook directed against all efforts at assimilation by its Russian overlords. At the bottom of the social hierarchy were the original natives of the country – the Letts, a severe, industrious, oppressed population of Lutheran peasants, who at this time began to generate the beginnings of an intelligentsia, and were making strides particularly in the graphic and plastic arts. In the interstices of this social structure was to be found the small official Russian establishment which governed the Baltic provinces, and finally the Jews, who were divided into the upper stratum of those whose language and habit were German (together with some surviving descendants of the community of pre-Petrine Swedish times) and the lower stratum of the mainly Yiddish-speaking Russian Jews, whose children spoke Russian and were moving in the main directions which divided Russian Jewry at that period: liberal bourgeois, socialist and Zionist.

Isaac Landoberg, we are told by his nearest relations, looked upon all these movements and strata of population with equal contempt. He was filled with the romantic ideal of personal self-realisation: this took, in the first place, the form of physical self-perfection; that once achieved, he turned towards moral and intellectual self-education. He cut himself off from his parents, who were by this time divorced – he despised his mother's second husband, Isaac Ginzburg, and hardly ever spoke of him – and with such money as his father had left him, determined to make his own life and career. An expert in nothing save boxing, wrestling and football, he was too lazy and too bohemian by nature to wish to acquire any kind of professional skill. Consequently he decided to become an art dealer – this would shock his milieu, and afford him an opportunity, as he supposed, of a free and imaginative life, meeting painters and sculptors and other free spirits and living an independent, gay and, above all, Gentile life, free from the cramped, over-intellectual, orthodox life of the Jewish merchants and scholars of whom his family was composed.

His mode of life was extraordinary: his shop remained closed in the mornings, which he devoted to boxing, organising football matches, wrestling and posing as a model for painters and sculptors. He was proud of his appearance, and the fact that his well-built body at times attracted the interest of some of the young naturalistic painters and sculptors who were then to be found in Riga flattered him greatly, and he took pleasure in the thought of how profoundly outraged his mother and relations would be by accounts of this pagan activity. He had read Nietzsche and determined to cultivate the Dionysiac side of his nature. Sexually he seems to have been perfectly continent at this period, although later he was to become a lover celebrated for his infidelities.

In 1912 he married my father's sister Evgenia (Zhenya) Berlin, his first cousin: their mothers were sisters.[1] This lady, the very opposite of Landoberg in every respect, a socialist who proposed to devote her life to the improvement of the lives of workers and peasants, a graduate of two faculties, humourless, earnest, respectable, idealistic, without any feminine attainments, exceedingly plain, with a cast in one of her eyes which gave her a peculiarly governessy appearance, fell passionately in love with the splendid savage whom Landoberg delighted to impersonate. He did not reciprocate her passion, but was impressed by her intellectual attainments, by the fact that she had braved the anger of her parents and respectable friends by taking part in the revolutionary activities of 1905, that she was sought after by the police for two years; consequently he permitted her to marry him. The wedding, which relieved their common relatives by its respectability, was celebrated in the best bourgeois style at an immense party at which the bridegroom became somewhat intoxicated, to the mingled horror and pride of the bride. The life of boxing, wrestling, art dealing continued until 1914.

As soon as war broke out Landoberg immediately volunteered for service in the army. As he was an only son and a married man it

---

[1] I was taken to his wedding, but I am told that there were so many guests and the music was so loud that I burst into tears and said 'I hate this screaming music' and had to be removed. I never saw him on that occasion.

was not legally necessary for him to become a soldier: his rich relations promptly bought him out of the army. He allowed himself to be brought back to his doting wife and child, a daughter called Asia; after a few weeks of tranquillity he deserted his wife and secretly joined the army again. He was 'bought back' again. He did this for a third time and disappeared – his relatives were discouraged by the two earlier flights and ceased to trouble about him.

In 1917 he appeared in Petrograd as a member of the Socialist Revolutionary Party, dedicated to the peasants' cause, armed with an enormous Mauser revolver and an arm-band proclaiming him to be a member of the People's Militia. He was at this stage filled with revolutionary zeal and childish pride in his new uniform, his pistol and the intoxication of the Revolution. He appeared in the Petrograd flat of his very respectable brother-in-law and cousin, Mendel Berlin, and his wife Marie – my parents – and boasted about his revolutionary exploits with such innocence and charm, such infantile delight in the violent upheaval then in progress, that he enchanted us all. His hostess, also a cousin, took his revolver away and plunged it in a bath of cold water as if it was a bomb which might go off. He allowed himself to be disarmed and sat in our flat till three or four in the morning regaling his goggling relations with his own and his comrades' exploits as heroes of the Revolution, under the ultimate command of Pinchas (in those days Petr) Rutenberg, whose view of Lenin and Trotsky he shared: he told us, I remember, that they were a couple of dangerous fanatics and should be suppressed. His wife took a more serious view of events, but allowed herself to be carried away by his exuberance and his utter unconcern and irresponsibility.

He was a man of considerable temperament, a gifted actor, and a great wooer of others, particularly women. He was followed by adoring ladies and addressed revolutionary meetings, although those who heard him could never remember anything in particular that he said. He was a natural orator, fiery, convinced, rhetorical and inspiring: with this went a quality of gay and cynical frivolity, not unlike that of the greatest of all Russian revolutionary tribunes, Mikhail Bakunin, in the nineteenth century. Like Bakunin, Landoberg was fundamentally a pleasure-loving anarchist, irked by all ties and frontiers, heartless, as innocent children are heartless, in pursuit of some goal on which he has fixed his fancy, but, like a child, naïve, transparent and affectionate.

He stormed round Petrograd in 1917, and probably effected nothing. After the Bolshevik Revolution he disappeared again. For some months his wife had no idea where he was and had to be supported by her relations. He left her with no means of subsistence and appeared to take not the slightest interest in either her or his child. He was subsequently discovered to have joined the Red Guard – simply from love of action, as he later told me – and to have wandered about with his detachment in Central and then Southern Russia. Then he reappeared in Petrograd, went to see his wife in Moscow, where by this time she was living with her brothers; she was overjoyed to see him and asked no questions – he showed concern about his child's illness, but almost at once disappeared again, promising to come back very soon. He duly deserted the Red Guard, whom he found too violent and too brutal, and somewhere joined a detachment of Whites at the beginning of 1919. His mother, meanwhile, had died, but this appeared a matter of no concern to him. One of his half-brothers had been shot for commercial speculation, and another had become a member of the Cheka or secret police. Neither of these facts caused him the slightest anxiety; he communicated with neither brother and wandered about with merry unconcern, proclaiming the evils of Communism. With a White regiment he reached the outskirts of Theodosia, on the shores of the Black Sea.

At this point his wife, who had with the greatest difficulty traced his movements, joined him with their child. He expressed delight at seeing them and managed to get the White commander to quarter them in one of the unused flats deserted by the inhabitants in the port town. The little girl was visibly worse, and was in fact dying of the croup. Her mother, who had no eyes but for her husband, nursed her as well as a distracted, unpractical bluestocking could, torn between thoughts of revolution, the peasantry, the workers, the rival claims of Marxism and anti-Marxism, and her husband's peculiar tergiversations between Reds and Whites. They discussed the possibility of joining the Green armies – wild marauding bands of peasants who belonged to an anarchist movement directed equally against Whites and Reds – and in the course of these discussions Asia, his daughter, died. Her mother was broken by this, but Landoberg appeared to feel little.

He developed an immense passion for music at this time, and when not marching or counter-marching listened to an amateur quartet, in which Nicolas Nabokov, later an eminent composer and writer on music, took part. Nabokov remembered him well as one of the small informal audience which gathered to listen to this quartet in the midst of the civil war on the shores of the Black Sea, and recollects that he was a man of irresistible spontaneity, warmth and charm.

Landoberg took part in several indecisive battles between Reds and Whites. Then one night, as he sat near a camp fire with a small group of White officers, he listened to one of the staple themes of White soldiers – their hatred of the Jews as members of an international conspiracy, sworn to destroy Russia, murderers of the Tsar, to be exterminated at all costs, both in the immediate future and when victory was finally achieved over the forces of darkness.

This frightened him: there and then he determined to get away from these dangerous allies, and collecting his wife he bluffed his way into a ship carrying refugees from ports in the Black Sea to Turkey. It is not clear how he managed to make his way into a ship of this type without the necessary documents: but he was a man of infinite resource, and his artless charm, then and later, evidently melted the hearts of those in charge.

He determined to go to Palestine. He had never been a Zionist: indeed he had regarded that as a typical piece of bourgeois Jewish folly, an attempt on the part of victims to create a respectable liberal State or community, of the stuffiest, most Victorian type, and to perpetuate all the most philistine and socially mean and iniquitous characteristics of their oppressors. Nevertheless he suddenly decided that a new world was opening in Palestine for the Jews, rediscovered his Jewish origins and emotions, and joined the Zionist pioneer group Hechalutz in the Crimea. Inevitably, he became its leader after the celebrated soldier, Joseph Trumpeldor, who had organised Jewish self-defence against pogrom-makers in Russia, had left the Crimea for Palestine.

He landed in Jaffa at the head of a group of thirty-one pioneers, at the beginning of 1920, with his wife and a small bundle of luggage, and two devalued Russian roubles in his pocket. They travelled with a collective visa granted by the British authorities. He later said that they represented themselves as returning refugees from Palestine; when asked how long they had been refugees, they replied 'two thousand years'. This was very much in the spirit of Russian Zionists of those days.

In common with other immigrants they were taken to a Zionist reception camp. They were kindly treated and he was asked what profession he wished to choose. He indicated that physical labour was what he preferred. This wish was granted. He became a navvy engaged in breaking stones in a quarry. He is next heard of as taking part in the anti-British riots in Jaffa, together with the followers of the revisionist Jewish leader, Jabotinsky, whose by this time violent romantic nationalism was the very opposite of what Landoberg and his wife believed. However, where there was violence, thither he was irresistibly attracted. The British stood for all that was moderate, limited, dull, official, pompous and dead. Moreover they were for the most part pro-Arab and attracted by Middle Eastern semi-feudalism. The revisionists belonged to the extreme right wing of Zionism and stood for passion, militancy, resistance, self-assertion, pride and a nationalist mystique. He never actually joined the revisionists, and remained identified with the Haganah.

Landoberg was a man not permanently wedded to any ideal or any person. He changed his views, his mode of life, everything about himself, easily, with pleasure, delighting in everything new, exulting in his own capacity for beating any drum, wearing any suit of clothes, provided they were sufficiently gaudy – life was a carnival in which one changed one's disguise to raise one's own spirits and those of other people. He was duly arrested for taking part in the riots, and found himself in prison. Lady Samuel, the wife of the then High Commissioner of Palestine, Sir Herbert Samuel, was a prison visitor, and asked him what he had done. 'I am Lady Samuel,' she began. 'I am Isaac Landoberg,' he answered at once, and glared at her with amiable insolence. 'What is your crime?' she asked. 'I fight for liberty everywhere,' he answered. 'All officials are my enemies. I fought with the Reds against the Whites, I fought with the Whites against the Reds, I fight with the Jews against the British. I am prepared to conceive that one day I may fight with the Arabs against the Jews, or anyone else.' This was held to be inexcusable insolence. His sentence was doubled.

After his release from prison he broke stones to such effect that he was soon appointed manager of one of the quarries of the Jewish co-operative enterprise, Solel Boneh. His family had heard nothing about him. In 1924 he wrote a letter to my father, who by this time was living in London, saying that he was a happy, patriotic Zionist, with a bright future before him, urging all the members of his family to settle in this new and splendid land, where equality, fraternity and, one day, liberty would reign – a small country in which it was possible to do things impossible in larger, more unwieldy territories.

In the same year he appeared as the representative of the Palestine Jews in the Palestine pavilion at the Wembley Empire Exhibition in London. He was in the happiest possible mood. He visited my father and presented me, then a schoolboy, with a text of Ovid, whom he loved (Latin was among his few, curious scholastic attainments), and a book by Warde Fowler entitled *Social Life in Rome in the Time of Cicero*, which he thought a good book for a schoolboy to read. He was full of vitality, of wonderful talk; he had tremendous gusto and great charm; he was gay, insouciant and the most delightful company in the world. He taught us the latest Hebrew songs. He taught me a new tune for the song 'B'tzet Yisrael Mimitzraim' ('De exitu Israel de Aegypto', which has also been set by Mendelssohn in a very different fashion) and other new Hebrew songs, pre- and post-war. He talked with immense life and imagination, in the richest possible Russian, about a vast variety of subjects. I was completely charmed, and have remained so for the rest of my life. He invited the family to see the Palestine pavilion in Wembley. There we found him seated cross-legged on the stone relief map of Palestine – watched with fascination and horror by the representatives of the Palestine Arabs, who uncomfortably shared the pavilion with the Jews – eating sandwiches composed of Palestine produce, and drinking bottle after bottle of wine.

Unlike most of the Jews of his generation, he was a boon companion with an infectious wit and a most amiable disposition. His wife, gloomy, aware that her husband's eye was straying elsewhere, not convinced of the value of Zionism, inasmuch as it was a nationalistic patriotic conception, not allied to the social-democratic ideals for which she had suffered in 1905 and which she still carried in her heart, tried to enter his moods of unrestrained gaiety, but did not succeed. This irritated him. He complained to my father about the arid, unimaginative, doctrinaire character of his sister, and said that if this situation continued, he would be forced, in the interests of his duty to his new country, which he must serve with all his heart, to leave her; unable to fly herself, she clipped his wings. My father reasoned with him, fearing what would happen to his sister if she were abandoned; she continued to love her husband with a most violent and ever-increasing passion, despite his lack of interest in her and complaints about her lack of *joie de vivre*.

After Wembley he returned to Palestine and continued in his quarries. In due course he abandoned his wife and took up with a number of other ladies who were only too delighted with the companionship of this attractive, unbridled, romantic figure of more than ordinary human size. His feeling about the Jews was, in a sense, wholly external; although he was one by birth and education, his behaviour was that of a happy fellow-traveller, whom pure accident had brought to an unfamiliar shore, who found the people and their ideals sympathetic, so that although he did not feel bound to them by any profound emotion, despite the ties of blood, he was ready to collaborate with them and forward their ends with the greatest good will.

All this may have been transformed by the years during which no certain information about his psychological state can be obtained. His qualities of leadership, his reckless, lion-hearted courage, the total absence of any physical or any other fear (despite his flight from the Whites, which indicated that he had some self-protective instinct), his rich imagination and love of his fellows, his very childlikeness endeared him to many. Dr Weizmann, when he visited Palestine in 1936, had him assigned to himself as body-guard, and found him an agreeable, lively and intelligent Russian, a welcome relief from the tense and worried faces he saw round him, and from the political problems and political intrigue to which he was normally condemned. They remained friends until the end. Not so David Ben-Gurion, who looked on him, mistakenly it seems to me, as a dangerous power-seeker.

His wife, despairing of recapturing his affection, returned to Moscow to her brothers, where she duly wore herself out in good works and faded towards an untimely death. His relations found it difficult to forgive Landoberg for abandoning her; judging him in terms of their own morality, they showed, as might be expected, blindness to his heroic attributes. He was a guerrilla by nature, and the rules of settled, non-nomadic populations did not apply to him. In the 1930s, when self-defence units among the Jews gradually coalesced into the Haganah – the underground Jewish army – he was a natural recruit and became its principal trainer in shock tactics. He was a chief architect of the Palmach – the *force de frappe*, the successor in 1941 of earlier units – which he saw as the heart of resistance, battling against alien rule. I imagine that the Arabs entered his mind no more than they did that of the Yishuv.

He became one of the principal leaders of the Haganah. At the outbreak of war he fought with the British Army (with which the Haganah was allied), was called 'Big Isaac', and fought the Vichy forces in Lebanon and Syria. After the War was over, he grew a beard, went into hiding, and took part in the Jewish resistance to the Mandatory British authorities. A price was put on his head, but he was never caught.

I had tried to find him when I went to Palestine for the first time, in 1934, but no one I knew could tell me where he was. He was presumably at this time engaged in creating the beginning of what later became the Palmach, but of that I was to know nothing at that time. I next met him in 1947, while I was staying with Dr Weizmann at Rehovot. Somehow the conversation turned on my relatives in Russia. I mentioned Yitzhak Sadeh (he had begun to use this name in 1938), and Weizmann said he knew him, and was greatly taken by him: he referred to him, with a smile, as 'Reb Yitzhok'. The fact that Reb Yitzhok did not greatly care for David Ben-Gurion did not distress Weizmann too deeply. He said he thought he could find out where my uncle and cousin was. It was not too easy, because the Palestine police were looking for him. But I succeeded in meeting him clandestinely in the back of a café in Tel Aviv, and had a very good two hours with him. He was in the best of spirits. He told me about his exploits with the British Army. He assured me that no one would inform on him to the authorities. He proved right.

As for his relations to the British, he said that he had no feeling against them, he liked some of them and greatly admired their qualities; but since their policies were what they were, there was no alternative – they had to be fought tooth and nail. Submission to the Arabs – which the Colonial Office plainly wanted – was unthinkable. He said that the Palestine administration in the 1920s and 1930s really was too much for him: the officials, even when well-meaning and not overtly anti-Jewish or anti-Zionist, were too mean-minded, too pedantic, too narrow. Above all they were philistine; they lacked what he called genuine culture; with few exceptions, it was impossible to talk to them about books, ideas, music, history, particularly the long Jewish tradition with consciousness of which the Jews, of course, were filled. There was no contact: it was never and could never be a marriage, the sooner there was complete divorce the better – perhaps relations would improve after that.

When I first knew Sadeh, he was slender, elegant and had a certain pride in his appearance: now he was plump, had grown a beard, his clothes were ragged, and he plainly did not care what he looked like – he was totally uninterested in the amenities of life, what he adored was action – he enjoyed his hunted existence quite enormously. He was certainly a happy man when I met him in this café, with no sign of the slightest nervousness, fear or real concern about the future – every day brought its own problems, every day brought its own pleasures – he simply went from adventure to adventure with the greatest appetite for life.

In 1948, after the British left Palestine, he became a commander of a mobile unit, and captured Egyptian fortresses, and took prisoners. His method, as we learn from those under his command (for example, a grandson of the very Lady Samuel to whom he was so insolent), simply consisted of rushing Egyptian outposts with a grenade in each hand, shouting loudly and telling his men to do likewise. The Egyptians duly fled, leaving their shoes behind. Little blood was shed. He gathered up whatever weapons caught his eye.

The trophies he collected – guns, daggers, yataghans – afterwards proudly adorned his house in Jaffa. I met him there after the War of Independence. By this time he was something of a national hero. He showed me a great many photographs of himself in action against Egyptian troops and strongholds. When I told him that he was a kind of Jewish Garibaldi – the famous Italian national hero who fought the Austrians in the nineteenth century – he was delighted.

He turned out to know all about Garibaldi: his life and campaigns had always fascinated him, he said, and in the postcard he wrote me shortly afterwards he signed himself 'Garibaldi'. He kept a goat tethered to a tree in the garden, not because he needed its milk, but simply because this was forbidden by the new Israeli laws, and he believed in defying idiotic regulations. He seemed to me totally unchanged. His by this time considerable fame had not gone to his head; he remained simple, informal, with an undiminished gaiety and verve, above all vitality, a love of life in all its phases, a love of action, a love of change, events, a love of whatever might happen, a hatred of peace and quiet and boredom and a settled life. He had a large bottle of vodka on the table – 'I keep that for the Soviet Ambassador,' he said.

His part in Israeli politics had exactly the same quality of insouciance and irresponsibility as everything else that he did. Adoring children gazed at him rapturously in the streets. Fellow-travellers and Communists gathered in his Sabbath salon. He drank with members of the Soviet Embassy and wondered if he ought to pay a visit to Moscow to see what had happened in his absence. He explained his pro-Soviet attitude by his conviction that the Americans and British would never bomb Israel, but the Russians might: hence the need to keep in with them – he disclaimed ideological sympathies. He said to me in Jaffa: 'The Russians would like a large Arab federation to include our little State – but that is impossible – we shall never be Communists. The Israeli Communist Party is a ridiculous party, and the Arabs will not be Communists either, whatever they may say. Good relations with the Soviet Union are possible, Communism never. Our problem is not political, our problem is relations with the Arabs, which is a moral and personal problem. At one time I believed in the possibility of a bi-national State of Jews and Arabs, but I see it is impossible – they hate us too much, and I quite understand that. We must live separate lives. Of course, we shall try to treat our Arab minority as well as possible, but I am afraid that will not reconcile them. Still, one never knows – the future is the future, all kinds of things can happen, one must not give up hope, above all one must not be afraid, one must simply regard everything as material out of which to build one's life, and make it as rich and full as possible.'

He took particular pride in his friendship with his disciples, as he thought of them, Moshe Dayan and Yigal Allon, both of whom he adored – there is a famous photograph, at one time on public sale, showing him with his arms round the shoulders of the two warriors. He was determined not to be taken altogether seriously. He adored telling of his exploits, like a retired revolutionary Mexican general – but even there he displayed qualities of vanity so simple, and so attractive, that no one was moved to jealousy.

He was by this time happily married to a well-known partisan lady, having abandoned many others in his victorious course. He enquired tenderly, when I visited him, after his family, and regaled me with stories of his magnificent past. In a country filled with tensions and anxiety and earnest purpose, as all pioneering communities must be, this huge child introduced an element of total freedom, unquenchable gaiety, ease, charm and a natural elegance, half bohemian, half aristocratic, too much of which would ruin any possibility of order, but an element of which is something which no society should lack if it is to be free or worthy of survival.

He was one of life's irregulars, wonderful in wars and revolutions and bored with peaceful, orderly, unexciting existence. Trotsky once said that those who wanted a quiet life did badly to be born into the twentieth century. Yitzhak Sadeh certainly did not want a quiet life. He enjoyed himself enormously, and communicated his enjoyment to others, and inspired them and excited them and delighted them. I liked him very much.

His exploits – his training of, and friendship with, other Israeli soldiers, his emergence as a legendary hero – are not part of this story: they belong to the history of the War of Independence and the foundation of the State of Israel. All I have attempted to do is to present some recollections of my close relation, and some facts about his early life. He was a generous and adventurous man who played his part in the history of his nation, whose weaknesses attracted me at least as much as his virtues, and to whose memory I dedicate this modest and deeply affectionate memorial. *Zikhrono livrakha.*[1]

---

[1] 'May his memory be blessed.'

# L. B. NAMIER

THIS ACCOUNT of Lewis Namier is based upon no research and is composed purely from memory. Namier was one of the most distinguished historians of our time, a man of fame and influence. His achievement as a historian, still more his decisive influence on English historical research and writing, as well as his extraordinary life, deserve full and detailed study. For this task I am not qualified. My sole purpose is to describe to the best of my ability the character and some of the opinions of one of the most remarkable men that I have ever known. I was not at any time one of his intimate friends; but his immediate intellectual and moral impact was such that even those who, like myself, met him infrequently but regularly, and spoke with him, or rather were addressed by him, on matters in which he was interested, are unlikely to forget it. It is this impression that I should like to record for the benefit of those who did not know him and may be curious about the kind of man that he was.

I first came across his name as an undergraduate at Oxford, in, I think, 1929. Someone showed me an article by him in the *New Statesman* on the condition of the Jews of modern Europe.[1] It was the best and most arresting piece on that subject that I or, I suspect, anyone had ever read. Much was being written on that topic then; for the most part it was competent journalism: a combination of intellectual power, historical sweep and capacity for writing clear and vigorous prose was seldom, if ever, to be found among the writers on this subject, whether Jews or Christians. This essay was of an altogether higher quality. In reading it one had the sensation – for which there is no substitute –

---

[1] 'Zionism', *New Statesman*, 5 November 1927, 103–4; reprinted in *Skyscrapers and Other Essays* (London, 1931). Cf. 'The Jews', *The Nineteenth Century and After* 130 (July–December 1941), 270–7; reprinted in *Conflicts* (London, 1942).

of suddenly sailing in first-class waters. Namier compared the Jews
of Eastern Europe to a glacier, part of which remained frozen; part
of which had evaporated under the influence of the rays of the
Enlightenment; while the rest had melted and formed violent
nationalist or socialist-nationalist torrents. He developed this thesis
with incomparable imagination and a power of incisive historical
generalisation that was at once factually concrete and had great
historical sweep, with no attempt to play down disturbing
implications. I wondered who the author might be. I was told that
he was a historian whose work had caused some stir in the world
of learning, at most a respected specialist, but not a scholar of the
same order as Tout or Barker or Fisher, not to speak of Halévy or
Trevelyan. That was that: the author was a minor historical expert
with a fairly high reputation in his own profession. I heard no
more until 1932 when I was elected to All Souls.

There I found that a higher opinion of Namier was entertained
by my new historical colleagues – G. N. Clark, Richard Pares,
A. L. Rowse and others. From them I learnt something of Namier's
real achievement. My election to All Souls had evidently intrigued
Namier, who had failed to secure election himself some years
before the First World War.[1] I received a note in which, in huge
majuscule letters, the author informed me that he proposed to call
on me one afternoon in the following week and hoped that I would
be free to receive him. The letter was signed 'L. B. Namier'. When
he arrived, he said in his slow, deliberate, ponderous voice that he
wished to see me because his friend Richard Pares had told him
that I was interested in Karl Marx, of whom he held a low opinion.
He wished to know why I was engaged in writing a book about
him. He had some respect for the Fellows of All Souls. He believed
them, for the most part, with certain exceptions which he did not
wish to mention, to be intellectually qualified to do genuine
research work. Marx appeared to him unworthy of such attention:
he was a poor historian and a poor economist, blinded by hatred.
Why was I not writing about Freud? Freud's importance for
historical and biographical science had still been insufficiently
appreciated. Freud's books were, unlike those of Marx, works of
genius, and far better written. Besides which, Freud was still alive

[1] 'I have always had a certain grudge against Grant Robertson, who, as
examiner, had preferred Cruttwell to myself,' Namier said to me in the late 1930s,
'but when I think of what he has done for the German-Jewish refugees – I forgive
him.'

and could be interviewed. Marx, fortunately, was not; his followers, especially in Russia, which was now intellectually dead, had
used up far too much printer's ink, and were comparable in this
respect with German philosophers, who suffered from an equal
lack of sense of proportion and of literary talent and taste.

He stood in the middle of my room and spoke his words in a
slow, somewhat hypnotic voice, with great emphasis and in a
continuous unbroken drone, with few intervals between the
sentences, a strongly Central European accent and a frozen
expression. He kept his eyes immovably upon me, frowning now
and then, and producing (I realised later that this was how he drew
his breath without seeming to do so) a curious mooing sound
which blocked the gaps between his sentences and made interrup-
tion literally impossible. Not that I dreamt of interrupting: the
entire phenomenon was too strange, the intensity of the utterance
too great; I felt that I was being eyed by a stern and heavy
headmaster who knew precisely what I was at, disapproved, and
was determined to set me right and to get his instructions obeyed.
Finally he stopped and glared in silence. I begged him to sit down.
He did so, and went on glaring. I made a halting defence of what I
was, in fact, doing. He scarcely listened. 'Marx! Marx!' he kept
intoning, 'a typical Jewish half-charlatan, who got hold of quite a
good idea and then ran it to death just to spite the Gentiles.' I asked
whether Marx's origin seemed to him relevant to his views. This
turned out to be the stimulus that he needed to plunge into his own
autobiography. The next two hours were full of interest. He spoke
almost continuously.

He told me that he was born the son of a man called Bernstein
(or Bernsztajn), the Jewish administrator of a large Polish estate,
and that his father had been converted to the Roman Catholic faith,
which, he said, was common enough in his family's class and
circumstances. He had himself been given the education of a young
Polish squire, for his parents believed that assimilation to a Polish
Catholic pattern was a feasible and desirable process if one wanted
it strongly enough. They supposed that the only barrier between
Jews and Gentiles was the difference of religion, that if this were
abolished, the social and cultural obstacles which it had historically
brought about would fall with it. Conversion could bring about
the total integration of the Jews into the prevailing social texture,
and would put an end to the insulation, ambiguous status and,
indeed, persecution of Jews sensible enough to follow this rational

course. His parents' theory was essentially the same as that which had moved Börne and Heine, as well as Heinrich Marx and Isaac d'Israeli – two fathers of famous sons – to embrace Christianity. The hypothesis was, in his view, baseless and degrading; and he, Ludwik Bernsztajn as he then was, came to understand this when he was still quite young, sixteen or seventeen. He felt himself in a false position, and realised that the converted Jews in his circle lived in an unreal world – had abandoned the traditional misery of their ancestors only to find themselves in a no man's land between the two camps, welcome to neither. His father's conventional, bourgeois outlook repelled him in any case. He decided to return to the Jewish community – at any rate in his own mind – partly because he believed that to attempt to cut oneself off from one's own past was self-destructive and shameful, and in any case impracticable; partly because he wished to show his contempt for his family and their unworthy ideals. His father thought him ungrateful, foolish and perverse, and refused to support him. He went to England, which to him as to many Central and Eastern European Jews appeared the most civilised and humane society in the world, as well as one respectful of traditions, including his own. As part of his general revolt against his father's way of life, which was in his mind associated with the mixture of corruption, hypocrisy and oppression by which the Austro-Hungarian Empire was governed, he was attracted to socialism. The false and humiliating lives lived by his parents and their society seemed to him largely due to systematic delusion about themselves and their position, and, in particular, the attitude towards them of the Poles, whether Austrianised or nationalist, among whom they lived. Marxism was the leading philosophy which attempted to explain away and to refute such liberal fantasies as so many disguises intended to conceal an irrational and unjust social order, and one based on ignorance or misinterpretation of the real (largely economic) facts.

When he arrived in London, he became a student at the London School of Economics, then dominated by the Webbs, Graham Wallas and their followers, who, if not Marxists, were socialists and militantly anti-Liberal. However, in due course he realised that he had simply left one set of delusive ideologies for another. The principles and generalisations of socialism were as silly and unrealistic as those it sought to supplant. The only reality was to be found in the individual and his basic desires – conscious and unconscious, particularly the latter, which were repressed and rationalised by a series of intellectual subterfuges, which Marxism had detected, but for which it had substituted illusions of its own. Individual psychology, not sociology, was the key. Human action – and social reality in general – could be explained only by fearless and dispassionate scientific examination of the roots of individual human behaviour – basic drives, permanent human cravings for food, shelter, power, sexual satisfaction, social recognition and so on. Nor was human history, and in particular political history, to be explained in any other way.

He was not disappointed in England. It took, as he had supposed, a humane, civilised and, above all, sober, undramatised, empirical view of life. Englishmen seemed to him to take account, more than most men, of the real ends of human life – pleasure, justice, power, freedom, glory, the sense of human solidarity which underlay both patriotism and adherence to tradition; above all they loathed abstract principles and general theories. Human motives could be illuminated by attention to unexamined, occult causes which Freud and other psychologists had begun to investigate. Nevertheless, even such overt considerations as were present to the mind of an average Englishman, far more than to that of, say, an average German or an average Pole, accounted for a great deal of human behaviour – a far larger sector of it than had been explained by the 'ideologists'. At some point in this discourse, delivered with a kind of controlled ferocity, Namier spoke – as he often later spoke – of the absurdity of those who attempted to account for human behaviour by invoking the influence of ideas. Ideas were mere interpretations by the mind of deep-seated drives and motives which it was too cowardly, or too conventionally brought up, to face. Historians of ideas were the least useful kind of historians. 'Do you remember', he asked me, 'what Lueger, the anti-Semitic Mayor of Vienna, once said to the municipality of Vienna when a subsidy for the natural sciences was asked for? "Science? That is what one Jew cribs from another."[1] That is what *I* say about *Ideengeschichte*, history of ideas.' Perhaps he saw a discontented expression on my face, for I well remember that he repeated all this

[1] He quoted this with much relish in German: 'was ein Jud' vom andern Juden abschreibt'. But for once he appears to have been inaccurate. The real author, I have since learnt, appears to have been Hermann Bielohlawek, a member of Lueger's Christian-Social party in the Austrian parliament, of Czech origin, who apparently once said 'Literatur ist was ein Jud' vom andern abschreibt.'

again in still more formidable accents, and emphasised it over and over again in a slow, heavy, drawling voice, as he often did on later occasions.

The London School of Economics was not the England that he had admired from afar, and he felt this still more strongly when he met it face to face. It was a pathetic offshoot of the worst continental nonsense. He migrated to Balliol College, Oxford, and was there taught history by A. L. Smith and others. Oxford (he continued) had less truck with ideologies: here he could freely profess what he thought to be the deepest factor in modern history – the historically grounded sense of nationality. The notion that rational men, Jews or Gentiles, could live full lives either by dedication to a religion (organised falsification – rabbis were worse than priests, and lived on and by deception), or by abandoning their religion, or by emigrating to lands beyond the sea, or by any means other than those by which all other human communities had done so, that is, by organising themselves into political units and acquiring a soil of their own – all such notions were sheer nonsense. Self-understanding was everything, both in history and in individual life; and this could be achieved only by scrupulous empiricism, the continuous adaptation of one's hypotheses to the twisted and obscure windings of individual and social lives. Hence his respect for Freud and other psychological theorists – including graphologists, in whom his faith was very strong – and his lack of respect for Marx, who had, indeed, correctly diagnosed the disease, but then had offered a charlatan's nostrum. Still, that was better than Burke or Bentham, who peddled mere ideas rooted in nothing, and were rightly distrusted by sensible, practical politicians.

He returned to his autobiography: he had not been too well treated by England. He deserved a permanent post in Oxford, which he had not obtained. Scant recognition had been shown him by many established scholars, because they knew that he could 'show them up'. Nevertheless, it was the only country to live in. It was less fanatical and closer to empirical reality than other nations, and there was in its political tradition a certain realism – some called it cynicism – which was worth all the vapid idealism and idiotic liberalism of the Continent. There were Englishmen who were taken in by continental '-isms' – here followed names of some eminent contemporaries – but they were relatively few and not too influential: the majority wisely went by habit and well-tried

practical rules and kept clear of theory, thereby avoiding much
nonsense in their ideas and brutality in their action. He could not
talk to English Jews about Zionism. The Jews of England were
victims of pathetic illusions – ostriches with their heads in some
very inferior sands – foolish, ridiculous creatures not worth saving.
But Englishmen understood its appeal and its justification. The
only Jew he had ever met who in this respect could be compared to
an Englishman was Weizmann – indeed, he was the only Zionist
for whom he had complete respect. Upon this note he ended, and
having, as must be supposed, diagnosed me sufficiently – although
he took not the slightest notice of my occasional queries – he
marched out of my room to tea with Kenneth Bell of Balliol,
'whose family is very fond of me', he added.

I felt flattered by his visit, as well as deeply impressed and
slightly bewildered by his lecture. In the five or so years before the
War I met him more than once. He spoke bitterly about the policy
of appeasement. He felt that their sense of reality and their
empiricism had evidently deserted the ruling classes in England:
not to understand that Hitler meant everything he said – that *Mein
Kampf* was to be taken literally, that Hitler had a plan for a war of
conquest – was self-deception worthy of Germans or Jews. The
Cecils were 'all right', they understood reality, they stood for what
was most characteristic of England. So was Winston Churchill. The
men who opposed Zionism were the same as those who were
against Churchill and the policy of national resistance – Geoffrey
Dawson, the editor of *The Times*, Chamberlain, Halifax, Toynbee,
the officials of the Foreign Office, Archbishop Lang, the bulk
of the Conservative Party, most trade unionists. The Cecils,
Churchill, true aristocracy, pride, respect for human dignity,
traditional virtues, resistance, Zionism, personal grandeur, no-
nonsense realism, these were fused into one amalgam in his mind.
Pro-Germans and pro-Arabs were one gang.

He spoke a good deal about Zionism to me, no doubt because he
thought (rightly) that I was sympathetic. Gradually I became
convinced that this was the deepest strain in him: and that he was
fundamentally driven into it by sheer pride. He found the position
of the Jews to be humiliating: he disliked those who put up with
this or pretended that it did not exist. He wanted a free and
dignified existence. He was intelligent enough to realise that to
shed his Judaism, to assume protective colouring and disappear
into the Gentile world, was not feasible, and a pathetic form of

self-deception. If he was not to sink to the level of the majority of his brethren (whom on the whole he despised), if he had to remain one of them, as was historically inevitable, then there was only one way out – they must be pulled up to his own level. If this could not be achieved by slow, gradual, peaceful, kindly means, then it must be achieved by rapid and, if need be, somewhat drastic ones. He had not believed this to be wholly possible until he had met Weizmann, whom he admired to the point of hero-worship: here at least was a Jew whom he did not find it embarrassing to associate with, indeed, even to follow. But the other Zionist leaders appeared nonentities to him and he did not trouble to conceal this. He called them 'the rabbis' and said that they were no better than priests and clergymen – to him, then, terms of abuse. His Zionist colleagues valued his gifts but could scarcely be expected to enjoy his open and highly articulate contempt. Despite Weizmann's favour, he was never made a permanent member of the World Zionist Executive – a fact that rankled with him for the rest of his life. Despite all his talk of realism and his historical method, he had the temperament of a political romantic. I am not sure that he did not indulge in day-dreams in which he saw himself as a kind of Zionist d'Annunzio riding on a white horse to capture some Trans-Jordanian Fiume. He saw the Jewish national movement as a Risorgimento; if he was not to be its Garibaldi, he would serve as the adviser and champion of its Cavour – the sagacious, realistic, dignified, Europeanised, the almost English Weizmann.

Privately I used to think that in character, if not in ideas, Namier was not wholly unlike his *bête noire*, Karl Marx. Namier too was an intellectually formidable, at times aggressive, politically minded intellectual – and his hatred of doctrine was held with a doctrinaire tenacity. Like Marx, he was vain, proud, contemptuous, intolerant, quick to give and take offence, master of his craft, confident of his own powers, not without a strain of pathos and self-pity. Like Marx, he hated all forms of weakness, sentimentality, idealistic liberalism; most of all he hated servility. Like Marx, he fascinated his interlocutors and oppressed them too. If you happened to be interested in the topic which he was discussing (Polish documents relating to the revolution of 1848, or English country houses), you were fortunate, for it was not likely that you would again hear the subject expounded with such learning, brilliance and originality. If, however, you were not interested, you could not escape. Hence those who met him were divided into some who looked on him as a man of genius and a dazzling talker and others who fled from him as an appalling bore. He was, in fact, both. He aroused admiration, enthusiasm and affection among his pupils and those who were sympathetic to his opinions; uneasy respect and embarrassed dislike among those who did not. If he came across latent anti-Semitism he stirred it into a flame; London clubmen (whom he often naïvely pursued) viewed him with distaste. Academics and civil servants, whom he bullied, loathed and denigrated him. Scholars looked on him as a man of prodigious powers and treated him with deep, if at times somewhat nervous, admiration.

I never experienced boredom in his company, not even when he was at his most ponderous. All the subjects that he discussed appeared to me, at any rate while he spoke about them, interesting and important; when in form he spoke marvellously. He spoke with sovereign, and often wholly unmitigated, contempt about other scholars, and indeed most other human beings. The only living persons wholly exempt from his disparagement were Winston Churchill, who could do no wrong; Weizmann, in whose presence Namier was simple, childlike, reverent, uncritical to the point of worship; and his great friend Blanche Dugdale, Balfour's niece. He was said to be transformed in her presence, but I never saw them together. Nor do I know how he felt and what he said in the country houses which he visited for the purpose of examining their muniments and family papers. His pleasure in staying in them was part of the romantic Anglomania which remained with him to the end of his days. The English aristocracy was for him bathed in a heavenly light. His interest in history is certainly not alone sufficient to explain this radiant vision. Rather it is probably the other way about: his interest in the history of individual members of the English Parliament during a time when many of them were members of (or closely connected with) a powerful and gifted Whig aristocracy was due to his idealisation of this style of life. He has, at times, been accused of being a snob. There is something in this; but Namier's snobbery was of the Proustian kind – peers, members of the aristocracy, rich, proud, self-possessed, independent, freedom-loving to the point of eccentricity – such Englishmen were for him works of art which he studied with devoted, indeed, fanatical attention and discrimination. He was not carried away by the fascination of this world, as Oscar Wilde, or even Henry James, appear to have been. He was content to remain an outsider. He gloried in his vision of the English national character, its strengths and its foibles, and remained a lifelong passionate addict to a single human species, to the analysis and, inevitably, celebration of which his life – for psychological reasons which Freud had certainly not helped him to understand – was devoted. He studied every detail in the life of the English governing class, as Marx studied the proletariat, not as an end in itself, as an object of fascinated observation, but as a social formation; in each case from an outside vantage-point, which neither bothered either to emphasise or to deny.

His origins obsessed him. His morbid hatred of obsequiousness, which may have had something to do with his memories of Poles and Jews in Galicia, often took ferocious forms. Meeting me in the corridor of a train, he said, apropros of nothing: 'I have been visiting Lord Derby. He said to me: "Namier, you are a Jew. Why do you write our English history? Why do you not write Jewish history?" I replied, "Derby! There *is* no modern Jewish history, only a Jewish martyrology, and that is not amusing enough for me." ' He spoke of Jews as 'my co-racials', and clearly enjoyed the embarrassing effect which this word produced on Jew and Gentile alike. In All Souls one afternoon someone in his presence – he was in the common room at tea as a guest – defended the German claim to colonies, a topic then much in the air. Namier rose, glared round the room, fixed a basilisk-like eye on one of his fellow-guests, whom he had, mistakenly as it turned out, assumed to be a German, and said loudly, 'Wir Juden und die andere Farbingen denken anders.'[1] He savoured the effect of these startling words with great satisfaction. He was an out-and-out nationalist, and did not disguise his far from fraternal feelings towards the Arabs in Palestine, about whom his position was more intransigent than that of the majority of his fellow Zionists. I well recollect a meeting to interview candidates for a post in English in the University of Jerusalem, at which Namier would fix some timid lecturer from, say, Nottingham, with his baleful, annihilating glare, and say: 'Mr Levy, can you shoot?' – the candidate would mutter something – 'Because if you take this post, you will have to shoot. You will have to shoot our Arab cousins. Because if you do not shoot them, they will shoot you.' Stunned silence. 'Mr Levy, will you please

[1] 'We Jews and the other coloured peoples think otherwise.'

answer my question: can you shoot?' Some of the candidates withdrew. No appointment was made.

As the 1930s wore on and the position of the West steadily deteriorated, Namier grew steadily gloomier and more ferocious. He would visit me in All Souls, and later in New College, and say that as war was now inevitable, he proposed to sell his life as dearly as possible, and paint imaginary pictures involving the extermination of a good many Nazis by all kinds of diabolical means. The position of Zionism – one of the victims of British foreign policy at this time – depressed him further. The villains in his eyes were not so much the Conservative leaders – some of those were members of the aristocracy and as such enjoyed a certain degree of exemption from blame – but the Arab-loving 'pen-pushers of the Foreign Office' and the 'hypocritical idiots of the Colonial Office'. He would lie in wait for these – particularly the latter – in the Athenaeum. There he would drive some unsuspecting official into the corner of the smoking-room, where he would treat him to a terrifying homily which the victim would not soon forget, and which would probably increase his already violent antipathy to Zionism in general and Namier in particular.

Sir John Shuckburgh, then the Permanent Under-Secretary of the Colonial Office, was a not infrequent target for Namier when he was on the war-path. I was once present when Namier, in his soft but penetrating and remorseless voice, addressed Shuckburgh, who made every effort to escape; in vain. Namier followed him out of the room, on to the steps, into the street, and so on – down the Duke of York's Steps, probably to the door of the Colonial Office itself. Politically he was as great a liability to his party as he was an asset to it intellectually. His final and most savagely treated victim was Malcolm MacDonald, the Colonial Secretary himself. In 1939, after the Chamberlain government's White Paper on Palestine, which seemed to put an end to all Zionist hopes, Namier came to lunch with Reginald Coupland at All Souls. Coupland was the effective author of the Peel Report on Palestine, probably the most valuable document ever composed on that agonising subject. Coupland had spoken bitterly of the shameful betrayal of the Palestine Jews by the British Government, and said that he would write a letter to *The Times* pointing out the shortcomings of both Chamberlain and Malcolm MacDonald. Namier said that he had his own method of dealing with such cases. He had met Malcolm MacDonald somewhere in London. 'I spoke to him. I began with a jest. I said that in the eighteenth century peers made their tutors Under-Secretaries, whereas in the twentieth Under-Secretaries made their tutors peers. He did not seem to understand. I did not bother to explain.[1] Then I said something he would understand. I said to him, "Malcolm" – he is, you know, still Malcolm to me – I know him quite well – "I am writing a new book." He said, "What is it, Lewis?" I replied, "I will tell you what it is. I have called it *The Two MacDonalds: A Study in Treachery*." ' I do not know whether Namier had actually said this; he supposed that he had and he was certainly capable of it. It was, again, not unlike Karl Marx at his most vindictive, and, like Marx's insults, was intended to draw blood. Yet he was surprised by the fact that he was feared and disliked so widely.

In 1941 I was employed by the Ministry of Information in New York, and there I met a man who threw a good deal of light on Namier's younger days. His name was Max Hammerling, and his father had been associated with Josef Bernsztajn, Namier's father, in the management of his estate near Lemberg in Galicia, long before the First World War. The younger Hammerling was a warm sympathiser with the British cause, and got in touch with me to offer his help at a time when Britain was fighting Hitler alone. In the course of general conversation he asked me if I knew a man called Professor Namier, and was surprised to hear that I did. He said that he used to see him in earlier years, but that since then the connection had ended and he was anxious to hear what had happened to the son of his father's associate. Hammerling Senior had, so his son told me, emigrated to America and acquired control of one or more of the foreign-language periodicals of New York in the years before the First World War. The young Namier first arrived in New York in 1913 with very little money – supplied by his father – to engage in research on the American War of Independence. Josef Bernsztajn had made an arrangement with his old associate under which Hammerling engaged Namier to write leading articles to be syndicated and translated for a section of his publications. Namier wrote these articles at night, and worked in the New York Public Library in the daytime, and in this way kept

[1] Only Namier would have supposed that the average educated Englishman (or Scotsman) would realise that he was referring to the fact that the philosopher Locke had been made an Under-Secretary by his ex-pupil, Lord Shaftesbury, and that Godfrey Elton, who had been Malcolm MacDonald's tutor at Queen's College, Oxford, had recently been elevated to the peerage.

body and soul together. According to Max Hammerling, Namier viewed the continued existence of the Dual Monarchy with extreme disfavour, and was a vigorous champion of the *Entente Cordiale*. Hammerling Senior had many Roman Catholic readers and had no great wish to alienate the Roman Church in the United States, which was on the whole pro-Austrian and isolationist. When Namier's articles became too violently interventionist, he was told to moderate them: he ignored hints and requests; matters came to a head, and his employment came to an end in the spring of 1914. It was then that Namier, without any obvious means of subsistence, returned to England and was given a grant by Balliol College which enabled him to continue his research. Namier told me that the news of the assassination of the Archduke Franz Ferdinand was brought to the editor of *The Times*, Geoffrey Dawson, in All Souls after dinner. Namier, who happened to be there too, announced to Dawson and his friends that war was now imminent. Dawson indicated that he did not believe this (he laboured under similar delusions in 1938–9) and turned to other topics.

When war was declared Namier volunteered for the British Army. He was evidently not a perfect soldier. Some intelligent person took him out of the army, and put him into the Foreign Office as adviser on Polish affairs attached to the Historical Adviser to the Foreign Office, Sir John Headlam-Morley. 'I remember', said Namier to me, 'the day in 1918 when the Emperor Karl sued for peace. I said to Headlam-Morley: "Wait." Headlam-Morley said to Balfour: "Wait." Balfour said to Lloyd George: "Wait." Lloyd George said to Wilson: "Wait." And while they waited, the Austro-Hungarian Empire disintegrated.[1] I may say that I pulled it to pieces with my own hands.'

Apart from feeling convinced that the Polish National Democratic Party was plotting his assassination, Namier enjoyed his work in the Foreign Office. The Foreign Office showed no desire to retain Namier on its staff after the War, nor did the Treasury, with which he also was temporarily connected. Nor did Balliol College, Oxford, which made him a temporary lecturer for a while – his most devoted Oxford pupils date from this period. Thereupon he left England for Vienna, and there made a few thousand

---

[1] Namier pronounced this word very slowly, syllable by syllable, which heightened the dramatic climax of his narrative.

pounds. In the early 1920s he came back to London with his exiguous capital. Here his extraordinary character showed itself at its fullest. He did not do what others might have been tempted to do: he did not try to spend as little as possible while looking for a means of subsistence; he knew that he had it in him to write an original and important book and decided to do so. He spoke of this to friends and allies (some of them connected with the Round Table group of Liberal Imperialists with whose ideas Namier had been in sympathy during the War). He told them that he needed money to write a book; he held out no promise of repayment: the money was to be regarded as an investment in learning and in that alone. Philip Kerr, who was among those approached, told me (in Washington in 1940 where he was by then Lord Lothian and British Ambassador) that he did not find Namier congenial company, but was overawed by his leonine personality and felt him to be a man of unusual intellectual power. He and his friends obtained a grant for him; he was also supported by at least one private person. Namier felt no false shame in accepting such patronage: this was usual enough in that best of all periods, the later years of the eighteenth century. He felt that he had as good a claim as Burke, or any other talented writer of the past, whom the rich and the powerful should be proud to support; and he bound his spell upon his 'patrons', who, as he had always known, had no cause to regret their generosity. The books that he wrote did what he wished them to do: they transformed the standards of historical scholarship (and to some degree the style of historical writing) in England for at least a quarter of a century.

Having discharged this intellectual obligation, Namier threw himself, in the later 1920s, with passion and ferocity into political work in the Zionist Organisation. This gave full play to his formidable gifts: his polemical skill, his sense of history, his pride, his nationalism, his passion for exposing weakness, cowardice, lies and unworthy motives. He derived deep satisfaction from these labours. In the course of them he managed to irritate and humiliate his less talented collaborators, to impress some members of the British intelligentsia, astonish and anger others, and permanently upset and infuriate a number of influential officials in the Foreign and Colonial Offices. After the Second World War, when it became plain that his unwavering and withering contempt for most of his Zionist colleagues had made it certain that if an independent Jewish establishment ever emerged he would not be amongst its

guides, he turned his back upon Zionist politics, without changing
his moral or political convictions. He returned to the study of
history. He hoped and expected, not without reason, that he might
yet be appointed to a post by his *alma mater*. This was not to be.
Whenever a Chair in History (or International Relations, on
which, too, he had made himself a leading expert) fell vacant, his
name inevitably came up and was duly dismissed. Those responsible for such appointments in Oxford often said that it was a crying
shame that some other group of electors had failed to appoint
Namier to one or other of the three or four Chairs for which his
distinction fitted him pre-eminently. But when their own turn
came, such electors or advisers acted precisely like their predecessors. He was invariably passed over. Various reasons were
adduced: that his field of specialisation was too narrow; that he was
politically intemperate, as his Zionism or his low opinion of pre-
war British foreign policy plainly showed; that he would be too
arrogant to his colleagues or too exacting to his students; that he
would be a terrible bore, intolerable at mealtimes to the Fellows of
this or that college. The quality of his genius was not seriously
disputed: but this was not regarded as a sufficiently weighty factor.
He had made some implacable enemies. Yet, despite his acuteness,
he was an unworldly man, and in personal matters clumsy,
innocent and childlike. He was easily deceived: he took flattery for
true coin. He often had no notion of who was covertly working
against him: he was totally incapable of manoeuvre or intrigue. He
achieved everything by the sheer weight of his huge intellectual
armour. He misjudged motives and often could not tell friends
from ill-wishers. He fell into traps and remained to his dying day
unaware of this. He was an Othello who retained confidence in
more than one minor academic Iago. His failure to obtain an
Oxford Chair ate into his soul, as it has into those of others
similarly treated. 'I will tell you how they make professors in
Oxford,' he said bitterly to me during the period when he was
delivering the Waynflete Lectures at Magdalen College shortly
after the end of the Second World War. 'In the eighteenth century
there was a club called the Koran Club. The qualification for
membership was to have travelled in the East. Then it was found
that there were various persons whom it was thought desirable to
make members of the club and who had not travelled in the East.
So the rules were changed from "travelling in the East" to
"expressing a wish to travel in the East". That is how they make

professors in Oxford. Do not', he added, 'let this story go too far.'
He continued to teach at Manchester, but finally moved to London
and was entrusted with the formidable enterprise of the History of
Parliament, to be done in his own fashion – by means of detailed,
microscopically examined lives of all who ever were members of it.
Honours were showered upon him in England and abroad, but
nothing made up for the Oxford disappointment. Balliol made him
an Honorary Fellow. Two honorary doctorates were conferred
upon him by the University. He delivered the Romanes Lecture.
But although this pleased him, as did his knighthood, the old scar
remained and troubled him.

It was at this period that he married for the second time (his first
marriage had not lasted long – his wife is said to have been a
Muslim and died during the Second World War). He was
converted to the Anglican faith, and his marriage to Julia de
Beausobre finally ended the period of acute loneliness and bitter
personal unhappiness, mitigated by rare moments of pride and joy,
which had begun for him after the First World War. Friedrich
Waismann, an eminent Austrian philosopher whom he had met
during his years in Vienna, told me that he had never in his life met
an intellectually more gifted, penetrating and fascinating man, or
one more deeply plunged in the most hopeless misery and solitude.

His conversion to Christianity cost him the friendship of
Weizmann, who did not wish to examine the reasons for this step,
but reacted instinctively, as his fathers would have done before
him, to what he regarded as an act of apostasy for which no decent
motive could exist. This, of course, hurt Namier deeply, but his
marriage had created a new life for him and he bore such things
more easily. He visited the State of Israel after Weizmann's death,
was profoundly moved, but remained implacably opposed to the
rabbis and complained of clerical tyranny. When I made light of
this to him he turned upon me sternly and said 'You do not know
rabbis and priests as I do – they can ruin any country. Clergymen
are harmless. Nobody ever speaks of being in the hands of the
clergymen as they do of the Jesuits and, I fear, now should do of
the rabbis.' During this period I would receive occasional visits
from him in Oxford. He had grown mellower with age; he was
happier because his domestic life was serene, and because adequate
recognition had been given him at last. He took criticism as
painfully as ever: when his friend and disciple Alan Taylor wrote
an insufficiently respectful review of a collection of his essays in

the *Manchester Guardian*, he, like Marx, took this as a symptom of failing powers on the part of the critic.

He invested a great deal in his few personal relationships, and breaches were particularly painful to him. His relations with Taylor suffered further deterioration, in large part as a result of the role which Taylor believed him to have played in the choice of the successor to V. H. Galbraith as Regius Professor of History in Oxford. Taylor was not appointed; he blamed Namier for failing to support him sufficiently when he could have done so, and broke off relations. Namier was genuinely fond of him – fonder of him than of most men. He told me that some of his happiest hours had been spent at Taylor's house; that one must be careful – more careful than he had been – in one's human relations; but that Taylor, whose gifts were so extraordinary, had disappointed him by what he considered his addiction to popular journalism. 'And if I have hurt *your* feelings,' he said to me, 'I apologise also. I am not always too careful': this was a touching and handsome reference to the fact that I had sent him the printed version of a lecture on an abstract subject, which he had acknowledged with the words 'You must indeed be a very clever man to understand what you write.' This was a characteristic gibe aimed at the philosophy of history – a subject which he believed to be bogus, and which had been the subject of my lecture. I was delighted by his letter, which could not have been regarded as offensive by any normal person, still less by anyone who knew Namier and took pleasure in his prejudices and absurdities. E. H. Carr, who was a common friend, came to visit me on the day when I received it, and I read him Namier's letter with great relish. Shortly afterwards Namier's comment appeared in a gossip column of the *Daily Express*. Namier was horrified, and wrote to me immediately to explain that he had not, of course, meant to insult either me or the subject of my lecture. My reassurances did not convince him: he suspected Carr – quite baselessly, since Carr flatly denied this – of communicating the gibe to the *Daily Express*; serious journalism was, of course, another matter. How could such serious, learned, gifted men, Taylor, Carr, Fellows of the British Academy, who had it in them to give so much to historical study, compromise the dignity of their calling – and of academic life generally – by associating with the enemies of learning, however entertaining and informative? And in so public a fashion? At least Butterfield, than whom no one was more mistaken, did not dabble in this. Namier's suspicions were often (as in this case) without foundations; but he clung to them. My defence fell on deaf ears: an idealised image, which he had carried with him for the greater part of his life – the image of the scholar, and perhaps also of the Englishman – had in some way been damaged, and this was almost more painful than a personal attack.

He spoke often of the dignity of learning: of the need to keep scholarship pure, to protect it from its three greatest enemies: amateurism, journalistic prostitution, and obsession with doctrine. 'An amateur', he declared in one of his typical apophthegms, 'is a man who thinks more about himself than about his subject', and he mentioned a younger colleague whom he suspected of a wish to glitter. He passionately believed in professionalism in every field: he denounced fine writing, and, still more, a desire to startle or shock the reader, whether he was a member of the general public or of the world of scholars. He spoke with indignation about those who had accused him of wishing to reassess the character and historical influence of George III out of a desire to dish the Whigs and attack their values and their heroes. He would solemnly and with deep sincerity assure me that his sole purpose was to reconstruct the facts and explain them by the use of well-tested, severely empirical methods; that his only reason for distrusting party labels and professions of political ideals in the eighteenth century was his conviction – based on incontrovertible documentary and other factual evidence – that such labels and professions disguised the truth, often from the agents themselves. His own psychological tenets, on which these exposures were in part based, seemed to him confirmed over and over again by the historical evidence – the actual transactions of the politicians and their agents and their kinsfolk – which were susceptible of one and only one true explanation. Whether or not he was mistaken in this, he believed profoundly that he was guided not by theories but by the facts and by them alone. As for the question of what was a fact, what constituted evidence, this was a philosophical issue – something from which he shied with all the force of his whole abstraction-hating, anti-philosophical nature.

Journalism – the desire to *épater*, to entertain, to be brilliant – was, in a man of learning, mere irresponsibility. 'Irresponsible' was one of the most opprobrious terms in his vocabulary. His belief in the moral duties of historians and scholars generally was Kantian in its severity and genuineness. As for doctrinaire obsessions, that again appeared to him as a form of culpable self-indulgence – wanton escape from the duty of following minutely, wherever they led, the often complex, convoluted empirical paths constituted by the 'facts', into some symmetrical pattern invented by the historian to indulge his own metaphysical or moral predilection; alternatively it was a quasi-pathological intellectual obsession which rendered the historian literally incapable of seeing 'wie es eigentlich gewesen'. Hence Namier's distaste for, and ironies at the expense of, philosophical historians; and the emphasis on material factors and distrust of ideal ones. This was odd in a man who was himself governed by so many ideals and indeed prejudices: nationalism and national character, love of traditional 'roots', *la terre et les morts*, disbelief in the efficacy of intellectuals and theorisers, faith in individual psychology, even in graphology, as a key to character and action. But it was so.

It is not perhaps too extravagant to classify his essentially deflationary tendency – the desire to reduce both the general propositions and the impressionism of historians to hard pellet-like 'facts', to bring everything down to brass tacks – to regard this as part of the dominant intellectual trend of his age and milieu. It was in Vienna, after all, that Ernst Mach enunciated the principles of 'economy of thought' and tried to reduce physical phenomena to clusters of identifiable, almost isolable, sensations; that Freud looked for 'material', empirically testable causes of psychical phenomena; that the Vienna Circle of philosophers generated the verification principle as a weapon against vagueness, transcendentalism, theology, metaphysics; that the Bauhaus with its clear, rational lines had its origin in the ideas of Adolf Loos and his disciples. Vienna was the centre of the new anti-metaphysical and anti-impressionist positivism. Whether he knew this or not – and nobody could protest more vehemently against such ideological categorisation – this was the world from which Namier came. Its most original thinkers had reacted violently against German metaphysics and had found British empiricism sympathetic. In philosophy they achieved a celebrated and fruitful symbiosis with British thought. Namier was one of the boldest and most revolutionary pioneers of the application of this very method to history. The method – especially in the work of his followers – has been criticised as having gone too far – 'taken the mind out of history'. This kind of criticism has been levelled no less at the corresponding schools of philosophy, art, architecture, psychology. Whether the charge is just or not, even its sharpest critics can scarcely deny the value and importance of the early impact of the new method. It opened windows, let in air, revealed new horizons, made men see what they had not seen before. In this great constructive-destructive movement Namier was a major figure.

Namier's most striking personal characteristics were an unremittingly active intellectual power, independence, lack of fear, and an unswerving devotion to his chosen method. This method had yielded him rich fruit, and he would not modify it merely because it seemed to eclectics or philistines to be extreme or fanatical. Like Marx, like Darwin, like Freud, he was severely anti-eclectic. Nor did he believe in practising moderation or introducing qualifications simply in order to avoid charges of extremism, to please men of good sense. Indeed, anxiety to please in any fashion, still less appeasement of critics, was remote from his temperament. He believed that objective truth could be discovered, and that he had found a method of doing so in history; that this method consisted in a sort of *pointillisme*, 'the microscopic method', the splitting up of social facts into details of individual lives – atomic entities, the careers of which could be precisely verified; and that these atoms could then be integrated into greater wholes. This was the nearest to scientific method that was attainable in history, and he would adhere to it at whatever cost, in spite of all criticism, until and unless he became convinced by internal criteria of its inadequacy, because it had failed to produce results verified by research. This psychological Cartesianism was his weapon against impressionism and dilettantism of every kind. Kant had said that nature would yield up her secrets only under torture, only if specific questions were put to her. Namier believed this of history. The questions had to be formulated in such a way as to be answerable.

He was a child of a positivistic, deflationary, anti-romantic age, and his deep natural romanticism came out in other – political – directions. Dedicated historian that he was, he deliberately confined himself to his atomic data. He did indeed split up and reduce his material to tiny fragments, then he reintegrated them with a marvellous power of imaginative generalisation as great as that of any other historian of his time. He was not a narrative historian, and underestimated the importance and the influence of ideas. He admired individual greatness, and despised equality, mediocrity, stupidity. He worshipped political and personal liberty. His attitude to economic facts was at best ambivalent: and he was a very half-hearted determinist in his writing of history, whatever he may have said about it in his theoretical essays. Materialism, excessive determinism, were criticisms levelled against him, but they fit better those historians who, using the method without the genius, tend towards pedantry and timidity, where he was boldly constructive, intuitive and untrammelled. He thought in large terms. The care with which he examined and described the individual trees did not obscure his vision of the wood for the sake of which the huge accumulation and the minute analyses had been undertaken; the end, at any rate in the works of his best period, is never lost to view; the reader is not cluttered with detail, never feels that he is in the grasp of an avid fact-gatherer who cannot let anything go, a fanatical antiquary who can no longer distinguish between the trivial and the important. Perhaps, towards the end of his life, trees and even shrubs did begin to obscure his vision of the wood. But when he was at his best he might well have said, echoing Marx, for whom he had so little respect and by whose method he was in practice much influenced: 'Surtout, je ne suis pas namier-iste.'

# FELIX FRANKFURTER AT OXFORD

I FIRST met Felix Frankfurter in, I think, the first or second week of the autumn term of 1933 at Oxford in the rooms of Roy Harrod in Christ Church, where I called one afternoon in October, in order to return a book. I was followed into the room by Sylvester Gates, then a lawyer in London, whom I knew; he was accompanied by a small, neat, dapper figure, who was introduced as Professor Frankfurter. His name, I am ashamed to say, was then scarcely familiar to me: I vaguely connected it with the New Deal and Roosevelt, though in no clear fashion; but this may merely be evidence of my own provincialism and lack of acquaintance with world affairs. I do not know whether the impending arrival of Felix Frankfurter as visiting Eastman Professor had caused a stir in the Law Faculty at Oxford, but I can testify to the fact that his visit was otherwise unheralded. Visits by eminent professors from foreign universities were not unusual at Oxford, then as now; and no matter how distinguished, such visitors were not, and are not, lionised; indeed, at times too little notice is taken of them. (Whatever the sociological explanation of this phenomenon, it is one that brings relief to some and much chagrin and disappointment to others.) At any rate, when I was introduced to Frankfurter, I wondered about his identity and attributes. I knew Gates to be a man of exceptionally fastidious taste – indeed, one of the cleverest, most intellectual, most civilised men I had ever met. He had brought a friend – a professor of law, doubtless distinguished in his own field – and that was all. Within five minutes, however, a conversation sprang up, about politics, personalities, Mr Stimson (whom the professor evidently knew well), Sir John Simon, Sacco and Vanzetti, the Manchurian invasion, President Lowell and his behaviour to Harold Laski, to all of which the unknown professor contributed with such vivacity, and so extraordinary and attractive a mixture of knowledge and fancy, that although I had not intended to stay, I listened (although I am, by nature, liable to interrupt) in a state of complete and silent fascination. After an hour or so an urgent appointment did finally force me to leave, without giving me an opportunity of enquiring about who this remarkable personage might be.

A few days later he dined at All Souls, which was my own college. His host on this occasion was, I think, Geoffrey Dawson, the editor of *The Times*, and one of the most influential political figures in England in his day. By this time I had discovered the identity of the remarkable stranger, nor was there, at All Souls, any way of avoiding this knowledge: Dawson and his circle (he had invited guests and got his friends to do so also) looked on Frankfurter, as I perceived, less as an academic figure than as a man of influence in Washington, an intimate friend and adviser of the President of the United States, and a man whom it was for obvious public reasons evidently desirable to cultivate. He responded to this treatment with the greatest naturalness and lack of self-consciousness. I do not suppose that he disliked being made an object of such attention – it was not surprising at All Souls, which, at that time particularly, was a meeting-place of a good many persons prominent in public life, among whom there were some very powerful men – but he did not display the slightest sign of grandeur, did not pontificate, did not speak in that measured and important fashion which often characterises the speech of one eminent person conscious of discussing affairs of State with other, equally weighty figures. He talked copiously, with an overflowing gaiety and spontaneity which conveyed the impression of great natural sweetness; his manner contrasted almost too sharply with the reserve, solemnity and, in places, vanity and self-importance of some of the highly placed persons who seated themselves round him and engaged his attention. He spoke easily, made his points sharply, stuck to all his guns, large and small, and showed no tendency to retreat from views and political verdicts some of which were plainly too radical for the more conservative of the public personages present; they were hailed with the greatest approval by the majority of our generation of fellows – then very young – who formed the outer circle of Frankfurter's audience, and were divided from most of their elders by irreconcilable differences of view on most of the political and social issues of that day – Manchuria, the 'Bankers' Ramp', Fascism, Hitler, unemployment, slumps, collective security (Abyssinia and Spain were still to come).

After something like two hours of talk on grave issues, Frankfurter cast a sharp look round the room and decided to make a break for freedom. Fidgeting visibly, he rose from his chair and made as if towards the table on which decanters of whisky and brandy and small chemist's bottles of seltzer water stood in rows. But long before he reached it – he was evidently in no need of artificial stimulation – he almost literally buttonholed a junior fellow who looked lively and sympathetic, and engaged him in frivolous conversation of some sort. Dawson, Simon, Lionel Curtis and other mandarins tried to bring him back to great Anglo-American issues. In vain. He would not be detached from this junior fellow – I think it was Penderel Moon, who was afterwards to play so original, fearless and admirable a part in India – and insisted on involving himself in some purely intellectual controversy that was clearly of no interest to the statesmen. Presently he drifted over into the corner of the room where the junior fellows were talking among themselves. Here he behaved with so gay, childlike and innocent a warmth of feeling, and talked with such enjoyment of, it seemed, everything, that the young men were charmed and exhilarated, and stayed up talking with him until the early hours of the morning.

Whenever I met him at dinner elsewhere in Oxford, I observed the same phenomenon: a certain amount of firm cultivation of him by those who felt it their right and duty to be talking to him as a representative of influential American circles in the law or government; the same polite but unenthusiastic response by the Eastman Professor; apparent unawareness on his part that some people were much more important than others; and affectionate familiarity in his dealings with everyone, which lightened the atmosphere in the most portentous milieux and delighted those who were young and observant.

Oxford in the 1920s and early '30s was stiffer, more class-conscious, hierarchical and self-centred than it is now (it may, of course, be only because I was young that I think so – but there is, I believe, a good deal of objective evidence for this too), and Felix Frankfurter had an uncommon capacity for melting reserve, breaking through inhibitions, and generally emancipating those with whom he came into contact. Only the genuinely self-important and pompous resented this, and they did so most deeply. I heard Maynard Keynes, who was himself a famous and merciless persecutor of pretentiousness and humbug, and a

considerable expert on the subject, accord recognition to Frankfurter as a master of this craft: indeed, he said that he placed him
first among Americans of his acquaintance in this respect, although
he supposed that Holmes had been even more formidable and less
inclined to mercy.

Indeed, Frankfurter had his blind spots. He was a genuine
Anglomaniac: the English, whatever he thought of their public
policies, individually could do little wrong in his eyes. It needed a
great deal of stupidity, wickedness or personal nastiness or
rudeness on an Englishman's part to arouse unfriendly sentiment
in Felix Frankfurter's breast. In general, he liked whatever could be
liked, omnivorously, and he greatly disliked having to dislike.
Everything delighted him: the relations of one ex-military fellow of
a college to another; C. K. Ogden's attitude to London restaurants;
unequal success in the wooing of their academic hosts achieved by
various German exiles then in England and the socially ludicrous
consequences of this; Salvemini's deflation of Harold Laski's
rhetorical homage to Burke; his own progress in London and
Oxford. His sense of the ridiculous was simple but acute, his
enjoyment of incongruities irrepressible. He was not what is
known as a good listener: he was too busy; like a bee, carrying
pollen from an unbelievable number of flowers (and what seemed
to some mere weeds), he distributed it and caused plants which had
never been seen to do so to burst into sudden bloom. The short
memoranda, several lines long, scribbled in pencil, and often
accompanied by cuttings or offprints, stirred pools that had not
been known to move before; this social gift he displayed to the
point of genius.

But to return to Oxford. Those who were sensitive to status, and
suffered from fears that their own might not be adequately
recognised, and dreaded irreverence in all its forms, complained of
the Eastman Professor's unseasonable frivolity, his lack of taste,
his noisy laughter, his childishness, his Americanisms, his immature
enthusiasm, his insensitivity to the unique qualities of Europe in
general, and Oxford in particular – a lack of *gravitas*, a deliberate
defiance of the genius of the place – and so on. These strictures
were certainly groundless: our guest did not practise irreverence
for its own sake. He admired Oxford, if anything, too deeply and
devotedly, and with a sensibility that exceeded that of his critics.
He understood what there was to understand. If he struck sharp
notes occasionally, he did so intentionally, and they were not

discordant in the ears of most of those who turned out, in the next quarter of a century, to be the bearers of the central traditions of Oxford, and of much of the intellectual life of England both before and after the Second World War. I do not know what impact he made on Oxford lawyers or the undergraduates who went to his lectures. So far as I and my friends were concerned, his genius resided in the golden shower of intellectual and emotional generosity that was poured forth before his friends, and liberated some among them who needed the unlocking of their chains. Whenever, during his first and subsequent visits, I met him at dinner in colleges or private houses, the same phenomenon was always to be observed: he was the centre, the life and soul of a circle of eager and delighted human beings, exuberant, endlessly appreciative, delighting in every manifestation of intelligence, imagination or life. He was (to use the phrase of a man he did not like) life-enhancing in the highest degree. No wonder that even the most frozen monsters in our midst responded to him and, in spite of themselves, found themselves on terms of both respect and affection with him. Only the vainest, and those most 'alienated' (a term then not in common use) from their fellow men, remained unaffected by his peculiar type of vitality or positively resented it. Attitudes towards him seemed to me a simple but not inadequate criterion of whether one was in favour of the forces of life or against them. I do not intend this as a moral judgement, or a judgement of value at all: there are moral, aesthetic and intellectual qualities of the rarest value which seem incompatible with a positive attitude to life; I mean this distinction only as a statement of fact.

He came to us twice again, once on a purely private visit, once to receive an honorary degree, and the welcome in each case from his friends and the friends of his friends was justifiably rapturous. I recollect no particularly memorable observations or epigrams by him, or about him, then or at any time, but two occasions stand out in my recollection as characteristic. One was a dinner party in Christ Church. I cannot now remember who was host – perhaps it was again Roy Harrod. All that I recollect is that a charade was acted by some of us after dinner, and such was the degree of vitality infused by the guest of honour that the acting (if I remember rightly, it had something to do with a jealous eighteenth-century French marquis and his peccant wife) became passionately expressive. I shall not reveal the identities of the actors; they have all attained to celebrity since. Felix applauded the performance and egged the actors on until the realism of the actors reached a maximum degree of intensity. I do not think I shall ever forget the expressions on the faces, the gestures, the inflections of voices on this extraordinary occasion. For Oxford dons – the most self-conscious, inhibited human beings in an already intensely self-conscious and inhibited society – to have broken out of their prisons to such a degree was something that only the most potent force could achieve – an elixir powerful enough to break through the most sacred spells. This liberating power seems to me evident in all Felix's dealings, from the most intimate to the most public, ever since the beginning of his career. Oxford, made by nature and art to be the greatest possible obstacle to this force, proved it indeed to be literally irresistible.

The second occasion is one that he mentions himself in his reminiscences: a dinner party held by him and his wife[1] at Eastman House, then situated in Parks Road, attended among others by Sylvester Gates, Freddie and Renée Ayer, Goronwy Rees, Maurice Bowra and one or two others, including, I think, the famous expatriate Guy Burgess, who was then staying in Oxford, and was pursuing a profession about which we were not clear – I think he published a city letter of financial advice, or something of the kind – at any rate, he was excellent company and, in those days, a friend of mine and of several of the others present.

It is always difficult to convey to others what it is about a particular occasion – particularly a private one – that makes it delightful or memorable. Nothing conveys less to the reader or (rightly) nauseates him more than such passages as 'How we laughed! Tears rolled down our cheeks', or 'His irresistible manner and his inimitable wit drew gusts of merry laughter from us all! How happy we were then, so young, so gay, such high spirits! How little did we see the shadows gathering over us all! How sad to reflect on the subsequent fate of X.Y.Z.! What a summer it was, etc.' The evening terminated, as Felix himself reports a little inaccurately, in a bet between Freddie Ayer and Sylvester Gates

---

[1] I have said nothing here of Marion Frankfurter. This is a deliberate omission: her distinction in every respect was too great to be treated in what would inevitably have been a marginal manner. That she deserves a full-length portrait to herself, none of those who were admitted to her friendship would, I think, deny. I have proceeded on the principle that a blank is better than an unworthy sketch.

about whether the sentence of the philosopher Ludwig Wittgenstein 'Whereof one may not speak, thereon one must preserve
silence [*Wovon man nicht sprechen kann, darüber muß man
schweigen*]' occurs once or twice in his *Tractatus Logico-Philo-
sophicus*. Freddie said that he could have said it only once. He was
then sent in a taxi to consult the text in his own flat in the High
Street, and came back to report that Wittgenstein had indeed, as
Gates maintained, said it twice, once in the preface[1] and once in
the main body of the text, and paid ten shillings' forfeit.

Why was this so memorable? Only because the mixture of
intellectual gaiety and general happiness generated at this and other
dinner parties was too uncommon in so artificial an establishment
as the University of Oxford – where self-consciousness is the
inevitable concomitant of the occupations of its inhabitants – not
to stand out as a peak of human feeling and of academic
emancipation. Courage, candour, honesty, intelligence, love of
intelligence in others, interest in ideas, lack of pretension, vitality,
gaiety, a very sharp sense of the ridiculous, warmth of heart,
generosity – intellectual as well as emotional – dislike for the
pompous, the bogus, the self-important, the *bien-pensant*, for
conformity and cowardice, especially in high places, where it is
perhaps inevitable – where was such another combination to be
found? And then there was the touching and enjoyable Anglomania – the childlike passion for England, English institutions,
Englishmen – for all that was sane, refined, not shoddy, civilised,
moderate, peaceful, the opposite of brutal, decent – for the liberal
and constitutional traditions that before 1914 were so dear to the
hearts and imaginations especially of those brought up in Eastern
or Central Europe, more particularly to members of oppressed
minorities, who felt the lack of them to an agonising degree, and
looked to England and sometimes to America – those great citadels
of the opposite qualities – for all that ensured the dignity and
liberty of human beings. That which has sometimes been taken for
snobbery in Felix Frankfurter – a profound possible misreading of
his character – was, in fact, precisely this. His feeling for England
was subjected to strain during the troubles in Palestine: he was a
stout-hearted Zionist, and his conversations in Oxford on this
topic with Reginald Coupland – the principal author of the Royal

[1] [Though here 'reden' appears in place of 'sprechen' at the end of the main
text. I.B. took Ayer's side in the bet, and also paid a forfeit. Ed.]

Commission's report, which to this day is the best account of the Palestine issue of its time – are still unrecorded. Coupland frequently remarked that Frankfurter had taught him more on this subject than the officials instructed to brief him, and had doubtless made enemies by the courage and candour of his views. His part in this, like his contributions to the law, his influence on the policies of the New Deal, his work in United States government departments before he became professor, his advocacy of Sacco and Vanzetti, his public life and influence in general, may be worthier of comment and commendation than the personal qualities upon which I have dwelt here. But it is these last, and not the attributes which made him important to the leading political men in England by whom he was assiduously entertained, that made their deepest impact upon the academic community in Oxford.

No one had ever captivated so many unlikely and resistant members of an apparently forbidding fortress so swiftly. Obituaries often refer to the deceased's 'genius for friendship'. Not the dubious quality indicated by this cliché, but an unrivalled power of liberation of human beings imprisoned beneath an icy crust of custom or gloom or social terror – this seems to me to be Felix Frankfurter's rarest single personal gift. It was this that penetrated our defences – ramparts that have kept out and needlessly frustrated many a good and interested and intelligent and well-intentioned man.

# RICHARD PARES

WHEN I first knew Richard Pares, in the early 1930s, he was an unmarried Research Fellow of All Souls, and lived an ordered life, governed by strict, self-imposed rules, dedicated to teaching and to scholarship. He looked much younger than his years, like a shy, distinguished, clever undergraduate; this alert and youthful look he retained to the end of his life. His intellect, clear, formidable and with a fine cutting edge, left no one in doubt of its elegance and power. With this he possessed charm of manner, a discriminating (at times almost feminine) love for whatever possessed style and form, and an ironical humour which alternately delighted and alarmed his more impressionable colleagues. He lived behind doors through which none but his intimate friends were permitted to enter; but his gifts, his distinction both as a scholar and as a human being, still more his uncompromising moral and intellectual principles, and his originality and strength of character, made him a natural leader of the younger, reforming party in All Souls. His moral influence upon his colleagues was very great. He talked very well: and his ascendancy was in part founded on his talent as a college orator. Few who heard it will forget the blend of original thought, caustic wit and controlled passion, expressed in apt and classically lucid sentences, that more than once altered the tone and direction of a college debate. I remember no one, old or young, who failed to respect his intelligence, his unsleeping integrity, or the combination of piety towards traditions and institutions with his own independent judgement which he brought to the defence of whatever he deeply believed in – historical scholarship, the sanctity of personal relations, the maintenance of rigorous stand-ards in the College or the University. Yet, with all his pride, his talent, his fastidious intellect and temper, he was kind, affectionate and gay. His moral feelings, which he did not trouble to conceal, did not make him censorious or priggish; they were allied to his deep and critical aesthetic sense. He chose the eighteenth century as his field of historical study, partly because he was attracted by order and formal beauty (he later occasionally complained that the human beings he found in it proved more brutal, coarse, bleak and repulsive than he had conceived possible). He read and reread Jane Austen, Emily Dickinson, Virginia Woolf; he adored Mozart, and this aesthetic sensibility and understanding entered into all his relationships.

With all this, he belonged to the central stream of Winchester and still more of Balliol: he had a tender social conscience; he respected earnestness and public spirit; he was very just; he was a willing and lifelong slave of self-imposed obligations; and in consequence wore himself out by his devotion to research, his pupils, and later his service to the State. But he was not dulled by this stern self-discipline; he liked to be amused and exhilarated; he delighted in every form of artistic and intellectual virtuosity. As is sometimes the case with delicate and slightly wintry natures, he needed, and was sustained by, the greater vitality of others, and rewarded it with grateful and lasting affection. He had a keen sense of pleasure, and, despite his Wykehamical piety towards established values and his careful judgement and sense of measure, he welcomed eagerly almost any kind of original gift, however extravagant or eccentric, if it raised his own at times somewhat melancholy spirits.

But he did not, I think, count on such moments; when they occurred, they were for him a kind of windfall; he did not hope for much. To his mediocre pupils, he remained a conscientious, acute, sympathetic and stimulating tutor. He never allowed himself to intimidate or pillory the weaker among them, or to ignore them, or treat them with disdain. He disliked only the idle and fraudulent. But to those among them who displayed exceptional gifts he responded beyond their expectations: they found the most sensitive understanding and wide encouragement to the freest play of their imagination. Imagination, but not ideas. His distaste for philosophy, which he acquired as an undergraduate reading for Greats, developed into distrust of all general ideas. He disliked speculation and preoccupation with questions capable of no clear answers. There was always a predictable limit beyond which he declined to move. His values were fixed by the good sense and the authority of the moral and social order in which he consciously believed. Attempts to raise fundamental issues, whether personal or historical, were stopped with a few dry words, and, if pressed, with growing impatience and even irritation.

He was perhaps the most admired and looked up to of the Oxford teachers of his generation. He was attached to his pupils, and followed their subsequent careers with sympathy. But he avoided intimacy and kept himself apart, surrounded by a reserve that few dared to violate. He did not seek to dominate, to form a school, to bask in the easily acquired worship of undergraduates. In the outer field of political or social views he was prepared to be influenced; in the inner citadel of personal life and scholarship he remained self-sufficient, untouched and proudly independent.

He had, in a full sense, belonged to the great decade that followed the First World War. When he was an undergraduate of Balliol he became a close friend of Francis Urquhart and a member of the celebrated group that met in his rooms in Balliol and in his Alpine chalet. In particular Humphrey Sumner, Roger Mynors, Tom Boase, Christopher Cox, John Maud became his friends. And Sligger's own disciplined life, his deep convictions and tolerance of others, made a lasting impression on him. At the same time he was on terms of intimacy with the leading *beaux esprits* of his generation: Cyril Connolly, Evelyn Waugh, John Sutro were his close friends, and indeed formed a society in his honour; and although he subsequently, by an act of will, turned away from these companions of his youth, to make himself an austere and dedicated scholar, his taste remained incurably and admirably sophisticated to the end of his days. He renounced what he had admired, even though he continued to admire what he had renounced. He fostered thoroughness, application, the disinterested pursuit of the truth; he told himself that there were no a priori reasons for supposing that the truth, when discovered, would necessarily prove interesting. He defended the duller virtues: he had always detested romantic rhetoric, ostentation, journalism. This became, to the point of pedantry, his conviction and his doctrine, but he was never solemn, was capable of moments of marvellous gaiety and high spirits, and had a strain of childlike innocence and fancy that went oddly but delightfully with the cultivated quality of his taste and intellect.

His lifelong belief in academic life and academic values was the faith of a convert; he wanted no recognition or reward outside its bounds. He was endowed by nature with a wide and generous vision, was very imaginative, and understood almost everything; it was therefore a deliberate self-narrowing – an act of self-imposed stoicism – by which he chose the life of a don, and adhered to it to the exclusion of many other interests. Universities were his home and his world. He was an excellent civil servant during the War; there, too, his colleagues regarded him with deep respect, admiration, and a liking not unmixed with awe. But he returned to academic life with relief. His professorial lectures at Edinburgh were, as always, fresh, first-hand, just; he earned the love and admiration of his pupils and colleagues there as everywhere. But when All Souls offered him the most distinguished research fellowship at its disposal, he resigned the professorship which his progressive paralysis made it hard for him to carry, and came back gladly. His academic distinctions – the Fellowship of the British Academy, the Ford Lectures, the honorary Fellowship of Balliol – gave him abiding pleasure. He was most happily married and delighted in his daughters. He took as full a part in the life of All Souls as his physical condition made possible. From his wheelchair he made pungent and effective speeches at college meetings, and carried all his old authority. His conversation was as clever and delightful as ever.

Great learning, tireless labours, unswerving pursuit of truth, even brilliant powers of exposition are qualities, if not frequently, yet sufficiently often found in combination not to constitute a unique claim. What was astonishing in Pares was the union of extreme refinement of mind and heart, an intellect of the first order, and rigorous self-discipline with acute perceptiveness and understanding of others, rare personal charm, an unflagging ironical pleasure in the comedy of life, and a disposition to gay and brilliant play of the imagination characteristic of a certain type of artistic genius. And with all this a sense of honour, greatness of soul, an unsullied purity of character, and a capacity for love and devotion which made his moral personality unique, and his example and his influence dominant in his generation.

Until the end he took a conscientious interest in public issues, but they were not central in his life. He was – so far as he had clear-cut political views – a moderate socialist, somewhat right of centre; but his heart was not in politics. He lived his life within the frontiers of a deliberately circumscribed world, a formal garden which he could shape according to his own desire for order and unity, harmonious and enclosed: a universe that consisted of the study of history, of personal relations, and of his own full inner life. In this private world – perhaps the final flowering of Winchester and the Balliol of the 1920s – everything had its place, its own private name, its own particular relationship to himself. It was not an attempt on his part to protect his life against the chaos of the public world: within this *hortus inclusus* he demarcated carefully the realm of objective truth from that of his own sensibility and fancy.

His full height became revealed in the last year of his life, when he gradually lost control of his body, limb by limb, muscle by muscle, and, tended by, as he himself had called it, the loving-kindness of his wife, and by his children, he faced his end, which he knew to be near, with a noble serenity which no words of mine are fit to describe. He had not always been, but he died, a believing Christian. He was the best and most admirable man I have ever known.

# HUBERT HENDERSON AT ALL SOULS

WHEN Hubert Henderson first came to All Souls in 1934 he was not known to many of its Fellows. D. H. Macgregor, the Drummond Professor, who, like Henderson, had come from Cambridge, had, I think, some acquaintance with him; R. H. (later Lord) Brand and Sir Arthur Salter knew him well, and one or two of the relatively senior Fellows had come into contact with him in the course of his public activities. But to the majority of the junior and academical Fellows who formed the bulk of the College he was virtually unknown. He appeared gentle, shy and a trifle vague. He was courteous, amiable, but reserved; and seemed a little bewildered. All Souls was, and still is, *sui generis*, and the effect it will have upon those who come to it in middle life is difficult to foretell. Henderson had been deeply involved in public life both as editor of the *Nation* and as Joint Secretary of the Economic Advisory Council. All Souls must have seemed to him a curious private world, exceedingly unlike either Cambridge or the larger world which he had inhabited. It took him a little time to assimilate, but when he did so he came to occupy a distinguished and unique position in the College. He liked conversation; he was interested in many topics and was glad to speak about them with anyone who responded to his own detached, disinterested, and essentially middle-road notions; he did not particularly expect or take pleasure in agreement. He was a man of deep convictions, which he held with clarity and a kind of tranquil passion; in argument he was eloquent, lucid and tenacious; and since he was free from solemnity and priggishness, and liked to discuss whatever interested him, he took equal pleasure in analysing personalities and in dissecting abstract topics or political issues, and treated them always in the same scrupulous, and sometimes animated, fashion. He talked well, and with a courtesy of manner which never abandoned him even in moments of acute provocation; nor were either his juniors or his seniors ever made to feel that he put them into any category or box, or that he was conscious of being in one himself. This made the experience of talking with him, whether *à deux* or in company, particularly delightful and profitable. Nobody, I think, felt about him that he belonged specially to any one section of the College, of the Senior Fellows, or of the Junior Fellows, or of academics or of 'Londoners', or of conservatives or of progressives. He had a genuinely independent personality, and held sharp ideas and opinions both about persons and about issues, and spoke about them without rancour, without self-consciousness, moderate in judgement, intellectually intense, and naturally civil.

I dwell upon the quality of his talk because All Souls has been, as long as anyone remembers, a college of talkers, and his own genuine love of conversation and debate caused him to fit into it without effort. He liked to talk an issue through and he liked argument; he wished to make his own views entirely clear to others and grasp theirs as fairly and as accurately as he could; and since he had an intellect of exceptional acuteness and integrity, and a genuine desire to establish the truth, and sincerely believed that this could sometimes be done by means of rational discussion, he used to argue on and on, with tenacity and absorption, and infectious spontaneity. His face would assume a puzzled, sometimes bewildered or incredulous expression when, as occasionally happened, his opponent seemed to him to advance opinions which no sane or well-informed person could conceivably hold. He would ruffle his hair, his voice would rise in pitch, he would make gestures of despair, but, whatever the hour, he would go on. He would never willingly let go. He would never grow angry, or rude, or waspish, no matter how maddening his opponent seemed to him to be. The hour would grow late, it would be past midnight, and the ashtray beside him would become filled and over-filled with the stubs of du Maurier cigarettes. If, as sometimes happened, the argument broke down under a hail of mere counter-assertions, he would simply grow silent and avert his thoughts; if the tone grew too sharp he would look at a newspaper or quietly leave the room. He was not at his ease save in an atmosphere of courtesy, intelligence, moderation, and a modicum of intellectual goodwill.

He had an acute sense of humour, and, in particular, of the ridiculous, which found free play in Oxford, together with a boyish sweetness of disposition, and a genuine hatred of all forms of sentimentality and humbug. For those younger than himself (of whom alone I can speak with confidence) he was easier to be with than almost any other of their seniors: he was not in the least pompous, not in the least vain, not in the least difficult; he had an open mind and a natural fund of sympathy and kindness. He treated all men as equals, and contact with him was direct and delightful. One was never reminded, by some unconscious phrase on his part, of his own eminence in the world of affairs, or of particular convictions or prejudices which it was not safe to touch upon. He liked to be amused, he was not censorious or disapproving of high spirits or gaiety or even of a degree of silliness and nonsense in others, and he was not put off by eccentricity; in short, he was in favour of the flow of life, he enhanced it and was a cause of it in others. What he liked above all was a combination of imaginative ideas and practical knowledge, and at All Souls he found these in sufficient quantity. On committees his good judgement, freedom from bias, clear principles, fearlessness and unruffled good temper (the high falsetto to which his voice rose in moments of excitement sometimes belied him) were a great asset, particularly at moments when these qualities seemed to be on the ebb; at college meetings he spoke with authority. All Souls is a large college, and to be effective at its meetings one must have a certain degree of oratorical power. This Henderson did not possess, but his speeches were listened to with respect because his impartiality and independence were evident and because he was widely liked and admired. I doubt whether he knew how widespread this feeling was until he was elected Warden: he was not a man who spent time on reflecting about other people's attitudes or feelings towards him; this went with his freedom from vanity and neurotic preoccupation with his own personality or status. He had, to everyone's sorrow, had a breakdown in health some time before the last war, but had seemed to make a complete recovery and continued to play his part in College, as a member of committees, and as a frequent assistant examiner in economics in the fellowship elections. His shrewd judgement as an examiner was always much trusted and has vindicated itself, so far as I remember, on all occasions.

After the untimely death of Warden Sumner in 1951 he was elected to succeed him in June of that year. He certainly did not seek the office. If ever there was a popular 'draft' of a reluctant candidate, this was an instance of it; for a long time he did not wish to be considered, and when in the end he allowed himself to be discussed, it was due not to ambition, nor even to a sense of duty (for I am sure he did not consider it anyone's particular duty to seek or hold such office), but because it was part of his inherent modesty not to resist too violently the pressure of his friends. I doubt if he asked himself whether he had much chance of being elected; I am sure that he did not care in the least how great or small it was. I remember very well his air after his election, which was, as so often in moments of crisis, slightly bewildered and incredulous; he was deeply moved by this token of corporate trust and affection.

He scarcely entered upon his reign. A few days after his election he had a heart attack in the Sheldonian Theatre, on the day of the Encaenia. I went to visit him at the Acland Nursing Home and he was, as always, charming and cheerful; with, as the Vice-Chancellor so well said of him in his commemorative remarks, 'his quiet gaiety and his transparent goodness'.[1] To goodness he added purity of character, distinction of intellect and of feeling, a sense of public duty, and a devotion to personal relations and private life, as well as, beneath his vagueness and gentleness, a foundation of Scottish granite which gave him an unsuspected strength of will. He possessed a blend of characteristics which All Souls, in the view of some, should aim at producing: he was intellectual – he was interested in general ideas – but he was neither woolly-minded nor pedantic, nor locked in an ivory tower. He was involved in public affairs, and took a lifelong interest in public issues, but he was not a philistine and did not judge an academic world by the standards drawn from public life, nor vice versa. He admired practical good sense and administrative ability, and respected all experts and *métiers* as such, and was very suspicious of abstractions and theories in his own subject, which he regarded as essentially applied and not 'pure'. On the other hand, he was not militantly anti-intellectual; he liked any evidence of mental power or elegance; and suffered from neither of those two notorious occupational 'complexes' of dons – a repressed yearning for spectacular worldly success and influence, and a resentful *odium academicum* of those who aspire to it.

His attitude to the great world was balanced and harmonious. He was little worried by official reputations and liked associating

[1] *Oxford University Gazette* 83 (1952–3), 85.

Winston Churchill on his way to 10 Downing Street, 1940

Franklin D. Roosevelt

Chaim Weizmann in 1945

Albert Einstein in Christ Church Meadow, Oxford, 1932

Yitzhak Sadeh

L. B. Namier

Felix Frankfurter in his office in the Supreme Court
*George James/NYT Pictures*

Richard Pares

Hubert Henderson

J. L. Austin in 1952

John Plamenatz

Maurice Bowra in Oxford, 1950

Lord David Cecil and the author in the
cloisters, New College, Oxford, 1950

Virginia Woolf

Edmund Wilson, *c.*1953

Auberon Herbert in the garden at
Pixton, his home in Somerset

Aldous Huxley

Anna Akhmatova and Boris Pasternak at a public reading in Moscow, 1946

with anyone whom he regarded as intelligent, enjoyable or interesting; and of these qualities he was a very good judge. He avoided fools and bores but gave even them little reason for offence. He liked thinking for its own sake and had a streak of imaginative poetry which used to emerge when, in the intimacy of sympathetic company, he would describe old friends or episodes in his Cambridge or London life. His behaviour was always wonderfully normal; there were no antics, no idiosyncrasies, no virtuoso flights, no conscious exercise of charm, no display; yet he felt neither jealousy of such behaviour nor disapproval. He did not resent or dislike cleverness or temperament in others, nor did he resent dimness or pedantry. But he disliked histrionic exhibitions, and every form of hollowness and falsity; he liked the dry and not the wet, the clear and not the obscure, however rich and suggestive. When an occasion presented itself, he took obvious pleasure in torpedoing arguments or schemes which appeared to him foolish or pretentious. He had an acute, ironical humour, was obstinate under attack, and could not be either snubbed or bullied. Ambition he did not seem to me to have, but he had much dignity and a proper sense of his own worth which was never obtruded, but emitted quiet radiations of its own. He did not speak unless he had something to say, and because he often had, talked a great deal, and because he had no fondness for small talk, was also often silent. His mind was just, acute and liberal, free from all personal and social prejudice, distinguished, serious, humane; above all, he was an exceptionally nice man, who remained detached from the normal academic categories, an independent human being on his own; and his premature death was a very great loss to his College and to his University.

# J. L. AUSTIN AND THE EARLY BEGINNINGS
# OF OXFORD PHILOSOPHY

THE PHILOSOPHICAL trend which afterwards came to be called 'Oxford Philosophy' originated principally in weekly discussions by a small group of young Oxford philosophers – the oldest was twenty-seven – which began some time in 1936–7. They were suggested by J. L. Austin, who remained their leading spirit until the War brought them to an end. Austin was elected to a Fellowship at All Souls in the autumn of 1933. He had not then fully decided on a philosophical career. He was convinced, so he used to say, that philosophy, as taught in Oxford, was an excellent training for young men; there was no better way of making them rational – in those days his highest term of praise – if only because it generated in them a critical, indeed a sceptical, attitude, the only antidote, in his view, to what he called 'being chuckle-headed'. He was to modify his view later: even philosophy as he taught it proved, in his view, helpless against the traditional pieties and naïve beliefs of some of his most gifted pupils. He complained that, so far from undermining their conventional opinions, all his efforts left the majority of them incurably respectable and dully virtuous. He knew that he possessed exceptional capacities as a teacher, but he also had a strong desire to do something more concrete and more practical, a job of work, something for which, at the end of the day, there was more to show. He used to tell me that he regretted that he had spent so much time on the classics instead of learning to be an engineer, or an architect. However, it was now too late for that: he was resigned to remaining a theorist. He had a passion for accurate, factual information, rigorous analysis, testable conclusions, the ability to put things together and to take them to pieces again, and detested vagueness, obscurity, abstraction, evasion of issues by escape into metaphor or rhetoric or jargon or metaphysical fantasy. He was from the beginning determined to try to reduce whatever could be so reduced to plain prose.

Despite his admiration for practical experts, he was, in fact, himself preoccupied by purely philosophical questions, and, when he first came to All Souls, appeared to think about little else. The two living philosophers whom he most admired were Russell and Prichard, the first for his original genius, independence of mind, and powers of exposition; the second because he seemed to him the most rigorous and minute thinker to be found in Oxford at that time. Austin accepted neither Prichard's premisses nor his conclusions, but he admired the single-mindedness and tautness of his arguments, and the ferocity and the total lack of respect for great names with which Prichard rejected obscurity and lack of consistency in philosophy, ancient and modern. His own doctrine of the performative function of words seems to me to owe a good deal to Prichard's painful self-questionings, about, for example, the logical character of promises. 'People say that if I say "I agree" to this or that I create rights that were not there before,' Prichard would say. '*Create* rights? What does this mean? Blowed if I know.' Austin did not think this, or Prichard's discussion of the nature of moral obligation, to be either unimportant or ill formulated, and talked about it (to me) a great deal in 1933–5.

Our conversations usually began after breakfast in the smoking room at All Souls. When I had pupils to teach I left him by 11 a.m.; but on other mornings I seem to recollect that we often talked until lunch-time. He had at that time no settled philosophical position, no doctrine to impart. He would simply seize on some current topic of the day, some proposition uttered by a writer or a lecturer, and cut it into smaller and smaller pieces with a degree of skill and intellectual concentration which I met in no one else until I listened to G. E. Moore. The most admired philosopher of the 1930s in Oxford was, I should say, Henry Price, whose lucid, ingenious and beautifully elegant lectures fascinated his audiences, and were largely responsible for putting problems of perception in the centre of Oxford philosophical attention at this time. The counter-influence, so far as the young philosophers were concerned, was the mounting revolt against the entire traditional conception of philosophy as a source of knowledge about the universe. It was led by A. J. Ayer, whose paper on Wittgenstein's *Tractatus*, read, I think, in the spring of 1932, was the opening shot in the great positivist campaign. *Language, Truth and Logic* had not yet been published; nor had Ryle's views yet advanced, publicly at any rate, beyond 'Systematically Misleading Expressions'.[1] Nevertheless the positivist attack, especially in the form of the early articles by John Wisdom at that time appearing in *Mind*, became a source of illumination and excitement to the younger philosophers, and of considerable scandal to their elders. A sweeping anti-metaphysical empiricism was gaining converts rapidly. Price alone, at this time, while in some respects an Oxford realist, showed understanding and sympathy for the new movement, and was regarded by its members as something of an ally in the adversary's camp.

The movement grew apace. It had invaded the pages of *Mind*, and had its own house journal in *Analysis*. This was a source of deep distress and indeed despair to the most influential among the older Oxford philosophers – Prichard, Joseph, Joachim. They reacted very differently. Joachim, who was one of the last and most scrupulous and civilised representatives of moderate Continental Idealism, and lived in a world inhabited by Aristotle, Spinoza, Kant, Hegel and Bradley, ignored this wave as an aberration, a temporary recession to a crude barbarism and irrationality – a view expressed in their different fashions and more passionately by Collingwood and Mure, although Collingwood thought Ayer a much worthier and indeed more dangerous opponent than Joseph, Prichard and their disciples. As for Prichard, he evidently felt contempt for and lack of interest in what appeared to him to be the recurrence of fallacies long exposed, something that belonged to a far cruder order of thought than that of the great sophists who opposed the realist philosophy when he was a young man – Bradley and Bosanquet. But he was so intensely preoccupied by his own continuous effort to 'worry things out', as he called it, and so painfully conscious of his own inability to arrive at adequate formulations of the answers to the questions that tormented him, both epistemological and ethical – the former derived from Cook Wilson, the latter from Kant and the Protestant tradition – that he had no time for dealing with the confusions and errors of his juniors, most of whom he suspected of wasting their time, and in none of whom he was much interested.

The man who suffered most deeply was probably Joseph. He had a very acute sense of the true tradition which he felt it his duty to defend – a tradition which he received at the hands of his deeply

[1] *Proceedings of the Aristotelian Society* 32 (1931–2), 139–70; reprinted in Ryle's *Collected Papers* (London, 1971), vol. 2.

admired master Cook Wilson, whose name and fame, despite all his disciples' efforts, are still confined – so far as they survive at all – to Oxford. Plato, Aristotle, to some degree the rationalists, and again Cook Wilson – these Joseph defended to the end of his days. The deadliest enemies of this kind of realist metaphysics were no longer the Idealists, whose day, he agreed with his pupil Prichard, was done, but the empiricists and sceptics headed by the father of fallacies, Hume, followed by Mill, William James, Russell and other intellectually and morally subversive writers whose doctrines he conceived it as his duty to refute and root out. All his life he had been engaged on the great task of weeding the garden of philosophy; and I believe that there were times when he thought that the great task to which he had been called, of restoring the ancient truths, was at last being achieved, at least in the English-speaking world. But as the 1920s wore on, and the '30s began, he saw with horror that rank weeds were springing up again, and not least in Oxford itself, mainly from seeds wafted across from Cambridge – blatant fallacies propagated by Ramsey, Braithwaite, Ayer and their allies, aided and abetted by various pragmatists in the United States. All these ancient heresies were abroad once more, and evidently influenced the young, as if their shallowness and speciousness had not been exposed over and over again by the faithful band of Cook Wilson's disciples. His last lecture, held in New College garden, was a tremendous onslaught on Russell and Co. He died, I suspect, in a state of intellectual despair – the truth was drowning in a sea of falsehoods, a disaster which he was never able to explain to himself.

Austin was himself one of these dangerous empiricists, although he was not a militant controversialist at this stage; nor was his empiricism inhibited by fidelity to any particular tradition. He was not doctrinaire. He did not hold with programmes. He did not wish to destroy one establishment in the interests of another. He treated problems piecemeal as they came, not as part of a systematic reinterpretation. That effort, in so far as it was made (and of course he did try to develop a coherent doctrine of philosophical method), took place much later. I do not think that I ever heard him say anything during this period, that is, before the beginning of the War, which sprang from, or was clearly intended to support, any kind of systematic view. I do not know whether his pupils in Magdalen will bear me out, but it seems to me that he addressed himself to the topics which were part of the then normal curriculum in Oxford with no conscious revolutionary intent. But, of course, he had a very clear, acute and original intellect, and because, when he spoke, there appeared to be nothing between him and the subject of his criticism or exposition – no accumulation of traditional commentary, no spectacles provided by a particular doctrine – he often produced the feeling that the question was being posed clearly for the first time: that what had seemed blurred, or trite, or a play of conventional formulae in the books had suddenly been washed away: the problem stood out in sharp relief, clear, unanswered and important, and the methods used to analyse it had a surgical sharpness, and were used with fascinating assurance and apparently effortless skill.

He always, in those days at any rate, answered one in one's own terminology when he understood what was said to him; he did not pretend that it was not clear until it had been translated into his own language, some special set of terms of his own. In private he used no rhetorical tricks of any kind, and displayed an extraordinary power of distinguishing what was genuine or interesting in what his collocutor said from what was not – from ideological patter, or nervous confusion, or the like. This was not always so in public: opposition made him combative, and in classes or meetings of societies he plainly wished to emerge victorious. But this did not happen, so far as my own experience goes, in private conversation, at any rate not in the presence of those with whom he felt comfortable and unthreatened. I do not mean to say that he was not by temperament dogmatic: he was. But he argued patiently and courteously, and if he failed to convince one, returned to the topic over and over again, with new and highly imaginative examples and first-hand arguments which were intellectually exhilarating whether they produced conviction or not. He still remained throughout this time sceptical about the value of philosophy, except as an educational instrument; but he could not break himself from it: whenever we met during the 1930s he invariably found opportunity of raising some philosophical question, and left one not so much with a set of firm and well-argued positions as with a series of philosophical question-marks strewn along the path, which stopped those who listened to him from resting in the comfortable beds of accepted opinion. I think he was much more authoritarian after the War, and did not, at any rate in public, move his pieces until the entire plan of campaign had been thoroughly thought out, and he felt secure against any possible refutation. One of the criticisms made of him – I think a just one – was that he refused to advance rather than face the smallest possible risk of successful counter-argument. Even so, this did not hold so much in private (I speak only for myself); in the 1930s his pride and his sense of his own position were not so evidently in play, nor did he conceive philosophy as a set of doctrines and a method to which it was his mission to convert the ignorant and the mistaken. It was not until a later period that his philosophical activity became a consciously planned campaign for the dissemination of the truth.

When Ayer's *Language, Truth and Logic* was published in 1936, Austin expressed great admiration for it, and then proceeded to criticise it, during our afternoon walks, page by page and sentence by sentence, without wishing to score points (he did not get far beyond the first chapter, so far as I can remember). Certainly his later polemical ferocity was less in evidence, at any rate so far as the works of his contemporaries – the articles in *Mind* or in *Analysis* on which we fed – were concerned. In 1936, after he had been at Magdalen for about a year he came to my rooms in All Souls one evening and asked me what I had been reading. Had I been reading any Soviet philosophy, and was any of it worth reading? He had visited the Soviet Union as a tourist and had been impressed by his experience. He was attracted by the austerity and sternness and dedication of the grey, impersonal-looking men and women whom he had seen there, had detected the growth of nationalism (of which he did not disapprove) and of admiration (which he shared) for the great men who had worked against gigantic odds, Marx and Lenin for example. His admiration for the founders of Communism was, I think, short-lived. His favourite examples of intellectual virtue in later years were Darwin and Freud, not because he particularly admired their views, but because he believed that once a man had assured himself that his hypothesis was worth pursuing at all, he should pursue it to its logical end, whatever the consequences, and not be deterred by fear of seeming eccentric or fanatical, or by the control of philistine common sense. If the logical consequences were in fact untenable, one would be able to withdraw or modify them in the light of the undeniable evidence; but if one failed to explore a hypothesis to its full logical conclusions, the truth would for ever be defeated by timid respectability. He said that a fearless thinker, pursuing a chosen path unswervingly against mutterings and warnings and criticism, was the proper object of admiration and emulation; fanaticism was preferable to cowardice, and imagination to dreary good sense.

What about Soviet thought? I replied that I had not read anything by any contemporary Communist philosopher which I could genuinely recommend to him – nothing since Ralph Fox, the only English Marxist Austin had read or thought worth reading. But I had, a year or two before, read an interesting book on philosophy called *Mind and the World-Order* by C. I. Lewis, a professor at Harvard of whom I had not previously heard. It says much for the philosophical insulation and self-centredness of Oxford (and other English universities at that time) that so little about American philosophy should have been known to my colleagues and myself. I had come across this book by pure chance on a table in Blackwell's bookshop, had opened it and thought that it looked interesting. I bought it, read it, and thought that its pragmatist transformation of Kantian categories was original and fruitful. I lent it to Austin, who left me almost immediately. He told me that instead of playing his violin – he used to go through unaccompanied Bach partitas evening by evening – he began reading it at once. Three days later he suggested to me that we should hold a class on this book, which had also impressed him.

I may be mistaken about this, but I think that this was the first class or seminar on a contemporary thinker ever held in Oxford. Austin's reputation as a teacher was by this time considerable, and a relatively large number of undergraduates came once a week to our class in All Souls. I had no notion how joint classes were held, and assumed that their holders would begin by a dialogue on points provided by the text, in which they would show each other the almost exaggerated respect which was then common form at philosophical debates among dons. Austin opened by inviting me to expound a thesis. I selected Lewis's doctrine of specific, sensible characteristics – what Lewis called *qualia* – and said what I thought. Austin glared at me sternly and said, 'Would you mind saying that again.' I did so. 'It seems to me', said Austin, speaking slowly, 'that what you have just said is complete nonsense.' I then realised that this was to be no polite shadow-fencing, but war to the death – my death, that is. There is no doubt that Austin's performance at our class had a profound and lasting effect upon some, at any rate, of those who attended it. Some of them later became eminent professional philosophers and have testified to the extraordinary force and fertility of Austin's performance. For a performance it undoubtedly was: as much so as Moore's annual classes held at the joint meetings of the Aristotelian Society and Mind Association. Slow, formidable and relentless, Austin dealt firmly with criticism and opposition of the intelligent and stupid alike, and, in the course of this, left the genuine philosophers in our class not crushed or frustrated, but stimulated and indeed excited by the simplicity and lucidity of the nominalist thesis which he defended against Lewis. 'If there are three vermilion patches on this piece of paper how many vermilions are there?' 'One,' said I. 'I say there are three,' said Austin, and we spent the rest of the term on this issue. Austin conducted the class like a formidable professor at the Harvard Law School. He put questions to the class. If, petrified by terror, everyone remained silent, he would extend a long, thin finger, and after oscillating it slowly to and fro for a minute, like the muzzle of a pistol, would suddenly shoot it forward, pointing at some man, chosen at random, and say in a loud, nervous voice: '*You* answer!' The victim would, at times, be too terrorised to utter. Austin would realise this, answer himself, and return to our normal conditions of discussion. Despite these somewhat terrifying moments, the class remained undiminished in numbers and intensity of interest. We spent the term on nominalism. It was the best class that I have ever attended, and seems to me to mark the true beginning of Austin's career as an independent thinker.

At the end of the summer of 1936 Austin suggested that we hold regular philosophical discussions about topics which interested us and our contemporaries among Oxford philosophers. He wished the group to meet informally, without any thought of publishing our 'results' (if we ever obtained any), or any purpose but that of clearing our minds and pursuing the truth. We agreed to invite Ayer, Macnabb and Woozley, all of whom were at that time teaching philosophy at Oxford; to these Stuart Hampshire, who had been elected to All Souls, and Donald MacKinnon, who had become a Fellow of Keble, were added. The meetings began some time in 1936–7 (I think in the spring of 1937). They took place on Thursdays in my rooms in All Souls after dinner, and continued, with a few intervals, until the summer of 1939. In retrospect they seem to me the most fruitful discussions of philosophy at which I was ever present. The topics were not carefully prepared, nor necessarily announced beforehand, although I think we knew from week to week what we were likely to talk about. The principal topics were four in number: perception – theories of sense data as Price and Broad discussed them; a priori truths, that is, propositions which appeared necessarily true or false, and yet did not appear reducible to rules or definitions and what these entailed; the verification and logical character of counter-factual statements, which I think, in those days, we called unfulfilled hypotheticals or contra-factuals; and the nature and criteria of personal identity, and the related topic of our knowledge of other minds.

When I mentioned perception as one of our subjects, I should have said that what we talked about was principally phenomenalism and the theory of verification with which it was closely bound up, topics on which Ayer held strong, characteristically clear, and well-known opinions. Austin attacked the entire sense-datum terminology, and asked what the criteria of identity of a sense datum were: if one's field of vision contained seven yellow and black stripes like a tiger-skin, did it contain, or consist of, let us say, seven black data and seven yellow ones, or one continuous striped datum? What was the average size of a datum, and what was its average life-span? When could it be said that a single datum changed colour or faded or vanished, or were there as many data as there were hues or saturations of colours or timbres or pitches of sounds? How did one count them? Were there *minima sensibilia* and did they vary from observer to observer? All this apart from the by that time familiar question of how the concept of the observer was itself to be analysed.

Ayer defended positivism and wished to know, if phenomenalism were abandoned, what was to be put in its place. Did Austin suppose that there existed impalpable substrata either in the old, crude Lockean sense, or in the sense in which some modern scientists and philosophers, who were no less confused and much less consistent or honest than Locke, maintained or presupposed the existence of equally unverifiable and metaphysical entities? I cannot remember that Austin ever tried to furnish any positive answers to these questions, or, to begin with at any rate, to formulate any doctrine of his own; he preferred, undoubtedly, to drill holes into solutions provided by others. It was, I think, in the course of one of these sceptical onslaughts, after four or five formulations of the reductionist thesis of pure phenomenalism had been shot down by Austin, that Ayer exclaimed: 'You are like a greyhound who doesn't want to run himself, and bites the other greyhounds, so that they cannot run either.'[1]

There was certainly something of this about Austin. I do not remember that he did altogether, before the War, come out of the wood on phenomenalism; but he did begin saying even then that he could not see that there was all that much wrong with ordinary language as used about the external world. The problems raised by, for example, optical illusions – double images, sticks bent in water, tricks of perspective and the like – were due to the ambiguities of language, mistakenly analysed by philosophers, and not to implausible non-empirical beliefs. Berkeley, whom he admired as against Locke and Hume, was, in his view, right about this. A stick that was 'really' bent was of course something quite different from a stick 'bent in water', and once the laws of the refraction of light were discovered, no confusion need occur: being bent was one thing, and looking bent was another; if a stick were plunged in water and did *not* look bent, then indeed there would be occasion for surprise. The sense-datum language was a sub-language, used for specific purposes to describe the works of impressionist painters, or called for by physicians who asked their patients to describe their symptoms – an artificial usage carved out of ordinary language – language which was sufficient for most everyday purposes and did not itself tend to mislead.

As may be imagined, Ayer, and perhaps others amongst us, stoutly resisted this frontal attack upon the views of Moore and Russell, Broad and Price, and the rejection of the entire apparatus and terminology of the English school of the theory of perception. These discussions led to the emergence of 'Oxford Analysis', not so much as a consequence of Austin's specific theses, as from the appeal to common linguistic usage which was made by us all, without, so far as I recollect, any conscious reference at the time to Wittgenstein's later doctrines, even though the 'Blue Book' was already in circulation in Cambridge, and had, I think, by 1937 or so, arrived in Oxford.

Similar methods were used in discussing counter-factual statements – their extension and their relation to the verification

---

[1] This may have been stimulated by a remark made by Donald Macnabb to the effect that our discussions reminded him of nothing so much as a pack of hounds in full cry (after, presumably, the truth).

principle[1] – as well as the problems of personal identity and its relation to memory. If I remember rightly, the principal example of the latter that we chose was the hero of Kafka's story *Metamorphosis*, a commercial traveller called Gregor Samsa, who wakes one morning to find that he has been transformed into a monstrous cockroach, although he retains clear memories of his life as an ordinary human being. Are we to speak of him as a man with the body of a cockroach, or as a cockroach with the memories and consciousness of a man? 'Neither,' Austin declared. 'In such cases we should not know what to say. This is when we say "Words fail us" and mean this literally. We should need new words. The old ones just would not fit. They aren't meant to cover this kind of case.' From this we wandered to the asymmetry, or apparent asymmetry, between the analysis of propositions made by the speaker about himself and those made by him about others; this was treated from correspondingly differing standpoints by Austin and Ayer, who gradually became the protagonists of two irreconcilable points of view. Austin's particular philosophical position was developed, it seems to me, during those Thursday evenings, in continuous contrast with, and opposition to, the positivism and reductionism of Ayer and his supporters. I do not mean to imply that Austin and Ayer entirely dominated the discussions, and that the rest of us were scarcely more than listeners. We all talked a great deal,[2] although if I asked myself what I myself said or believed, apart from criticising the verification principle, and pure Carnapian logical positivism, I should find it hard to say. All I can recollect is that there was no crystallisation into permanent factions: views changed from week to week, save that Ayer and Austin were seldom, if ever, in agreement about anything.

The discussion of what, for short, I shall call a priori statements

[1] As an example, I might say 'If a horse called Sylvia runs in this race it will undoubtedly win.' Suppose no such horse ran or even existed, and I am subsequently asked why I thought that it would win. If I answer that I believed this although – or even because – it was an irrational proposition, that I felt inclined to gamble on its truth because I like gambling, that I had not the slightest desire to know whether there was, or could be, any evidence for the proposition, it seems to follow that the meaning of the counter-factual is detached from 'the means of its verification' in however 'weak' a sense, even if the question of its truth is not.

[2] And interrupted each other unceremoniously; so much so that Austin, with his passion for order, proposed that we acquire 'a buzzer' to introduce discipline. The suggestion was not taken up.

arose out of a paper read by Russell in 1935 to the Cambridge Moral Sciences Club, which Austin and I attended, on 'The Limits of Empiricism'.[1] The thesis was that while such propositions as 'The same object [or surface, or portion of my visual field, or whatever was substituted for this] cannot be red and green at the same time in the same place' appeared to be incontrovertibly true beyond the possibility of falsification, their contradictories did not seem to be self-contradictory. This was so because their truth did not appear to follow from verbal definitions, but from the meaning of colour words, the use of which was learnt or explained by acts of pointing – was fixed by means of what, in those days, used to be called 'ostensive definitions'. The contradictories of such propositions, therefore, seemed better described as absurd or meaningless or unintelligible, and not as contradictions in terms. This stimulated long discussions about verbal and non-verbal definitions, the relation of Carnap's syntactical properties to semantic ones, the difference between the relations of words to words and the relations of words to things, and so on.

The dissimilarity of approach between Austin and Ayer once more showed itself very clearly. Ayer, if he perceived that a given theory entailed consequences which, he was certain, were false or absurd, for example, the existence of impalpable entities or some other gross breach of the verification principle, even in its so-called 'weak' form, felt that the whole argument must be proceeding on fallacious lines, and was prepared to reject the premises, and try to think of new ones from which these undesirable consequences would not follow. Austin looked at whatever was placed before him, and was ready to follow the argument wherever it led.

It was later maintained by some of his critics (at least in conversation) that this philosophical spontaneity and apparent freedom from preconceived doctrine were not altogether genuine: that in fact they were elaborate Socratic devices which concealed a fully worked-out positive doctrine which he was not yet ready to reveal. I believe this to be false. In 1936–9 he had a philosophically open mind. Indeed, at that time he was full of suspicion of any cut and dried doctrine; if anything, he seemed to take active pleasure in advancing propositions which appeared to him true or at any rate plausible, whatever havoc they might wreak with the systematic

[1] The paper was read on 28 November 1935, and published in the *Proceedings of the Aristotelian Society* 36 (1935–6), 131–50.

ideas of writers in, say, *Erkenntnis* or *Analysis*. He was certainly not free from a certain degree of malicious pleasure in blowing up carefully constructed philosophical edifices – he did like stopping the other greyhounds – but his main purpose seemed to me, then and afterwards, to be the establishing of particular truths with a view to generalising from them, or eliciting principles at a later stage. He certainly wished to 'save the appearances', and in this sense was a follower of Aristotle and not of Plato, of Berkeley and not of Hume. He disliked clear-cut dichotomies – between, for instance, universals and particulars (as distinguished in C. I. Lewis's book), or descriptive and emotive language, or empirical and logical truths, or verifiable and unverifiable, corrigible and incorrigible expressions – all such claims to clear and exhaustive contrasts seeming to him incapable of doing the job they were expected to do, namely to classify the normal use of words. It seemed to him then, as it did later, that types and distinctions of meaning were often reflected in ordinary language. Ordinary language was not an infallible guide; it was at best a pointer to distinctions in the subject-matter which language was used to describe, or express, or to which it was related in some other fashion; and these important distinctions tended to be obliterated by the clear-cut dichotomies advanced by the all-or-nothing philosophies, which in their turn led to unacceptable doctrines about what there was, and what men meant. Hence when Russell or others gave examples of propositions asserting irreducible incompatibilities between Lewis's *qualia* – colours, sounds, tastes and the like – propositions which did not seem either analytic or empirical; or when, to take another example, it was maintained that singular counter-factual statements could be not only understood, but actually believed, even though it was difficult to see how they could be verified, even in principle – Austin seized on these examples and developed them with great force and brilliance, partly, I suspect, from a desire to discover negative instances which would blow up general propositions that had been brought to bear too easily, like distorting moulds, on the complex and recalcitrant nature of things. He had an immense respect for the natural sciences, but he believed that the only reliable method of learning about types of action, knowledge, belief, experience consisted in the patient accumulation of data about actual usage. Usage was certainly not regarded by him as sacrosanct, in the sense of reflecting reality in some infallible fashion, or of being a guaranteed nostrum against confusions and fallacies. But it was neglected at our peril: Austin did have a Burkean belief that differences of usage did, as a rule, reflect differences of meaning, and conceptual differences too, and thus offered a valuable and relatively neglected path towards establishing distinctions of meaning, of concepts, of possible states of affairs, and in this way did help to clear away muddles and remove obstacles to the discovery of truth. Above all, philosophy was not a set of mechanisms into which untutored expressions had to be fed, and from which they would emerge classified, clarified, straightened out, and cleansed of their delusive properties.

In this sense Austin did not much believe in a specifically philosophical technology – the proliferation of gadgets to deal with difficulties. No doubt his insatiable interest in language and philology as such had something to do with this, and his superb classical scholarship fed his inordinate collector's curiosity, at times at the expense of genuinely philosophical issues. Nevertheless, his implicit rejection of the doctrine of a logically perfect language, which was capable of reflecting the structure of reality, sprang from a philosophical vision not dissimilar to that of Wittgenstein, whose then unpublished but illicitly circulated views he might possibly have looked at, though he did not, I think, pay serious attention to them before the War. Certainly his first published contribution to philosophy – the paper on a priori concepts in which a good deal of his positive doctrine is embodied[1] – owes, so far as I know, nothing to any acquaintance with Wittgenstein's views, unless perhaps, very indirectly, via John Wisdom's articles, which he certainly read.

Occasionally those who met on Thursday evenings talked about moral problems, but this was regarded as an escape, not to be repeated too often, from the sterner demands of the subject. We certainly discussed freedom of the will, in the course of which Austin said to me, *sotto voce*, so as not to provoke Freddie Ayer, who was at that time a convinced determinist, 'They all *talk* about determinism and *say* they believe in it. I've never met a determinist in my life, I mean a man who really did believe in it as you and I believe that men are mortal. Have you?' This endeared him to me

[1] 'Are there a priori concepts?', *Proceedings of the Aristotelian Society* supplementary vol. 18 (1939), 83–105; reprinted in Austin's *Philosophical Papers* (Oxford, 1961; 3rd ed., 1979).

greatly. So did his answer to a question that I once put to him during a walk. I asked: 'Supposing a child were to express a wish to meet Napoleon as he was at the battle of Austerlitz, and I said "It cannot be done", and the child said "Why not?", and I said "Because it happened in the past, and you cannot be alive now and also a hundred and thirty years ago and remain at the same age", or something of the kind; and the child went on pressing and said "Why not?", and I said "Because it does not make sense, as we use words, to say that you can be in two places at once or 'go back' into the past", and so on; and this highly sophisticated child said "If it is only a question of words, then can't we simply alter our verbal usage? Would that enable me to see Napoleon at the battle of Austerlitz, and also, of course, stay as I am now, in place and time?". – What [I asked Austin] should one say to the child? Simply that it has confused the material and formal modes, so to speak?' Austin replied: 'Do not speak so. Tell the child to try and go back into the past. Tell it there is no law against it. Let it try. Let it try, and see what happens then.' It seems to me now, as it seemed to me before the last war, that Austin understood the nature of philosophy, even if he was over-pedantic and over-cautious, and insisted on making over-sure of his defences before plunging into the arena – understood, better than most, what philosophy was.

These discussions were fruitful for several reasons: because the number of those who took part in them was small (it never rose above seven and was usually smaller than that); because the participants knew each other well, talked very freely, and were in no sense on show; they were totally spontaneous, and knew that if they went down some false path which led to a precipice or a marsh it did not matter, for they could retrace their steps, whenever they pleased, in the weeks to come. Moreover the intellectual freshness and force, both of Austin and of Ayer, were such that although they were in a state of almost continuous collision – Ayer like an irresistible missile, Austin like an immovable obstacle – the result was not a stalemate, but the most interesting, free and lively discussions of philosophy that I have ever known.

One of the shortcomings of these meetings is something that seems to me to apply to Oxford philosophy in general, at least in those days. We were excessively self-centred. The only persons whom we wished to convince were our own admired colleagues.

There was no pressure upon us to publish. Consequently, when we succeeded in gaining from one of our philosophical peers acceptance or even understanding of some point which we regarded as original and important, whether rightly or, as was more often the case at any rate with me, in a state of happy delusion, this satisfied us completely, too completely. We felt no need to publish our ideas, for the only audience which was worth satisfying was the handful of our contemporaries who lived near us, and whom we met with agreeable regularity. I don't think that, like Moore's disciples at the beginning of the century, of whom Keynes speaks in a memoir on his early ideas,[1] any of us thought that no one before us had discovered the truth about the nature of knowledge or anything else; but, like them, we did think that no one outside the magic circle – in our case Oxford, Cambridge, Vienna – had much to teach us. This was vain and foolish and, I have no doubt, irritating to others. But I suspect that those who have never been under the spell of this kind of illusion, even for a short while, have not known true intellectual happiness.

[1] 'My Early Beliefs', in John Maynard Keynes, *Two Memoirs* (London, 1949); reprinted in *The Collected Writings of John Maynard Keynes* (London, 1971–89), vol. 10, *Essays in Biography*.

# JOHN PETROV PLAMENATZ

JOHN PLAMENATZ was born in 1912 in Cetinje, the capital of Montenegro. Both his parents belonged to the ruling families of that old, pre-industrial, half-pastoral society, and although his life was lived almost entirely in England, his imagination and his feelings were dominated by his deep attachment to his native land. In 1917, when he was five years old, he was taken by his father to France, and soon after that to England, where he was placed in Clayesmore School, near Winchester, whose headmaster his father knew. There he stayed for the next eleven years, while the school moved from place to place, until he came to Oriel College, Oxford, in 1930. From time to time his parents summoned him to visit them during his school holidays, to Marseilles or Vienna, but for long stretches of time he lived apart from his family, and became used to solitude. He spent four years at Oriel; illness prevented him from completing his papers in PPE and he obtained an *aegrotat*; and, a year later, a First in History. In 1936 he was elected to All Souls, the first Fellow to be elected by thesis since Dearle, early in the century.

He spent the rest of his life in Oxford, and his work and his influence are part of the intellectual history of Britain and of that university. But there is a sense in which he remained in exile all his life. He was never wholly assimilated either to England or to Oxford: when he said 'we' – 'This is the way we think', or 'This is how it is with us' – he usually meant Montenegrins. He once said to me that he had made personal friends among individual English people; that he could feel at home with two or three at a time; but that when more than two or three were gathered in a room, he would become aware of a relationship *between* them, from which he felt excluded. He explained this by saying that he was rooted in a remote culture, that the sudden break in early childhood – the emigration to an alien environment – had forced him to turn, to some degree, in upon himself. Those who knew him can testify to the fact that, like Joseph Conrad (whom in some ways he resembled), all his life he displayed the pride and independence of a noble exile.

'Displayed' is the wrong term: John Plamenatz displayed nothing; he was reserved and reticent; he did not seek to put himself forward or impose his personality in any way on any occasion that I know of. He spoke his mind with candour and precision, and with the great natural courtesy that was an essential attribute of his character; yet, at times, one could not be sure about what was going on inside his mind – there was something remote and unapproachable about him; but when one came to know him well, this melted – he was a warm and affectionate friend. But neither friendship nor its absence ever blinded him to human character and motives; he was acutely perceptive – that somewhat myopic eye saw a very great deal. He was occasionally deceived by persons and situations, but not often. Above all, he was not anxious to judge. At times he commented upon individuals, or on the social scene, with amused irony, but in general he showed the kind of tolerance that only deeply civilised or saintly people can achieve. But, of course, there were qualities he found unbearable: he disliked shoddiness, triviality, ostentation, stridency, vulgarity and opportunism of every sort; he detested rudeness; he was upset by lack of manners, the sources of which he found it difficult to comprehend. He prized privacy and personal relations above all. He was gentle, dignified and wholly uncompetitive; he was interested in the character of others, and sensitive to their feelings, particularly to the feelings of those who, like himself, wished to walk by themselves and found it difficult to fit in with established social patterns. He spoke to such people more easily, and defended them against the criticisms of those who thought them farouche or unattractive. He understood loneliness, unhappiness, vulnerability better, I think, than anyone I have ever known. All Souls, in the years before the War, was full of animated talk by politicians and academics about the burning social and political questions of the day: John Plamenatz avoided such gatherings; his interest in the problems was just as great as that of a good many others, and his understanding of them sometimes more sensitive, but he disliked the noise, the jokes, the rivalry, the repartee, the high spirits – genuine or false – of such exchanges. He seldom attended gaudies.

College meetings were another matter. These he took very

seriously and, though he spoke little, when he did intervene the effect was sometimes decisive: he spoke quietly, with obvious conviction, without the slightest hint of rhetoric. He did not speak unless he had something of central relevance to say or ask: his motives were so completely free from any touch of calculation, his sincerity was so evident, that his apparently simple statements or questions, penetrating as they often did to the heart of some debated issue, tended to have a devastating effect. The word 'integrity' might have been invented for him. His words were listened to with deep respect, and on the rare occasions when he felt genuinely moved, he almost always carried the day. The independence, the scrupulous regard for the truth, the shining impartiality of his judgement were a unique moral asset to every society of which he was a member. It was so at All Souls, and, I am told, it was so at Nuffield also.

It was a singular irony, therefore, that the D.Phil. thesis that he submitted should have been failed by the examiners, on the ground, it was rumoured, of 'lack of judgement'. This was the very thesis on the strength of which he was, a little later, elected to All Souls. When it was published, its quality was plain for all to see. He came to be critical of it himself in later years. Nevertheless, it was, in the opinion of competent critics, probably the best work on political theory produced by anyone in Oxford since the First World War.[1] It was the first in a long line of books that did more than any other single factor to transform the level of the entire discussion of political theory in Oxford. His work served to raise its standards to that of serious philosophical argument. The judgement passed upon it was perhaps the greatest miscarriage of academic justice known to my generation. He was, of course, hurt by it at the time, but in the end ignored it – it left no obvious wound.

His intellectual weapons were derived from that sober, pre-positivist, pre-linguistic, realist tradition in moral philosophy to which his tutor, W. G. Maclagan, belonged, and which was dominant in Oxford in the early 1930s. The purpose of its method was to state the arguments – one's own or those of others, particularly the great thinkers of the past – in the clearest possible fashion – to avoid all vagueness, obscurity, rhetoric, confusion; to expose incoherence; to arrive, by the use of rational methods, at

[1] *Consent, Freedom and Political Obligation* (London, 1938).

conclusions acceptable to reasonable and self-critical beings. He believed in this method and defended it, and used it all his life. His purpose was to elucidate and criticise the ideas of those writers who seemed to him to address themselves to problems that were central to men everywhere and at all times. Like Machiavelli, he found a door into a timeless world of the great figures of the past, and questioned them, and sought to understand their basic concepts, their views of man and of society, of what they were and should be. He was never pedantic, and he did not niggle. If the thinkers whom he examined seemed to him dark or confused or even dishonest, he persevered with them if they appeared to him to reveal even glimpses of something important or profound about man's nature, his goals, or his moral or political experience or needs. And while he found clear writers like Machiavelli or Hobbes or the Utilitarians, if not more congenial, at least easier to deal with, he struggled with formidable and difficult theorists in whom he perceived glimmers of genius – Hegel, Marx and his followers – like Jacob wrestling with the Angel of the Lord, who could not let him go until he had received his reward.

His chapters on Hegel and Marx are among the clearest and most valuable expositions of these thinkers in the English language. He worked on these texts with immense tenacity, reading and rereading, writing and rewriting, paying the most scrupulous attention to the criticisms of friends and colleagues, and was more critical of his own work than others were. When argued with, he held on to his own positions with great stubbornness, but nevertheless went back to the texts and to his own commentaries; if the criticisms appeared to him to have any element of justice, he acknowledged them fully and altered his views; the second edition of his book on utilitarianism contains his own review of the first edition, far more severe than anything said by others. His purpose was not to detect inconsistencies in the thought of others, or merely to expose error, or to interpret, but to achieve at least the beginnings of some vision of the complex and elusive truth which thinkers whom he respected seemed to him to approach from this side and from that. His works greatly added to the dignity of the entire subject in England, and indirectly in every English-speaking country.

He was admired by his pupils, and respected by the most distinguished of his opponents, but he occupied no recognisable position and founded no school. Perhaps this was so because he simply said and wrote what seemed to him to be true, in his own unemphatic, careful prose, with all the qualifications that the truth seemed to demand; he did not modify or shape his thought to make it fit into a system, he did not look for a unifying historical or metaphysical structure, he did not exaggerate or over-schematise in order to obtain attention for his ideas – so that those who looked for a system, an entire edifice of thought to attach themselves to, went away dissatisfied. He had no ambition to shine, or to defeat rivals, or to proselytise or found a movement. He only wanted to discover and tell the truth. His methods were essentially English, and indeed local, characteristic of the Oxford of his youth: but they were superimposed on a temperament and outlook very different from the masters who impressed him, Prichard, Ross and the others. His view of human nature and its purposes and its potentialities was taken not only from his reading of the classical philosophers, but equally from his upbringing, from solidarity with, and indeed much nostalgia for, his native land, the customs and outlook of that almost pre-feudal community; and also from his lifelong love of French literature and thought, which he found more sympathetic than its English counterpart. He responded to Donne, Herbert, Wordsworth, but the prose of Montesquieu gave him physical pleasure. The French theatre of the eighteenth century – Marivaux, Jean-Baptiste Rousseau, Beau-marchais – moved him to enthusiasm. His letter to a journal defending Marivaux against charges of shallowness and artificiality, and praising him for true insight and exquisite description of the movements of the shy and innocent human heart, was itself a masterpiece of literary sensibility.

He understood best lonely and unhappy thinkers, who showed the deepest understanding of what men live by, and what frustrates them, of solitude and alienation – he loved best of all Pascal, Jean-Jacques Rousseau – solitary thinkers, given to painful moral and spiritual self-inquisition rather than rational self-examination. He praised Proudhon for knowing what the workers, or the *petit bourgeois*, need, what makes them miserable, because he truly understood them, as the far more gifted Marx, who fitted them into a vast theoretical model, did not bother to do. His acceptance of British empiricism, together with a deeply un-British, romantic vision of the human predicament, imparted to his work a tension that nothing else in English seems to me to have. It was never wholly impersonal: thus, after many pages of sober, Oxford exposition and argument, there would suddenly occur a sharp, original, highly characteristic comment – as when he remarks, 'Passing from German to Russian Marxism, we leave the horses and come to the mules.'[1] In these sudden, often ironical, asides his own authentic voice can be clearly heard. There is something wonderfully fresh, and often devastatingly direct, about these personal passages. Indeed, all his writing was authentic and, as it were, hand-made: it was balanced, unexaggerated, carefully quali-fied, but nothing in it was mechanical, derived from a model. His books give the impression of being written as if no book on the subject had ever been written before. So, too, with testimonials he wrote for pupils: never over-stated, never conventional, they were illuminated by flashes of acute psychological insight, and carried total conviction. It is this first-hand quality that, added to all its other attributes, lends his work peculiar and irresistible charm.

The War interrupted his work. On Lionel Curtis's advice, he became a member of a somewhat peculiar anti-aircraft battery, which gave full scope for the play of his irony. In time he was transferred to the service of the Yugoslav Embassy, and became a member of the War Cabinet of King Peter. He wrote a pamphlet to answer the detractors of General Mihailovic (it was published in a private, limited edition).[2] After the War he returned to All Souls as a Research Fellow and began to produce a series of essays and books on political thought. In 1951 he was elected to a Fellowship of Nuffield, and in 1967 to the Chair of Social and Political Theory at All Souls.

He told me that a few years later he was visited by some Montenegrin relatives of his, who were engaged in smuggling, I believe, somewhere in the Balkans. They said to him, 'You are a Professor at Oxford – that is a very strange thing for a Montenegrin to be doing.' He added that he thought that they were right. He said he did not feel himself a professor. He found administrative duties a burden; he forced himself to perform them; he attended committees and examined, but without pleasure or satisfaction. He wished to read, to write, to teach. He developed warm personal relations with his pupils; he was an excellent colleague; private life meant far more to him than the busy life of institutions. All Souls suited him better than Nuffield if only

[1] *German Marxism and Russian Communism* (London etc., 1954), p. 191.
[2] *The Case of General Mihailovic* ([London], 1944).

because it made fewer demands on his time. He was grateful to Nuffield, which had come to his aid at a difficult moment; some of his closest friendships were made there. Looking after the college garden gave him genuine pleasure. But what he loved best was privacy. He might have agreed with Pascal that many of the ills of mankind come because men will not stay quietly in a room.

In certain respects he was happier with Americans than he was with the English: like many inward-looking, reticent scholars he was liberated by the openness, the responsiveness, the warmth, the uninhibited natural candour, the unblasé attitude of American students and colleagues, by the deep and genuine desire for the truth with which they sought for answers to intellectual or political problems, by the fact that they took the trouble to understand what he thought and said. He was particularly happy at Columbia University. Yet during the seven long years of his Professorship he longed to be released from it. He was not discontented. Indeed, during his last three or four years, he seemed to me to have grown lighter-hearted, and to have come into something like his own. Friendship, and above all the love and devotion of his wife, were everything to him. He told me that he preferred to live in a village because there relations with neighbours seemed more natural and satisfactory to him – more like the life that human beings have led at all times, everywhere, than artificial existence in an academic enclave.

The heart attack which ultimately proved fatal was the first illness he had had since 1933. He died on 19 February 1975, the very day and month when, fifty-six years before, he had landed at Dover.

His independence, his remoteness from all the least attractive aspects of the life of universities – the idea of trying to involve him in some intrigue was unthinkable – his generous, uncalculating character, his refusal to compromise with whatever seemed to him to distort or ignore or even embellish experience, his distinction as a thinker, his nobility as a human being, were recognised by the academic world here and abroad. He had much pride, but was free from all vanity and snobbery, and treated all men alike: he made no differences between the young and the old, the important and the unimportant, the brilliant and the dull, but behaved towards everyone with the same grave courtesy. He possessed what I can only describe as a quality of moral charm that made all dealings with him delightful. His writings – and this was true of the authors he most admired – were altogether unlike any others. So, in the best and rarest sense, was he.

# MAURICE BOWRA

MAURICE BOWRA, scholar, critic and administrator, the greatest English wit of his day, was, above all, a generous and warm-hearted man, whose powerful personality transformed the lives and outlook of many who came under his wide and life-giving influence. According to a contemporary at Cheltenham, he was fully formed by the time he left school for the army in 1916. In firmness of character he resembled his father, of whom he always spoke with deep affection and respect; but unlike him he was rebellious by temperament and, when he came up to New College in 1919, he became the natural leader of a group of intellectually gifted contemporaries, passionately opposed to the conventional wisdom and moral code of those who formed pre-war Oxford opinion. He remained critical of all establishments for ever after.

Bowra loved life in all its manifestations. He loved the sun, the sea, warmth, light, and hated cold and darkness, physical, intellectual, moral, political. All his life he liked freedom, individuality, independence, and detested everything that seemed to him to cramp and constrict the forces of human vitality, no matter what spiritual achievements such self-mortifying asceticism might have to its credit. His passion for the Mediterranean and its cultures was of a piece with this: he loved pleasure, exuberance, the richest fruits of nature and civilisation, the fullest expression of human feeling, uninhibited by a Manichean sense of guilt. Consequently he had little sympathy for those who recoiled from the forces of life – cautious, calculating conformists, or those who seemed to him prigs or prudes who winced at high vitality or passion, and were too easily shocked by vehemence and candour. Hence his impatience with philistine majorities in the academic and official and commercial worlds, and equally with cultural coteries which appeared to him thin, or old-maidish, or disapproving. He believed in fullness of life. Romantic exaggeration, such as he found in the early 1930s in the circle formed round the German poet Stefan George, appealed to him far more than British reticence. With a temperament that resembled men of an older generation – Winston Churchill or Thomas Beecham – he admired genius, splendour, eloquence, the grand style, and had no fear of orchestral colour; the chamber music of Bloomsbury was not for him. He found his ideal vision in the classical world: the Greeks were his first and last love. His first and best book was a study of Homer; this, too, was the topic of his last book, had he lived to complete it.[1] Despite the vast sweep of his literary interests – from the epic songs of Central Africa to the youngest poets of his own day – it is Pindar, Sophocles, the Greek lyric poets who engaged his deepest feelings. Murray and Wilamowitz meant more to him than scholars and critics of other literatures.

Endowed with a sharp, quick brain, a masterful personality, an impulsive heart, great gaiety, a brilliant, ironical wit, contempt for all that was solemn, pompous and craven, he soon came to dominate his circle of friends and acquaintances. Yet he suffered all his life from a certain lack of confidence: he needed constant reassurance. His disciplined habits, his belief in, and capacity for, hard, methodical work, in which much of his day was spent, his respect for professionalism and distaste for dilettantism, all these seemed, in some measure, defensive weapons against ultimate self-distrust. So, indeed, was his Byronic irony about the very romantic values that were closest to his heart. The treatment of him at New College by that stern trainer of philosophers, H. W. B. Joseph, undermined his faith in his own intellectual capacity, which his other tutor in philosophy, Alick Smith, who did much for him, and became a lifelong friend, could not wholly restore.

Bowra saw life as a series of hurdles, a succession of fences to take: there were books, articles, reviews to write; pupils to teach, lectures to deliver; committees, even social occasions, were so many challenges to be met, no less so than the real ordeals – attacks by hostile critics, or vicissitudes of personal relationships, or the hazards of health. In the company of a few familiar friends, on whose loyalty he could rely, he relaxed and often was easy, gentle and at peace. But the outer world was full of obstacles to be taken

[1] Nine out of ten chapters were found after his death, and the book (*Homer*) was published in London in 1972. His first book was *Tradition and Design in the Iliad* (Oxford, 1930).

at a run; at times he stumbled, and was wounded: he took such reverses with a stiff upper lip; and then, at once, energetically moved forward to the next task. Hence, it may be, his need and craving for recognition, and the corresponding pleasure he took in the many honours he received. The flat, pedestrian, lucid, well-ordered but, at times, conventional style and content of his published writings may also be due to this peculiar lack of faith in his own true and splendid gifts. His private letters, his private verse, and above all his conversation, were a very different matter. Those who know him solely through his published works can have no inkling of his genius.

As a talker he could be incomparable. His wit was verbal and cumulative: the words came in short, sharp bursts of precisely aimed, concentrated fire, as image, pun, metaphor, parody seemed spontaneously to generate one another in a succession of marvellously imaginative patterns, sometimes rising to high, wildly comical fantasy. His unique accent, idiom, voice, the structure of his sentences became a magnetic model which affected the style of speech, writing, and perhaps feeling, of many who came under its spell. It had a marked effect on some among the best-known Oxford-bred writers of our time. But his influence went deeper than this: he dared to say things which others thought or felt, but were prevented from uttering by rules or convention or personal inhibitions. Maurice Bowra broke through some of these social and psychological barriers, and the young men who gathered round him in the 1920s and '30s, stimulated by his unrestrained talk, let themselves go in their turn.

Bowra was a major liberating force: the free range of his talk about art, personalities, poetry, civilisations, private life, his disregard of accepted rules, his passionate praise of friends and unbridled denunciation of enemies, produced an intoxicating effect. Some eyebrows were raised, especially among the older dons, at the dangers of such licence. They were wholly mistaken. The result, no matter how frivolous the content, was deeply and permanently emancipating. It blew up much that was false, pretentious, absurd; the effect was cathartic; it made for truth, human feeling, as well as great mental exhilaration. The host (and he was always host, whether in his own rooms or those of others) was a positive personality; his character was cast in a major key: there was nothing corrosive or decadent or embittered in all this talk, no matter how irreverent or indiscreet or extravagant or unconcerned with justice it was.

As a scholar, and especially as a critic, Bowra had his limitations. His most valuable quality was his deep and unquenchable love of literature, in particular of poetry, of all periods and peoples. His travels in Russia before the Revolution, when as a schoolboy he crossed that country on his way to his family's home in China, gave him a lifelong interest in Russian poetry. He learnt Russian as a literary language, and virtually alone in England happily (and successfully) parsed the obscurest lines of modern Russian poets as he did the verse of Pindar or Alcaeus. He read French, German, Italian and Spanish, and had a sense of world literature as a single firmament, studded with works of genius, the quality of which he laboured to communicate. He was one of the very few Englishmen equally well known to, and valued by, Pasternak and Quasimodo, Neruda and Seferis, and took proper pride in this. It was all, for him, part of the war against embattled philistinism, pedantic learning, parochialism. Yet he was, with all this, a stout-hearted patriot, as anyone could testify who heard him in Boston, for example, when England was even mildly criticised. Consequently, the fact that no post in the public service was offered him in the Second World War distressed him. He was disappointed, too, when he was not appointed to the Chair of Greek at Oxford (he was offered chairs by Harvard and other distinguished universities). But later he came to look on this as a blessing in disguise; for his election as Warden of Wadham eventually made up and more than made up for it all.

Loyalty was the quality which, perhaps, he most admired, and one with which he was himself richly endowed. His devotion to Oxford, and in particular to Wadham, sustained him during the second, less worldly, portion of his life. He did a very great deal for his college, and it did much for him. He was intensely and, indeed, fiercely proud of Wadham, and of all its inhabitants, senior and junior; he seemed to be on excellent terms with every undergraduate in its rapidly expanding population; he guided them and helped them, and performed many acts of kindness by stealth. In his last decades he was happiest in his Common Room, or when entertaining colleagues or undergraduates; happiest of all when surrounded by friends, old or young, on whose love and loyalty he could depend.

After Wadham his greatest love was for the University: he served it faithfully as Proctor, member of the Hebdomadal Council, and of many other committees, as Delegate of the Press, finally as Vice-Chancellor. Suspected in his younger days of being a cynical epicure (no less cynical man ever breathed), he came to be respected as one of the most devoted, effective and progressive of academic statesmen. He had a very strong institutional sense: his presidency of the British Academy was a very happy period of his life. Under his enlightened leadership the Academy prospered. But it was Oxford that claimed his deeper allegiance: the progress of the University filled him with intense and lasting pride. Oxford and Wadham were his home and his life; his soul was bound up with both. Of the many honours which he received, the honorary doctorate of his own University gave him the deepest satisfaction: the opinion of his colleagues was all in all to him. When the time for retirement came, he was deeply grateful to his college for making it possible for him to continue to live within its walls. His successor was an old personal friend: he felt sure of affection and attention.

Increasing ill health and deafness cut him off from many pleasures, chief among them committees and the day-to-day business of administration, which he missed as much as the now less accessible pleasures of social life. Yet his courage, his gaiety, his determination to make the most of what opportunities remained did not desert him. His sense of the ridiculous was still acute; his sense of fantasy remained a mainstay. New faces continued to feed his appetite for life. Most of all he now enjoyed his contact with the young, whose minds and hearts he understood, and whose desire to resist authority and the imposition of frustrating rules he instinctively shared and boldly supported to the end. They felt this and responded to him, and this made him happy.

He was not politically minded. But by temperament he was a radical and a nonconformist. He genuinely loathed reactionary views and had neither liking nor respect for the solid pillars of any establishment. He sympathised with the unions in the General Strike of 1926; he spoke with passion at an Oxford meeting against the suppression of socialists in Vienna by Dollfuss in 1934; he detested oppression and repression, whether by the right or by the left, and in particular all dictators. His friendship with Hugh Gaitskell was a source of pleasure to him. If political sentiments which seemed to him retrograde or disreputable were uttered in his presence, he was not silent and showed his anger. He did not enjoy the altercations to which this tended to lead, but would have felt it shameful to run away from them; he possessed a high degree of civil courage. He supported all libertarian causes, particularly minorities seeking freedom or independence, the more unpopular the better. Amongst his chief pleasures in the late 1950s and '60s were the Hellenic cruises in which he took part every year. But when the military regime in Greece took over, he gave them up.

His attitude to religion was more complicated and obscure: he had a feeling for religious experience; he had no sympathy for positivist or materialist creeds. But to try to summarise his spiritual outlook in a phrase would be absurd as well as arrogant. As Warden he is said scarcely ever to have missed Chapel.

The last evening of his life was spent at a convivial party with colleagues and undergraduates. This may have hastened the heart attack of which he died; if so, it was as he would have wished it to be: he wanted to end swiftly and tidily, as he had lived, before life had become a painful burden.

He was, in his prime, the most discussed Oxford personality since Jowett, and in every way no less remarkable and no less memorable.

# DAVID CECIL

LORD DAVID CECIL was born the second son of the fourth Marquess of Salisbury, and spent his boyhood and much of his youth at the family house at Hatfield. His earliest memories, as a boy, were of a house full of talk – sharp, articulate, amusing. He spoke of the atmosphere of total freedom and spontaneity in which everything was discussed at his parents' hospitable table, in particular, as was very often the case, when his uncles Robert and Hugh – the political sons of the great Victorian Prime Minister – and the future Bishop of Exeter, William, were present. Politics, history, religion, stories about the behaviour of British cabinets, episodes in Parliament (serious and comical), elaborate analyses of the personal relations of public personalities – all this was part of the daily pabulum of this famous and dominant clan.

When their cousin the Prime Minister, Arthur Balfour, came to stay, as he often did, the talk became particularly lively and vehement and indiscreet and intimate – but interspersed with discussions of moral and religious principles and issues – with the result that David Cecil's naturally keen and eager mind and wit developed early, and he acquired opinions, the capacity for clear and articulate expression, and a tendency to relate abstract ideas to the vicissitudes of public, social and personal lives, and the interplay of individual characters and doctrines to their public environment and their place in history – all this as a naturally uninhibited process.

Books were everywhere, prose and poetry; he read them at odd moments, at various times, in no particular order, and so became familiar with Clarendon, Dickens, Spenser, Shakespeare, Jane Austen, Carlyle, Lamb, Byron, Shelley, Macaulay, Disraeli; he had absorbed volumes or chapters or fragments of these writings by the time he went to Eton. He had, as a schoolboy, from all evidence, unusual charm and ease of manner, intellectual gaiety and delight in human gifts and foibles. But he was a bookish boy, and this did not stand him in particularly good stead at Eton. He did not like his years there. His contemporary, Edward Sackville-West, later a well-known musical critic, said that Cecil truly blossomed only when he left Eton and came to Oxford, and entered Christ Church. The strongest cultural influence on him at Eton was probably Aldous Huxley, who was a temporary master there during the First World War, and opened his eyes to realms of poetry which were new to him; his love of English poetry, particularly Christian poetry, stayed with him for the rest of his life.

At Oxford Cecil became deeply interested in English history, particularly the Stuarts and the rise of the Tory Party, with which his family's fortunes were so deeply bound up – this was strongly encouraged by his learned and sensitive history tutor, Keith Feiling, who thought him one of the cleverest as well as one of the most attractive undergraduates he had ever known. And indeed Cecil's reputation for natural charm, combined with a very sharp and nimble intelligence, both clear- and hard-headed, critical both of what he read and of what he wrote, and an unflagging interest in people (more than ideas) and imagination (more than intellect), characterised him at all times.

He was always conscious of his origins and his social position in the hierarchical structure of British society. He once said that it was difficult for English aristocrats to be original artists or writers because, unless their circumstances were very unusual, they tended to be brought up to be all things to all men, and this, he thought, was an obstacle to the withdrawal and concentration needed for original artistic creation – Tolstoy and Byron and perhaps Shelley were exceptions. Those brought up as he was, he thought, were tempted to take too much interest in the lives, both personal and social, by which they were surrounded to dedicate themselves to hard, life-absorbing tasks. He was, all his life, too deeply fascinated by too great a variety of individual experiences, as well as books, above all novels and poetry, stories and literary essays, to be able to do more than describe them and the worlds they expressed, give his own impressions, convey what they seemed to him to say and be; and this left no room for the self-disciplined, preoccupying creative labour after which, at times, he hankered.

After his First in History at Oxford he attempted All Souls, but was not taken, and was elected to a Fellowship at Wadham

College, where he remained from 1924 until 1930. He taught English literature (and sometimes history) there – it was then that he began to exercise his extraordinary capacity for understanding casts of mind and for eliciting from pupils and making them aware of the precise content of what they thought and felt and groped for, their roots and their goals, and, conversely, conveying his own vividly imaginative and concrete sense of what he himself thought and understood and knew about the writers and works which were being discussed. This gift for seeing in stunted-seeming seeds the particular kinds of blooms that might be encouraged to grow made him (especially after he became a tutor at New College, and then, from 1939 to 1970, Professor) a remarkable influence on his pupils, an unusually large number of whom became distinguished teachers of English literature themselves, at Oxford and other universities, and held him in affection and admiration for ever after. At least five among the most distinguished literary luminaries at Oxford alone acknowledged a deep intellectual and personal debt to him as a wonderfully sympathetic and inspiring teacher. Until fashions changed, his lectures were vastly attended.

His interest did not lie in scholarship, but he did not look down on the minutiae of learning, on the most scrupulous textual or philological investigations, let alone creative reconstruction of the past: he respected this deeply, and looked on as masters and personal friends some of the best-known literary scholars in Oxford at this time – C. S. Lewis, J. R. R. Tolkien, Helen Gardner, F. P. Wilson, Helen Darbyshire, L. P. Wilkinson, Nevill Coghill – who, in turn, liked him greatly and respected his judgement. But his heart was not in learning. He had a very definite doctrine of the proper aim of the study of literature, at least as he conceived of it, though he did not exclude other possibilities. He was not favourable to historical, biographical, sociological, sociolinguistic approaches to a writer, and the interpretation of his work in the light of them. His approach was aesthetic. Like T. S. Eliot, he thought that works of art shone by their own radiance, and that knowledge of the artist's life added little. Like Proust, he was against Sainte-Beuve's methods. He did not care for Edmund Wilson or the semantics of I. A. Richards, or the cultural moralism of F. R. Leavis (who duly attacked him). This was not what he wished to do, even when he admitted that it was, in its own way, well done. He thought that the task of a critic, and of a teacher of literature, was to make clear to himself and convey to others the creative process of the writer, the process of the particular imaginative act of composition, whether it obeyed rules or departed from them, or derived from examples, or was directed against other modes of expression, or created its own. He thought that this task resembled that of a teacher of composition in a musical *conservatoire* who describes the process of evolution of successive drafts of a Beethoven sonata, or Wagner's development of the organisation of orchestral forces and the relationship of this to his mythological invention. This entailed a degree of imaginative insight, as well as accurate knowledge where it was available, which alone could bring out the inwardness, and, in particular, convey the specific quality, of a piece of writing, its inner pulse, its poetic imagery and changing forms, which were part and parcel of its meaning, of the artist's way of achieving artistic effects. It was this wish to see nothing between him and the object of attention, and a consequent distaste for theories of literature, systems of aesthetics – sociological, psychological, philosophical, methodological approaches – that gave Cecil's teaching and his writing their particular character. It was this, too, that often enabled him to encourage a particular approach, and suggest further steps along the grain of a pupil's mind or imagination. He made no attempt to indoctrinate or impose correct methods, as some of his less formidable colleagues seemed, in the 1930s and late '40s, keen to do.

Cecil's books, which reflect his deepest interests, both in literature and life, show that what he loved best was what was most English in English life and letters, and everything outside England which seemed closest to its, to him, most valuable qualities – a sense of lives as they are lived, the inwardness, the awareness of the poetry of quiet existence in the country, the often complex self-absorption of solitary lives, as well as their part in and interplay with the facets of various kinds of English social life, particularly when the observation is authentic, and concerned with the personal and private, and the effects of distortion or destruction by disasters or false values. His first important work, *The Stricken Deer* (1929), is a beautifully written, deeply sympathetic study of a melancholy, introspective, semi-solitary, lyrical Christian poet living out his life in the country. Cecil had a natural affinity with uneasy, cloistered, fantasy-filled, inwardly rich lives, and the deep, unquenchable lyrical impulse which they fed – Cowper, Gray, Lamb, the Brontës (as in his *Early Victorian Novelists* of 1934), Dorothy Osborne in an earlier century (*Two Quiet Lives*, 1948) – and this is conveyed by the best pages of *Poets and Story-Tellers* (1949), by his essay on Walter de la Mare, and especially by his excellent, original and deeply-felt lectures on Thomas Hardy, perhaps the best of all his books.

But he was not confined to this genre: he gave an interesting account of Scott's early grasp of the collision of social classes, of conflicts of individuals in societies in flux, which owed nothing to Lukács. His lecture on Walter Pater in 1955 is something else again – an exquisite appreciation of the aesthetic approach to life, which meant a very great deal to him, and which he defended in an unfavourable climate, as emerged in his Inaugural Lecture. Against the current streams of the time, in 1949 and again in 1957, he declared that the central purpose of art was to give delight, not to instruct, nor to disturb, nor to explain, nor to praise or condemn a movement, an idea, a regime, nor to help build a better world in the service of a Church, a party, a nation, a class, but to irradiate the soul with a light which God had granted the artist the power to shed, and the reader or listener to absorb, understand, delight in, and thereby be drawn nearer its divine creator.

The true love of his life was, of course, Jane Austen. He wrote about her during his freelance life in London in 1935, and after he retired from Oxford in 1978: the *Portrait of Jane Austen* was his most finished study of her. Everything in her appealed to him: the dry light upon, and profound understanding of, the human heart; the unswerving pursuit of what she perceived to be the real nature of human beings and the world they lived in; the calm good sense and unalterably just appraisals; the steady gaze; the light but calculated weight; the perfection of marksmanship of every word; the pervasive irony, the deceptively quiet tone; the capacity to convey the nuances of every tremor of feeling and passion and painful thought in these well-mannered, genteel, provincial heads and hearts. He laughed at the strictures of social, especially Marxist, critics – what, no mention of the French or the Industrial Revolutions? Nothing about the condition of the poor? Or Napoleon? Or class warfare? Or the technological transformation which altered everything in the society about which she purported to write? Nothing but individual experience, personal relationships, children, adolescents, marriage, a thousand indescribable feelings, intimations? As if this were not enough, not the essence of life and of art.

She wrote of an England he knew and understood, and he responded to those who described it with genius. He felt this in a smaller degree about Mrs Gaskell and, in his own time, Jean Rhys. George Eliot was a genius, he knew, but for him too unaesthetic and too ideological. For this he was reproached by members of the Bloomsbury coterie, but he was defiantly unrepentant.

He was, of course, well acquainted with Bloomsbury; he had married the daughter of Desmond MacCarthy, who was brought up at the heart of it, and he went to Bloomsbury parties. He delighted in the wit and irreverence of its members. Lytton Strachey did have a strong and lasting influence upon him – he believed that Strachey was the creator of biography as a conscious art form alongside the novel, and as a biographer he confessed himself to be his disciple. *The Young Melbourne* and its successor, *Lord M.*, probably his most widely read works, owe a great deal to Strachey; the sure touch with which the brilliant world of the Whig aristocracy is brought to life has surely some foundation in Cecil's familiarity with his own social world before the War, and is perhaps a trifle anachronistic, as Tolstoy's society in *War and Peace* is, for much the same reason. Both volumes are most enjoyable reading – Strachey would have been much more ironical, mischievous, cruel, would have played with the facts to the point of caricature, but the genre is similar: Cecil is at once more high-spirited, kinder and more conventional. He liked the Partridges, thought E. M. Forster very clever, amusing, skilful, but recoiled from their moral values – they conflicted obviously with his own religious and perhaps more worldly ones. He compared Forster unfavourably with Turgenev, who seemed to him equally gifted, indeed, more so, equally clever, amusing, perceptive and humane, but with a lyrical imagination denied, in his view, to Forster.

He looked on Bloomsbury with some irony, as a kind of sect, a self-contained, unreal little society which had its own orthodoxies and its own experts on everything, rather like the Roman Catholic or Marxist or Freudian establishments. But the person in Bloomsbury he most deeply admired, and, indeed, looked up to almost uncritically, was, of course, Virginia Woolf. He thought her novels works of undeniable genius, but what meant most to him was *The Common Reader*, her critical essays. These formed his ideal model – the revelation of the varieties of the actual processes of creation, the literary analogue to the teaching of musical composition – in which he so deeply believed, and which he tried to write, all his life. He shared his sense of Woolf's dazzling genius with his lifelong friend, Elizabeth Bowen, whose novels spoke to him directly. He thought Elizabeth Bowen, as well as his intimate friend the novelist L. P. Hartley, to be endowed beyond others with a sensibility to the texture of life as it is lived, a gift which, for him, Chekhov possessed to a supreme degree. He loved Tolstoy – he preferred his sunlit world – 'Tolstoy was surely the cleverest man who ever lived', he said of him – to the crushing misanthropy of Flaubert or the unceasing discords and infernal regions of Dostoevsky. The most valuable quality for him in people was, I think, a capacity for self-understanding – for knowing what one could and could not be and do. Genius as she was, Virginia Woolf did not completely possess that – and Vita Sackville-West, for example, and indeed, the rest of Bloomsbury, then a dominant literary influence, not at all. He was too hard-headed and undeceivable not to look on this literary mandarinate with amused detachment, and mocked at the snobbishness, both social and artistic, of most of its members (acute even in his heroes, Strachey and Woolf) as being a genuine defect.

Towards the end of his life he did many other things. He wrote an excellent life of Max Beerbohm (*Max*), which Max, on his deathbed, had asked his widow to propose to him. He wrote about his own family and their house, first in the early 1950s, then again in his later years, in 1973. He wrote about his father-in-law, Desmond MacCarthy; and he edited anthologies, of Christian verse in 1940, and of his own choice (*Library Looking-Glass*) in 1935. He wrote *Visionary & Dreamer*, about the painters Samuel Palmer and Burne-Jones (1969), on whom he had lectured in the United States. He took no interest in 'the modern movement' – T. S. Eliot, James Joyce, Wyndham Lewis, Ezra Pound and their successors. The new schools – deconstruction and its successors, formalism, neo-Freudianism, neo-Marxism and the rest – seemed to him arid, academic exercises, or else dark mysteries conjured up by foreign mystagogues, which he was only too happy not to seek to penetrate.

All in all he was one of the most intelligent, irresistibly attractive, gifted, life-enhancing, shrewd and brilliant literary personalities of his time. He confined himself to what he liked, admired and enjoyed, and described it and his reasons for it with great talent. He saw through pretence and sham quickly and infallibly. Some declared that he wrote with undeniable charm, style and distinction, but with a lack of originality, that his opinions were often familiar enough though 'ne'er so well expressed'. This is not just. His pen had a very sharp edge, and often cut deeper than cruder, if stronger, weapons. However this may be, he was certainly the most delightful human being that anyone could ever hope to meet.

# MEMORIES OF VIRGINIA WOOLF

I REMEMBER that in 1933 Virginia Woolf was invited to stay the night by her first cousin H. A. L. Fisher, Warden of New College.

Mrs Fisher told me that she did not care for her much, as she thought her somewhat arrogant, but Herbert Fisher had a high regard for her, apart from his close relationship. The dinner party was given in the Warden's Lodgings, and there were present, apart from the guest of honour and the host and Mrs Fisher, John Sparrow, then a Fellow of All Souls (as, indeed, was I), Richard Crossman, whom Mrs Fisher greatly liked, C. S. Lewis, who could not bear feminine company and disapproved of women writers particularly, and a classical tutor from Brasenose College called Alan Carr, who was, I think, a friend of the Fisher family. Virginia Woolf, who was certainly the most beautiful woman I had ever seen, then or perhaps even later, looked exceedingly nervous and unseeing – she did not exactly stumble against the furniture, but she made her way to the table very uncertainly. I sat at Fisher's left, she on his right. Mrs Fisher, flanked by Crossman and Lewis, was at the other end of the table. Mary Fisher (now Mrs Bennett), Fisher's daughter, who fell totally under her cousin's spell, and her friend Rachel Walker were also present.

Mrs Woolf twitched nervously, and when her neighbour, the don from Brasenose, asked whether Mr Woolf would be coming also, did not reply. The explanation apparently was that Leonard Woolf was convinced that Fisher had been responsible, at any rate in part, for inventing the Black and Tans to quell the Irish rebellion in 1921, and refused to be in the same room with so wicked a member of Lloyd George's Cabinet.

Mrs Woolf was silent, so was the host. Then, to break the silence, he said, 'Do you do much reading, Virginia? Have you been reading novelists at all – Scott, for example?' To which she replied, 'No, not Scott, I think it's all terrible rubbish. I know that

David Cecil has just published a lecture about him, God knows what he finds in him, I didn't like the lecture either.' After that, another silence.

'Do you go for walks at all, Virginia?' asked Fisher a little desperately. 'Yes, I do. Not much in London. Mostly in the country.'

'What do you notice most on your walks?'

'I think mostly goats on hillsides, they look so ecclesiastical.'

Meanwhile, at the other end of the table, in loud voices, the company was saying how much they liked Uppingham (I do not vouch for my recollection of the actual words spoken).

'I like hearty schools,' said Crossman, 'none of your arty-tarty people there – there were some at Winchester when I was there, but not all that many. Eton, of course, is much worse.' Mrs Fisher, I think, agreed.

Lewis said he found it difficult to teach introverts at Magdalen – 'Arty-tarty, that's very good: Betjeman, Pryce-Jones, I found they had no genuine grasp of either prose or poetry, either modern or old – I was greatly relieved when they left.'

Mrs Woolf winced at the tone, the loudness, the sentiments, and Fisher quickly tried to intervene. They talked about people they had known, about travel in Italy and the like – I have no recollection of what either of the young women said. Then we went to the drawing room, where no fewer than forty or fifty graduates and undergraduates of New College who were thought suitable had been gathered to see and hear the great writer.

She stood in front of them, silent, nervous, her gaze fixed on some distant point, unable to utter – it was a little like an execution, or perhaps like a very shy bishop about to confirm a class of schoolboys or undergraduates. Finally she spoke.

'Has anyone here ever read *Jane Eyre*?' she said, looking at the ceiling, then at the windows, trying not to look at anyone's face.

One young man raised his hand. 'Can you tell me the plot?' said Mrs Woolf.

The young man did his best, he took ten minutes or so over it.

'Has anyone here read *Wuthering Heights*?'

The same process followed.

'What about *The Moonstone*?' Someone had read that too.

'Do you like reading detective stories?' There were mixed answers about that. Then, looking really at her wits' end, she said,

'I cannot go on talking like this, I am so sorry. Let us mingle like human beings.' And we did so.

It was by now near 10 o'clock, and Mrs Fisher announced that she was going to bed, but that those who wished to stay could do so. Fisher asked Mrs Woolf whether she liked Handel, Mozart, Haydn, Beethoven. She said she liked them all – 'What a very catholic taste you have,' he said. After that we broke up into little groups and she talked most amiably in a corner with two or three young women, perhaps her cousin Mary among them, and we all went to bed.

Much later, I think in 1938, Mrs Woolf asked me to dinner in her house in Tavistock Square. On her postcard she wrote: 'If you knock on my little grey door I shall open it.'

Apart from myself the only persons present were Leonard, Ben Nicolson and Sally Graves, niece of Robert Graves, by then married as Mrs Chilver, who later became Principal of Lady Margaret Hall in Oxford – Mrs Woolf obviously had a passion for her and had been cross-examining her (so Mrs Chilver told me) about whether there was much free love going on among young people: was lesbianism known at all? And so on. I rather think she must have cross-examined her nieces about that kind of thing too – she had a feeling that she knew too little about the contemporary world in England.

She began describing a visit which one of the Royal Princesses, I think Princess Beatrice, had paid to Duncan Grant's studio, and how delightful this was. Leonard, who, with a trembling hand, was fumbling to light the gas fire, said, 'I don't know why you think that – royalty are exactly like everybody else, there's no difference between them and ordinary people.' 'You are quite wrong, Leonard,' she said, 'they are quite different. Quite wonderful. Quite marvellous. Not at all like ordinary people. I was very excited on that occasion and I'm not ashamed of it.' Then she turned to Ben Nicolson – there was always someone she evidently liked to tease – and said, 'Ben, do tell us [he was the Assistant Keeper of the King's pictures], do you have to wear knee-breeches when you go to Buckingham Palace or Windsor? Do you bow very low? Do you go down on one knee? Do you ever speak before you are spoken to? Do you ever ask any questions? When you leave the King's presence do you walk backwards?' And so on.

Ben answered as best he could, without smiling, quite solemnly as was his way, and did finally burst out, 'You always tease me,

Virginia. I'll never forget when you asked poor Hugh Walpole whether his car was lined with gold.'

She then turned to me. 'What is that book that you came in with? I saw it.'

I said it was Henry James's book on Hawthorne.

'I expect there are no bats in your belfry, Mr Berlin,' she said, 'I can see that – you don't look to me like someone interested in dreams or fancies – or are you?'

I cannot remember what I answered. I expect I faltered out of pure terror at her presence. She did convey the presence of genius, and her conversation, which I cannot hope to reproduce, was full of wonderful images and analogies, and was more fascinating to listen to than that of I think anyone I have ever met – Pasternak was the only person who came close to it.

'Henry James,' she said, 'well everybody reads him now, of course, but by the time I met him he was nothing but a frozen-up old monster. I don't read many modern novels, not even those that we publish, Leonard and I. Stephen Spender told us how marvellous he thought *In a Province* by Laurens van der Post was – we published it, you know. Quite decent, I thought, but wonderful? No. Have you read *Murder in the Cathedral*, or seen it? I rather liked it.'

'I walked out of it in the middle, I couldn't bear it,' said Leonard, 'Tom Eliot is too obscurantist for me. All that religious nonsense.'

I can remember no more, but I spent three of the most wonderful hours of my life in the presence of that not entirely sympathetic and certainly not very kind, but wonderfully gifted writer, a writer of genius, as I still regard her – more and more so as I reread the works of her middle period.

# EDMUND WILSON AT OXFORD

I MET Edmund Wilson, I think, sometime in the early spring of 1946, after I had come back from Moscow to finish the job I was doing at the British Embassy in Washington. I had been in Washington during the war years, and my friend the Russian composer Nicolas Nabokov, who, like his cousin Vladimir, was a friend of Wilson's, thought that he might like to meet me (I had expressed my intense admiration for *Axel's Castle* and *The Triple Thinkers*) and talk about Russian literature and other topics. Wilson refused. He was convinced that any British official could want to meet him only in order to rope him into the British propaganda machine. He was acutely isolationist: his Anglophobia, which in any case had been fairly acute, was increased by the reflection that England had once again managed to drag America into a dreadful and totally unnecessary war, and he had no wish to meet any representative of that country. However, once the War was over he evidently decided that he was no longer in any danger of being inveigled into pro-British activities, and asked me to lunch at the Princeton Club in New York.

I was, I own, rather taken aback by his appearance. I do not know what I had imagined a distinguished literary critic to look like, but there stood before me a thickset, red-faced, pot-bellied figure, not unlike President Hoover in appearance; but once he began to talk, almost before we had sat down, I forgot everything save his conversation. He spoke in a curiously strangled voice, with gaps between his sentences, as if ideas jostled and thrashed about inside him, getting in each other's way as they struggled to emerge, which made for short bursts, emitted staccato, interspersed with gentle, low-voiced, legato passages. He spoke in a moving and imaginative fashion about the American writers of his generation, about Dante, and about what the Russian poet Pushkin had meant to him. He described his visit to the Soviet Union in 1935 and the appalling effect which this had had upon him, for, like many other members of the American intelligentsia, he had once tended to idealise the Communist regime.

The climax of his visit was a meeting with Prince D. S. Mirsky. Mirsky was a brilliant, highly original émigré writer in English on Russian literature who had become a convert to Marxism in England; he then returned to Russia and soon after this published a book denouncing British writers and intellectuals, some of whom had befriended him. Wilson found him in Moscow in a very low and wretched state (two years later he was arrested and sent to a camp, where he died). Mirsky's downfall and pathetic condition had made an indelible impression on Wilson, and he spoke long and bitterly about the passing of his own political infatuation. He then talked about Russian literature in general, and particularly about Chekhov and Gogol, as well as I have ever heard anyone talk on any literary topic. I was completely fascinated; I felt honoured to have met this greatly gifted and morally impressive man. We became friends. I did not return to the United States until 1949, when I went to teach at Harvard, and stayed a night with Wilson at Wellfleet, where he was living with his wife Elena. I went to see them both on subsequent visits in the 1950s.

In 1954 he came to England and telephoned virtually from the airport to tell me that he wished to come to Oxford and stay with me for a day or two. I welcomed this. Since I was not married then, I was living in All Souls College. Wilson did stay two nights with me in a not very attractive college room (which he describes with characteristic acerbity in his diary).[1] He was in a splendidly Anglophobic mood. On the first morning, before lunch, we went for a walk to look at the colleges. When we passed Christ Church, he looked at the decaying building of the Library (not then yet refaced, as it would be later, with the assistance of the Rockefeller Foundation) and said, 'Oh, most of these buildings look in very poor shape – I think they're actually falling down', and looked delighted. 'I think that's the case with a lot of England,' he went on, 'I think your country deserves a bit of this.'

He then launched into a sweeping attack on academic life and academics in general as murderers of all that was living and real in literature and art – classical, medieval, modern. I asked him

[1] Edmund Wilson, The Fifties, ed. Leon Edel (New York, 1986), p. 135 (entry for 20–21 January 1954).

whether there were no academics he liked or admired. He said that there were indeed a few: one was Christian Gauss, his teacher at Princeton, whose lectures he had greatly admired and whom he had liked and deeply respected as a man; another was Norman Kemp Smith, who had been a professor of philosophy at Princeton in his day and was now living in retirement in Scotland. (Wilson had gone to see him during a visit to England in 1945, the visit on which the pages about England in *Europe Without Baedeker* were founded.) Apart from these he could for the moment think of no one.

The diatribe continued (I had no idea of whether this was a passing mood, induced by Oxford, or a permanent attitude): he could wish for no worse fate for anyone than to hold a job at a university, particularly if it were connected with literary studies; he had heard that Archibald MacLeish contemplated becoming, or had become, a professor somewhere, was it Harvard? It was a fate that that ass deserved (I had read Wilson's devastating parody, 'The Omelet of A. MacLeish', and had realised that this poet was not one of his favourites). Then there had been the ridiculous Ted Spencer at Harvard, who tried to seek him out but had died before any relationship could be attempted; and there was also Spencer's protégé, Harry Levin – a clever man, and widely read, with interesting things to say, who had had it in him to become something if only he had not chosen to make a career at Harvard, which had turned him into a pedantic schoolmaster, buried in trivial detail, a Dryasdust, who turned everything into dust, a kind of coloured dust. 'Oh, but I can't explain it,' he said, 'I talked to him about Howells – he doesn't think Howells is any good at all.' He went on to say that Harry Levin was, in spite of all this, not a bad fellow; he could be highly perceptive and interesting, but he was ridiculous about Howells. I was under the impression that they were friends (as I feel sure in fact they were), and was taken aback by these remarks about Levin, whom I admired and whose essay on Stendhal I thought a remarkable piece of work. But he would not relent. His next target was Perry Miller; then C. S. Lewis; he went on and on in a ferocious fashion. Perhaps Tennyson talked about Churton Collins in this way when he called him a louse in the locks of literature. I saw no reason to doubt that he spoke of me in similar fashion; it was obviously part of him; I loved him as he was.

He asked me whether it was to be his fate to meet more

academics at lunch or dinner. I relieved his fears about lunch by saying the guests would be Stephen Spender and another man of letters (I cannot remember who); in the evening, however, if he wished to dine in All Souls as he had suggested, he might well meet some academics. Would he prefer to dine in a restaurant? No, he said, he wished to plumb the depths of old, decayed, conservative English academic life in its death-throes. I remember his words: 'It can't be long now,' he said ominously, 'I think we're in at the kill.' I did not ask him to develop this theme, but tried to divert him on to other subjects. No good. He said that in England – London – writers and the like formed little cliques, jealous coteries engaged in keeping each other out; there was no real literary world; Evelyn Waugh could not be in a room with Peter Quennell, a perfectly decent man of letters; both had spoken ill of Cyril Connolly; Auden was ostracised; nobody had a kind word to say about MacNeice or Angus Wilson; and so on and so on. Most of this seemed absurdly misconceived to me. To get him off this topic I asked him – unwisely, as it turned out – what his last visit to England had been like. But by then it was time for lunch. He seemed to enjoy the company, denounced the writers of the *Partisan Review*, said that Philip Rahv was able enough but, like the rest of them, used literature to make political points, and praised V. S. Pritchett as one of the few critics whose thought was free and who had something to say.

After lunch he reminded me of my earlier question and told me what had occurred during his previous London visit. He had arrived as a kind of war correspondent, and the wartime British Ministry of Information had detached the well-known publisher Hamish Hamilton, who was then a member of that ministry and was half American, to look after him. Hamilton had organised a party of eminent members of the British literary establishment. According to Wilson, he saw at the party, among others, T. S. Eliot, one or two Sitwells, Cyril Connolly, Siegfried Sassoon, Harold Nicolson, Peter Quennell and, I think, Rosamond Lehmann. He wished to talk to none of these. 'T. S. Eliot', he said, 'is a gifted poet, but somewhere inside him there is a scoundrel. When I see him, which is not often, I just cannot take him. I do not wish to meet him, although I think some of his poetry is wonderful – it repels me, but it is poetry.' The Sitwells he dismissed as being of no interest. The only person there that he was able to speak to was Compton Mackenzie – they swapped stories about life before and during the First World War, and he found the appearance, manner and conversation of the old buccaneer quite entrancing.

I gradually realised that there is a sense in which Wilson belonged to an earlier generation than the literary intelligentsia of England at that time; that the kind of people he preferred were the Edwardians – full-blooded, masculine men of letters, with sometimes coarse (and even to some degree philistine) but vital personalities – and that this was the world to which Compton Mackenzie truly belonged. Desmond MacCarthy had once described to David Cecil and myself a typical dinner he had attended some years before the First World War in a London club – the Reform, or it may have been the Travellers'. Present were Rudyard Kipling, H. G. Wells, Max Beerbohm, Hilaire Belloc, G. K. Chesterton, Arnold Bennett and Bernard Shaw, as well as Henry James and the young Hugh Walpole. There was no talk about literature or the arts, or friendship or nature or morality or personal relations or the ends of life – the kinds of things that were discussed in Bloomsbury. There was not a touch of anything faintly aesthetic – the talk was hearty, concerned with royalties, publishers, love-affairs, absurd adventures, society scandals, and anecdotes about famous persons, accompanied by gusts of laughter, puns, limericks, a great deal of mutual banter, jokes about money, women and foreigners, and a great deal of drink. The atmosphere was that of a male dining-club of vigorous, amusing, sometimes rather vulgar friends. These were the best-known authors of the time, the 'blind leaders of the blind' so much disliked and disapproved of by Bloomsbury. It seemed to me that Edmund Wilson, for all his unerring sense of quality and his moral preoccupations, had an affinity with these masters. I do not think that he would have greatly enjoyed tea with Virginia Woolf or an evening with Lytton Strachey.

Hence the literary party in London did not suit him at all, and, after a few perfunctory words with E. M. Forster about Jane Austen, he told Hamish Hamilton that he wanted to get away from it as soon as possible. After the conversation with Compton Mackenzie he swiftly withdrew, to the disappointment, so Hamilton told me, of some of those invited. All he wished to do was to go to Scotland and see his mentor, Kemp Smith. Hamish Hamilton, who had probably never heard of this Kantian scholar, did his best to arrange for the journey to Scotland. Wilson did manage to see him – he told me that he had had a good time with him, that they had talked about the old times with great pleasure and had discussed the decline in the standards of European scholarship. Then he came back to London to be met at the station by the courteous and indefatigable Hamilton, who tried to persuade him to get into a taxi to go to his hotel. It was evening; Wilson had become convinced (so he told me) that what Hamilton was mainly anxious to do was to prevent him from seeing the prostitutes who then walked the streets of London in exceptional numbers (so he had been told). He did his best to evade Hamilton, for whom he had by then conceived one of his violent, irrational dislikes (by this time reciprocated by Hamilton, who told me on a later occasion that Wilson was one of the most unpleasant and difficult people he had ever encountered). Wilson did get into a taxi, but, by God, he got out of it after five minutes, and he *did* walk the streets, particularly Park Lane, and he *did* see prostitutes, and he felt that he had scored off the officials who had been sent to escort him, almost, he thought, in the manner of the Russian secret police.

I tried to persuade him that all that Hamish Hamilton had attempted to do was to extend the kind of courtesies which cultural institutions thought to be his due. Wilson would have none of that: he was certain that an attempt was being made to bear-lead him in London, to prevent him from meeting unsuitable people whom in fact he might have liked to meet. This conviction – that there was a general conspiracy in England, of a Soviet type, not to let him meet unsuitable people – obsessed him, and was to surface later in Oxford. I asked him if he had disliked every literary person he had met in London. He said, 'No, I like Evelyn Waugh and Cyril Connolly best.' Why? 'Because I thought they were so nasty.' Perhaps this referred to later meetings, because I do not know if Evelyn Waugh was in London during the War, in which he served as a soldier. He had also taken to Angus Wilson because he reminded him of the heartfelt human feelings of the kind of Americans with whom he felt at home. It was the aestheticism, the prissiness, the superciliousness, the cliquishness, the thin, piping voices, the bloodlessness, the preoccupation with one's own emotions both in life and in literature – all of which he (no less than D. H. Lawrence) attributed to Bloomsbury – that irritated him. He thought the whole of English literary life was infected by this. I don't know what he would have said about J. B. Priestley – I think that he was, perhaps, below his angle of vision. He could not bear the thought of the Huxleys, Aldous or Julian.

Evening fell, and it was time for dinner in the Common Room of All Souls College. He had me on one side and the senior Fellow dining, the historian A. L. Rowse, on the other. He hardly spoke to Rowse, although Rowse tried to speak to him. He turned to me brusquely and engaged in conversation about mutual friends in America – Justice Felix Frankfurter and his wife, Nicolas Nabokov and his wives, the playwright Sam Behrman, Mary McCarthy (to whom Wilson had been married), Conrad Aiken, Arthur Schlesinger, Judge Learned Hand and others. Reluctantly he turned to his other side and allowed himself to be addressed by Rowse. He answered in monosyllables. After coffee, when we came back to my rooms, he complained that a flood of British nationalist propaganda had been poured over him by Rowse at dinner, that he had not come to Oxford to be made a victim of cultural chauvinists. I think that on a later occasion, when Rowse went to see him in the United States, they may have got on a little better – but on this occasion he was in a grumpy mood and would not let up.

He said that he realised why the All Souls college servants removed the plates so rapidly, hardly letting him finish a single dish – he spoke of a Barmecide feast – it was because they were acutely class-conscious, hated their masters, wanted to serve them as gracelessly as possible and get away from their hated presence as quickly as they could. He had noticed, he said, that class-consciousness was clearly rampant in this ancient establishment. I did not argue with him – he was, I think, past convincing on this and most other points. What he said was characteristic wonderful nonsense, of course. The majority of scouts (servants) in Oxford were certainly then, and perhaps are still, among the most conservative of its inhabitants; they were conscious carriers of ancient college traditions, old retainers if ever there were such, who for the most part – certainly at that time – refused to be unionised, on the ground that this was an insult to what they conceived to be their status and very special function. The servants at All Souls exemplified this type almost to the point of caricature.

It was plain that Wilson on that day – as on many others – lived in a world of angry fantasy, particularly in the case of anything British, and although I was devoted to him, felt deep admiration and respect for him to his dying day, and remain intensely proud of the friendship that bound us, I knew that it was useless to argue with him once he got the bit between his teeth. This was certainly the case during his stay with me in Oxford. After dinner I had invited my colleague David Cecil, the novelist Iris Murdoch and her husband the critic John Bayley, and the philosopher Stuart Hampshire to meet him. It was not a happy evening. He took against everyone in the room. He mistook Bayley for the critic Humphry House (with whom he might well have got on) and virtually ignored him and everyone else. He became listless, answered in monosyllables, gurgled, drank a great deal of whisky, and looked with hateful eyes at everyone. Although Iris, who is the soul of courtesy and kindness, tried to make things go, and John Bayley, a beguiling talker, did his best, the old bear remained in his lair, glaring balefully from time to time and trying to drown his boredom in drink. The evening came to an early end. At the end of it he burst out about these feeble creatures – aristocrats who dabbled in literature were useless; the dons were all bloodless monks, cut off from all that mattered. Why could I not have invited one of the few academics with guts, like A. J. P. Taylor, whom he wanted to meet because he liked his radical polemics? I said that I knew and liked Taylor, despite a slight *froideur* caused by a somewhat disparaging review he had written of a small book I had just published, but that I would gladly arrange a meeting between them – and did so on the following day.

Taylor was most amiable to us both. Wilson said that he had quite enjoyed his visit to Taylor's rooms in Magdalen College. But then Taylor had taken him to a lecture by Steven Runciman on a Byzantine subject, which bored him stiff; once again he heard the over-refined and, to him, deeply depressing accents of Bloomsbury, those high, thin voices which he could not bear. (I do not know how many of these voices he had ever actually heard.) I also arranged for him to see the Jewish historian Cecil Roth, because at this time he took an increasing interest in Jewish history and was learning Hebrew – it was not long before the publication of his book on the Dead Sea Scrolls. That visit also went well, particularly as I had warned him that Roth was something of a bore, though a worthy and learned antiquary; those mildly disparaging words were enough to make Wilson like him. He muttered something about being kept from people he admired by persons (myself) who for some reason decided to 'blackball' them – more fantasy, more mild paranoia.

Once he had formed a sociological and psychological hypothesis, he held on to it grimly with a kind of pleased deliberate perversity, against all evidence. He told me that the only persons he had truly enjoyed meeting in England, apart from his old friend Sylvester Gates, whom he had known at Harvard many years before, were Connolly (again because what he said was so malicious), Taylor, Roth and Angus Wilson. The rest seemed to him repellent. 'And Compton Mackenzie? And Kemp Smith?' Yes, indeed, these too, but that was all. The most hateful figure to him in England, he said, was Winston Churchill, who was nothing but a typical low-grade American journalist. If it were not for Sylvester Gates and myself he would not have come to England. Did Oxford still contain a ridiculous puffed-up fellow called Maurice Bowra, whom he had met with Gates and who, for all his knowledge of languages, had no understanding whatever of literature? He loved literature – that was evident – a pity that he had nothing of interest to say about it; he gathered that he was a friend of mine: how could this be? His conversation was banal and empty to a degree, just a lot of shouting. He could not understand how such writers as Cyril Connolly and Evelyn Waugh could be said to owe so much to this inflated philistine – they were at least gifted, he was a caricature John Bull. The diatribes went on. By this time he had drunk a great deal and his eyes were almost closed. I managed to get him to his bedroom, not without some difficulty.

Next day he was serene and gentle. We talked about Russian writers, about his life in Talcottville, which he pressed me to visit with him, about Hebrew tenses and the structure of the Hungarian language (which he contemplated acquiring), about his intense admiration for the poetry of W. H. Auden, about the interesting position of the *New Yorker* in American cultural life, about the monstrously patronising attitude of Europeans, not only the despicable English but the French and even the Italians, towards American culture, towards such great poets as Walt Whitman and such prose writers as Herman Melville and Henry James – they were recognised, but the fact that they were Americans had always, it seemed to him, to be explained away or apologised for. But America would show them. There was a wonderful generation of young technologists and engineers coming up in America, confident, gifted, clear-headed, uncluttered men in thin drill suits (I remember this odd description), inventors of excellent new gadgets; these men were building a new, fresh, highly practical civilisation that would respond to new human needs and would open prospects of wonderful new comforts of life, and this would supersede the decay and self-conceit and squalor of a fast-declining, petty-minded European culture. Nevertheless, these *boutades* of his were less violent than on the day before, and rarer. Wilson was in a calmer and happier mood, quite relaxed. He explained that his life was, and always had been, literature and writers, that music[1] and even painting meant less, even though they did mean a great deal: Malraux was marvellous on sculpture. Nothing had contributed so much to his ideas about life and art – to what seemed to him to matter, politics and all – as the great Russian masters. Pushkin had begun to move him more than Shakespeare, but not more than Dante; what terrible nonsense Orwell had written about Tolstoy and *Lear*. He said that his distaste for the English had been increased by the knock-kneed creatures he met in London and Oxford. Did I know his friend Jason Epstein? He was, he thought, himself misanthropic enough, but Epstein outdid him – his dislike of mankind was phenomenal. He liked Epstein, and liked that in him.

After which he left. It could not be regarded as a successful visit. In spite of this, he did come back to Oxford with his wife Elena to stay for a couple of days with me and my wife – by that time we were living in a house of our own – and I took care not to invite Oxford academics to meet him, however great their eagerness and admiration. I preferred to meet him in Boston, London and New York.

He was, in my eyes, a great critic, and a noble and moving human being, whom I loved and respected and wanted to have a good opinion of me; I was deeply touched when, not long before he died, he made me inscribe a line from the Bible with a diamond upon the window-pane of his house in Wellfleet, a privilege reserved for friends. The line was a verse from Isaiah, with whom, he insisted, I had obviously identified myself – another ineradicable fantasy, like his obstinate insistence that I had written as I did about Tolstoy only because I, too, was a fox, longing to be, indeed believing myself to be, a hedgehog. Nothing said to deny this absurdity made the faintest impression on him. He knew that 'like

[1] I once asked him, I cannot think why, whether he liked Wagner. He said, I think, 'Yes, yes, I did, yes, when I was much younger, but it is not the kind of stuff I can listen to now.'

all Jews' I sought unity and a metaphysically integrated organic world; in fact, I believe the exact opposite. The constructions of his inner world withstood all external evidence. He was prey to wild fantasies, to absurd conjectures, to irrational hatreds and loves. The fact that my prejudices largely coincided with his own was, of course, an immense source of sympathy and endearment. It was perhaps this more than anything else that brought us together.

His judgements were often erratic, and he was prey to delusions, but his humanity and integrity were total. When he went off on a tangent it might end anywhere. His review in the *New Yorker* of Pasternak's *Doctor Zhivago* was the best and most understanding, I think, in any language; but his speculation in a later article on the meaning of various names and symbols in the novel was crazy to a degree.[1] He managed to combine profound insight and extraordinary vision into cultures not his own with turbulent prejudices, hatreds and a great deal of pure nonsense; he sometimes misfired totally and missed the target by miles; yet most of his denunciations were deserved. He was the last major critic in the tradition of Johnson, Sainte-Beuve, Belinsky and Matthew Arnold; his aim and practice were to consider works of literature within a larger social and cultural frame – one which included an absorbed, acutely penetrating, direct, wonderfully illuminating view of the author's personality, goals and social and personal origins, the surrounding moral, intellectual and political worlds, and the nature of the author's vision – and to present the writer, the work and its complex setting as interrelated, integrated wholes. He told me during his visit that the modern tendency towards purely literary scholarship, towards an often deliberate ignoring of the texture of the writer's life and society, for him lacked all genuine content. I agreed with him, fervently. Art shone for him, but not by its own light alone. He is gone, and has not left his peer.

---

[1] The two articles are 'Doctor Life and his Guardian Angel', *New Yorker*, 15 November 1958, 201–26, and (with Barbara Deming and Evgenia Lehovich) 'Legend and Symbol in "Doctor Zhivago" ', *Nation* 188 No 16 (18 April 1959), 363–73, and *Encounter* 12 No 6 (June 1959), 5–16; both were reprinted in Wilson's *The Bit Between My Teeth: A Literary Chronicle of 1950–1965* (London, [1966]).

# AUBERON HERBERT

IN THE early spring of 1946, when I was still a government official, I had occasion to go to Paris for a few days, and was staying as a guest in the British Embassy, then presided over by the infinitely hospitable Duff and Diana Cooper. At dinner on my last night in Paris I found myself sitting opposite an officer in uniform, proclaimed by the metal strip on his shoulder to be a member of the Polish Army. He was tall, generously built, with a fine Roman bust and head, looking like (as someone once described him) a kindly Nero. For a Pole, which I took him to be, he seemed to me to speak English with remarkable purity and a rich and imaginative vocabulary; some question on my part about where he had served stimulated him to a magnificent outpouring of words reminiscent in style of an older and more stately world. Although I am far from taciturn myself, I was, for once, perfectly content to listen. The stream of vivid, somewhat formal, eloquence flowed on like a mountain torrent, carrying all before it; at moments it was diverted this way and that by questions or interruptions by the other guests, but not for long: it always returned to its original course, sweeping away, or twisting round, every obstacle in its path, until a full account had been given of the picaresque adventures of his wartime experience.

He continued to talk to me, to my great pleasure, after dinner. Held, like the wedding guest, by this strange and plainly gifted Pole, who plied me with drink after drink long after the hosts had gone to bed, I finally made my excuses and made my way to my bedroom for a few hours' sleep, until the car that was to take me to Boulogne arrived at five in the morning. This was not to be. My new friend followed, settled himself on the edge of my bed and continued to talk. Some might have found this excessive. I did not; I thought it a strange but delightful experience.

By this time I had discovered that he was Auberon Herbert; that

his father had died before he could know him, that he was devoted
to his mother and his sisters; that he had joined the Polish forces
because he had been rejected on medical grounds by those of his
own country. I learnt, too, that he had, not very long before, nearly
lost his life in a fracas with some Canadian soldiers, which he
described in horrifying detail, mitigated by his rolling Victorian
periods. His gift for languages was remarkable: he spoke Polish,
Ukrainian, Dutch, as well as French and German, a little Russian
(enough to indicate his extreme disapproval of the regime of that
country), some Czech, and, of course, Italian, since he had spent
many months in his family's house in Portofino. (He could manage
some Genoese and Provençal too.) We turned out to have a good
many acquaintances in common, of each of whom he was prepared
to provide pungent vignettes; and he judged them by the ancient
criteria of the traditional ruling classes of many lands: whether they
had courage, moral or intellectual distinction, nobility of character,
generosity, personal beauty, charm, breeding, and – most important of all – correct political and religious beliefs. These standards
were applied in a confident, direct, unswerving fashion, with fine
extravagance of speech and expression. I found that on a good
many of our common friends and acquaintances his judgements at
times diverged sharply from my own. He listened to my
qualifications courteously, but without much attention: everyone
he knew had his and her place in the coherent and vividly coloured
world constructed by his fervid imagination, which now and again
seemed to me to exist at a certain distance from the world of what
most of us regard as reality.

This chance meeting resulted in an acquaintance which ripened
into friendship. We met occasionally in London and Oxford; from
time to time he would invite me (I was then single) to Pixton, but
something always intervened. Ten years passed since our first
meeting in Paris. In 1956 I married, and that September my wife
and I, with some friends, came to stay in Portofino. There we saw a
good deal of Mary Herbert and Auberon, who was most
hospitable to us all; we greatly delighted in their company. In
Portofino even more than in England, Auberon's quixotic qualities
became overwhelmingly evident. He was high-souled and morally
fastidious, fearless in his devotion to noble, knightly virtues, and
the order in which alone they could flourish, deeply repelled as he
was by the modern world, from which he sought refuge in an
imaginary older world, to which his social, moral and religious

code could be made to apply. Like Don Quixote, he was, above and beyond everything – to use that obsolescent concept – a gentleman. He was totally free from anything in the least small-minded, ignoble, petty, opportunist – anything that in Bloomsbury used to be called 'squalid'. His passion for the causes of the oppressed, which he supported in his own exceedingly individual-istic manner, seemed to me to stem mainly from his religious convictions, with which his chivalrous instinct was closely inter-woven. Don Quixote may not have achieved worldly success, but his life was nothing if not a triumphant affirmation of the Christian soul in a workaday society. Neither Don Quixote nor Auberon were realists. But then, when men say 'I am afraid I am rather a realist', what they often mean is that they are about to tell a lie or do something shabby. From this Auberon was immeasurably remote. Everything that was eccentric and, at times, comical about him sprang from his inability to compromise with the exception-ally 'realistic' values of some of the times and places in which he spent his not altogether happy life.

This was very evident in Portofino. The inhabitants of that portion of the Ligurian coast are not given to exaggerated idealism. They are dry-eyed, tough-minded, not liable to excessive compas-sion, and concerned with their immediate interests, beyond, perhaps, those of other Italian provinces. Auberon was, in a sense, well aware of this – he talked about it often and amusingly, but his penchant for living in an idealised universe led him to magnify the minor intrigues of the inhabitants of this resort, as well as his own relationships with neighbouring landowners and peasants, into dramatic feuds or wonderful alliances, conducted in a world drawn from the pages of Scott or Manzoni or Mary Renault, or at times even from the fantasies of J. R. R. Tolkien, to whose works he was deeply addicted; and this enabled him to live his life at a level at which he could breathe without too much moral discomfort. His vision of life was filled with plots and counter-plots, sinister political conspiracies, secret alliances and mysterious operations of men engaged sometimes in local purposes in Portofino or Genoa or Rome, around the papal throne, or in far-flung world-wide political or financial schemes into which ruthless and wicked men lured innocents to their destruction – schemes which, at any rate at the local Ligurian level, he believed himself able to penetrate and even to foil and turn to his own or other good people's advantage.

All this was done with immense gaiety, fancy, and sometimes

obsessive saga-spinning (which not everyone was always prepared to hear out to the end), but also with a certain unexpected half-awareness of its incomplete reality: moments of fancy (which stimulated some of his 'business' activities) were, it seemed to me, succeeded by periods of clear-eyed vision in which he knew that the world, as he described it to himself and others, was not perhaps wholly what he insisted on its being. Heroes and martyrs who had died for his faith populated his world; so, of course, did the oppressed peoples whose causes he took up zealously: Poles, Ukrainians, Belorussians. What the members of these movements in fact thought of him I do not know, but they were fortunate to find someone who was prepared to work for them so passionately, so disinterestedly, and to involve so many of his bemused friends, bemused but loyal to him, and therefore prepared, against all motives of prudence, to be wafted by him into all kinds of unlikely predicaments, on public platforms and stranger places, in pursuit of some usually Utopian goal.

Auberon was not only pure-hearted, generous, honourable, and a generator of marvellous Chestertonian fantasies, but warm-hearted, morally perceptive, and always responsive to the states of mind and fortune, the feelings, the moods, the joys and the miseries of his friends. Passionate and unswerving as his political convictions were – no one who approved of the Yalta agreement could be spoken to, at any rate with comfort; as for those who were tolerant of the totalitarian regimes east of the Iron Curtain, they were either fools or knaves and to be treated accordingly – the claims of friendship transcended even these barriers. Although he saw the world politically in terms of black and white, this nevertheless did not blind him to the true character of the human beings he met and came to know. More often than not he recognised honesty, goodness, purity of heart when he met them, however deplorable the political or religious opinions of those who possessed these properties; but sometimes he was deceived, and found his trust betrayed, especially by those he helped, who, at least on one occasion, exploited him shamelessly and used him ill. He bore no grudges and harboured no resentment. He was entirely free from malice and from ill will. But if my words tend to suggest the character of a remote dreamer, self-absorbed, detached from common concerns, living in a feudal Middle Age of his own, I have failed to convey a true image of Auberon. He was the very opposite of a prig or prude, noble but humourless, not of this world. Unlike Don Quixote, he possessed an acute sense of the incongruous, and, indeed, of the ridiculous, even in his own knight-errantry. He knew that his efforts to be elected to Parliament were not likely to bear fruit, and gave highly entertaining, self-deprecating accounts of his political ambitions and activities. There was a sense in which he knew that he could do relatively little for the Polish or Ukrainian groups which he supported, that a good many of the persons who clustered round him were less worthy than he told himself and others that they must surely be; and that the entire undertaking, however great its moral worth, had rickety foundations in the world of serious social and political action.

It is, perhaps, a property of the romantic temperament to be at once dedicated to pursuing unattainable goals, demanding of the world what it can never give – to develop a kind of spiritual maximalism – and also to remain ironically aware that such claims bear little relation to what can be achieved on earth. It is this that enabled Auberon not to be shocked or offended when he perceived that others, among them persons he liked and respected, stopped their ears to his propaganda, or looked on him as politically inept, whether or not they were personally fond of him, or were touched by his stout-hearted integrity. He was at once prepared to make light of his own endeavours and yet persist with them. The universe of his imagination, the semi-feudal, nostalgic, historical romance which he lived out so movingly, so gallantly and painfully, had become second nature to him, and perhaps, despite moments of penetrating self-awareness – the bitter moments when reality broke through the fantasy – had become one with his basic character and nature.

He was talented, civilised, very well bred, and hated moderation in all things. He was fiercely anti-utilitarian, pursued ends for their own sakes, to extremes, and despised those who did not. He disliked philistines, policemen, cowards and hypocrites more than liars, barbarians or cunning adventurers. More than almost anything he liked style, dash, lunatic courage. He was highly cultivated in an eighteenth-century sort of way. Apart from his gift for languages, he explored byways of philology, preferably of languages and dialects spoken by semi-submerged local populations – Basques or Genoese or Maltese or Lusatian Sorbs, or Dalmatians, or Greek enclaves in Magna Graecia – and had accumulated an extraordinary store of out-of-the-way historical knowledge which fed his past-directed imagination and his acute aesthetic sense. His taste, expressed in the delightful disorder of his life and the charm and distinction of the houses he inhabited in England and in Italy, remained impeccable; so were his manners, whether he was tipsy or sober. He made excellent jokes. Nothing he said could ever make one wince. He was sometimes monotonous and glazed, never embarrassing. He was a loyal and affectionate friend and behaved beautifully to those who worked for him.

His life at Pixton, the management of the broad but not on the whole rich lands which he owned, his country concerns, his hunting and the open-handed hospitality dispensed by his mother – to whom he remained utterly and deeply, perhaps too deeply, devoted – and which continued after her death, not long before his own, were as much as he could do to keep the traditions of an older world going, a world in which he breathed more freely and suffered less acutely. He was visited by a sense of frustration, desolation and, still more, acute loneliness. His faith (if someone as remote from it as I am may speak of it), which was deep, childlike, beset by no genuine doubts, and the supreme value which guided his entire being, preserved him and kept him from ultimate despair. He was, above all, an extraordinarily good man. This shone through everything he did and said. I was not among his intimates, but I knew him, loved and admired him, and mourn his passing, and the world of fantasy which vanished with him.

# ALDOUS HUXLEY

THE CLASSICAL and History Middle and Upper Eighth forms at St Paul's School were, in the middle and late 1920s, an unusually sophisticated establishment. This was not directly induced by the masters, who were (with one exception – an obscure, eccentric, devoted contemporary and follower of Lytton Strachey) solid, sentimental and unimaginative. While the most civilised among them recommended Shaw, Wells, Chesterton, Gilbert Murray, Flecker, Edward Thomas, Sassoon and the *London Mercury*, we read Joyce, Firbank, Edward Carpenter, Wyndham Lewis, Schiller's Logic,[1] Havelock Ellis, Eliot, the *Criterion* and, under the impulsion of Arthur Calder-Marshall, whose elder brother was then in America and favoured them, the works of H. L. Mencken, Carl Sandburg, Sherwood Anderson; we also took an interest in Cocteau, *transition*, the early surrealists. We looked down on *Life and Letters*, edited by Desmond MacCarthy, as tame and conventional. Among our major intellectual emancipators were J. B. S. Haldane, Ezra Pound, Aldous Huxley.

I cannot myself claim to have been liberated by anyone; if I was in chains then, I must be bound by them still. But, as men of letters – led by Voltaire, the head of the profession – rescued many oppressed human beings in the eighteenth century; as Byron or George Sand, Ibsen and Baudelaire, Nietzsche, Wilde and Gide and perhaps even Wells or Russell have done since; so members of my generation were assisted to find themselves by novelists, poets and critics concerned with the central problems of their day. Social and moral courage can, on occasion, exercise a more decisive influence than sensibility or original gifts. One of my own contemporaries, a man of exceptional honesty, intellectual power

[1] F. C. S. Schiller, *Formal Logic: A Scientific and Social Problem* (London, 1912).

and moral responsiveness, inhibited and twisted by an uncertain social position and bitter puritanism on the part of his father, was morally freed (as others have been by psychoanalysis, or Anatole France, or living among Arabs) by reading Aldous Huxley: in particular *Point Counter Point*, and one or two short stories. Light had been thrown for him on dark places, the forbidden was articulated, intimate physical experience, the faintest reference to which used to upset him profoundly and affect him with a feeling of violent guilt, had been minutely and fully described. From that moment my friend advanced intellectually, and became one of the most admired and productive men of learning of our day. It is not this therapeutic effect, however, that appealed to the young men of my generation so much as the fact that Huxley was among the few writers who, with all his constantly commented upon inability to create character, played with ideas so freely, so gaily, with such virtuosity, that the responsive reader, who had learnt to see through Shaw or Chesterton, was dazzled and excited. The performance took place against a background of relatively few simple moral convictions; they were disguised by the brilliance of the technical accomplishment, but they were there, they were easily intelligible, and, like a monotonous, insistent, continuous ground bass slowly pounding away through the elaborate intellectual display, they imposed themselves on the minds of the boys of seventeen and eighteen – still, for the most part, eager and morally impressionable, no matter how complex or decadent they may in their *naïveté* have conceived themselves to be.

I suspect that the impact diminished as the ground bass – the simple repetitive pattern of Huxley's moral and spiritual philosophy – became increasingly obsessive in his later novels, and destroyed the exhilarating, delightfully daring, 'modern', neo-classical upper lines of the music, in combination with which alone his novels seemed such masterpieces. The grave, noble, humane, tolerant figure of the 1940s and '50s inspired universal respect and admiration. But the transforming power – the impact – was that of the earlier, 'cynical', God-denying Huxley, the object of fear and disapproval to parents and schoolmasters, the wicked nihilist whose sincere and sweetly sentimental passages – especially about music – were swallowed whole, and with delight, by those young readers who supposed themselves to be indulging in one of the most dangerous and exotic vices of those iconoclastic post-war times. He was one of the great culture heroes of our youth.

When I met him in 1935 or 1936, in the house of a mutual friend, Lord Rothschild, in Cambridge, I expected to be overawed and perhaps sharply snubbed. But he was very courteous and very kind to everyone present. The company played intellectual games, so it seemed to me, after nearly every meal; it took pleasure in displaying its wit and knowledge; Huxley plainly adored such exercises, but remained uncompetitive, benevolent and remote. When the games were over at last, he talked, without altering his low, monotonous tone, about persons and ideas, describing them as if viewed from a great distance, as queer but interesting specimens, odd, but no odder than many others in the world on which he seemed to look as a kind of museum or encyclopaedia. He spoke with serenity and disarming sincerity, very simply. There was no malice and very little conscious irony in his conversation, only the mildest and gentlest mockery of the most innocent kind. He enjoyed describing prophets and mystagogues, but even such figures as Count Keyserling, Ouspensky and Gurdjieff, whom he did not much like, were given their due and indeed more than their due; even Middleton Murry was treated more mercifully and seriously than in the portrait in *Point Counter Point*. Huxley talked very well: he needed an attentive audience and silence, but he was not self-absorbed or domineering, and presently everyone in the room would fall under his peaceful spell; brightness and glitter went out of the air, everyone became calm, serious, interested and contented. The picture I have attempted to draw may convey the notion that Huxley, for all his noble qualities, may (like some very good men and gifted writers) have been something of a bore or a preacher. But this was not so at all, on the only occasions on which I met him. He had great moral charm and integrity, and it was these rare qualities (as with the otherwise very dissimilar G. E. Moore), and not brilliance or originality, that compensated and more than compensated for any lack-lustre quality, and for a certain thinness in the even, steady flow of words to which we all listened so willingly and respectfully.

The social world about which Huxley wrote was all but destroyed by the Second World War, and the centre of his interests appeared to shift from the external world to the inner life of men. His approach to all this remained scrupulously empirical, directly related to the facts of the experience of individuals of which there is record in speech or in writing. It was speculative and imaginative only in the sense that in his view the range of valuable human experience had often been too narrowly conceived; that the hypotheses and ideas which he favoured about men in their relations to each other and to nature illuminated the phenomena commonly described as paranormal or supernormal better than much conventional physiology or psychology, tied to inappropriate models as they seemed to him to be. He had a cause and he served it. The cause was to awaken his readers, scientists and laymen alike, to the connections, hitherto inadequately investigated and described, between regions artificially divided: physical and mental, sensuous and spiritual, inner and outer. Most of his later writings – novels, essays, lectures, articles – revolved round this theme. He was a humanist in the most literal and honourable sense of that fearfully abused word; he was interested in human beings as objects in nature in the sense in which the *philosophes* of the eighteenth century had been, and he cared about them as they had. His hopes for men rested on the advance of self-knowledge: he feared that humanity would destroy itself by over-population or by violence; from this only greater self-understanding would save them – above all, understanding of the intimate interplay of mental and physical forces, of man's place and function in nature, on which so much alternate light and darkness seemed to him to have been cast both by science and by religion.

He was sceptical of all those who have tried to systematise the broken glimpses of the truth that had been granted to mystics and visionaries, whom he thought of as uncommonly sensitive or gifted or fortunate men whose power of vision could be cultivated and extended by devoted, assiduous practice. He recognised no supernatural grace; he was not a theist, still less an orthodox Christian believer. In all his writings, whether inspired by Malthusian terrors, or by hatred of coercion and violence, or by opposition to what he called idolatry – the blind worship of some single value or institution to the exclusion of others, as something beyond rational criticism or discussion – or by Hindu and Buddhist classics, or by Western mystics and writers gifted with capacity for spiritual or psychological insight – Maine de Biran, Kafka, Broch (Huxley was a remarkable discoverer of original talent) – or by composers, sculptors, painters, or by poets in all the many languages that he read well – whatever his purpose or his mood, he always returned to the single theme that dominated his later years: the condition of men in the twentieth century. Over and over again he contrasted on the one hand their new powers to create works of unheard-of power and beauty and live wonderful lives – a future far wider and more brilliant than had ever stretched before mankind – with, on the other hand, the prospect of mutual destruction and total annihilation, due to ignorance and consequent enslavement by irrational idols and destructive passions – forces that all men could in principle control and direct, as some individuals had indeed already done. Perhaps no one since Spinoza has believed so passionately or coherently or fully in the principle that knowledge alone liberates, not merely knowledge of physics or history or physiology, or psychology, but an altogether wider panorama of possible knowledge which embraced forces, open and occult, which this infinitely retentive and omnivorous reader was constantly discovering with alternate horror and hope.

His later works, novels and tracts – the frontiers were at times not clear – were everywhere respectfully received; respectfully, but without marked enthusiasm. Those who saw him as a latter-day Lucian or Peacock complained that the wit, the virtuosity, the play of facts and ideas, the satirical eye had disappeared; that the sad, wise, good man who lived in California was but the noble ghost of the author who had earned himself an assured place in the history of English letters. In short, it was alleged that he had turned into a lay preacher, who, like other poets and prophets, had been abandoned by the spirit, so that, like Newton and Robert Owen, Wordsworth and Swinburne, he had ended with little to say, and went on saying it earnestly, honourably, tediously, to an ever-dwindling audience. Such critics were mistaken in at least one fundamental respect: if he was a prophet, he was so in a literal sense. Just as Diderot's *Le Rêve de d'Alembert* and the *Supplément au voyage de Bougainville* (particularly the former) anticipated biological and physiological discoveries of the nineteenth and twentieth centuries, and expressed in the form of audacious speculation some of the major advances in the natural sciences, so Aldous Huxley, with that special sensibility to the contours of the future which impersonal artists sometimes possess, stood on the edge of, and peered beyond, the present frontiers of our self-knowledge. He was the herald of what will surely be one of the great advances in this and following centuries – the creation of new psychophysical sciences, of discoveries in the realm of what at present, for want of a better term, we call the relations between body and mind; a field in which modern studies of myth and ritual, the psychological roots of social and individual behaviour, the relations of the physiological and the logical foundations of linguistics, as well as the phenomena of paranormal psychology, psychical therapy and the like, are but the earliest and most rudimentary beginnings.

Huxley was well aware of this. There is a sense in which he knew that he stood on the frontier between the old astrology that was passing and the new astronomy that was beginning in the sciences of man; and he therefore bore the frequent accusations of betraying his original rationalism in favour of a confused mysticism, of a sad collapse into irrationalism as a means of escape from his own private miseries and the bleakness of his particular world, of a weak abandonment of his old belief in the clear, the precise, the tangible, for the comforting obscurity of hazy, facile, pseudo-religious speculation – he bore these charges with great sweetness and patience. He was perfectly aware of what was being said: no one could have composed a better caricature of precisely these attitudes if he had wished. He persisted not because of some softening of a once gem-like intellect, but because he was convinced that his chosen field was the region in which the greatest and most transforming advance would be made by mankind.

On the last occasion on which I met him, he would – at least in public – speak of nothing but the need for the re-integration of what both science and life had divided too sharply: the restoration of human contact with non-human nature, the need for antidotes to the lopsided development of human beings in the direction of observation, criticism, theory, and away from the harmonious development of the senses, of the 'vegetative soul', of that which man has in common with animals and plants. Others have spoken of this. The great modern protest against alienation springs as much from a sense of isolation from natural processes as from lack of social harmony and common purpose. But Huxley did not, it is evident, believe in the possibility of repairing the texture through institutional change, whether gradualist or revolutionary; nor solely through psychological therapy, though he attached great importance to it. He believed that there were regions in the world, among primitive peoples and in non-European cultures, where forms of life persisted, or had at any rate not been wholly lost, the rediscovery of which would offer a shorter and surer path, based as it was on tradition and experience, than Acts of Parliament or social revolutions or mechanical inventions, or even educational innovations in which he deeply believed. Much of what he said may one day seem vague or unreal in the light of the future experiences of men. Much of it, too, may prove delusive, or fantastic, as often happens with pioneers and those who have an intuitive sense of what is to come. But I must own that I think him wholly right to have directed his excellent mind towards the problems of psychophysical relationships and the control of mental – or what he would have preferred to call spiritual – factors, in which he thought that the Indians, ancient and modern, had advanced beyond the West.

His warnings, whether in *Brave New World*, which is certainly the most influential modern expression of disillusionment with purely technological progress, or in his other novels and essays, and his premonitions, even at their flattest and least artistic, have enough genius to have created a new genre, the pessimistic, frightening Utopia – a vision of unintended consequences of what a good many uncritical liberals and Marxists still conceive, in E. H. Carr's complacent words, as 'old-fashioned belief in progress'. These novels create a genuine uneasiness by getting near the bone (the rotting bone, he would have said) of the contemporary experience of the West. He was a victim of a deep and universal malaise, against which he rightly perceived that too many contemporary antidotes were and are useless because they are too practical and therefore too short-sighted, or operate with concepts which are too shallow, too crude and ephemeral, too vulgar and insulting to the nature of man, particularly to those – to him all-important – still concealed and neglected powers in it about which he wrote. He was conscious of this fatal inadequacy in much contemporary politics, sociology and ethics. There is no coherent body of doctrine, no systematic exposition in his works. But that he had a sense of what men stood and stand in need of, and a premonition of the direction in which, if mankind survives at all, it will be moving – of that I feel convinced. If I am right, justice will one day be done to those very pages over which even his admirers at present shake their heads, some sadly, others patronisingly.

I was delighted to meet him in India in 1961, when he and I found ourselves as delegates at the same congress in New Delhi. He spoke on his usual theme, the poet as *vates* – a man with powers of discerning what other eyes could not see – the poet's claims to prophetic powers in a literal sense. He was received, of course, with immense respect in a country with which his beliefs gave him special ties. We – Huxley, the American delegate Louis

Untermeyer and I – went to a reception at which six or seven hundred students came to do him homage and collect his autograph. There was dead silence as he stood, distinguished and embarrassed, looking beyond their heads. An ironical young man broke the silence with some such words as these: 'After the late Mr Gandhi the Taj Mahal is certainly the most precious possession of the Indian people. Why then did you, Mr Huxley, in your book *Jesting Pilate*, speak in so disparaging a fashion of it? May I enquire, Sir, if you continue to adhere to this unfavourable view?' Huxley was amused and faintly put out. He said that perhaps he had spoken a little too harshly about the Taj Mahal, that he had not intended to wound anyone's feelings, that aesthetics was an uncertain field, that tastes were incommensurable, and then he gradually slid from this perilous ground to his central Tolstoyan theme – the unnatural lives that men lead today. But he wondered afterwards whether perhaps he had been unjust, and so we decided to revisit Agra. We travelled separately: he and his wife with the well-known Indian novelist Mulk Raj Anand; my wife and I in a separate car. We met in Agra and went together to Fatehpur Sikri, Akbar's dead city. Huxley adored it. He moved with the slow, sure-footed, slightly gliding steps of a somnambulist: his grave and urbane charm was moving and very delightful.

On the way to Fatehpur Sikri, he described his earlier visit to India in the 1920s, when he had stayed with one of his Oxford contemporaries, now a member of the Upper House in India, a distinguished man who had welcomed him on this occasion too. He described Jawaharlal Nehru's father, Motilal, who, he said, was a man of exquisite appearance and manners, and sent his shirts to be washed in Paris; he had belonged to the rich and power-loving aristocracy that had sought to use Gandhi for its purposes; but they found that he had outwitted them, that the attempt to harness this great force, or at any rate the flood of popular emotion which Gandhi had brought into being, proved fruitless, that Gandhi ended by controlling them and not, as they had hoped, the other way about. Huxley described the relations of these distinguished and autocratic Brahmins to Gandhi with a kind of benevolent irony, even-toned, slow, deliberate and exceedingly entertaining. He went on to an elaborate enumeration of the wiles and stratagems that he used, whether in California or in India, to escape the bores by whom his life was menaced. He was very simple, very serene, very easy to talk with. The fact that, a few weeks before, his house and all his books had been destroyed by fire seemed hardly to trouble him at all, nor did he by the slightest allusion reveal the fact that he knew that he was suffering from a mortal disease; he complained of his eyesight – his old, familiar infirmity – but said nothing about the cancer that was ultimately to end his life.

When he finally saw the Taj Mahal again, he relented; and decided that it was not as unsightly as he had supposed, but on the contrary, except for the minarets – 'chimney pots' which he still thought a mistake – it was a creditable building after all. We spent the evening together; I think that Jean Guéhenno, the French writer, was also there part of the time. Guéhenno, a melancholy, interesting and idealistic man, was not likely – nor did he intend – to raise anyone's spirits; and the lights in the hotel were very low owing to some permanent power failure. One might have thought that the whole occasion would be one of extreme, if dignified, gloom and depression. But it was not. Huxley was simple, natural and unselfconscious, what he said was unusual and absolutely authentic. Everything about him was so sincere and so interesting that the occasion was wholly enjoyable, and inspired, at any rate in me, a lasting affection and a degree of respect bordering on veneration.

Huxley had spent a great deal of his time collecting facts; he much preferred to be told facts rather than opinions – opinions he could form for himself. But despite this he did not, contrary to common belief, talk like an encyclopaedia. Nor were the hatred of the flesh, the puritanical streak, the ascetic's obsession with scatological detail which his writings sometimes betray, ever in evidence; nor was his conversation strewn with oddly assorted bric-à-brac of abstract knowledge; nor did he ever behave like a writer conscious of his status as a great man. He was courteous, serious and charming, and his movements and his words possessed a dignity and humanity wholly unrelated to the popular image of him in the 1920s. He seemed to be more interesting, and his thought, despite his deliberate manner, seemed to be more direct, spontaneous and moving, more personal and authentic than his writings, which even at their best have something mechanical and derivative. But the recollection that will remain in my mind for the rest of my life is that of a wholly civilised, good and scrupulous man, and one of the greatest imaginable distinction.

# MEETINGS WITH RUSSIAN WRITERS
# IN 1945 AND 1956

Every attempt to produce coherent memories amounts
to falsification. No human memory is so arranged as
to recollect everything in continuous sequence. Letters
and diaries often turn out to be bad assistants.

Anna Akhmatova[1]


## I

IN THE SUMMER of 1945, while I was working as a temporary
official in the British Embassy in Washington, I was informed that
I was to be seconded to our Moscow Embassy for a few months;
the reason given was that it was short-handed, and since I knew
Russian, and had, at the San Francisco Conference (and long before
it), learnt something of official and unofficial American attitudes to
the Soviet Union, I might be of some use in filling a gap until the

I wish to acknowledge my gratitude to Miss Amanda Haight, Dr George
Katkov, Dr Aileen Kelly, Dr Robin Milner-Gulland, Professor Dimitri Obolensky, Mr Peter Oppenheimer, Mrs Josephine Pasternak, Mrs Lydia Pasternak-
Slater, Mr John Simmons and Mrs Patricia Utechin, all of whom were kind
enough to read the first draft of this account. I have greatly profited by their
suggestions, nearly all of which I have followed. For all the faults that remain, I
am, of course, solely responsible. I have never kept a diary, and this account is
based on what I now remember, or recollect that I remembered and sometimes
described to my friends during the last thirty or more years. I know only too well
that memory, at any rate my memory, is not always a reliable witness of facts or
events, particularly of conversations which, at times, I have quoted. I can only say
that I have recorded the facts as accurately as I can recall them. If there is
documentary or other evidence in the light of which this account should be
amplified or corrected, I shall be glad to learn of it. I.B. 1980.
[1] Quoted from L. A. Mandrykina, 'Nenapisannaya kniga: "Listki iz dnevnika"
A. A. Akhmatovoi' ('An Unwritten Book: Anna Akhmatova's "Pages from a
Diary" '), in *Knigi, Arkhivy, Avtografy* (Moscow, 1973), pp. 57–76; the quotation
appears on p. 75. Mandrykina's article is based on material in the archive of A. A.
Akhmatova in the V. I. Lenin State Library in Moscow (archive 1073, Nos 47–69);
the quotation appears in No 47, sheet 2.

New Year, when someone less amateur would be free to come. The War was over. The Potsdam Conference had led to no overt rift among the victorious allies. Despite gloomy forebodings in some quarters in the West, the general mood in official circles in Washington and London was cautiously optimistic; among the general public and in the Press it was much more hopeful and even enthusiastic: the outstanding bravery and appalling sacrifices of Soviet men and women in the war against Hitler created a vast wave of sympathy for their country which, during the second half of 1945, silenced many of the critics of the Soviet system and its methods; mutual understanding and co-operation at every level were very widely and ardently desired. It was during this season of good feeling, which, one was told, reigned equally in the Soviet Union and in Britain, that I left for Moscow.

I had not been in Russia since my family left in 1920 (when I was eleven years old) and I had never seen Moscow. I arrived in the early autumn, was given a table in the Chancery, and did such odd jobs as were assigned to me. Although I reported for work at the Embassy every morning, the task (the only one I was ever asked to do) of reading, summarising and commenting on the content of the Soviet Press was not exactly arduous: the contents of periodicals were, by comparison with the West, monochrome, predictable and repetitive, and the facts and propaganda virtually identical in them all. Consequently I had plenty of spare time on my hands. I used it to visit museums, historic places and buildings, theatres, book-shops, to walk idly about the streets, and so on; but unlike many foreigners, at any rate non-Communist visitors from the West, I had the extraordinary good fortune to meet a number of Russian writers, at least two among them persons of outstanding genius. Before I describe my meetings with them, I should say something about the background of the literary and artistic situation in Moscow and Leningrad as it appeared to me during the fifteen weeks that I spent in the Soviet Union.

The magnificent flowering of Russian poetry which had begun in the 1890s – the bold, creative, numerous, vastly influential experiments in the arts at the beginning of the twentieth century, the main currents within the new movements, the symbolist, post-impressionist, cubist, abstract, expressionist, futurist, suprematist and constructivist movements in painting and sculpture; their various tributaries and confluences in literature, as well as Acmeism, ego- and cubo-futurism, imagism, 'trans-sense' (the *zaumnye*) in poetry; realism and anti-realism in the theatre and the ballet – this vast amalgam, so far from being arrested by war and revolution, continued to derive vitality and inspiration from a vision of a new world. Despite the conservative artistic tastes of the majority of the Bolshevik leaders, anything that could be represented as a 'slap in the face' to bourgeois taste was in principle approved and encouraged: and this opened the way to a great outpouring of exciting manifestos and audacious, controversial, often highly gifted experiments in all the arts and in criticism, which, in due course, were to make a powerful impact on the West. The names of the most original among the poets whose work survived the Revolution, Alexander Blok, Vyacheslav Ivanov, Andrey Bely, Valery Bryusov and, in the next generation, Mayakovsky, Pasternak, Velemir Khlebnikov, Osip Mandel'shtam, Anna Akhmatova; of the painters, Benois, Roerich, Somov, Bakst, Larionov, Goncharova, Kandinsky, Chagall, Soutine, Klyun, Malevich, Tatlin, Lissitzky; of the sculptors, Arkhipenko, Gabo, Pevsner, Lipchitz, Zadkine; of the producers,[1] Meyerhold, Vakhtangov, Tairov, Eisenstein, Pudovkin; of the novelists, Aleksey Tolstoy, Babel', Pil'nyak – all these became widely known in the West. They were not isolated peaks, but were surrounded by foothills. There was a genuine renaissance, different in kind from the artistic scene in other countries, in Russia during the 1920s. Much cross-fertilisation between novelists, poets, artists, critics, historians, scientists took place, and this created a culture of unusual vitality and achievement, an extraordinary upward curve in European civilisation.

Plainly all this was too good to last. The political consequences of the devastation of war and civil war, of the famine, the systematic destruction of lives and institutions by the dictatorship, ended the conditions in which poets and artists could create freely. After a relatively relaxed period during the years of the New Economic Policy, Marxist orthodoxy grew strong enough to challenge and, in the late 1920s, crush all this unorganised revolutionary activity. A collectivist proletarian art was called for; the critic Averbakh led a faction of Marxist zealots against what was described as unbridled individualistic literary licence – or as formalism, decadent aestheticism, kowtowing to the West, opposition to socialist collectivism.

[1] Today called 'directors'.

Persecution and purges began; but since it was not always possible to predict which side would win, this alone, for a time, gave a certain grim excitement to literary life. In the end, in the early 1930s, Stalin decided to put an end to all these politico-literary squabbles, which he plainly regarded as a sheer waste of time and energy. The leftist zealots were liquidated; no more was heard of proletarian culture or collective creation and criticism, nor yet of the non-conformist opposition to it. In 1934 the Party (through the newly created Union of Writers) was put in direct charge of literary activity. A dead level of State-controlled orthodoxy followed: no more argument; no more disturbance of men's minds; the goals were economic, technological, educational – to catch up with the material achievements of the enemy – the capitalist world – and overtake it. If the dark mass of illiterate peasants and workers was to be welded into a militarily and technically invincible modern society, there was no time to be lost; the new revolutionary order was surrounded by a hostile world bent on its destruction; vigilance on the political front left no time for high culture and controversy, or concern for civil liberties and basic human rights. The tune must be called by constituted authority; writers and artists, the importance of whose influence was never denied or ignored, must dance to it.

Some conformed, some did not, to a lesser or greater degree; some felt state tutelage to be oppressive, others accepted and even welcomed it, since they told themselves, and one another, that it conferred upon them a status denied them by the philistine and indifferent West. In 1932 there were some symptoms of a coming relaxation; it did not come. Then came the final horror: the Great Purge, heralded by the repression which followed the assassination of Kirov in 1934 and the notorious political show trials, and culminating in the Ezhov Terror of 1937–8, the wild and indiscriminate mowing down of individuals and groups, later of whole peoples. While Gorky, with his immense prestige in the Party and the nation, was alive, his mere existence may have exercised some moderating influence. The poet Mayakovsky, whose fame and reputation as a voice of the Revolution were almost equal to Gorky's, had committed suicide in 1930 – Gorky died six years later. Soon after that Meyerhold, Mandel'shtam, Babel', Pil'nyak, Klyuev, the critic D. S. Mirsky, the Georgian poets Yashvili and Tabidze – to mention only the most widely known – were arrested and done to death. A few years later, in 1941, the poetess Marina Tsvetaeva, who had not long before returned from Paris, committed suicide. The activities of informers and false witnesses exceeded all previously known bounds; self-prostration, false and wildly implausible confessions, bending before, or active co-operation with, authority, usually failed to save those marked for destruction. For the rest it left painful and humiliating memories from which some of the survivors of the Terror were never completely to recover.

The most authentic and harrowing accounts of the life of the intelligentsia during that murderous period, neither the first nor, probably, the last in the history of Russia, are to be found in Nadezhda Mandel'shtam's and Lydia Chukovskaya's memoirs; and, in a different medium, in Akhmatova's poem *Requiem*. The number of writers and artists exiled and destroyed was such that in 1939 Russian literature, art and thought emerged like an area that had been subjected to a terrible bombardment, with some splendid buildings still relatively intact, but standing bare and solitary in a landscape of ruined and deserted streets. Finally Stalin called a halt to the proscriptions: a breathing space followed; nineteenth-century classics were again treated with respect, old street-names replaced revolutionary nomenclature. The period of convalescence was virtually blank so far as the creative and critical arts were concerned.

Then came the German invasion, and the picture changed again. Such authors of distinction as had survived the Great Purge and had managed to retain their human semblance responded passionately to the great wave of patriotic feeling. Some degree of truth returned to literature: war poems, not only those by Pasternak and Akhmatova, sprang from profound feeling. In the days when all Russians were caught up in the high tide of national unity, and the nightmare of the purges was succeeded by the tragic but inspiring and liberating sense of patriotic resistance and heroic martyrdom, writers, old and young, who expressed it, particularly those who had a vein of genuine poetry in them, were idolised as never before. An astonishing phenomenon took place: poets whose writing had been regarded with disfavour by the authorities, and who had consequently been published rarely and in very limited editions, began to receive letters from soldiers at the fronts, as often as not quoting their least political and most personal lines. I was told that the poetry of Blok, Bryusov, Sologub, Esenin, Tsvetaeva, Maya-kovsky was widely read, learnt by heart and quoted by soldiers and officers and even political commissars. Akhmatova and Pasternak, who had for a long time lived in a kind of internal exile, received an amazingly large number of letters from the front, quoting from both published and unpublished poems, for the most part circulated privately in manuscript copies; there were requests for autographs, for confirmation of the authenticity of texts, for expressions of the author's attitude to this or that problem. In the end this did not fail to impress itself on some of the Party leaders: the value of such writers as patriotic voices of which the State might one day be proud came to be realised by the bureaucrats of literature. The status and personal security of the poets were improved in consequence.

During the immediate post-war years, and, indeed, until the end of their lives, the most distinguished among the older writers found themselves in an odd condition of being objects of simultaneous worship on the part of their readers and of a half-respectful, half-suspicious toleration by the authorities: a small, diminishing Parnassus, sustained by the love and admiration of the young. Public readings by poets, as well as the reciting from memory of poetry at private gatherings and parties of all kinds, had been common in pre-revolutionary Russia; what was novel was a fact described to me by both Pasternak and Akhmatova, that when they read their poems before the vast audiences who packed assembly halls to hear them, and occasionally halted for a word, there were always scores of listeners present who prompted them at once – with passages from works both published and unpub-lished (and in any case not publicly available). No writer could help being moved or could fail to draw strength from this most genuine form of homage; they knew that their status was unique, that this absorbed attention was something that poets in the West might well envy; and yet, despite this sense of contrast, which most Russians feel between what they regard as the open, passionate, spontaneous, 'broad' Russian nature and the dry, calculating, civilised, inhibited, sophisticated approach usually attributed to the West (enormously exaggerated by Slavophils and populists), a good many among them still believed in the existence of an unexhausted Western culture, full of variety and free creative individuality, unlike the grey on grey of daily life in the Soviet Union, broken only by sudden acts of repression; nothing I could say – I speak of more than thirty years ago[1] – could shake this passionate conviction.

However this may be, famous poets were, at this time, heroic figures in the Soviet Union. It may well be so still. What is certain is that the vast increase in literacy, together with the wide circulation of the best-known Russian and foreign literary classics, particularly of translations into the various national languages of the USSR, created a public the responsiveness of which was, and probably still is, unique in the world. There is plenty of evidence that the majority of the avid readers of foreign masterpieces tended at that time to think that life in England and France was similar to that described by Dickens or Balzac; but the intensity of their vision of the worlds of these novelists, their emotional and moral involvement, their often childlike fascination with the lives of characters in these novels, seemed to me to be more direct, fresh, un-used-up, far more imaginative, than the corresponding response of the average readers of fiction in, say, England or France or the United States. The Russian cult of the writer as hero – which began early in the nineteenth century – is bound up with this. I do not know how it is today: perhaps it is all quite different – I can testify only that in the autumn of 1945 the crowded bookshops, with their understocked shelves, the eager literary interest – indeed, enthusiasm – of the government employees who ran them, the fact that even *Pravda* and *Izvestiya* sold out within a few minutes of their appearance in the kiosks, argued a degree of intellectual hunger unlike that found elsewhere. The rigid censorship which, with so much else, suppressed pornography, trash and low-grade thrillers such as fill railway bookstalls in the West, served to make the response of Soviet readers and theatre audiences purer, more direct and naïve than ours; I noticed that at performances of Shakespeare or Sheridan or Griboedov members of the audience, some of them obviously country folk, were apt to react to the action on the stage or to lines spoken by the actors – rhyming couplets in Griboedov's *Woe from Wit*, for example – with loud expressions of approval or disapproval; the excitement generated was, at times, very strong and, to a visitor from the West, both unusual and touching. These audiences were, perhaps, not far removed from those for which Euripides or Shakespeare wrote; my neighbours in the theatre,

---

[1] This essay, written in 1980, contains several references to the then present which have mostly not been altered in the light of more recent events. Ed. 1997.

when they talked to me, often seemed to look on the dramatic action with the sharp and unspoilt eyes of intelligent adolescents – the ideal public of the classical dramatists, novelists and poets. It may be that it is the absence of this kind of popular response that has made some avant-garde art in the West at times seem mannered, contrived and obscure – in the light of this the condemnation of much modern literature and art by Tolstoy, however sweeping, dogmatic and wrong-headed, becomes more intelligible. The contrast between the extraordinary receptivity and interest, critical and uncritical, of the Soviet public in anything that seemed authentic, new, or even true, and the inferiority of the pabulum provided by government-controlled purveyors, astonished me. I had expected a far greater degree of colourless, depressing conformity at all levels. At the official level, which included critics and reviewers, this was indeed so; but not among those to whom I spoke in theatres and cinemas, at lectures, football matches, in trains and trams and bookshops.

When, before my journey to Moscow, I was given advice by British diplomats who had served there, I was warned that meetings with Soviet citizens were difficult to achieve. I was told that a certain number of carefully selected high bureaucrats were to be met at official diplomatic receptions, and that these tended by and large to repeat the Party line and avoid all real contact with foreigners, at any rate those from the West; that ballet-dancers and actors were occasionally permitted to attend such receptions because they were thought to be the simplest-minded and least intellectual among artists, and consequently least likely either to be infected by unorthodox thoughts or to give anything away. In short, the impression I received was that, apart from linguistic obstacles, the general fear of association with foreigners, in particular those coming from capitalist countries, together with specific instructions to members of the Communist Party not to engage in such activities, left all Western missions culturally insulated; that their members (and most journalists and other foreigners) lived in a kind of zoo, with intercommunicating cages, but cut off by a high fence from the outside world. I found that this was to a large extent true, but not as much as I had been led to expect. I did, during my brief stay, meet not only the same well-regimented group of ballet-dancers and literary bureaucrats who were to be seen at all receptions, but also a number of genuinely gifted writers, musicians and producers, among them two poets of genius. One of these was the man I most of all wished to meet, Boris Leonidovich Pasternak, whose poetry and prose I deeply admired. I could not bring myself to seek his acquaintance without some excuse, however transparent. Fortunately I had met his sisters, who were living in Oxford, and one of them had asked me to take a pair of boots for her brother the poet. This was the pretext I needed, and I was most grateful for it.

I arrived in Moscow just in time to attend a dinner arranged by the British Embassy to celebrate an anniversary of its Russian-language publication, *The British Ally*, to which Soviet writers had been invited. The guest of honour was J. B. Priestley, who was then regarded as a firm friend by the authorities of the Soviet Union; his books were much translated, and two of his plays were, I seem to recollect, then being performed in Moscow. That evening Priestley seemed out of humour: he was, I think, exhausted by being taken to too many collective farms and factories – he told me that although he had been well received, he had found the majority of these official visits inconceivably tedious; in addition to this, his royalties had been blocked, conversation through interpreters was horribly stilted, in short he was not enjoying himself, was very tired and longed to go to bed. So, at any rate, his interpreter and guide from the British Embassy whispered to me; he proposed to accompany the guest of honour back to his hotel, and asked me if I would try to do something to fill the awkward gap left by Mr Priestley's early departure. I readily agreed and found myself sitting between the famous director Tairov and the equally distinguished literary historian, critic, translator and inspired writer of children's verse, Korney Chukovsky. Opposite me was the best known of all Soviet film directors, Sergey Eisenstein. He looked somewhat depressed: the reason for this, as I learned later, was not far to seek.[1] I asked him to what years of his life he looked back

[1] A short while before he had been severely reprimanded by Stalin, who had been shown the second part of his film *Ivan the Terrible*, and had expressed his displeasure, mainly, I was told, because Tsar Ivan (with whom Stalin may, to some degree, have identified himself) had been represented as a deeply disturbed young ruler, violently shaken by his discovery of treason and sedition among his boyars, tormented by the need to apply savage measures if he was to save the State and his own life, and transformed by this experience into a lonely, gloomy despot, suspicious to the point of neurosis, even while he was raising his country to a pinnacle of greatness.

with the greatest pleasure. He replied that the early post-revolutionary period was far and away the best in his own life as a creative artist, and in the lives of many others. It was a time, he said wistfully, when wild and marvellous things could be done with impunity. He remembered with particular delight an occasion at the beginning of the 1920s when pigs covered with grease were let loose among the audience of a Moscow theatre, who leapt on to their seats, terrified; people shrieked, the pigs squealed. 'This was just what was required by our surrealist spectacle. Most of us who were active in those days were happy to be living and working then; we were young and defiant and full of ideas; it did not matter whether we were Marxists or formalists or futurists – painters, writers or musicians – we all met and quarrelled, sometimes very bitterly, and stimulated each other; we really did enjoy ourselves, and produced something, too.'

Tairov said much the same. He, too, spoke wistfully about the experimental theatre of the 1920s, about the genius of both Vakhtangov and Meyerhold; about the boldness and vitality of the short-lived Russian modern movement, which, in his view, was far more interesting than anything achieved on the stage by Piscator or Brecht or Gordon Craig. I asked him what had brought the movement to an end: 'Things change,' he said, 'but it was a wonderful time; not to the taste of Stanislavsky or Nemirovich, but absolutely wonderful.' The actors of the Moscow Art Theatre were not now educated enough, he said, to understand what Chekhov's characters were really like: their social status, their attitudes, manners, accents, their entire culture, outlook, habits were a closed book to the rising actors and actresses of the present; no one had been more aware of this than Chekhov's widow, Olga Knipper, and, of course, Stanislavsky himself; the greatest actor who survived from those days was the peerless, but rapidly ageing, Kachalov; he would soon retire and then, with modernism gone and naturalism in decay, would something new spring up? He doubted it: 'A few minutes ago I said to you "Things change." But they also do not change. This is even worse.' And he fell into gloomy silence.

Tairov proved right on both scores. Certainly Kachalov was the best actor I have seen in my life. When he was on the stage as Gaev in Chekhov's *Cherry Orchard* (he played the part of the student in the original performance) he literally fascinated the audience, nor did the other actors take their eyes off him: the beauty of his voice and the charm and expressiveness of his movements were such that one wished to go on looking at him and listening to him for ever; this may have distorted the balance of the play, but Kachalov's performance that night, like Ulanova's dancing in Prokofiev's *Cinderella*, which I saw a month later (and Chaliapin in *Boris Godunov* many years before), remains in my memory as an unsurpassed summit in terms of which to judge all later performances. So far as power of expression on the stage is concerned, these Russians still seem to me to have no equals in the twentieth century.

The neighbour on my right, the critic Korney Chukovsky, talked with rare wit and charm about writers, both Russian and English. He said that his brisk dismissal by the guest of honour reminded him of the visit to Russia of the American journalist Dorothy Thompson. She came with her husband, Sinclair Lewis, whose fame in Russia in the 1930s was very great: 'Several of us called on him in his hotel room – we wished to tell him how much his wonderful novels had meant to us. He sat with his back to us, typing away on his machine, and did not once turn his head to look at us; he did not utter a sound. This had a certain sublimity.' I did my best to assure him that his own works were read and greatly admired by Russian scholars in English-speaking countries; by Maurice Bowra, for example (who, in his memoirs, gives an account of meeting him during the First World War), and by Oliver Elton – the only English writers interested in Russian literature whom at that time I knew personally. Chukovsky told me of his two visits to England, the first at the beginning of the century when he was very poor and earned a few shillings by casual work – he had learned English by reading Carlyle's *Past and Present* and *Sartor Resartus*, the second of which he had bought for one penny, and which he extracted for me there and then out of his waistcoat pocket. He was a frequenter in those days, he told me, of the Poetry Bookshop, whose celebrated owner, the poet Harold Monro, befriended him and introduced him to various British men of letters including Robert Ross, Oscar Wilde's friend, of whom he retained an agreeable memory. He felt, he said, at ease in the Poetry Bookshop, but nowhere else in England; like Herzen, he admired and was amused by the social structure and the manners of the English, but like him had made no friends among them. He loved Trollope: 'What wonderful parsons [*popy*], charming, eccentric –

nothing like that here, in old Russia; here they were sunk in sloth and stupidity and greed. They were a miserable crew. The present ones, who have had a difficult time since the Revolution, are a much better lot: at least they can read and write; some are decent and honourable men. But you will never meet our priests – why should you want to? I am sure that English clergymen are still the most delightful people in the world.' He then told me about his second visit, during the First World War, when he came with a party of Russian journalists to report on the British war effort; they were entertained by Lord Derby, with whom he had found little common ground, at a weekend at Knowsley, of which he also gave an exceedingly entertaining and not very respectful account.

Chukovsky was a writer of high distinction who had made his name before the Revolution. He was a man of the left, and welcomed the Revolution; like all intellectuals of any independence of mind, he had had his share of harassment by the Soviet authorities. There are more ways than one of preserving one's sanity under a despotism: he achieved his own by a kind of ironical detachment, careful behaviour and considerable stoicism of character; the decision to confine himself to the relatively calm waters of nineteenth-century literature in Russian and in English, of children's verse, of translation, may have saved himself and his family, if only just, from the dreadful fate of some of their closest friends. He informed me that he had one overmastering wish; if I could satisfy it he would do almost anything for me in return: he longed to read Trollope's autobiography. His friend Ivy Litvinov, the wife of Maxim Litvinov, the former Foreign Minister and Ambassador to the United States, who was living in Moscow, could not find her own copy and thought it unsafe to order one from England in view of the extreme suspicion in which all relations with foreign countries were held; could I supply it? I did so a few months later, and he was delighted by it. I said that what I in my turn wished for most of all was to meet Boris Pasternak, who was living in the writers' village of Peredelkino, where Chukovsky, too, had a cottage. Chukovsky said that he admired Pasternak's poetry deeply; personally, although he loved him, he had had his ups and downs with him – his interest in Nekrasov's civic poetry and in populist writers of the late nineteenth century had always irritated Pasternak, who was a pure poet out of tune with the Soviet regime, with a particular distaste for committed – *engagé* – literature of any kind; nevertheless, he was at the moment on good terms with him, would arrange a meeting, and warmly invited me to visit him too, on the same day.

This was, as I was soon to discover, a courageous, not to say foolhardy, act: contact with foreigners – especially members of Western embassies, all of whom were regarded by the Soviet authorities, and particularly by Stalin himself, as spies – was, to say the least, strongly discouraged. Realisation of this fact led me later, in some cases too late, to exercise caution in meeting Soviet citizens informally – it placed them in a degree of danger which not all those who wished to see me seemed fully to realise; some did so, and knew that in meeting me they were taking a risk, but took it because their desire to be in contact with life in the West was overwhelming. Others were less reckless, and I respected their well-grounded fears and met fewer Soviet citizens, especially those not protected to some extent by their fame abroad, than I could have wished, for fear of compromising them. Even so, I probably did inadvertent harm to innocent people whom I met accidentally, or because they assured me, in some cases, as it turned out, mistakenly, that it involved no risk for them. Whenever I hear of the subsequent fate of some of these, I feel qualms of conscience, and blame myself for not having resisted the temptation of meeting some of the most unspoilt, delightful, responsive, moving human beings I have ever come across, with a quality of intellectual gaiety astonishing in their circumstances, consumed, for the most part, with an enormous curiosity about life beyond the frontiers of their country, anxious to establish a purely human relationship with a visitor from that outer world who spoke their language and, it seemed to them, understood them and was understood by them. I do not know of any case of imprisonment or worse, but I do know of cases of harassment and persecution to which meetings with me may have contributed. It is difficult to tell, for the victims often never knew why they were punished. One can only hope that survivors do not feel too bitterly towards the foreign visitors for the harm of which, unwittingly and perhaps too unthinkingly, we may have been a cause.

The visit to Peredelkino was arranged for a week after the dinner at which I met Korney Chukovsky. In the meanwhile, at another festivity in honour of Priestley (for whose presence I am still grateful, since it helped to open doors to me), I met Mme

Afinogenova, a Hungarian-American dancer, the widow of a playwright 'honourably' killed – in an air-raid on Moscow in 1941 – who was evidently authorised, and perhaps instructed, to organise a salon for foreign visitors with cultural interests. At any rate, she invited me to it, and there I met a number of writers. The best known among them was the poet Ilya Sel'vinsky ('Sel'vinsky had his hour, but it is, thank God, long past,' said Pasternak to me later), who had had the temerity to suggest that if socialist realism was the correct genre of imaginative writing, it might perhaps be equally compatible with Communist ideology to develop a literature of socialist romanticism – a freer use of the imagination, equally impregnated with total loyalty to the Soviet system. He had recently been harshly reproved for this, and when I met him was in an obviously nervous state. He asked me whether I agreed that the five greatest English writers were Shakespeare, Byron, Dickens, Wilde and Shaw; with perhaps Milton and Burns as runners-up. I said that I had no doubt about Shakespeare and Dickens, but before I could continue he went on to say that it was our new writers that they were interested in – what about Greenwood and Aldridge? What could I say about them? I realised that these were names of contemporary writers, but confessed that I had never heard of them – this was, perhaps, because I had been abroad during the greater part of the War – what had they written?

This was clearly not believed. I discovered later that Aldridge was an Australian Communist novelist and that Greenwood had written a popular novel called *Love on the Dole*; their works had been translated into Russian and published in large editions. Ordinary Soviet readers had little idea of what scales of values obtained in other societies, or sections of them; an official literary committee, directed by the cultural department of the Party's Central Committee, decided what was to be translated and how widely it was to be distributed, and modern British writing at that moment was in effect represented principally by A. J. Cronin's *Hatter's Castle,* two or three plays by Somerset Maugham and Priestley, and – so it seemed – the novels of Greenwood and Aldridge (the age of Graham Greene, C. P. Snow, Iris Murdoch and the 'angry young man' – who have since been extensively translated – had not yet dawned).

It was my impression that my hosts thought that I was less than honest when I said that I knew nothing of the two authors whom they mentioned, because I was an agent of a capitalist power, and therefore obliged to ignore the merits of left-wing writers, much as they themselves were committed to real or pretended ignorance of most émigré Russian writers and composers. 'I know,' said Sel'vinsky, speaking loudly, with great rhetorical force, as if he were addressing a much wider audience, 'I know that we are called conformists in the West. We are. We conform because we find that whenever we deviate from the Party's directives it always turns out that the Party was right and that we were wrong. It has always been so. It is not only that they say that they know better: they do; they see further: their eyes are sharper, their horizons are wider, than ours.' The rest of the company looked uncomfortable: these words were plainly intended for the concealed microphones without which we could scarcely have met as we did. Under dictatorships public and private expressions of opinion may differ; but Sel'vinsky's outburst was, perhaps because of the insecurity of his own position, too clumsy and overdone: hence the embarrassed silence which followed. I realised none of this at the time, and argued that free discussion, even of political issues, was no danger to democratic institutions: 'We are a scientifically governed society,' said a handsome lady who had once been one of Lenin's secretaries and was married to a famous Soviet writer, 'and if there is no room for free thinking in physics – a man who questions the laws of motion is obviously ignorant or mad – why should we, Marxists, who have discovered the laws of history and society, permit free thinking in the social sphere? Freedom to be wrong is not freedom; you seem to think that we lack freedom of political discussion; I simply do not understand what you mean. Truth liberates: we are freer than you in the West.' Lenin was quoted, so was Lunacharsky. When I said that I remembered propositions of this sort in the works of Auguste Comte, that this was the thesis of French positivists in the nineteenth century, whose views were surely not accepted by Marx or Engels, a chill fell upon the room, and we passed on to harmless literary gossip. I had learnt my lesson. To argue about ideas while Stalin was in power was to invite predictable answers from some, and to put those who remained silent in some jeopardy. I never saw Mme Afinogenova or any of her guests again. I had obviously behaved with conspicuous absence of tact, and their reaction was perfectly comprehensible.

II

A few days later, accompanied by Lina Ivanovna Prokofiev, the composer's estranged wife, I took the train to Peredelkino. Gorky, I was told, had organised this colony to provide recognised writers with an environment in which they could work in peace. Given the temperament of creative artists, this well-intentioned plan did not always lead to harmonious coexistence: some of the personal and political tensions could be sensed even by an ignorant stranger like myself. I walked down the tree-lined road which led to the houses inhabited by the writers. On the way there we were stopped by a man who was digging a ditch; he climbed out of it, said his name was Yazvitsky, asked after our names, and spoke at some length about an excellent novel that he had written called *The Fires of the Inquisition*; he warmly recommended it to us and told us that we should read an even better novel he was in the course of writing about Ivan III and medieval Russia. He wished us Godspeed and returned to his ditch. My companion thought it all somewhat uncalled-for, but I was charmed by this unexpected, direct, open-hearted and utterly disarming monologue; the simplicity and immediacy, even when it was naïve, the absence of formalities and small talk which seemed to hold everywhere outside official circles, was, and is, wonderfully attractive.

It was a warm, sunlit afternoon in early autumn. Pasternak, his wife and his son Leonid were seated round a rough wooden table in the tiny garden at the back of the dacha. The poet greeted us warmly. He was once described by his friend the poetess Marina Tsvetaeva as looking like an Arab and his horse: he had a dark, melancholy, expressive, very *racé* face, now familiar from many photographs and his father's paintings; he spoke slowly, in a low tenor monotone, with a continuous, even sound, something between a humming and a drone, which those who met him almost always remarked; each vowel was elongated as if in some plaintive, lyrical aria in an opera by Tchaikovsky, but with more concentrated force and tension.

With an awkward gesture I offered him the parcel that I was holding in my hands, and explained that I had brought him a pair of boots sent him by his sister Lydia. 'No, no, what is all this?' he said, visibly embarrassed, as if I were offering him a charitable gift: 'It must be a mistake, this must be for my brother.' I, too, became acutely embarrassed. His wife, Zinaida Nikolaevna, tried to put me at my ease and asked me whether England was recovering from the effects of the War. Before I could answer, Pasternak broke in: 'I was in London in the '30s – in 1935 – on my way back from the Anti-Fascist Congress in Paris. Let me tell you what happened. It was summer, I was in the country, when two officials, probably from the NKVD – not, I think, the Writers' Union – called – we were not quite so afraid of such visits then, I suppose – and one of them said "Boris Leonidovich, an Anti-Fascist Congress is taking place in Paris. You have been invited to it. We should like you to go tomorrow. You will go via Berlin: you can stay there for a few hours and see anyone you wish: you will arrive in Paris on the next day and will address the Congress in the evening." I said that I had no suitable clothes for such a visit. They said that they would see to that. They offered me a formal morning coat and striped trousers, a white shirt with stiff cuffs and a wing collar, a magnificent pair of black patent leather boots which, I found, fitted perfectly. But I somehow managed to go in my everyday clothes. I was later told that pressure had been brought to bear at the last minute by André Malraux, one of the chief organisers of the Congress, to get me invited. He had explained to the Soviet authorities that not to send me and Babel' might cause unnecessary speculation, since we were very well known in the West, and there were, at that time, not many Soviet writers to whom European and American liberals would be so ready to listen. So, although I was not on the original list of Soviet delegates – how could I possibly be? – they agreed.'

He went via Berlin, as arranged, where he met his sister Josephine and her husband, and said that when he arrived at the Congress many important and famous people – Dreiser, Gide, Malraux, Forster, Aragon, Auden, Spender, Rosamond Lehmann and other celebrities – were there. 'I spoke. I said "I understand that this is a meeting of writers to organise resistance to Fascism. I have only one thing to say to you about that. Do not organise. Organisation is the death of art. Only personal independence matters. In 1789, 1848, 1917 writers were not organised for or against anything; do not, I implore you, do not organise." I think they were very surprised. But what else could I say? I thought I would get into trouble at home after that, but no one ever said a word to me about it, then or now.[1] I went on from Paris to

---

[1] I asked André Malraux about this many years later. He said that he did not remember this speech.

London, where I saw my friend Lomonosov, a most fascinating man, like his namesake, a kind of scientist – an engineer. Then I travelled back to Leningrad in one of our boats, and shared a cabin with Shcherbakov, then the Secretary of the Writers' Union, who was tremendously influential.[1] I talked without ceasing, day and night. He begged me to stop and let him sleep. But I went on and on. Paris and London had awoken me, I could not stop. He begged for mercy, but I was relentless. He must have thought me quite deranged; it may be that I owe a good deal to his diagnosis of my condition.' Pasternak did not explicitly say that what he meant was that to have been thought a little mad, or at least very eccentric, might have helped to save him during the Great Purge; but the others present told me that they understood this all too well, and explained it to me later.

Pasternak asked me whether I had read his prose – in particular *The Childhood of Lüvers*, which I greatly admired. I said that I had. 'I can see by your expression', he said, quite unjustly, 'that you think that these writings are contrived, tortured, self-conscious, horribly modernist – no, no, don't deny it, you do think this and you are absolutely right. I am ashamed of them – not of my poetry, but of my prose – it was influenced by what was weakest and most muddled in the symbolist movement, which was fashionable in those years, full of mystical chaos – of course Andrey Bely was a genius – *Petersburg*, *Kotik Letaev* are full of wonderful things – I know that, you need not tell me – but his influence was fatal – Joyce is another matter – all I wrote then was obsessed, forced, broken, artificial, no good [*negodno*]; but now I am writing something entirely different: something new, quite new, luminous, elegant, harmonious, well-proportioned [*stroinoe*], classically pure and simple – what Winckelmann wanted, yes, and Goethe; and this will be my last word, and most important word, to the world. It is, yes, it is, what I wish to be remembered by; I shall devote the rest of my life to it.'

I cannot vouch for the accuracy of all these words, but this is how I remember them and his manner of speaking. This projected work later became *Doctor Zhivago*. He had in 1945 completed a draft of a few early chapters, which he asked me to read and take to his sisters in Oxford; I did so, but was not to know about the plan

[1] Shcherbakov later became a powerful member of Stalin's Politburo, and died in 1945.

for the entire novel until much later. After that, he was silent for a while; none of us spoke. He then told us how much he liked Georgia, Georgian writers, Yashvili, Tabidze, and Georgian wine, how well received he always was there. He then politely asked me about what was going on in the West; did I know Herbert Read and his doctrine of personalism? Here he explained that the doctrine of personalism basically derived from the moral philosophy – in particular the idea of individual freedom – of Kant, and of his interpreter Hermann Cohen, whom he had known well and greatly admired when he was his student in Marburg before the First World War. Kantian individualism – Blok had misinterpreted him completely, had made him a mystic in his poem *Kant* – did I know it? Did I know Stefan Schimansky, a personalist who had edited some of his, Pasternak's, work in translation? There was nothing here in Russia about which he could tell me. I must realise that the clock had stopped in Russia (I noticed that neither he nor any of the other writers I met ever used the words 'Soviet Union') in 1928 or so, when relations with the outer world were in effect cut off; the description of him and his work in, for instance, the Soviet Encyclopaedia, made no reference to his later life or work.

He was interrupted by Lydia Seifullina, an elderly, well-known writer who came in while he was in mid-course: 'My fate is exactly the same,' she said: 'the last lines of the Encyclopaedia article about me say "Seifullina is at present in a state of psychological and artistic crisis" – this has not been changed in the last twenty years. So far as the Soviet reader is concerned, I am still in a state of crisis, of suspended animation. We are like people in Pompeii, you and I, Boris Leonidovich, buried by ashes in mid-sentence. And we know so little: Maeterlinck and Kipling, I know, are dead; but Wells, Sinclair Lewis, Joyce, Bunin, Khodasevich – are they alive?' Pasternak looked embarrassed and changed the subject to French writers generally. He had been reading Proust – French Communist friends had sent him the entire masterpiece – he knew it, he said, and had reread it lately. He had not then heard of Sartre or Camus,[1] and thought little of Hemingway ('Why Anna Andreevna [Akhmatova] thinks anything of him I cannot imagine,' he said). He pressed me warmly to visit him in his Moscow apartment – he would be there from October.

---

[1] By 1956 he had read one or two of Sartre's plays, but nothing by Camus, who had been condemned as reactionary and pro-Fascist.

He spoke in magnificent, slow-moving periods, with occasional intense rushes of words; his talk often overflowed the banks of grammatical structure – lucid passages were succeeded by wild but always marvellously vivid and concrete images – and these might be followed by dark words when it was difficult to follow him – and then he would suddenly come into the clear again; his speech was at all times that of a poet, as were his writings. Someone once said that there are poets who are poets when they write poetry and prose-writers when they write prose; others are poets in everything that they write. Pasternak was a poet of genius in all that he did and was; his ordinary conversation displayed it as his writings do. I cannot begin to describe its quality. The only other person who seems to me to have talked as he talked was Virginia Woolf, who, to judge from the few occasions on which I met her, made one's mind race as he did, and obliterated one's normal vision of reality in the same exhilarating and, at times, terrifying way.

I use the word 'genius' advisedly. I am sometimes asked what I mean by this highly evocative but imprecise term. In answer, I can only say this: the dancer Nijinsky was once asked how he managed to leap so high. He is reported to have answered that he saw no great problem in this. Most people when they leapt in the air came down at once. 'Why should you come down immediately? Stay in the air a little before you return, why not?' he is reported to have said. One of the criteria of genius seems to me to be the power to do something perfectly simple and visible which ordinary people cannot, and know that they cannot, do – nor do they know how it is done, or why they cannot begin to do it. Pasternak at times spoke in great leaps; his use of words was the most imaginative I have ever known; it was wild and very moving. There are, no doubt, many varieties of literary genius: Eliot, Joyce, Yeats, Auden, Russell did not (in my experience) talk like this.

I did not wish to overstay my welcome: I left the poet, excited, and indeed overwhelmed, by his words and by his personality. I went on to Chukovsky's neighbouring dacha, and although he was charming, friendly, interesting, remarkably penetrating and, indeed, brilliantly amusing as a talker, I could think only about the poet with whom I had been an hour before. At Chukovsky's house I met Samuil Marshak, translator of Burns and also a writer of children's verse, who, by standing aside from the main stream of ideology and political storms, and, perhaps, because he enjoyed the protection of Maxim Gorky, managed to survive intact during the darkest days. He was one of the few writers permitted to meet foreigners. During my weeks in Moscow he showed me much kindness, and was, indeed, one of the nicest and most warm-hearted members of the Moscow intelligentsia whom it was my good fortune to meet; he talked freely and painfully about the horrors of the past, showed little faith in the future, and preferred to discuss English and Scottish literature, which he loved and understood, but about which he seemed to me to have little of interest to say. There were others there, among them a writer whose name, if it was mentioned, I had not taken in. I asked him about the Soviet literary scene: who were the most notable authors? He mentioned various writers, among them Lev Kassil'. I said, 'The author of *Shvambraniya* [a fantasy for adolescents]?' 'Yes,' he said, 'the author of *Shvambraniya*.' 'But that is a poor novel,' I said: 'I read it some years ago – I thought it had no imagination and was both dull and naïve – do you like it?' 'Yes,' he said, 'I do rather – it seems to me sincere and not badly written.' I disagreed. Some hours later, when darkness fell and I said that I was very bad at finding my way anywhere, he volunteered to accompany me to the railway station. As we were parting I said to him 'You have been wonderfully kind to me all day – I am so sorry that I never took in your name.' 'Lev Kassil',' he said. I stood rooted to the ground in shame and remorse, crushed by my gaffe. 'But', I said, 'why didn't you tell me? *Shvambraniya* . . .'. 'I respect you for saying what you really thought – the truth is not easy for us writers to come by.' I went on apologising until the train arrived. No one in my experience has ever behaved so admirably; I have never before or since met an author so free from vanity or *amour propre* of any kind.

While I was waiting for the train it began to rain. There were only two other persons on the platform, a young-looking couple, and we all huddled for cover under the only protection we could find – some planks jutting over an old, dilapidated fence. We exchanged a few words – they turned out to be young students – the young man said he was a chemist, the girl was a student of nineteenth-century Russian history, in particular of revolutionary movements. We were in complete darkness – the station had no light – and we could scarcely see each other's faces; consequently they felt reasonably secure with a total stranger and talked freely. The girl said that they were taught that in the last century the Russian Empire was a huge prison with no liberty of thought or expression: but although they thought this generally true, radicals did seem to have got away with quite a lot, and dissidence without actual terrorism did not then, as a rule, mean torture and death; and even terrorists escaped. 'Why', I said, I admit not altogether innocently, 'can people not speak their minds now on social issues?' 'If anyone tries,' said the young man, 'he is swept away as with a broom, and we do not know what happens to him; no one ever sees him or hears from him again.' We changed the subject and they told me that what young Russians at this time read most avidly were nineteenth-century novels and stories: not Chekhov, it turned out, nor Turgenev, who seemed to them antiquated and preoccupied with problems of little interest to them; nor Tolstoy – perhaps because (so they said) they were fed on *War and Peace* as the great national patriotic epic too insistently during the War. They read, when they could get them, Dostoevsky, Leskov, Garshin, and the more accessible foreign masters – Stendhal, Flaubert (not Balzac or Dickens), Hemingway and, somewhat unexpectedly, O. Henry. 'And Soviet writers? What about Sholokhov, Fedin, Fadeev, Gladkov, Furmanov?' I said, reeling off the first names of contemporary Soviet authors that came into my head. 'Do *you* like them?' the girl asked. 'Gorky is sometimes good,' said the young man, 'and I used to like Romain Rolland. I suppose you have great and marvellous writers in your country?' I said 'No, not marvellous', but they seemed incredulous, and may have thought that I was peculiarly jaundiced about British writers, or else was a Communist who did not care for bourgeois artists of any kind. The train arrived and we entered different carriages – the conversation could not have continued before others.

Like these students, many Russians (at least at that time) seemed convinced that in the West – England, France, Italy – there was a magnificent flowering of art and literature, inaccessible to them. When I threw doubts on this I was never really believed: at best, it was attributed to politeness or world-weary capitalist ennui. Even Pasternak and his friends were firmly convinced that there was a golden West where writers and critics of genius had created, and were creating, masterpieces concealed from them. This belief was very widespread. Most of the writers whom I met in 1945 and 1956, Zoshchenko, Marshak, Seifullina, Chukovsky, Vera Inber, Sel'vinsky, Kassil' and a dozen others, and not only writers but musicians like Prokofiev, Neuhaus, Samosud, producers like Eisenstein and Tairov, painters and critics whom I met in public

places, at official receptions given by VOKS (the Society for
Promoting Cultural Relations with Foreigners) and very occasionally in their own homes, philosophers whom I met at a session of
the Academy of Sciences which I was invited to address on the
initiative of none other than Lazar' Kaganovich, just before his fall
from grace and power – all these persons were not only immensely
curious about – indeed, hungry for news of – progress in arts and
letters in Europe (rather less in America), but were firmly
convinced that marvellous works of art and literature and thought
were ceaselessly being born there, hidden from their eyes by the
rigid Soviet censors. *Omne ignotum pro magnifico*. I had no wish
to denigrate Western achievements, but I tried to indicate that our
cultural development was less irresistibly triumphant than they
generously supposed. It may be that some of those who emigrated
to the West are still looking for this rich cultural life, or else feel
disillusioned. The campaign against 'rootless cosmopolitans' was
clearly directed in part against this extraordinary pro-Western
enthusiasm, aroused in the first place, perhaps, by rumours of life
in the West stemming from returned Soviet soldiers, both ex-
prisoners and the conquering battalions themselves, as well as
being the inevitable reaction to the steady and very crude campaign
of vilification of Western culture in the Soviet press and on the
radio. Russian nationalism used as an antidote against such
unhealthy interest on the part of, at any rate, the educated section
of the population, and fed, as so often, by ferocious anti-Semitic
propaganda, in its turn produced strong pro-Jewish and pro-
Western feeling which seemed to me to have taken deep root
among the intelligentsia. By 1956 there was rather less ignorance
about the West, and perhaps correspondingly less enthusiasm, but
still a great deal more than the reality justified.

After Pasternak returned to Moscow, I visited him almost
weekly and came to know him well. He always spoke with his
peculiar brand of vitality, and flights of imaginative genius which
no one has been able to convey; nor can I hope to describe the
transforming effect of his presence, his voice and gestures. He
talked about books and writers; I wish I had made notes at the
time. At this distance of years I can remember only that of modern
Western writers he loved Proust most of all, and was steeped in his
novel and in *Ulysses* (he had not read Joyce's later work). When,
some years later, I brought to Moscow with me two or three
volumes of Kafka in English, he took no interest in them, and later,

so he told me, gave them to Akhmatova, who admired them intensely. He spoke about French symbolists and about Verhaeren and Rilke, both of whom he had met and the second of whom he greatly admired as both a man and a writer. He was steeped in Shakespeare. He was dissatisfied with his own renderings, particularly of *Hamlet* and *Romeo and Juliet*: 'I have tried to make Shakespeare work for me,' he said early in the conversation, 'but it has not been a success.' And he then quoted examples of what he regarded as his own failures in translation, which, unfortunately, I have forgotten. One evening during the War, he told me, he was listening to the BBC and heard poetry being read aloud – he understood spoken English with difficulty but this seemed to him wonderful. He asked himself 'Who is this by?' – it seemed familiar. 'Why, it is by me,' he said to himself; but it turned out to be a passage from Shelley's *Prometheus Unbound*.

He grew up, he said, in the shadow of Tolstoy, whom his father knew well – to him an incomparable genius, greater than Dickens or Dostoevsky, a writer who stood with Shakespeare and Goethe and Pushkin. His father, the painter, had taken him to see Tolstoy on his deathbed, in 1910, at Astapovo. He found it impossible to be critical towards him: Russia and Tolstoy were one. As for Russian poets, Blok was of course the dominant genius of his time, but he did not find his quality of feeling sympathetic. He would not enlarge on this. Bely was closer to him, a man of strange, unheard-of insights, magical and a holy fool in the tradition of Russian Orthodoxy. Bryusov he considered a self-constructed, ingenious, mechanical musical-box, a clever, calculating operator, not a poet at all. He did not mention Mandel'shtam. He felt most tenderly towards Marina Tsvetaeva, to whom he had been bound by many years of friendship.

His feelings towards Mayakovsky were more ambivalent: he had known him well, they had been close friends, and he had learnt from him; he was, of course, a titanic destroyer of old forms but, he added, unlike other Communists, he was at all times a human being – but no, he was not a major poet, not an immortal god like Tyutchev or Blok, not even a demi-god like Fet or Bely; time had diminished him; he was needed, he was indispensable in his day, what those times had called for – there are poets, he said, who have their hour, Aseev, poor Klyuev – liquidated – Sel'vinsky – even Esenin – they fulfil an urgent need of the day, their gifts are of crucial importance to the development of poetry in their country, and then they are no more; Mayakovsky was far and away the greatest of these – *The Cloud in Trousers* had a central historical importance, but the shouting was unbearable: he inflated his talent and tortured it until it burst: the sad rags of the multicoloured balloon still lay in one's path if one was a Russian – he was gifted, important, but coarse and not grown up, and ended as a poster-artist; Mayakovsky's love-affairs had been disastrous for him as a man and a poet; he had loved Mayakovsky as a man – his suicide was one of the blackest days in his own life.

Pasternak was a Russian patriot – his sense of his own historical connection with his country was very deep. He told me again and again how glad he was to spend his summers in the writers' village, Peredelkino, for it had once been part of the estate of that great Slavophil, Yury Samarin: the true lines of tradition led from the legendary Sadko to the Stroganovs and the Kochubeys, to Derzhavin, Zhukovsky, Tyutchev, Pushkin, Baratynsky, Lermontov, to the Aksakovs, Tolstoy, Fet, Bunin, Annensky – to the Slavophils in particular – not to the liberal intelligentsia, which, as Tolstoy maintained, did not know what men lived by. This passionate, almost obsessive, desire to be thought a Russian writer with roots deep in Russian soil was particularly evident in his negative feelings towards his Jewish origins. He was unwilling to discuss the subject – he was not embarrassed by it, but he disliked it: he wished the Jews to assimilate, to disappear as a people. Apart from his immediate family, he had no interest in relatives, past or present. He spoke to me as a believing, if idiosyncratic, Christian. Among consciously Jewish writers he admired Heine, Hermann Cohen (his neo-Kantian philosophical mentor in Marburg), whose ideas – in particular, his philosophy of history – he evidently thought profound and convincing. If I mentioned Jews or Palestine, this, I observed, caused him visible distress; in this respect he differed from his father, the painter. I once asked Akhmatova whether others of her intimate Jewish friends – Mandel'shtam or Zhirmunsky or Emma Gerstein – were sensitive on this subject: she said that they had little liking for the conventional Jewish bourgeoisie from which they sprang, but did not deliberately avoid the subject as Pasternak was apt to do.

His artistic taste had been formed in his youth and he remained faithful to the masters of that period. The memory of Scriabin – he had at one time thought of becoming a composer himself – was sacred to him; I shall not easily forget the paean of praise offered by Pasternak and Neuhaus (the celebrated musician and former husband of Pasternak's wife Zinaida) to Scriabin, by whose music they had both been influenced, and to the symbolist painter Vrubel', whom, with Nicholas Roerich, they prized above all contemporary painters. Picasso and Matisse, Braque and Bonnard, Klee and Mondrian seemed to mean as little to them as Kandinsky or Malevich.

There is a sense in which Akhmatova and Gumilev and Marina Tsvetaeva are the last great voices of the nineteenth century (with Pasternak and, in his very different fashion, Mandel'shtam in some interspace between the centuries), and remain the last representatives of what can only be called the second Russian renaissance, for all that the Acmeists wished to relegate symbolism to the nineteenth century, and declared themselves poets of their own time. They seemed basically untouched by the modern movement – their contemporaries, Picasso, Stravinsky, Eliot, Joyce – even when they admired them, a movement which, like many others, was aborted in Russia by political events.

Pasternak loved everything Russian, and was prepared to forgive his country all her shortcomings, all save the barbarism of Stalin's reign; but even that, in 1945, he regarded as the darkness before a dawn which he was straining his eyes to detect, the hope expressed in the last chapters of *Doctor Zhivago*. He believed himself to be in communion with the inner life of the Russian people, to share its hopes and fears and dreams, to be its voice as, in their different fashions, Tyutchev, Tolstoy, Dostoevsky, Chekhov and Blok had been (by the time I knew him he conceded nothing to Nekrasov). In conversation with me during my Moscow visits, when we were always alone, before a polished desk on which not a book or a scrap of paper was to be seen, he repeated his conviction that he lived close to the heart of his country, and sternly and repeatedly denied this role to Gorky and Mayakovsky, especially to the former, and felt that he had something to say to the rulers of Russia, something of immense importance which only he could say, although what this was – he spoke of it often – seemed dark and incoherent to me. This may well have been due to lack of understanding on my part – although Anna Akhmatova told me that when he spoke in this prophetic strain, she, too, failed to understand him.

It was when he was in one of these ecstatic moods that he told me of his telephone conversation with Stalin about Mandel'shtam's arrest, the famous conversation of which many differing versions circulated and still circulate. I can only reproduce the story as I remember that he told it me in 1945. According to his account he was in his Moscow flat with his wife and son and no one else, when the telephone rang and a voice told him that it was the Kremlin speaking, and that comrade Stalin wished to speak to him. He assumed that this was an idiotic practical joke and put down the receiver. The telephone rang again and the voice somehow convinced him that the call was authentic. Stalin then asked him whether he was speaking to Boris Leonidovich Pasternak; Pasternak said that it was indeed he. Stalin asked whether he was present when a lampoon about himself, Stalin, was recited by Mandel'shtam:[1] Pasternak answered that it seemed to him of no importance whether he was or was not present, but that he was enormously happy that Stalin was speaking to him; that he had always known that this would happen, that they must meet and speak about matters of supreme importance. Stalin then asked whether Mandel'shtam was a master: Pasternak replied that as poets they were very different; that he admired Mandel'shtam's poetry but felt no affinity with it; but that in any case this was not the point at all.

Here, in recounting the episode to me, Pasternak again embarked on one of his great metaphysical flights about cosmic turning-points in the world's history, which he wished to discuss with Stalin – it was of supreme importance that he should do so – I can easily imagine that he spoke in this vein to Stalin too. At any rate, Stalin asked him again whether he was or was not present when Mandel'shtam read the lampoon. Pasternak answered again that what mattered most was his indispensable meeting with Stalin, that it must happen soon, that everything depended on it, that they must speak about ultimate issues, about life and death. 'If I were Mandel'shtam's friend I should have known better how to defend him,' said Stalin, and put down the receiver. Pasternak tried to ring back but, not surprisingly, failed to get through to the leader. The episode evidently preyed deeply upon him: he repeated to me the version I have just recounted on at least two later occasions, and told the story to other visitors, although, apparently, in somewhat different forms. His efforts to rescue Mandel'shtam, in particular

[1] See Nadezhda Mandelstam, *Hope Against Hope*, trans. Max Hayward (London, 1971), p. 13 and chapter 32.

his appeal to Bukharin, probably helped to preserve him at least for a time – Mandel'shtam was finally destroyed some years later – but Pasternak clearly felt, perhaps without good reason, but as anyone not blinded by self-satisfaction or stupidity might feel, that perhaps another response might have done more for the condemned poet.[1]

He followed this story with accounts of other victims: Pil'nyak, who anxiously waited ('was constantly looking out of the window') for an emissary to ask him to sign a denunciation of one of the men accused of treason in 1936, and because none came, realised that he too was doomed. He spoke of the circumstances of Tsvetaeva's suicide in 1941, which he thought might have been prevented if the literary bureaucrats had not behaved with such appalling heartlessness to her. He told the story of a man who asked him to sign an open letter condemning Marshal Tukhachevsky; when Pasternak refused and explained the reasons for his refusal, the man burst into tears, said that the poet was the noblest and most saintly human being that he had ever met, embraced him fervently, and then went straight to the secret police and denounced him.

Pasternak then said that despite the positive role which the Communist Party had played during the War, and not in Russia alone, he found the idea of any kind of relationship with it increasingly repellent: Russia was a galley, a slave-ship, and these were the overseers who whipped the rowers. Why, he wished to know, did a diplomat from a remote British 'territory', then in Moscow, whom I surely knew, a man who knew some Russian and claimed to be a poet, and visited him occasionally, why did this person insist, on every possible and impossible occasion, that he, Pasternak, should get closer to the Party? He did not need gentlemen who came from the other side of the world to tell him what to do – could I tell this man that his visits were unwelcome? I promised that I would, but did not do so, partly for fear of rendering Pasternak's none too secure position still more precarious. The Commonwealth diplomat in question shortly afterwards left the Soviet Union, and, I was told by his friends, later changed his views.

Pasternak reproached me too; not, indeed, for seeking to impose my political or any other opinions on him, but for something that

[1] Akhmatova and Nadezhda Mandel'shtam (according to Lydia Chukovskaya) decided that he deserved four out of five for his conduct in this situation.

to him seemed almost as bad: here we both were, in Russia, and wherever one looked everything was disgusting, appalling, an abominable pigsty, yet I seemed to be positively exhilarated by it, I wandered about and looked at everything (he declared) with bemused eyes – I was no better than other foreign visitors who saw nothing and suffered from absurd delusions, maddening to the poor miserable natives.

Pasternak was acutely sensitive to the charge of accommodating himself to the demands of the Party or the State – he seemed afraid that his mere survival might be attributed to some unworthy effort to placate the authorities, some squalid compromise of his integrity to escape persecution. He kept returning to this point, and went to absurd lengths to deny that he was capable of conduct of which no one who knew him could begin to conceive him to be guilty. One day he asked me whether I had read his wartime volume of poems *On Early Trains*; had I heard anyone speak of it as a gesture of conformity with the prevailing orthodoxy? I said truthfully that I had never heard this, that it seemed to me a ludicrous suggestion.

Anna Akhmatova, who was bound to him by the deepest friendship and admiration, told me that when she was returning to Leningrad from Tashkent, where in 1941 she had been evacuated from Leningrad, she stopped in Moscow and visited Peredelkino. Within a few hours of arriving she received a message from Pasternak that he could not see her – he had a fever – he was in bed – it was impossible. On the next day the message was repeated. On the third day he appeared before her looking unusually well, with no trace of any ailment. The first thing he did was to ask her whether she had read his latest book of poems: he put the question with so painful an expression on his face that she tactfully said that she had not read them yet; at which his face cleared, he looked vastly relieved and they talked happily. He evidently felt needlessly ashamed of these poems, which, in fact, were not well received by the official critics. It evidently seemed to him a kind of half-hearted effort to write civic poetry – there was nothing he disliked more intensely than this genre.

Yet, in 1945, he still had hopes of a great renewal of Russian life as a result of the cleansing storm that the War had seemed to him to be – as transforming in its own terrible fashion as the Revolution itself – a vast cataclysm beyond our puny moral categories. Such vast mutations cannot, he held, be judged; one must think and think about them and seek to understand as much of them as one can, all one's life; they are beyond good and evil, acceptance or rejection, doubt or assent; they must be accepted as elemental changes, earthquakes, tidal waves, transforming events which are beyond all moral and historical categories. So, too, the dark nightmare of betrayals, purges, massacres of the innocent, followed by an appalling war, seemed to him a necessary prelude to some inevitable, unheard-of victory of the spirit.

I did not see him again for eleven years. By 1956 his estrangement from his country's political order was complete. He could not speak of it, or its representatives, without a shudder. By that time his friend Olga Ivinskaya had been arrested, interrogated, maltreated, sent to a labour camp for five years. 'Your Boris,' the Minister of State Security, Abakumov, had said to her, 'your Boris detests us, doesn't he?' 'They were right,' Pasternak said to me: 'she could not and did not deny it.' I had travelled to Peredelkino with Neuhaus and one of his sons by his first wife, Zinaida Nikolaevna, who was now married to Pasternak. Neuhaus repeated over and over again that Pasternak was a saint: that he was too unworldly – his hope that the Soviet authorities would permit the publication of *Doctor Zhivago* was plainly absurd – martyrdom of the author was far more likely. Pasternak was the greatest writer produced by Russia for decades, and he would be destroyed, as so many had been destroyed, by the State; this was an inheritance from the tsarist regime – whatever the difference between Russia old and new, suspicion and persecution of writers were common to both. His former wife had told him that Pasternak was determined to get his novel published somewhere; he had tried to dissuade him, in vain. If Pasternak mentioned the matter to me, would I – it was important – more than important – perhaps a matter of life and death, who could tell, even in these days? – would I try to persuade him to hold his hand? Neuhaus seemed to me to be right: Pasternak probably did need to be physically saved from himself.

By this time we had arrived at Pasternak's house. He was waiting for me by the gate and let Neuhaus go in, embraced me warmly and said that after eleven years during which we had not met, much had happened, most of it very evil. He stopped and said 'Surely there is something you want to say to me?' I said, with monumental tactlessness (not to say unforgivable stupidity), 'Boris Leonidovich, I am happy to see you looking so well: but the main thing is that you have survived – it seemed almost miraculous to some of us' (I was thinking of the anti-Jewish persecution of

Stalin's last years). His face darkened and he looked at me with real anger: 'I know what you are thinking,' he said. 'What, Boris Leonidovich?' 'I know, I know it, I know exactly what is in your mind,' he replied in a breaking voice – it was very frightening – 'do not prevaricate, I can see more clearly into your mind than I can into my own.' 'What am I thinking?' I asked again, more and more disturbed by his words. 'You think – I know that you think – that I have done something for *them*.' 'I assure you, Boris Leonidovich, that I never conceived of this – I have never heard this suggested by anyone, even as an idiotic joke.' In the end he believed me. But he was visibly upset. Only after I had assured him that admiration for him, not only as a writer, but as a free and independent human being, was, among civilised people, world-wide, did he begin to return to his normal state. 'At least', he said, 'I can say, like Heine, "I may not deserve to be remembered as a poet, but surely as a soldier in the battle for human freedom." '[1]

He took me to his study. There he thrust a thick envelope into my hands: 'My book,' he said, 'it is all there. It is my last word. Please read it.' I began to read *Doctor Zhivago* immediately on leaving him, and finished it on the following day. Unlike some of its readers in both the Soviet Union and the West, I thought it was a work of genius. It seemed – and seems – to me to convey an entire range of human experience, to create a world, even if it contains only one genuine inhabitant, in language of unexampled imaginative power. When, two or three days later, I saw him again I found it difficult to say this to him, and only asked what he intended to do with his novel. He told me that he had given it to an Italian Communist, who worked in the Italian Section of the Soviet radio and at the same time acted as an agent for the Communist Milanese publisher Feltrinelli; he had assigned world rights to Feltrinelli – he wished his novel, his testament, the most authentic, most complete of all his writings – his poetry was nothing by comparison (although the poems in the novel were, he thought, perhaps the best he had written) – he wished his work to travel over the entire world, to 'lay waste with fire' (he quoted from Pushkin's famous poem *The Prophet*) 'the hearts of men'.[2]

[1] Cf. *Heinrich Heines Sämtliche Werke*, ed. Oskar Walzel (Leipzig, 1911–20), vol. 4, p. 306.

[2] 'Glagolom zhgi serdtsa lyudei!' A. S. Pushkin, *Sobranie sochinenii* (Moscow, 1974–8), vol. 2, p. 83. I have slightly amended Maurice Baring's translation in his *Russian Lyrics* (London, 1943), p. 2.

At some point during the day, while the famous raconteur Andronikov was entertaining the company with an elaborate account of the Italian actor Salvini, Zinaida Nikolaevna drew me aside and begged me with tears in her eyes to dissuade Pasternak from getting *Doctor Zhivago* published abroad without official permission: she did not wish her children to suffer; surely I knew what 'they' were capable of. Moved by this plea, I spoke to the poet at the first opportunity. I said that I would have microfilms of his novel made, and cause them to be buried in the four quarters of the globe – in Oxford, in Valparaiso, in Tasmania, Haiti, Vancouver, Cape Town, Japan – so that a text would survive even if a nuclear war broke out; was he resolved to defy the Soviet authorities, had he considered the consequences?

For the second time during that week he showed a touch of real anger in talking to me. He told me that what I said was no doubt well intentioned, that he was touched by my concern for his own safety and that of his family (this was said a trifle ironically), but that he knew what he was doing: that I was worse than that Commonwealth diplomat eleven years ago who had tried to convert him to Communism; he had spoken to his sons; they were prepared to suffer; I was not to mention the matter again – I had read the book, I surely realised what it, above all its dissemination, meant to him. I was shamed into silence.

After an interval, perhaps to lighten the atmosphere, he said, 'You know, my present position here is less insecure than you seem to think. My translations of Shakespeare, for example, have been acted with success: let me tell you an amusing story.' He then reminded me that he had once introduced me to one of the most celebrated of Soviet actors, Livanov (whose real name, he added, was Polivanov). Livanov was very enthusiastic about Pasternak's translation of *Hamlet*, and, some years ago, wished to produce it and act in it himself. He obtained official permission for this and rehearsals began. During this period he was invited to one of the regular banquets in the Kremlin, over which Stalin presided. It was Stalin's habit, at a certain point in the evening, to walk from table to table, exchanging greetings and offering toasts. When he approached Livanov's table, the actor asked him: 'Iosif Vissariono-vich, how should one play *Hamlet*?' He wanted Stalin to say something, anything; he could then carry this away under his arm and use it. As Pasternak put it, if Stalin had said 'You must play it in a mauve manner', Livanov could tell his actors that what they were doing was not mauve enough, that the Leader had distinctly ordered it to be mauve; he, Livanov, had alone grasped exactly what the Leader meant, and the director and everyone else would then be bound to obey. Stalin stopped and said 'You are an actor? At the Arts Theatre? Then you should put your question to the artistic director of the theatre; I am no expert on theatrical matters.' Then, after a silence, 'However, since you have put the question to me, I shall give you my answer: *Hamlet* is a decadent play and should not be performed at all.' The rehearsals were broken off on the next day. There was no performance of *Hamlet* until well after Stalin's death. 'You see,' said Pasternak, 'things have changed. They change all the time.' Another silence.

He then talked about French literature, as often before. Since our last meeting he had procured Sartre's *La Nausée* and found it unreadable, and its obscenity revolting. Surely after four centuries of creative genius this great nation could not have ceased to generate literature? Aragon was a time-server, Duhamel, Guéhenno were inconceivably tedious; was Malraux still writing? Before I could reply, one of his guests at lunch, a woman with an indescribably innocent and sweet expression of a kind perhaps more often found in Russia than in the West, a teacher who had recently returned after fifteen years in a labour camp, to which she had been condemned solely for teaching English, shyly asked whether Aldous Huxley had written anything since *Point Counter Point*; and was Virginia Woolf still writing? – she had never seen a book by her, but from an account in an old French newspaper which in some mysterious fashion had found its way into her camp, she thought that she might like her work.

It is difficult to convey the pleasure of being able to bring news of art and literature of the outer world to human beings so genuinely eager to receive it, so unlikely to obtain it from any other source. I told her and the assembled company all that I could of English, American, French writing: it was like speaking to the victims of shipwreck on a desert island, cut off for decades from civilisation – all they heard, they received as new, exciting and delightful. The Georgian poet Titsian Tabidze, Pasternak's great friend, had perished in the Great Purge; his widow Nina Tabidze, who was present, wanted to know whether Shakespeare, Ibsen and Shaw were still great names in the Western theatre. I told her that interest in Shaw had declined, but that Chekhov was greatly admired and often performed, and added that Akhmatova had said to me that she could not understand this worship of Chekhov: his universe was uniformly drab; the sun never shone, no swords flashed, everything was covered by a horrible grey mist – Chekhov's world was a sea of mud with wretched human creatures caught in it helplessly – it was a travesty of life. Pasternak said that Akhmatova was wholly mistaken: 'Tell her when you see her – we cannot go to Leningrad freely, as you probably can – tell her from all of us here that all Russian writers preach to the reader: even Turgenev tells him that time is a great healer and that kind of thing; Chekhov alone does not. He is a pure artist – everything is dissolved in art – he is our answer to Flaubert.' He went on to say that Akhmatova would surely talk to me about Dostoevsky and attack Tolstoy. But Tolstoy was right about Dostoevsky: 'His novels are a dreadful mess, a mixture of chauvinism and hysterical religion, whereas Chekhov – tell Anna Akhmatova that, and from me! I love her deeply, but I have never been able to persuade her of anything.' But when I saw Akhmatova again, in Oxford in 1965, I thought it best not to report his judgement: she might have wished to answer him; but Pasternak was in his grave. In fact, she did speak to me of Dostoevsky with passionate admiration.

But let me return to 1945 and describe my meetings with the poet (she detested the word 'poetess') in Leningrad. It happened in the following way. I had heard that books in Leningrad, in what in the Soviet Union were called 'antiquarian bookshops', cost a good deal less than in Moscow; the terrible mortality and the possibility of bartering books for food during the siege of that city had led to a flow of books, especially those of the old intelligentsia, into government bookshops. Some of the inhabitants of Leningrad, one was told, weakened by illness and undernourishment, became too feeble to carry entire books, and so had had torn out for them by friends chapters and pages of poems: books and fragments of books had found their way into the second-hand departments of the shops and were on sale. I should have done my best to go to Leningrad in any case, for I was eager to see again the city in which I had spent four years of my childhood; the lure of books added to my desire. After the usual delays I was granted permission to spend two nights in the old Astoria hotel, and in company with the British Council representative in the Soviet Union, Miss Brenda Tripp – a most intelligent and sympathetic organic chemist – I reached Leningrad on a grey day in late November.

III

I had not seen the city since 1920, when I was eleven years old and my family was allowed to return to our native city of Riga, the capital of a then independent republic. In Leningrad my recollections of childhood became fabulously vivid – I was inexpressibly moved by the look of the streets, the houses, the statues, the embankments, the market-places, the suddenly familiar broken railings of a little shop in which samovars were mended below the house in which we had lived – the inner yard of the house looked as sordid and abandoned as it had done during the first years of the Revolution. My memories of specific events, episodes, experiences, came between me and the physical reality: it was as if I had walked into a legendary city, myself at once part of the vivid, half-remembered legend, and yet, at the same time, viewing it from some outside vantage-point. The city had been greatly damaged, but still in 1945 remained indescribably beautiful (it seemed wholly restored by the time I saw it again eleven years later).

I made my way to the object of my journey, the Writers' Bookshop of which I had been told, in the Nevsky Prospekt. There were then – I expect there still are – two sections in certain Russian bookshops: the outer room for the general public, in which one asks for books across the counter, and an inner room, with free access to the shelves, for recognised writers, journalists and other privileged persons. Because we were foreigners, Miss Tripp and I were admitted to the inner sanctum. While looking at the books, I fell into casual conversation with someone who was turning over the leaves of a book of poems. He turned out to be a well-known critic and literary historian; we talked about recent events, and he described the terrible ordeal of the siege of Leningrad and the martyrdom and heroism of many of its inhabitants, and said that some had died of cold and hunger, others, mostly the younger ones, had survived: some had been evacuated. I asked him about the fate of writers in Leningrad. He said, 'You mean Zoshchenko and Akhmatova?' Akhmatova to me was a figure from a remote past; Maurice Bowra, who had translated some of her poems, spoke about her to me as someone not heard of since the First World War. 'Is Akhmatova still alive?' I asked. 'Akhmatova, Anna Andreevna?' he said: 'Why yes, of course, she lives not far from here on the Fontanka, in Fontanny Dom [Fountain House]; would you like to meet her?' It was as if I had suddenly been invited to meet Miss Christina Rossetti; I could hardly speak; I mumbled that I should indeed like to meet her. 'I shall telephone her,' my new acquaintance said; and returned to tell me that she would receive us at three that afternoon; I was to come back to the bookshop and we would go together. I returned to the Hotel Astoria with Miss Tripp, and asked her if she would like to meet the poet – she said that she could not, she was otherwise engaged that afternoon.

I returned at the appointed hour. The critic and I left the bookshop, turned left, crossed the Anichkov Bridge and turned left again, along the embankment of the Fontanka. Fountain House, the palace of the Sheremetevs, is a magnificent late baroque building with gates of exquisite ironwork for which Leningrad is famous, and built around a spacious court, not unlike the quadrangle of a large Oxford or Cambridge college. We climbed up one of the steep, dark staircases to an upper floor, and were admitted to Akhmatova's room. It was very barely furnished – virtually everything in it had, I gathered, been taken away – looted or sold – during the siege; there was a small table, three or four chairs, a wooden chest, a sofa and, above the unlit stove, a drawing by Modigliani. A stately, grey-haired lady, a white shawl draped about her shoulders, slowly rose to greet us.

Anna Andreevna Akhmatova was immensely dignified, with unhurried gestures, a noble head, beautiful, somewhat severe features, and an expression of immense sadness. I bowed – it seemed appropriate, for she looked and moved like a tragic queen – thanked her for receiving me, and said that people in the West would be glad to know that she was in good health, for nothing had been heard of her for many years. 'Oh, but an article on me has appeared in the *Dublin Review*,' she said, 'and a thesis is being written about my work, I am told, in Bologna.' She had a friend with her, an academic lady of some sort, and there was polite conversation for some minutes. Then Akhmatova asked me about the ordeal of London during the bombing: I answered as best I could, feeling acutely shy and constricted by her distant, somewhat regal manner. Suddenly I heard what sounded like my first name being shouted somewhere outside. I ignored this for a while – it was plainly an illusion – but the shouting became louder and the word 'Isaiah' could be clearly heard. I went to the window and looked out, and saw a man whom I recognised as Randolph Churchill. He was standing in the middle of the great court, looking like a tipsy undergraduate, and screaming my name. I stood rooted to the floor for some seconds. Then I collected myself, muttered an apology and ran down the stairs: my only thought was to prevent him from coming to the room. My companion, the critic, ran after me anxiously. When we emerged into the court, Churchill came towards me and welcomed me effusively: 'Mr X,' I said mechanically, 'I do not suppose that you have met Mr Randolph Churchill?' The critic froze, his expression changed from bewilderment to horror, and he left as rapidly as he could. I never saw him again, but as his works continue to be published in the Soviet Union, I infer that this chance meeting did him no harm. I have no notion whether I was followed by agents of the secret police, but there could be no doubt that Randolph Churchill was; it was this untoward event that caused absurd rumours to circulate in Leningrad that a foreign delegation had arrived to persuade Akhmatova to leave Russia; that Winston Churchill, a lifelong admirer of the poet, was sending a special aircraft to take Akhmatova to England, and the like.

I had not met Randolph since we were undergraduates at Oxford. After hastily leading him out of Fountain House, I asked him what all this meant. He explained that he was in Moscow as a journalist on behalf of the North American Newspaper Alliance. He had come to Leningrad as part of his assignment; on arriving at the Hotel Astoria, his first concern had been to get the pot of caviare which he had acquired into an icebox: but as he knew no Russian and his interpreter had disappeared, his cries for help had finally brought down Miss Brenda Tripp. She saw to his caviare and, in the course of general conversation, told him that I was in the city. He said that he knew me and that in his view I would make an excellent substitute interpreter, and was then unfortunately told by Miss Tripp about my visit to the Sheremetev Palace. The rest followed: since he did not know exactly where I was to be found, he adopted a method which had served him well during his days in Christ Church (his Oxford college), and, I dare say, on other occasions; and, he said with a winning smile, it worked. I detached myself from him as quickly as I could and, after obtaining her number from the bookseller, telephoned Akhmatova to offer an explanation of my precipitate departure and to apologise for it. I asked if I might be allowed to call on her again. 'I shall wait for you at nine this evening,' she answered.

When I returned, her companion turned out to be one of her

second husband's – the Assyriologist Shileiko's – pupils, a learned lady who asked me a great many questions about English universities and their organisation. Akhmatova was plainly uninterested and, for the most part, silent. Shortly before midnight the Assyriologist left, and then Akhmatova began to ask me about old friends who had emigrated – some of whom I might know (she was sure of that, she told me later; in personal relationships, she assured me, her intuition – almost second sight – never failed her). I did indeed know some of them: we talked about the composer Artur Lurié, whom I had met in America during the War; he had been an intimate friend of hers and had set some of her and of Mandel'-shtam's poetry to music; about the poet Georgy Adamovich; about Boris Anrep, the mosaicist (whom I had never met); I knew little about him, only that he had decorated the floor of the entrance hall of the National Gallery with the figures of celebrated persons – Bertrand Russell, Virginia Woolf, Greta Garbo, Clive Bell, Lydia Lopokova and others. Twenty years later I was able to tell her that in the meantime Anrep had added a mosaic of her too, and had called it 'Compassion'. She did not know this, and was profoundly moved; and showed me a ring with a black stone which Anrep had given to her in 1917.

She asked after Salome Halpern, *née* Andronikova, whom she knew well in St Petersburg before the First World War – a celebrated society beauty of that period, famous for her wit, intelligence and charm, a friend of Russian poets and painters of the time. Akhmatova told me – what, indeed, I knew already – that Mandel'shtam, who had been in love with her, dedicated one of his most beautiful poems to her; I knew Salomeya Nikolaevna (and her husband Aleksandr Yakovlevich Halpern) well, and told Akhmatova something of their lives and friendships and opinions. She asked after Vera Stravinsky, the composer's wife, whom I did not then know; I answered these questions only in 1965, in Oxford. She spoke of her visits to Paris before the First World War, of her friendship with Amedeo Modigliani, whose drawing of her hung over her fireplace – one of many (the rest had perished during the siege); of her childhood on the Black Sea coast, a pagan, unbaptised land, she called it, where one felt close to an ancient, half-Greek, half-barbarian, deeply un-Russian culture; of her first husband, the celebrated poet Gumilev, who had done a great deal to form her – he had thought it ridiculous that a poet should be married to another poet, and on occasion had harshly criticised her writing, though he never humiliated her before others. On one occasion, when he was returning from one of his journeys to Abyssinia (the subject of some of his most exotic and magnificent poems), she had come to meet him at the railway station in St Petersburg (years later she told the story again, in the same words, to Dimitri Obolensky and me in Oxford). He looked severe: the first question he put to her was 'Have you been writing?' 'Yes.' 'Read it.' She did so: 'Yes, good, good,' he said, his eyebrows unknitting, and they went home; from that moment he accepted her as a poet. She was convinced that he had not taken part in the monarchist conspiracy for which he had been executed; Gorky, who had been asked by many writers to intervene on his behalf, disliked him and, according to some accounts,[1] did not intercede for him. She had not seen him for some time before his condemnation – they had been divorced some years before; her eyes had tears in them when she described the harrowing circumstances of his death.

After a silence she asked me whether I would like to hear her poetry: but before doing this, she said that she wished to recite two cantos from Byron's *Don Juan* to me, for they were relevant to what would follow. Even if I had known the poem well, I could not have told which cantos she had chosen, for although she read English, her pronunciation of it made it impossible to understand more than a word or two. She closed her eyes and spoke the lines from memory, with intense emotion; I rose and looked out of the window to conceal my embarrassment. Perhaps, I thought afterwards, that is how we now read classical Greek and Latin; yet we, too, are moved by the words, which, as we pronounce them, might be wholly unintelligible to their authors and audiences. Then she spoke her own poems from *Anno Domini*, *The White Flock*, *From Six Books* – 'Poems like these, but far better than mine, were the cause of the death of the best poet of our time, whom I loved and who loved me . . .' – whether she meant Gumilev or Mandel'shtam I could not tell, for she broke down in tears and could not go on. She then recited the (at that time) still unfinished *Poem Without a Hero*. There are recordings of her readings, and I shall not attempt to describe them. Even then I realised that I was listening to a work of genius. I do not suppose that I understood that many-faceted

[1] For example, that of Nadezhda Mandel'shtam; see her *Hope Abandoned*, trans. Max Hayward (London, 1974), p. 88.

and most magical poem and its deeply personal allusions any better than when I read it now. She made no secret of the fact that it was intended as a kind of final memorial to her life as a poet, to the past of the city – St Petersburg – which was part of her being, and, in the form of a Twelfth Night carnival procession of masked figures *en travesti*, to her friends and their lives and destinies and her own – a kind of artistic *nunc dimittis* before the inescapable end which would not be long in coming. The lines about the Guest from the Future had not then been written, nor the third dedication. It is a mysterious and deeply evocative work. A tumulus of learned commentary is inexorably rising over it. Soon it may be buried under its weight.

Then she read the *Requiem*, from a manuscript. She broke off and spoke of the years 1937–8, when both her husband and her son had been arrested and sent to prison camps (this was to happen again), of the queues of women who waited day and night, week after week, month after month, for news of their husbands, brothers, fathers, sons, for permission to send food or letters to them – but no news ever came, no message ever reached them – when a pall of death in life hung over the cities of the Soviet Union while the torture and slaughter of millions of innocents were going on. She spoke in a dry, matter-of-fact voice, occasionally interrupting herself with 'No, I cannot, it is no good, you come from a society of human beings, whereas here we are divided into human beings and . . .'. Then a long silence. 'And even now . . .'. I asked about Mandel'shtam: she was silent, her eyes filled with tears, and she begged me not to speak of him: 'After he slapped Aleksey Tolstoy's face it was all over . . .'. It took some time for her to collect herself; then, in a totally changed voice, she said 'Aleksey Tolstoy liked me; he wore lilac shirts *à la russe* when we were in Tashkent, and spoke of the marvellous time he and I would have together when we came back. He was a very gifted and interesting writer, a scoundrel, full of charm, and a man of stormy temperament; he is dead now; he was capable of anything, anything; he was abominably anti-Semitic; he was a wild adventurer, a bad friend, he only liked youth, power, vitality, he didn't finish his *Peter the First* because he said that he could only deal with Peter as a young man; what was he to do with all those people when they were old? He was a kind of Dolokhov, he called me Annushka – that made me wince – but I liked him, even though he was the cause of the death of the best poet of our time, whom I loved and who loved me.'

(Her words were identical with those she had used earlier; it now seemed clear to me to whom, on both occasions, she was referring.)

It was, I think, by now about three in the morning. She showed no sign of wishing me to leave. I was far too moved and absorbed to stir. The door opened and her son Lev Gumilev entered; it was plain that his relation to his mother and hers to him were deeply affectionate; he explained that he had been a student of the famous Leningrad historian Evgeny Tarle, and his field of study now was the history of the ancient tribes of central Asia (he did not mention the fact that he was there originally in a prison camp); he had become interested in the early history of the Khazars, Kazakhs and earlier peoples; he had been allowed to join a prisoners' unit of anti-aircraft gunners and had just returned from Germany. He seemed cheerful and confident that he could once more live and work in Leningrad, and offered me a dish of boiled potatoes, which was all that they had. Akhmatova apologised for the poverty of her hospitality. I begged her to let me write down the *Poem Without a Hero* and *Requiem*. 'There is no need,' she said: 'a volume of my collected verse is to appear next February; it is all in proof; I shall send you a copy to Oxford.' The Party, as we know, ruled otherwise, and she was denounced by Zhdanov (in a phrase that he had not wholly invented) as 'half nun, half harlot',[1] as part of the condemnation of other 'formalists' and 'decadents' and of the two periodicals in which their work had been published.

After Lev Gumilev left us, she asked me what I read: before I could answer, she denounced Chekhov for his mud-coloured world, his dreary plays, the absence in his world of heroism and martyrdom, of depth and darkness and sublimity – this was the passionate diatribe, which I later reported to Pasternak, in which she said that in Chekhov 'no swords flashed'. I said something about Tolstoy's liking for him. 'Why did Anna Karenina have to be killed?' she asked. 'As soon as she leaves Karenin, everything changes: she suddenly becomes a fallen woman in Tolstoy's eyes, a *traviata*, a prostitute. Of course there are pages of genius, but the basic morality is disgusting. Who punishes Anna? God? No,

[1] A similar formula had been used, in a very different context, by the critic Boris Eikhenbaum, in *Anna Akhmatova: opyt analiza* (Petersburg, 1923), p. 114, to describe the mingling of erotic and religious motifs in Akhmatova's early poetry. It reappeared in 1930, in a caricatured form, in an unfriendly article on her in the Soviet Literary Encyclopaedia, whence it found its way into Zhdanov's anathema of 1946.

society; that same society the hypocrisy of which Tolstoy is never tired of denouncing. In the end he tells us that she repels even Vronsky. Tolstoy is lying: he knew better than that. The morality of *Anna Karenina* is the morality of Tolstoy's wife, of his Moscow aunts; he knew the truth, yet he forced himself, shamefully, to conform to philistine convention. Tolstoy's morality is a direct expression of his own private life, his personal vicissitudes. When he was happily married he wrote *War and Peace*, which celebrates family life. After he started hating Sofia Andreevna, but was not prepared to divorce her because divorce is condemned by society, and perhaps by the peasants too, he wrote *Anna Karenina* and punished her for leaving Karenin. When he was old, and no longer lusted so violently after peasant girls, he wrote *The Kreutzer Sonata*, and forbade sex altogether.'

Perhaps this summing up was not meant too seriously: but Akhmatova's dislike of Tolstoy's sermons was genuine. She regarded him as an egocentric of immense vanity, and an enemy of love and freedom. She worshipped Dostoevsky (and, like him, despised Turgenev); and after Dostoevsky, Kafka ('He wrote for me and about me,' she told me in 1965 in Oxford – 'Joyce and Eliot, wonderful poets, are inferior to this profoundest and most truthful of modern authors'). She said of Pushkin that of course he understood everything: 'How did he, how could he have known it all? This curly-haired youth in Tsarskoe, with a volume of Parny under his arm?' Then she read me her notes on Pushkin's *Egyptian Nights*, and talked about the pale stranger, the mysterious poet who offered, in that story, to improvise on themes drawn at random. The virtuoso, she had no doubt, was the Polish poet Adam Mickiewicz; Pushkin's relation to him became ambivalent – the Polish issue divided them, but he always recognised genius in his contemporaries. Blok was like that, with his mad eyes and magnificent genius – he too could have been an *improvisateur*. She said that Blok, who had, on occasion, praised her verse, had never liked her, but that every schoolmistress in Russia believed, and would go on believing, that they had had a love-affair – 'and historians of literature will believe this too – all this is probably based on my poem *A Visit to the Poet* which I dedicated to him in 1914; and perhaps on the poem on the death of *The Grey-Eyed King*, although that was written more than ten years before Blok died; there were other poems, too, but he did not like any of us' – she was speaking of the Acmeist poets, above all Mandel'shtam,

Gumilev and herself – and added that Blok did not like Pasternak either.

She then spoke about Pasternak, to whom she was devoted. She said that it was only when Pasternak was in a low state that he would express a wish to be with her; and then he would come, distraught and exhausted, usually after some passionate involvement, but his wife would swiftly follow and take him home. Both Pasternak and Akhmatova were apt to fall in love easily. Pasternak had occasionally proposed to her, but she had not taken this seriously; they had never been genuinely in love with one another; not in love, but they loved and adored each other and, after Mandel'shtam's and Tsvetaeva's deaths, felt themselves alone. The idea that the other was alive and at work was a source of infinite comfort to them both; they criticised each other, but permitted no one else to do so. She admired Tsvetaeva: 'Marina is a better poet than I am,' she said to me; but now that Mandel'shtam and Tsvetaeva were gone she and Pasternak were living in a desert, alone, even though they were surrounded by the love and passionate devotion of countless men and women in the Soviet Union who knew their verse by heart, and copied it and circulated it and recited it; this was a source of pride and delight to them, but they remained in exile. Their deep patriotism was not tinged by nationalism; the thought of emigration was hateful to both. Pasternak longed to visit the West, but not at the risk of being unable to return to his native land. Akhmatova said to me that she would not move: she was ready to die in her own country, no matter what horrors were in store; she would never abandon it. Both were among those who harboured extraordinary illusions about the rich artistic and intellectual culture of the West – a golden world, full of creative life – both wished to see it and communicate with it.

As the night wore on, Akhmatova grew more and more animated. She questioned me about my personal life. I answered fully and freely, as if she had an absolute right to know, and she rewarded me by giving a marvellous account of her childhood by the Black Sea, her marriages to Gumilev and Shileiko and Punin, her relationships with the companions of her youth, and of St Petersburg before the First World War. It is in the light of this alone that the succession of images and symbols, the play of disguises, the entire *bal masqué* of the *Poem Without a Hero*, with its echoes of *Don Giovanni* and the *commedia dell'arte*, can be understood. Once again she spoke of Salomeya Andronikova (Halpern), her beauty, charm, acute intelligence, her incapacity for being taken in by the second- and third-rate poets ('they are fourth-rate now'), of evenings at the Stray Dog cabaret, performances at the Distorting Mirror theatre; of her reaction against the sham mysteries of symbolism, despite Baudelaire and Verlaine and Rimbaud and Verhaeren, whom they all knew by heart. Vyacheslav Ivanov was infinitely distinguished and civilised, a man of unerring taste and judgement, of the finest imaginable critical faculty, but his poetry was to her chilly and unsympathetic; so was Andrey Bely; as for Bal'mont, he was unjustly despised – he was, of course, ridiculously pompous, and self-important, but gifted; Sologub was uneven, but interesting and original; far greater than these was the austere, fastidious Tsarskoe Selo headmaster, Innokenty Annensky, who had taught her more than anyone, even more than Gumilev, his disciple, and who died largely ignored by editors and critics, a great, forgotten master: without him, there would have been no Gumilev, no Mandel'shtam, no Lozinsky, no Pasternak, no Akhmatova. She spoke at length about music, about the sublimity and beauty of Beethoven's last three piano sonatas – Pasternak thought them greater than the posthumous quartets, and she agreed with him, she responded with her whole nature to the violent changes of feeling within their movements. The parallel which Pasternak drew between Bach and Chopin seemed to her to be strange and fascinating. She found it easier to talk to him about music than about poetry.

She spoke of her loneliness and isolation, both personal and cultural. Leningrad after the War was for her nothing but a vast cemetery, the graveyard of her friends: it was like the aftermath of a forest fire – the few charred trees made the desolation still more desolate. She had devoted friends – Lozinsky, Zhirmunsky, Khardzhiev, the Ardovs, Olga Bergholz, Lydia Chukovskaya, Emma Gerstein (she mentioned neither Garshin nor Nadezhda Mandel'shtam, of whose existence I then knew nothing) – but her sustenance came not from them but from literature and the images of the past: Pushkin's St Petersburg; Byron's, Pushkin's, Mozart's, Molière's Don Juan; and the great panorama of the Italian Renaissance. She lived by translating: she had begged to be allowed to translate the letters of Rubens, and not those of Romain Rolland – permission had finally been granted; had I seen them? I asked whether the Renaissance was a real historical past to her, inhabited by imperfect human beings, or an idealised image of an imaginary world. She replied that it was of course the latter; all poetry and art, to her, was – here she used an expression once used by Mandel'shtam – a form of nostalgia, a longing for a universal culture, as Goethe and Schlegel had conceived it, of what had been transmuted into art and thought – of nature, love, death, despair and martyrdom, of a reality which had no history, nothing outside itself. Again she spoke of pre-revolutionary St Petersburg as the town in which she was formed, of the long dark night which had covered her thenceforth. She spoke without the slightest trace of self-pity, like a princess in exile, proud, unhappy, unapproachable, in a calm, even voice, at times in words of moving eloquence.

The account of the unrelieved tragedy of her life went far beyond anything which anyone had ever described to me in spoken words; the recollection of them is still vivid and painful to me. I asked her if she intended to compose a record of her literary life. She replied that her poetry was that, in particular the *Poem Without a Hero*; and then she read it to me again. Once more I begged her to let me write it down. Once again she declined. Our conversation, which touched on intimate details of both her life and my own, wandered from literature and art, and lasted until late in the morning of the following day. I saw her again when I was leaving the Soviet Union to go home by way of Leningrad and Helsinki. I went to say goodbye to her on the afternoon of 5 January 1946, and she then gave me one of her collections of verse, with a new poem inscribed on the flyleaf – the poem that was later to form the second in the cycle entitled *Cinque*. I realised that this poem, in this, its first version, had been directly inspired by our earlier meeting. There are other references and allusions to our meetings, in *Cinque* and elsewhere.[1]

These allusions were plain to me when I first read them: but Academician Victor Zhirmunsky, Akhmatova's close friend, an eminent literary scholar and one of the editors of the posthumous Soviet editions of her poems, who visited Oxford a year or two after Akhmatova's death, went through the text with me and confirmed my impressions with precise references. He had read the texts with the author: she spoke to him both about the three dedications, their dates and their significance, and about the 'Guest from the Future'. With some embarrassment, Zhirmunsky

[1] For details see the appendix on pp. 253–4 below.

explained to me why the last dedication of the poem, that to myself
– that this dedication existed was, so he informed me, widely
known to readers of poetry in Russia – had nevertheless to be
omitted in the official edition. I understood and understand the
reason for this only too well. Zhirmunsky was an exceptionally
scrupulous scholar, and a man of courage and integrity who had
suffered for his principles; he explained his distress at being obliged
to ignore Akhmatova's specific instructions in this regard, but
political conditions made it essential. I tried to persuade him that
this was of little consequence: it was true that Akhmatova's poetry
was to a high degree autobiographical, and that therefore the
circumstances of her life threw more light on the meaning of her
words than was the case with many other poets; nevertheless, the
facts were unlikely to be wholly forgotten – as in other countries
under rigorous censorship, an oral tradition was likely to preserve
such knowledge. The tradition might develop in various directions,
and might not be free from legend and fable, but if he wished to be
sure that the truth was known to a small circle of those likely to be
interested, he could write an account of it all and leave it with me
or someone else in the West to be published when it was safe to do
so. I doubt if he followed my advice; but he remained inconsolable
about his shortcomings as an editor under censorship, and
apologised for it again and again, whenever we met during his visits
to England.

The impact upon Akhmatova of my visit, such as it was, seems
to me to have been largely due to the fortuitous fact that I
happened to be only the second foreign visitor whom she had seen
since the First World War.[1] I was, I think, the first person from
the outside world who spoke her language and could bring her
news of a world from which she had been isolated for many years.
Her intellect, critical power and ironical humour seemed to exist
side by side with a dramatic, at times visionary and prophetic, sense
of reality; she seemed to see in me a fateful, perhaps doom-laden
messenger of the end of the world – a tragic intimation of the
future which made a profound impact upon her, and may have had
a part in creating a new outpouring of her creative energy.

I did not see her on my next visit to the Soviet Union, in 1956.
Pasternak told me that though Anna Andreevna wished to see me,

[1] Before me, she had met only one other non-Soviet citizen – Count Joseph
Czapski, the eminent Polish critic, whom she saw during the War in Tashkent.

her son, who had been rearrested some time after I had met him, had been released from his prison camp only a short while before, and she therefore felt nervous of seeing foreigners, particularly as she attributed the furious onslaught upon her by the Party at least in part to my visit in 1945. Pasternak said that he doubted whether my visit had done her any harm, but since she evidently believed that it had, and had been advised to avoid compromising associations, she could not see me; but she wished me to telephone her – this was safe, since all her telephone calls were certainly monitored, as were his own. He had told her, when he was in Moscow, that he had met my wife and me, that he thought my wife delightful, and told Akhmatova that he was sorry that she could not meet her. Anna Andreevna would not be in Moscow long, and I was to telephone her at once.

'Where are you living?' he asked me. 'At the British Embassy.' 'You must on no account telephone her from there – you must use a public call box – not my telephone.'

Later that day I spoke to her over the telephone. 'Yes, Pasternak told me that you were in Moscow with your wife. I cannot see you, for reasons which you will understand only too well. We can speak like this because then they know. How long have you been married?' 'Not long,' I said. 'But exactly when were you married?' 'In February of this year.' 'Is she English, or perhaps American?' 'No, she is half French, half Russian.' 'I see.' There followed a long silence. 'I am sorry you cannot see me, Pasternak says your wife is charming.' Another long silence. 'Have you seen a collection of Korean poems translated by me? With an introduction by Surkov? You can imagine how much Korean I know – a selection of poems, it was not I who selected them. I shall send them to you.'

After this she told me something of her experience as a condemned writer: of the turning-away of some whom she had considered faithful friends, of the nobility and courage of others; she had reread Chekhov, whom she had once condemned so severely, and said that at least in *Ward No 6* he had described her situation accurately, hers and that of many others. 'Pasternak [she always called him so when speaking to me, as has long been the habit among Russians, never 'Boris Leonidovich'] will probably have explained to you why I cannot see you: he has had a difficult time, but not as agonising as mine. Who knows, we may yet meet in this life. Will you telephone me again?' I promised to do so, but when I did, I was told that she had left Moscow, and Pasternak strongly advised against attempting to ring her in Leningrad.

When we met in Oxford in 1965, Akhmatova described the details of the attack upon her by the authorities. She told me that Stalin was personally enraged by the fact that she, an apolitical, little-published writer, who owed her security largely to having contrived to live comparatively unnoticed during the early years of the Revolution, before the cultural battles which often ended in prison camps or execution, had committed the sin of seeing a foreigner without formal authorisation, and not just a foreigner, but an employee of a capitalist government. 'So our nun now receives visits from foreign spies,' he remarked (so it is alleged), and followed this with obscenities which she could not at first bring herself to repeat to me. The fact that I had never worked in any intelligence organisation was irrelevant: all members of foreign embassies or missions were spies to Stalin. 'Of course,' she went on, 'the old man was by then out of his mind. People who were there during this furious outbreak against me, one of whom told me of it, had no doubt that they were speaking to a man in the grip of pathological, unbridled persecution mania.' On the day after I left Leningrad, on 6 January 1946, uniformed men had been placed outside the entrance to her staircase, and a microphone was screwed into the ceiling of her room, plainly not for intelligence purposes but to frighten her. She knew that she was doomed – and although official disgrace followed only some months later, after the formal anathema pronounced over her and Zoshchenko by Zhdanov, she attributed her misfortunes to Stalin's personal paranoia. When she told me this in Oxford, she added that in her view we – that is, she and I – inadvertently, by the mere fact of our meeting, had started the Cold War and thereby changed the history of mankind. She meant this quite literally; and, as Amanda Haight testifies in her book,[1] was totally convinced of it, and saw herself and me as world-historical personages chosen by destiny to begin a cosmic conflict (this is indeed directly reflected in one of her poems). I could not protest that she had perhaps, even if the reality of Stalin's violent fit of anger and of its possible consequences were allowed for, somewhat overestimated the effect of our meeting on the destinies of the world, since she would have felt this as an insult

[1] Amanda Haight, *Anna Akhmatova: A Poetic Pilgrimage* (Oxford, 1976), p. 146.

to her tragic image of herself as Cassandra – indeed, to the historico-metaphysical vision which informed so much of her poetry. I remained silent.

Then she spoke of her journey to Italy in the previous year, when she was awarded the Taormina Literary Prize. On her return, she told me, she was visited by officials of the Soviet secret police, who asked her for her impressions of Rome: had she come across anti-Soviet attitudes on the part of writers, had she met Russian émigrés? She said in reply that Rome seemed to her to be a city where paganism was still at war with Christianity. 'What war?' she was asked: 'Was the USA mentioned?' What would she answer when similar questions were put to her, as they inevitably would be, about England? London? Oxford? Did the poet who was honoured with her in the Sheldonian Theatre – Siegfried Sassoon – have any political record? Or the other honorands? Would it be best to confine herself to speaking of her interest in the magnificent font which Tsar Alexander I had given to Merton College when he was similarly honoured by the University, at the end of the Napoleonic Wars? She was a Russian, and to Russia she would return no matter what awaited her there: the Soviet regime, whatever one might think of it, was the established order in her country; with it she had lived and with it she would die – that is what being a Russian meant.

We returned to Russian literature. She said that the unending ordeal of her country in her own lifetime had generated poetry of wonderful depth and beauty, which, since the 1930s, had for the most part remained unpublished. She said that she preferred not to speak of the contemporary Soviet poets whose work was published in the Soviet Union. One of the most famous of these, who happened to be in England at this time, had sent her a telegram to congratulate her on her Oxford doctorate. I was there when it arrived – she read it, and angrily threw it into the waste-paper basket: 'They are all little bandits, prostitutes of their gifts and exploiters of public taste. Mayakovsky's influence has been fatal to them all.' She said that Mayakovsky was, of course, a genius, not a great poet but a great literary innovator, a terrorist, whose bombs blew up ancient structures, a major figure whose temperament outran his talent – a destroyer, a blaster of everything; the destruction was, of course, deserved. Mayakovsky shouted at the top of his voice because it was natural to him to do so, he could not help it: his imitators – here she mentioned a few names of living poets – had adopted his manner as a genre and were vulgar declaimers with not a spark of true poetry in them, rhetoricians whose talents were theatrical, and Russian audiences had got used to being screamed at by these 'masters of the spoken word' as they were called nowadays.

The only living poet of the older generation about whom she spoke with approval was Maria Petrovykh; but there were many gifted young poets in Russia now: the best among them was Joseph Brodsky, whom she had, she said, brought up by hand, and whose poetry had in part been published – a noble poet in deep disfavour, with all that that implied. There were others, too, marvellously gifted – but their names would mean nothing to me – poets whose verses could not be published, and whose very existence was testimony to the unexhausted life of the imagination in Russia. 'They will eclipse us all,' she said, 'believe me, Pasternak and I and Mandel'shtam and Tsvetaeva, all of us are at the end of a long period of elaboration which began in the nineteenth century. My friends and I thought we spoke with the voice of the twentieth century. But these new poets constitute a new beginning – behind bars now, but they will escape and astonish the world.' She spoke at some length in this prophetic vein, and returned again to Mayakovsky, driven to despair, betrayed by his friends, but, for a while, the true voice, the trumpet, of his people, though a fatal example to others; she herself owed nothing to him, but much to Annensky, the purest and finest of poets, remote from the hurly-burly of literary politics, largely neglected by avant-garde journals, fortunate to have died when he did. He was not read widely in his lifetime, but then this was the fate of other great poets – the present generation was far more sensitive to poetry than her own had been: who cared, who truly cared about Blok or Bely or Vyacheslav Ivanov in 1910? Or, for that matter, about herself and the poets of her group? But today the young knew it all by heart – she was still getting letters from young people, many of them from silly, ecstatic girls, but the sheer number of them was surely evidence of something.

Pasternak received even more of these, and liked them better. Had I met his friend Olga Ivinskaya? I had not. She found both Pasternak's wife, Zinaida, and his mistress equally unbearable, but Boris Leonidovich himself was a magical poet, one of the great poets of the Russian land: every sentence he wrote, in verse and prose, spoke with his authentic voice, unlike any other she had ever heard. Blok and Pasternak were divine poets; no Frenchman, no Englishman, not Valéry, not Eliot, could compare with them – Baudelaire, Shelley, Leopardi, that was the company to which they belonged; like all great poets, they had little sense of the quality of others – Pasternak often praised inferior critics, discovered imaginary hidden gifts, encouraged all kinds of minor figures – decent writers but without talent – he had a mythological sense of history, in which quite worthless people sometimes played mysterious, significant roles – like Evgraf in *Doctor Zhivago* (she vehemently rejected the theory that this mysterious figure was in any respect based on Stalin; she evidently found this impossible to contemplate). He did not really read the contemporary authors he was prepared to praise – not Bagritsky or Aseev, or Maria Petrovykh, not even Mandel'shtam (for whom he had little feeling as a man or a poet, though of course he did what he could for him when he was in trouble), nor her own work – he wrote her wonderful letters about her poetry, but the letters were about himself, not her – she knew that they were sublime fantasies which had little to do with her poems: 'Perhaps all great poets are like this.'

Pasternak's compliments naturally made those who received them very happy, but this was a delusion; he was a generous giver, but not truly interested in the work of others: interested, of course, in Shakespeare, Goethe, the French symbolists, Rilke, perhaps Proust, but 'not in any of us'. She said that she missed Pasternak's existence every day of her life; they had never been in love, but they loved one another deeply, and this irritated his wife. She then spoke of the 'blank' years during which she was officially out of account in the Soviet Union – from the mid-1920s until the late '30s. She said that when she was not translating, she read Russian poets: Pushkin constantly, of course, but also Odoevsky, Lermontov, Baratynsky – she thought Baratynsky's *Autumn* was a work of pure genius; and she had recently reread Velemir Khlebnikov – mad but marvellous.

I asked her if she would ever annotate the *Poem Without a Hero*: the allusions might be unintelligible to those who did not know the life it was concerned with; did she wish them to remain in darkness? She answered that when those who knew the world about which she spoke were overtaken by senility or death, the poem would die too; it would be buried with her and her century; it was not written for eternity, nor even for posterity: the past alone had significance for poets – childhood most of all – those were the emotions that they wished to re-create and relive. Vaticination, odes to the future, even Pushkin's great epistle to Chaadaev, were a form of declamatory rhetoric, a striking of grandiose attitudes, the poet's eye peering into a dimly discernible future, a pose which she despised.

She knew, she said, that she had not long to live: the doctors had made it plain that her heart was weak, and therefore she was patiently waiting for the end; she detested the thought that she might be pitied; she had faced horrors and knew the most terrible depths of grief, and had exacted from her friends the promise that they would not allow the faintest gleam of pity to show itself, to suppress it instantly if it did; some had given way to this feeling, and with them she had been obliged to part; hatred, insults, contempt, misunderstanding, persecution, she could bear, but not sympathy if it was mingled with compassion – would I give her my word of honour? I did, and have kept it. Her pride and dignity were very great.

She then told me of a meeting with Korney Chukovsky during the War, when they were both being evacuated to cities in Uzbekistan. Her feelings towards him had for years been somewhat ambivalent: she respected him as an exceptionally gifted and intelligent man of letters, and had always admired his integrity and independence, but did not like his cool, sceptical outlook, and was repelled by his taste for Russian populist novels and the committed literature of the nineteenth century, in particular for civic poetry; this, as well as the unfriendly ironies which he had uttered about her in the 1920s, had created a gulf between them; but now they were all united as fellow victims of Stalin's tyranny. She said that he had been particularly amiable to her on the journey to Tashkent, and that she was on the point of offering him a royal pardon for all his sins, when suddenly he said 'Ah, Anna Andreevna, that was the time – the '20s! What a wonderful period in Russian culture – Gorky, Mayakovsky, the young Alesha Tolstoy – that was the time to be alive!' The pardon she had so nearly extended was instantly withdrawn.

Unlike the survivors of the turbulent years of post-revolutionary experimentation, Akhmatova looked on these beginnings with deep distaste; to her it was a dishevelled, Bohemian chaos, the beginning of that vulgarisation of cultural life in Russia which sent true artists into bomb-proof shelters when they could find them: from which they emerged at times, only to be slaughtered.

Anna Andreevna spoke to me about her life with an apparent detachment, and even an impersonality, which only partially disguised passionate convictions and moral judgements against which there was plainly no appeal. Her accounts of the personalities and acts of others were compounded of sharp insight into the moral centre of both characters and situations – she did not spare her friends in this respect – together with a dogmatic obstinacy in attributing motives and intentions, particularly when they related to herself, which even to me – who often did not know the facts – seemed implausible, and indeed, at times, fanciful – but it may be that I did not sufficiently understand the irrational and sometimes wildly capricious character of Stalin's despotism, which makes normal criteria of what can and cannot be believed difficult to apply with confidence even now. It seemed to me that upon dogmatically held premisses Akhmatova constructed theories and hypotheses which she developed with extraordinary coherence and lucidity. Her unwavering conviction that our meeting had had serious historical consequences was an example of such *idées fixes*; she also believed that Stalin had given orders that she should be slowly poisoned, then countermanded them; that Mandel'shtam's belief, shortly before his end, that the food he was given in the labour camp was poisoned was well founded; that the poet Georgy Ivanov (whom she accused of having written lying memoirs after he emigrated) had at one time been a police spy in the pay of the tsarist government; that the poet Nekrasov in the nineteenth century must also have been a government agent; that Innokenty Annensky had been hounded to death by his enemies. These beliefs had no apparent foundation in fact – they were intuitive – but they were not senseless, not sheer fantasies; they were elements in a coherent conception of her own and her nation's life and fate, of the central issues which Pasternak had wanted to discuss with Stalin, the vision which sustained and shaped her imagination and her art. She was not a visionary; she had, for the most part, a strong sense of reality. She described the literary and social scene in St Petersburg and her part in it before the First World War with a sharp and sober realism which made it totally credible. I blame myself greatly for not having recorded in detail her views of persons and movements and predicaments.

Akhmatova lived in terrible times, during which, according to Nadezhda Mandel'shtam's account, she behaved with heroism. This is borne out by all available evidence. She did not in public, nor indeed to me in private, utter a single word against the Soviet regime: but her entire life was what Herzen once described virtually all Russian literature as being – one uninterrupted indictment of Russian reality. The widespread worship of her memory in the Soviet Union today, both as an artist and as an unsurrendering human being, has, so far as I know, no parallel. The legend of her life and unyielding passive resistance to what she regarded as unworthy of her country and herself, transformed her into a figure (as Belinsky once predicted about Herzen) not merely in Russian literature, but in Russian history in our century.

To return to the starting-point of this narrative: in a despatch for the Foreign Office written in 1945,[1] I wrote that, whatever the reason – whether it was innate purity of taste or the enforced absence of bad or trivial literature to corrupt it – it was a fact that there was, in our time, probably no country where poetry old and new was sold in such quantities and read so avidly as in the Soviet Union; and that this could not fail to act as a powerful stimulus to critics and poets alike. I went on to say that this had created a public whose responsiveness could only be the envy of Western novelists, poets and dramatists; so that if, by some miracle, political control at the top were relaxed, and greater freedom of artistic expression permitted, there was no reason why, in a society so avid for productive activity, in a nation still so eager for experience, still so young and so enchanted by everything that seemed to be unfamiliar or even true, above all a society endowed with a degree of vitality which could carry off blunders, absurdities, crimes and disasters fatal to a thinner culture, a magnificent creative art should not once again spring into life; and that the contrast between the appetite for anything that had signs of life in it, and the dead matter provided by most of the approved writers and composers, was perhaps the most striking phenomenon of Soviet culture of that day.

I wrote this in 1945, but it still seems to me to fit; false dawns have been many, but the sun has still not risen for the Russian intelligentsia. Even the most hateful despotism sometimes has the unintended effect of protecting the best against corruption, and of promoting a heroic defence of humane values. In Russia this has been, as often as not, combined, under all regimes, with an

[1] 'A Note on Literature and the Arts in the Russian Soviet Federated Socialist Republic in the Closing Months of 1945', in Public Record Office FO 371/56725.

extravagant and often subtle and delicate sense of the ridiculous, to be found in the entire field of Russian literature, at times at the heart of the most harrowing pages of Gogol or Dostoevsky; it has about it something direct, spontaneous, irrepressible, different from the wit and satire and carefully contrived entertainments of the West. I went on to say that it was this characteristic of Russian writers, even of loyal servants of the regime, when they were slightly off their guard, that made their bearing and their conversation so attractive to a foreign visitor. This seems to me to be no less true today.

My meetings and conversations with Boris Pasternak and Anna Akhmatova; my realisation of the conditions, scarcely describable, under which they lived and worked, and the treatment to which they were subjected, and the fact that I was allowed to enter into a personal relationship, indeed, friendship, with them both, affected me profoundly and permanently changed my outlook. When I see their names in print, or hear them mentioned, I remember vividly the expressions on their faces, their gestures and their words. When I read their writings I can, to this day, hear the sound of their voices.

APPENDIX

Some of the passages relevant to the 'Guest from the Future'[1] in the *Poem Without a Hero* occur in the poems listed below. References are to the collection in one volume of Akhmatova's poems edited by V. M. Zhirmunsky, *Stikhotvoreniya i poemy* (Leningrad, 1976) (hereafter Z). Included are page references to Anna Akhmatova, *Sochineniya*, ed. G. P. Struve and B. A. Filippov, 2 vols ([Munich], 1967 (2nd ed.), 1968) (hereafter SF I and SF II).[2]

*Cinque*, Z Nos 415–19: 1, 26 November 1945; 2 and 3, 20 December 1945; 4, 6 January 1946; 5, 11 January 1946 (Z pp. 235–7, notes pp. 412, 488; SF I pp. 283–5, notes p. 410).

*A Sweetbriar in Blossom: From a Burnt Notebook (Shipovnik tsvetet: iz sozhzhennoi tetradi)*, Z Nos 420–33; 1, *Burnt Notebook (Sozhzhennaya tetrad')*, 1961; 2, *In Reality (Nayavu)*, 13 June 1946; 3, *In a Dream (Vo sne)*, 15 February 1946; 4, *First Song (Pervaya pesenka)*, 1956; 5, *Another Song (Drugaya pesenka)*, 1956; 6, *A Dream (Son)*, 14 August 1956, near Kolomna; 7, untitled, undated; 8, untitled, 18 August 1956, Starki; 9, *In a Broken Mirror (V razbitom zerkale)*, 1956; 10, untitled, 1956 (1957 in SF), Komarovo; 11, untitled, 1962, Komarovo (Z pp. 238–43, notes pp. 412–13, 488–9; SF I pp. 288–95, notes pp. 411–12).

Z No 555, untitled, 27 January 1946 (Z pp. 296–7, notes p. 499; SF I p. 295, printed (on the authority of Lydia Chukovskaya) as poem 13 of *A Sweetbriar in Blossom* (see above), notes p. 412).

[1] See p. 242 above.
[2] A third volume, edited by G. P. Struve, N. A. Struve and B. A. Filippov, was published in Paris in 1983. A complete English translation of Akhmatova's poems is also now available: *The Complete Poems of Anna Akhmatova*, trans. Judith Hemschemeyer, ed. Roberta Reeder (Somerville, Mass., 1989 [English text only: 2nd ed. 1992] and 1990 [with parallel Russian text]); this edition includes translations of many of Zhirmunsky's notes. Ed. 1997.

*Midnight Verses: Seven Poems* (*Polnochnye stikhi: sem' stikho-tvorenii*), Z Nos 442–50: *In Place of a Dedication* (*Vmesto posvyashcheniya*), summer 1963; 1, *Elegy Before the Coming of Spring* (*Predvesennaya elegiya*), 10 March 1963, Komarovo; 5, *The Call* (*Zov*) (originally published with the epigraph 'Arioso dolente', the title of the third movement of Beethoven's piano sonata, op. 110), 1 July 1963; 6, *The Visit at Night* (*Nochnoe poseshchenie*), 10–13 September 1963, Komarovo (Z pp. 247–50, notes pp. 414–15, 490; SF I pp. 303–6, notes pp. 414–15).

Z No 456, untitled, 15 October 1959 (October 1959 in SF), Yaroslavskoe Chaussée (Z p. 253, notes pp. 415, 491; SF I pp. 320–1, notes p. 418) (Professor Zhirmunsky has no doubt that it should be included under this heading; I feel less certain of its relevance).

*From an Italian Diary* (*Iz italyanskogo dnevnika*) (Mecelli), Z No 597, December 1964 (Z pp. 311–12, notes p. 502).

Z No 598, untitled, February 1965, Moscow (Z p. 312, notes p. 502).

*A Song* (*Pesenka*), Z No 601, undated (Z p. 313, notes pp. 422–3, 502).

Z No 619, untitled, undated (Z p. 318, notes p. 503).

*Poem Without a Hero: A Triptych* (*Poema bez geroya: triptykh*), Z No 648, 1940–62 (Leningrad–Tashkent–Moscow in SF): *Third and Last Dedication* ([*Posvyashchenie*] *Tret'e i poslednee*), 5 January 1956 (*Le jour des rois*); *1913: A Petersburg Tale* (*Devyat'sot trinadsatyi god: petersburgskaya povest'*), lines 133–45 ('The White Hall' ('Belyi zal'), 210 (Z pp. 354–5, 358, 360, notes pp. 427, 513–14; SF II pp. 102–3, 107 (lines 82–93), 109 (line 166), notes pp. 357–70, 603–5); *Epilogue* (*Epilog*), lines 40–50 (SF II pp. 130–1).

The reader should be warned that some of the figures who occur in the *Poem Without a Hero*, and in the other poems referred to above, may represent a fusion of two or more persons, real, imaginary or symbolic.

This is as much assistance to scholars as I am able to provide. There is nothing that I wish to add.

# THE THREE STRANDS IN MY LIFE

WHEN THE NEWS of the award of the 1979 Jerusalem Prize became public, the Israel Broadcasting Service telephoned me in Oxford, and the interviewer asked me whether it was correct to say that I had been formed by three traditions – Russian, British and Jewish. I am not good at improvising answers to unexpected questions, and I was too greatly taken aback by this deeply personal enquiry to provide a coherent reply. I have never thought of myself as particularly important, or interesting as a topic for reflection, either to myself or others; and so I did not know what to answer. But the question itself lingered in my mind, and since it was asked, it deserves to be answered. I shall do my best to do this now.

I

To my Russian origins I think that I owe my lifelong interest in ideas. Russia is a country whose modern history is an object-lesson in the enormous power of abstract ideas, even when they are self-refuting – for example, the idea of the total historical unimportance of ideas in comparison with, let us say, social or economic factors. Russians have a singular genius for drastically simplifying the ideas of others, and then acting upon them: our world has been transformed, for good and ill, by the unique Russian application of Western social theory to practice. My fascination with ideas, my belief in their vast and sometimes sinister power, and my belief that, unless these ideas are understood, men can be their victims even more than of the uncontrolled forces of nature, or of their own institutions – these are reinforced daily by what goes on in the world. The French Revolution, the Russian Revolution, American democracy and American civilisation with its vast influence, the horrors of Hitler and of Stalin, the rise of the Third or decolonised World, of Islam, and the creation of the State of Israel – all these are transformations of world importance; and their effects in shaping men's lives are not intelligible without a degree of insight into the social, moral and spiritual visions embodied in them, whether noble and humane, or cruel and odious – or a mixture of the two – always formidable, often dangerous, forces for good and evil or for both. That is an element in my conception of history and society which I owe, I believe, to my Russian origins.

The oldest and most obsessive of these visions is, perhaps, that of the perfect society on earth, wholly just, wholly happy, entirely rational: a final solution of all human problems, within men's grasp but for some one major obstacle, such as irrational ideas in men's heads, or class war, or the destructive effects of materialism or of Western technology; or, again, the evil consequences of institutions – State or Church – or some other false doctrine or wicked practice; one great barrier but for which the ideal could be realised here, below. It follows that, since all that is needed is the removal of this single obstacle in the path of mankind, no sacrifice can be too great, if it is only by this means that the goal can be attained. No conviction has caused more violence, oppression, suffering. The cry that the real present must be sacrificed to an attainable ideal future – this demand has been used to justify massive cruelties. Herzen told us long ago that sacrifices of immediate goals to distant ends – the slaughter of hundreds of thousands today that hundreds of millions might be happy tomorrow – often means that hundreds of thousands are indeed slaughtered, but that the promised happiness of the hundreds of millions is no nearer, is still beyond the hills. Acts of faith – *autos-da-fé* – when they inflict misery and savage repression in the name of lofty ideals, have the effect of removing all sense of guilt from the perpetrators, but do not lead to the blessed state guaranteed to result from, and therefore the justification of, the appalling means. When all is said and done, we are never too sure – not even the wisest among us – of what is good for men; in the end we can only be reasonably sure of what it is that particular societies of individuals crave for: what makes them miserable and what, for them, makes life worth living.

Men's ultimate ends sometimes conflict: choices, at times agonising, and uneasy compromises cannot be avoided. But some needs seem universal. If we can feed the hungry, clothe the naked, extend the area of individual liberty, fight injustice, create the minimum conditions of a decent society, if we can generate a modicum of toleration, of legal and social equality, if we can provide methods of solving social problems without facing men with intolerable alternatives – that would be a very, very great deal. These goals are less glamorous, less exciting than the glittering visions, the absolute certainties, of the revolutionaries; they have less appeal to the idealistic young, who prefer a more dramatic confrontation of vice and virtue, a choice between truth and falsehood, black and white, the possibility of heroic sacrifice on the altar of the good and the just – but the results of working for these more moderate and humane aims lead to a more benevolent and civilised society. The sense of infallibility provided by fantasies is more exciting, but generates madness in societies as well as individuals.

## II

An effective antidote to passionate intensity, so creative in the arts, so fatal in life, derives from the British empirical tradition. It was this civilised sense of human reality, a quality of life founded on compromise and toleration as these have been developed in the British world, that seemed so marvellous to the half-emancipated children of the oppressed and impoverished Jews of Central and Eastern Europe in the nineteenth century. I confess to a pro-British bias. I was educated in England and have lived there since 1921; all that I have been and done and thought is indelibly English. I cannot judge English values impartially, for they are part of me: I count this as the greatest of intellectual and political good fortune. These values are the basis of what I believe: that decent respect for others and the toleration of dissent are better than pride and a sense of national mission; that liberty may be incompatible with, and better than, too much efficiency; that pluralism and untidiness are, to those who value freedom, better than the rigorous imposition of all-embracing systems, no matter how rational and disinterested, or than the rule of majorities against which there is no appeal. All this is deeply and uniquely English, and I freely admit that I am steeped in it, and believe in it, and cannot breathe freely save in a society where these values are for the most part taken for granted. 'Out of the crooked timber of humanity', said Immanuel Kant, 'no straight thing was ever made.'[1] And let me quote also the words of the

---

[1] 'Idee zu einer allgemeinen Geschichte in weltbürgerlicher Absicht' ['Idea for a Universal History with a Cosmopolitan Purpose'] (1784): p. 23, line 22, in *Kant's gesammelte Schriften* (Berlin, 1900– ), vol. 8.

eminent German-Jewish physicist, Max Born, who, in a lecture delivered in 1964, said: 'I believe that ideas such as absolute certainty, absolute exactness, final truth and so on are figments of the imagination which should not be admitted in any field of science ... the belief in a single truth, and in being the possessor thereof, is the deepest root of all evil in the world.'[1] These are profoundly British sentiments, even though they come from Germany – salutary warnings against impatience and bullying and oppression in the name of absolute certitude embodied in unclouded Utopian visions. Wherever in the world today there is a tolerable human society, not driven by hatreds and extremism, there the beneficent influence of three centuries of British empirical thought – not, unfortunately, of a good deal of British practice – is to be found. Not to trample on other people, however difficult they are, is not everything; but it is a very, very great deal.

### III

As for my Jewish roots, they are so deep, so native to me, that it is idle for me to try to identify them, let alone analyse them. But this much I can say. I have never been tempted, despite my long devotion to individual liberty, to march with those who, in its name, reject adherence to a particular nation, community, culture, tradition, language – the myriad unanalysable strands that bind men into identifiable groups. This seems to me noble but misguided. When men complain of loneliness, what they mean is that nobody understands what they are saying. To be understood is to share a common past, common feelings and language, common assumptions, the possibility of intimate communication – in short, to share common forms of life. This is an essential human need: to deny this is a dangerous fallacy. To be cut off from one's familiar environment is to be condemned to wither. Two thousand years of Jewish history have been nothing but a single longing to return, to cease being strangers everywhere; morning and evening, the exiles have prayed for a renewal of the days of old, to be one people again, living normal lives on their own soil – the only condition in which individuals can live unbowed and realise their potential fully. No people can do that if they are a permanent minority – worse still, a

[1] 'Symbol und Wirklichkeit' ['Symbol and Reality'], *Universitas*, German edition, 19 (1964), 817–34, at p. 830.

minority everywhere, without a national base. The proofs of the crippling effect of this predicament, denied though it sometimes is by its very victims, can be seen everywhere in the world. I grew up in the clear realisation of this fact; it was awareness of it that made it easier for me to understand similar deprivation in the case of other people and other minorities and individuals. Such criticisms as I have made of the doctrines of the Enlightenment and of its lack of sympathy for emotional bonds between members of races and cultures, and its idealistic but hollow doctrinaire internationalism, spring, in my case, from this almost instinctive sense of one's own roots – Jewish roots, in my case – of the brotherhood of common suffering (utterly different from a quest for national glory), and a sense of fraternity, perhaps most real among the masses of the poor and socially oppressed, especially my ancestors, the poor but literate and socially cohesive Jews of Eastern Europe – something that has grown thin and abstract in the West, where I have lived my life.

These are the three strands about which the Israeli radio interviewer asked me: I have done my best to answer her question.

# INDEX

*Compiled by Douglas Matthews*

# Survival
# in the Outdoors

*Also by Byron Dalrymple*

COMPLETE GUIDE TO HUNTING ACROSS
NORTH AMERICA
SPORTSMAN'S GUIDE TO GAME FISH
ALL YOU NEED TO KNOW ABOUT FISHING,
HUNTING, AND CAMPING
DOVE SHOOTING
ICE FISHING FOR EVERYBODY
PANFISH

*An Outdoor Life Book*

# Survival
# in the Outdoors

Byron Dalrymple

*Illustrated by*
Charles Waterhouse
Carl Sigman
Fergus Retrum

OUTDOOR LIFE · E. P. DUTTON & CO., INC.
NEW YORK

# *Contents*

# Survival
# in the Outdoors

# 1 / Orientation for Survival

INVARIABLY when survival is discussed, people think of a lost man trying to survive. To be sure, a number of persons venturing into the outdoors do become lost each year. But the idea of survival does not begin and end there. *Survival situations may occur even when you are not lost.*

Heading out on a jaunt, you probably don't think at all of any danger. Why should you? You've been on outdoor trips time after time. If you are going into a large region sparsely settled, you are cautioned undoubtedly not to get lost. But a great many other situations might arise that will suddenly place you in a position where you must, by your own astuteness, get out of a difficulty of survival proportions.

## When You Are Not Lost

Not long ago, for example, only a short distance from one of the largest cities in the Southwest, a group of five persons, children and adults, perished in the desert. Their vehicle had become stuck. They were not lost. All they had to do, and failed to do, was stay in its shade. Water was within a third of a mile, a paved highway only a quarter-hour on foot. They used improper judgment and did not have necessary, simple knowledge. Heat and exposure needlessly killed them.

Consider your transportation into any wilderness region, or for that matter into any wild but not necessarily far-removed region. You can backpack, ride a horse, use a motor vehicle such as 4WD, trail bike, or snowmobile. You can travel by plane or by boat. You may be an expert woodsman who realizes that emergencies can arise. And the emergency may have no bearing upon your expertness or ineptness.

Let us say that you are alone, backpacking, and you are suddenly snowed in. Or you injure a leg. Or you are riding a horse and it falls and breaks a leg. Perhaps you are in a motor vehicle and it breaks down. Or your trail bike has two ruined tires. Or the boat you used to get thirty miles back in the bush somehow gets cracked up. Or a plane crashes.

It is probable that in all but the plane situation you are not lost at all. But you do have to extricate yourself. Can you do it? Will you be *equipped* to do it, mentally as well as with basic gear? Physically, too? The majority of average outdoorsmen, even those who are deskbound most of the year, are tougher physically than they think, if they can control their mental state and use careful—and practiced—judgment to arrive at a sensible, cautious course of action.

Too much nonsense has been written about this subject. It is fine to know how to build a water-gathering trap in the desert. It is great to know that cattail roots are good to eat. However, the "there's-nothing-to-it-take-heart" bit has lured many a befuddled amateur woodsman into difficulty.

## Knowing Yourself

In my opinion, a broad category of survival lore begins with *you*, not with the cattail roots. Again, all of the woods lore is excellent to have, but a man who knows what survival is all about realizes that it begins and ends, really, in his own thinking processes. You can live longer than you think without food or on very little. The specifics of living off the country, making yourself comfortable and safe in emergency situations, and all the information needed to assist you in times of outdoor difficulty are important, but you can't live very long without using your head and knowing how to use it with firm discipline!

An honest evaluation of your mental and physical reactions and capabilities will help you to *cope with yourself*. This is the person, remember—you—who may well be the only one upon whom you can depend to surmount the emergency!

Perhaps you get lost easily. If so, don't be embarrassed. Don't pretend you don't. That's just asking for trouble. As a matter of fact, there are in my experience only three general classes of outdoorsmen so far as orientation is concerned. One type never gets lost, compass or none. I know several of these, but they are rare. Another is what might be termed "pretty good." Look out for these! They're real trouble! Third comes my class, the ones who long ago learned to rely on compass and map. Since I know I am one of these, I don't let myself get into situations where I must depend on my own sense of orientation.

You should know so much about *you* that in any situation of emergency you will be able to predict how you will react. For instance, does altitude bother you? Many people have startling reactions to altitude, mostly caused by low oxygen supply, but also by various phobias, the awesome expanses of mountains, high places and so on. I know precisely how high I can go before I begin to feel some kind of peculiar anxiety. I *know* it will occur, so I don't worry. Also, I know precisely at what altitude I begin to "run out of gas." At ten to twelve thousand feet I do not sleep well, my muscles ache and I never feel top notch. Often a shot of oxygen, a whiff from a portable container taken along, is an immense relief, indeed, a cure.

What happens to you when you enter dense thickets? Have you tried it and do you know? Some persons, though in no real danger, have such severe feelings of claustrophobia in such circumstances that they are physically ill. Others are only slightly discomfited, or not at all. People are indeed individuals.

What happens to your feet on a long hike? Supposedly, if your boots are proper and fit correctly and your socks are not mended or rent, your feet should not be troublesome. But certain persons literally suffer anguish from much steady hiking. The legs of others chronically give out on even a short climb. Very slow going with rest stops every few steps may well be the answer to such a problem. The point is, will you remember these things under strain of emergency?

There are also scores of outdoorsmen who admit to minor or major feelings of panic when they are left alone in the woods or any wild area. It is revealing to know what happens all too often to people who panic. They do strange and totally unreasonable things. A breakdown of a vehicle sends a panicked man off across a swamp instead of down the trail toward help. A hunter who is lost throws away his gun, races through brush, tearing his clothes to shreds. People in panic have been known to cross paved highways and keep on going. They are literally temporarily insane. There are instances of lost men actually hiding from their rescuers.

Don't deny these feelings to yourself. You don't have to dwell on them and enhance their importance. But if you admit them to yourself, and in certain cases even to a guide who is with you, a first step has been made toward dodging trouble.

## Survival Mentality

Any practicing and dedicated outdoorsman should form the habit of thinking of himself on all trips as always close to possible emergency. I do not mean that you should go about cowering and frightened, wondering what awful crisis is going to shape up, but you can prepare yourself mentally to realize that emergencies can occur.

Among most primitive peoples *worry* and *panic* as we know them are almost unknown. These peoples are stoic, fatalistic, and usually able to cope with whatever situation occurs, because they are much more familiar with their surroundings than we. The "calm mind of the primitives" is without any question the most important tool that *you* can use in extricating yourself from any emergency. It is so important that the lack of it may tip the balance toward life or death. This is the precise time *not* to let fear and panic grab you. It is a good idea, under many circumstances, to forget about your starting point. Tell yourself there is no hurry about getting back to that place. Where you are now is what's important, and your mental attitude under stress is what will make it possible, or impossible, to eventually return to your original position.

One of the best insurances against panic is to be well-informed beforehand as to just what sort of box you might get yourself into. If you have guts enough to face the truth, there are plenty of emergencies that are downright sticky. Being lost is one of them, because in so many people this particular emergency does induce panic and unfounded fears. Getting yourself out of serious emergencies is not simple, and it certainly isn't always easy or comfortable. You don't just pick a few berries, dig a hole and hit a cold spring, and have fun. Emergencies are too often true ordeals. You want to realize this and keep it always in mind, the better to control yourself if one occurs.

On the bright side, though survival may not be easy,

it is generally possible. If you understand that fact well beforehand, you are preparing your mind for the moment when the sudden realization hits home that you are in trouble. And, though you know it isn't going to be fun, you should try to acquire the attitude that when it happens it *can* be an *adventure*. In fact, it can be the greatest adventure of your life because the stakes are high and the reason for winning so great. How could there be any circumstance in which winning would be of greater consequence, or of more satisfaction!

There were times years ago in this country when wilderness emergencies were far more serious than they are today. One of the most reassuring thoughts any outdoorsman can carry with him is the knowledge that regardless of what variety of emergency turns up, he is almost certain to be found and helped within a short time. *But only if he does his part properly*. In almost all true wilderness regions today, and in many not remote, search and rescue teams are trained and on standby. State agencies such as game and fish departments are equipped with planes and helicopters, and their personnel, both wardens and wildlife biologists, know every square mile of their state or province intimately. In National Forests, the rangers are likewise informed. In serious emergencies, federal agencies such as the Army and Air Corps join in.

Keep solidly in mind that the one thing that will make the work of rescue personnel most difficult will be the errors committed by the person who is in difficulty. *Your* help is as important and probably more so than theirs. You cannot assist others to assist you if you panic. So, whatever difficulty you have got into, don't act immediately or impulsively. *Stay right where you are,* sit down and get hold of yourself. That is the first and most important act.

I have a friend who has spent a great deal of time in wilderness areas of the outdoors. He once told me that whenever he is in a tight spot his first step is to build a fire.

"Even on a hot day in midsummer and in desert-type terrain," he says, "if there is any available material for a fire, I build one. This gives me something to do for a few minutes to get my nerves in shape, rather than sitting and fretting. Also, there is something about a fire that is like 'home.' It is probably a primitive instinct. Where your fire is, that's camp. That's where you belong. After the fire is going, I sit down beside it and begin to plot my course. By then I am calm."

*Feeling at home,* then, regardless of emergency, is a vital step in winning the battle for survival. Consider that a moment before this emergency arose, you were happy and enjoying life. You might have been lost for some time, but you didn't realize it and so you were not afraid or anxious. But suddenly you realize your situation. This is indeed a jolt. But what has changed? Nothing except your mental attitude. Don't let it run away with you! When you are lost, you are only temporarily removed from the place where you belong *most of the time.* If you have taken with you the proper knowledge, and the proper basic equipment, and you now hang tight to your proper mental attitude, you simply have a problem to work out.

## Being Prepared

For years now I have done my best to be prepared for emergencies, not just mentally, but with useful items of equipment as well. The gear you take along must bear a sensible relationship to where you are going, the type of transport you will utilize, and how long you will be gone.

For example, when my boys and I go to our ranch for a day of hunting, we never worry about food or comfort. In an old house on the property we have some cheap iron cots. Occasionally when a hard rain comes, the creek is so high that we can't get out and nobody can get in, until it runs down. So we keep a few canned goods there. We also have a couple of caches under rocks here and there that contain, in tightly sealed glass jars, salt and matches.

We have several old-fashioned cane poles stashed, with lines and hooks attached. On occasion we've caught fish, built a fire, broiled the fish on sticks, salted them and had a meal when we were famished and waiting for the creek to run down. These measures are not actually survival measures. I used them only to illustrate the basic idea. Stretch this remote ranch situation to the true wilderness, and the same philosophy of preparedness applies.

We will discuss various gear specifically in another chapter. But here let me say that I would not pack in by vehicle, horse, boat or plane anywhere without thinking beforehand of how I could get out *without* transportation. On some trips this may mean squirreling away a full-blown backpack outfit suited to the place and the time of year. In fact, that's an easy way to pack most of your gear. In other situations it may be enough to toss in a small rucksack with a few basics for overnight comfort or an afternoon's hike.

## Fatigue

Old-fashioned fatigue, exhaustion, is probably one of the main causes of outdoor difficulties. A trout fisherman stays too long on the stream, until he can hardly lift his casting arm. Coming out he stumbles, falls and hits his head on a rock. A hunter going back to camp is so weary he can hardly stay upright. Eager to get in, he stumbles hurriedly along, and tumbles off a ledge and down a shale slide. A backpacker keeps on the trail for so many hours that his senses are dulled. Just tired, all of them. Dangerously tired. Fatigue slows reactions and can even lead to hallucinations. It furthers carelessness: you miss an obscure trail because you don't see it; you're not alert.

There is no valid reason for becoming overtired outdoors, although nearly everyone does it. Know your limits and stay within them. After all, being outdoors is supposed to be for enjoyment. When it ceases to be, and you are in trouble, it is even *more* important not to get overtired. Conserve your energy. Exhaustion is one more difficulty, and it leads to others.

Emergency is always possible, wherever you go. It's like the rock that remains precariously balanced for many years. One day it topples. I don't travel hoping for emergency, or worried over one. I just go ready—

and reasonably confident because I am ready! Perhaps this sounds as if I'm trying to frighten you. But it might be an excellent idea if more people who find recreation in the outdoors were frightened a bit. Once past that state, they begin to work toward preparedness, and the prepared outdoorsman doesn't need to be frightened. He knows how to take charge!

# 2 / Pre-Emergency Schooling: Learning to Observe

PRE-EMERGENCY schooling for any outdoorsman means learning how to observe: how to look, listen, and correctly interpret what you see and hear. The rifleman who learns how to judge range accurately in either mountains or plains can judge how far it is from landmark to landmark when he travels. If he is adept at using a binocular, or a scope on his rifle, he can spot something distant, raise the glass and place it "right on" instantly. It is surprising how many beginners cannot do this.

To the schooled observer, nothing in the terrain escapes notice. He can go into strange territory and in a few hours be perfectly at home. He has checked out various landmarks and the general direction of watershed flow. He has observed the most common types of

12

vegetation, and whether for example there is a good blueberry or acorn crop this season. He has noted tracks and filed away mentally what made them. He sees where a deer or elk has been bedded, and where a black bear has clawed a stump apart or broken low limbs on chokecherry scrub to get the fruit. If he is fishing along a stream, he soon knows whether or not the ruffed grouse or woodcock are plentiful there.

Watch for animal tracks in strange country and determine what made them. By identifying the deer tracks here, you would have clues to the vegetation and geography of the area.

Nothing escapes him. Even a small broken branch beside the trail means something and he pauses to assess its meaning.

I said earlier that there are three classes of outdoorsmen so far as orientation is concerned: those who rarely get lost, those who are just "pretty good," and those who get lost easily. Now it is a fact that some outdoorsmen have a better sense of direction than others. But in most cases the person who just can't be lost not only has an excellent natural directional feeling but is mainly, and more importantly, a topnotch observer.

## Who Is 'Accident Prone'?

I am sure everyone has heard of what are known as "accident prone" individuals. Are you one? Have you ever thought carefully about this?

I have a close friend who is an avid and very experienced outdoorsman. Once when I was hunting deer with him he fell in rocks, smashed the stock of his rifle and cut his palm so badly that numerous stitches had to be taken. He was hurrying. On another occasion he shot a rifle that had a bullet from a handload stuck in the chamber—it had come loose—and he rammed another home atop it and blew up the gun. By a great miracle he was not killed, but he was seriously injured. He has fallen off a trail horse onto rocks, been hospitalized with pneumonia after being caught in a blizzard while trying to get out of the wilderness back country. These are just a few of his accidents.

So his family calls him accident prone. Even his doctor has sagely agreed that this man has "it" always hanging over him. But I'll tell you something. I have been with this man on a number of occasions under wilderness conditions. And I won't ever go again, regardless of our friendship. The term "accident prone" is purely and simply an excuse.

There is no proof that any man is headed for continuous "accidents" because of his genes. The man I used as an illustration *is* accident-prone, you bet. And I'll tell you why. He is incautious, reckless, inept in judgment, overconfident, has too quick a temper, and though he is a delightful companion most times, he totally lacks good sense and good judgment. Astrologers believe that all this is in the stars, but as this is beyond proof, I will claim emphatically that for every "accident prone" person you show me, I will show you one —the same one—who has somehow not learned about *caution,* one in whose head nothing clicks that says, "Watch it, this can be trouble!" when trouble is standing smack in the path just begging to be dodged!

Some professional guides, more's the pity, are like this. Maybe you recognize yourself. Are you one of these? Are you foreordained to follow a path where boulders fall on your head, vipers appear from nowhere to smite you, holes suddenly yawn in the trail to snap your bones? Cheer up! You can be cured—by you! Fit yourself out to dodge emergencies and chances of having to cope with them are far less.

Some time ago a fisherman out in Aransas Bay on the Texas Gulf coast pulled his boat up to an oil installation platform, climbed up on it to fish. The boat got free and drifted off. The man, in his fifties, decided to swim after it. He drowned. Accident prone? This

poor man was simply unbelievably incautious. All he
had to do was sit still. He would have been found by
boat or Coast Guard plane within minutes after he
was missed.

All you have to do is learn what *caution* is all about,
school yourself to see an emergency in the making, and
*become* cautious and discerning. Think ahead. Do you

In desert terrain, the practiced outdoorsman
looking for a campsite stays clear of dry washes
and walks in the hottest, brightest sunlight as a
safeguard against snakes.

really *need* to drive that go-anywhere 4WD up that
especially precarious trail? Recently in Colorado several people rolled with theirs some hundreds of feet
and several were killed. The sheep or elk you're going
after isn't worth your life. If you can't judge what is
truly safe, be smart enough to doubt. Don't take the
chance.

So, the first lesson in pre-emergency schooling is to *see* possibilities and avoid emergencies. I've watched hunters walk in places they shouldn't, where a fall would have been serious trouble. I've watched them walk, in hot snake country, in the shady spots, whereas they should have been skirting these and staying in the patches of hottest, brightest sun. I've seen campers set up on gravel bars in streams during rainy seasons—one not long ago when the river rose seven feet in a few hours. The people made it to shore in time, but with not much to spare. I've also seen campers, in desert-mountain country, make camp in a dry wash, an open invitation to disaster even without a drop of rain falling on them. A heavy, distant rainfall on a dry slope could send a wall of water down on them.

## Training Your Interest in Nature

Some outdoorsmen are better natural observers than others. But all can learn to be sharp at it. You have to have a keen interest in all of nature, or else train yourself to have it. You must make a conscious effort to know the birds, plants, animals. And you have to make a conscious effort to see everything that goes on around you. It is absolutely amazing to me how deficient many outdoorsmen are in basic knowledge. What good does it do to know that certain plants are edible and nutritious if you don't have any idea what they look like or in what terrains or plant communities they grow? Of what value is it to know that certain woods are far better than others for emergency fires, if you can't identify the trees?

Several years ago, two young fellows in the Southwest, supposedly good outdoorsmen, got themselves into a jam with a 4WD vehicle and spent several exceedingly uncomfortable and hungry days getting out to civilization. They had a shotgun but their only shells were fine birdshot. They debated about trying to bag a deer for food. They said a waterhole near the vehicle was peppered with small deer tracks. But they decided they'd never get close enough to a deer to kill it with birdshot.

What they had actually seen were javelina tracks. This was verified by the people who eventually got their vehicle out. Javelina tracks do superficially resemble the tracks of fawns or small deer. But the hoof sections are rounded in front, and uneven. To a trained observer in the desert, they are unmistakable. All the two had to do was sit by the waterhole and wait. The birdshot would have knocked over a small javelina. It has been done on numerous occasions.

Learning to observe is not only important to the "sometime" when trouble may appear, it is also a grand means of outdoor entertainment and to the accomplished a matter of immense pride.

I have two friends, brothers, whom I consider among the best outdoor observers I know. I don't believe these gentlemen will ever get into serious outdoor difficulty. I have been with them in Canada, Mexico, the western mountains, the southwestern deserts. They see everything, hear everything. I have watched them check out a bad piece of trail to see whether or not their 4WD would be able to negotiate it, and exactly how the bad spot should be approached. I've watched them turn

When you travel by vehicle, stop and look over difficult spots of trail before continuing. It's better to detour than to risk serious breakdown.

down a good many such spots. They knew it would be foolhardy because of the type of soil, or the lack of anything to attach a winch cable to. When we hike anywhere together they are always *looking back*. Sure you know what the landmark you are heading toward

Even on short forays, look over your shoulder often to see what the landmark just passed will look like on the return trip.

looks like as you approach it, but how will it look when you're returning? The only way you can tell is to look back at it, and put into your mind how it appears from this side. Watching your back trail even on short jaunts where no big trouble but only brief inconvenience might occur, is the least practiced yet one of the most important acts of the observant outdoorsman. In wilderness situations *it is absolutely crucial!*

## Sounds and Smells

In addition to visual images, no sounds should go unnoticed. In a forest, the distant snarl of a chain saw has a message. It is also a directional point. A hunter lost in Wisconsin several years ago heard one plainly, he recalled later, the morning he went out but forgot about it after he became confused. There was a timber-cutting operation within less than a mile of him. The sound of traffic on a main highway, apt to be heavier in daytime, but likely to have loud big-truck sounds at night, is a sound to stow away for future reference. A friend of mine in Minnesota heard a distant "thud, thud, thud" partially obscured by a whimsical breeze. He took time to get on a knoll where he could hear better. He had wrecked his canoe on a float trip and needed help. The sound, as he evaluated it, just had to be someone chopping wood. It could be a camp. He took a compass bearing as closely as possible on it, knowing it probably wouldn't last long and that it could not be heard if it were very far away. It was a camp of fishermen on a small nearby lake and he walked right to it.

You should constantly listen for animal and bird sounds and learn what they mean. A hooting blue grouse, a rather naive species, in early spring could mean food to a desperate man. The sound of small pikas or coneys, those tiny rabbit-like animals of the high peaks, going "beep, beep" early and late, could lead to needed food in a bad situation, but only if the listener knows what makes the sound.

Perhaps you have never thought about it, but even a practiced sense of *smell* and an awareness that many smells are easily identifiable in the outdoor world can be of value. While hunting into the wind you can catch the scent of such animals as deer or elk, especially in the rut, and droves of javelina, from surprising distances. Patches of ripe strawberries give off a delectable and identifiable odor. So do several other varieties of wild fruits.

You should always be alert to the smell of smoke. It may mean a forest fire, or a campfire. A keenly attuned student of nature can smell a rattlesnake den when the snakes first come out in spring. It is even possible to smell spawning fish from a lakeshore or from a boat, when large concentrations, such as bluegills or other shallow-water spawners, are on their beds.

To be sure, many such scents may not have anything to do with survival, but again, *one might*. Having all of your senses alert at all times, trying constantly to learn and identify, builds up a storehouse of knowledge that may have endless uses. But more than that, the outdoorsman who approaches experience in every conceivable way is the one who is likely to be the most resourceful when the chips are down.

Nature lore is endless. The latitude and terrain have infinite bearing on it. I recall sitting with the two brothers previously mentioned in an evening camp in strange territory in a brushy area of the Southwest. We were listening to coyotes howling. They seemed especially plentiful.

"Must be a good year for rabbits," one of them remarked.

It was. Predator numbers rise and fall with the cycles of their forage. Sighting many hawks always means that the area has rodents and rabbits in abundance. Knowing the time of year when various crops of wild foods, from cactus fruits to wild persimmons to piñon nuts, are ripe is valuable. Even a knowledge of the times of year where certain species of fish spawn, especially those that run from lake into streams, is important. For example, in northern streams tributary to lakes, suckers jam by thousands even into small creeks. This occurs about the middle of May in northern Canada, earlier farther south. Smelt runs pack certain small creeks shortly after ice out. Both suckers and smelt under these conditions can be caught or flipped out on the bank by hand. Trout of several varieties, some of which spawn in spring and others in fall, can be trapped in small feeders by jerry-built small dams and caught by hand.

It will not do you much good to begin boning up on nature lore *after* you are in difficulty. Nor do you have to wait until you are on a wilderness trip to start. When you go pheasant hunting on somebody's farm, or trout fishing for a couple of hours along a stream close to which you have parked your car, keep fully alert. Practice. Look, listen and interpret. Every sight and sound in the environment is important to the whole, and important to you if you are to be fully at home in it. Learning and checking the authenticity of your observations is also most enjoyable. You see things no one else sees. You hear things your partners don't. You read signs they don't even see.

This recalls a hunt I made one season for Gambel's quail, those handsomely plumed desert runners. We were in desert country totally new to me, but I was with a native who knew it well. He kept stopping the car and getting out to check various places that might be used by quail. At first I didn't catch on to what he was doing. Finally he returned and got his dog out on leash.

"There's a good bunch around here somewhere," he said.

Suddenly I knew. He was checking for quail *tracks*. It was the first time I had ever heard of anybody looking for quail by their tracks. But in this soil and with sparse vegetation they were easy to see. He knew that quail coveys do not range widely. Birds were somewhere within a quarter mile of us.

### Reading Correctly

As you learn to read all of the sights and sounds around you, be certain your *interpretation* of what you see is correct. A somewhat amusing incident occurred one fall in Utah when I visited with a hunter who was after mule deer. It was early in the season, and I was headed with some other hunters for the high country and the aspen stands. The weather had been mild and the deer had not come down to the foothills yet. But this hunter insisted he was working an area where there were swarms of deer. They were, he told us, too smart for him. He had yet to see his first one.

We took time to look at this "hot" area. He had found plenty of sign, sure enough. Piles of droppings were scattered everywhere. But unfortunately in the dry air of this country the droppings do not change much in appearance, especially if damp from dew or a shower, over a long period. He was hunting the lower country winter range of the deer, and the sign was from the previous winter!

In a later chapter we will discuss weather in some detail. Along with other nature lore, bear in mind that weather is part of it. You should always be keenly aware of what the weather is doing, and what you suspect the signs mean it may do. I have traveled with many old-time "weather hands" who would say, "I don't like the feel of that wind." Or, "That breeze has got the smell of rain on it. Let's get out of here." Total awareness can be practiced and learned, and it is invaluable.

So, on every trip you make, no matter how short, practice being what is generally called a "good woodsman," even if you're just hunting cottontails on your back forty. The man who never cares about knowing one bush from another, who never sees tracks or feels a storm coming is almost certain to find himself in trouble when he needs such information. Conversely, the careful, sharp observer who has always schooled himself will be ready for that day when he may need all senses keenly honed, when what he sees and hears and properly interprets may be the very means to his survival.

# 3 / Where Emergencies May Occur

A NUMBER of outdoor-minded people pursue activities other than hunting and fishing. Some are rock hounds. Some backpack just for sheer enjoyment of wilderness hiking. A few make canoe trips or travel by rubber boats on remote rivers and lakes. Nonetheless, by far the majority of outdoorsmen who get into the back country are sportsmen, fishermen and hunters. These millions meet the most challenges by mass of numbers alone and face the possibilities of a major share of emergencies.

With transport so efficient today, thousands of sports-men who years ago would never have faced anything more rugged than a quail hunt or fishing trip after black bass near home find themselves taking off on high-country mule deer and elk hunts, flying to northern Canada after Arctic char, plunging into the bush on a bear hunt, or following hounds on a lion chase in southwestern desert mountains. Opportunities are almost endless and a great many persons in average circumstances can and do avail themselves of them.

This means that every year thousands are planning what to them will be new adventures. They will be thrusting themselves into outdoor situations with which they are wholly unfamiliar, getting involved in strange terrains. It seems to me therefore that all sportsmen should have a fundamental knowledge of what general *areas* of this continent and what *waters* are most likely to lead them into emergency situations. Relate this information to the various *species* of fish, game birds and game animals you will pursue. Because fish and game occupy the same habitats that outdoorsmen other than hunters and fishermen also visit, much material relating to the species will be just as valid for the non-sportsman.

### Fishing Hazards

We might begin with *fish,* chiefly because most sportsmen seldom consider that fish as well as big-game animals can lead them into trouble.

**Black bass.** The largemouth bass and its relative the smallmouth are the most popular freshwater sport fishes in the U.S. Odd as it may seem, their changing habitats over past years have gotten a good many anglers with boats into serious trouble.

Bass have been transplanted to the extent that their range today is nationwide. The construction of hundreds of large dams, forming impoundments of huge size, has progressed at such a pace that there is more surface acreage in these than in natural lakes. Today they are the foremost black bass waters.

Use caution on large, open lakes where stiff, unbroken winds can create extremely dangerous conditions for small craft.

The major share of these impoundments are scattered throughout the Mid-South, the Deep South, the Midwest, the Plains states and Texas. However, others now are found in such diverse locations as Oregon (Owyhee is an example), and Arizona-Utah-Nevada (Lake Mead, Lake Powell, Mojave, Havasu). To the unwary or incautious, these large manmade lakes can be very dangerous waters. Each extends across tens of thousands of surface acres, and commonly shorelines are hundreds of miles long. The danger for fishermen is rough water.

Consider that many of these lakes allow a stiff wind from a certain direction an uninterrupted path of fifty to one hundred miles straight up. I have seen such bass-renowned lakes as Falcon, on the lower Rio Grande, when a hard wind blowing for a couple of days made them literally too dangerous for anything less than a seaworthy cruiser of thirty to thirty-six feet. They are often more dangerous than open ocean expanses. Numerous bass fishermen and pleasure boaters have drowned in large impoundments simply because they badly underestimated them.

Strict adherence to all Coast Guard and state regulations is the first preventive. Having someone on shore know the general part of the lake where you'll be is next. And don't switch plans! Attention to storm warnings is mandatory. But if you are out on such a lake when a storm comes up, and you may be many miles from dock, unless you are positively equipped to ride it home, make for a protected cove immediately. Most impoundments have many, because flooding filled numerous small valleys and canyons. There are hundreds of spots where you can tie up, or get your light skiff ashore. Stay put, even if you have to stay overnight.

If you have an accident that disables your craft and you can get it to shore, again, stay right there. And relax. You will be found. Occasionally you may be near a marina or a dwelling and can get to a telephone. But on scores of the larger impoundments there are immense stretches of true or near wilderness areas along the shores, often in mountainous locales. Walking out can be rougher than you think and can lead to very serious consequences, for example in the deserts around such enormous expanses as Utah-Arizona's Lake Powell, or in the deep forests surrounding such a lake as the 182,000-acre Toledo Bend on the Texas-Louisiana line. "Stay with your boat" is the best advice you can get. And I repeat, have someone ashore know the general area where you are operating that day.

Dangerous situations may also arise in large swamps, such as the Everglades, where there is excellent bass fishing, or in a place like Okefenokee in southeast Georgia and across the line into Florida. Usually you will be guided in such places. By all means engage a

If your boat is disabled, find a protected area as quickly as possible and stay with your boat.

Beware of soft, slippery shorelines. Don't go wading unless you've checked to see that the bottom is firm.

guide. You can get hopelessly lost in these swamps, and even with a compass you'd be in bad trouble.

The last bass fishing warning concerns wading fishermen. Avoid soft shorelines. I once came close to losing my life while wading a lake shoreline in Michigan's Upper Peninsula. An old sawmill had been there years before. Some forty feet of decayed sawdust was under me and I was slipping and sliding on scattered slab cuttings atop it! As a rule, where such vegetation as lily pads grows, the bottom is very soft and may be treacherous. Where slender reeds grow, it is usually sandy or full of fine gravel, and firm.

**Panfish, walleyes, pike, muskellunge.** Most panfish are caught in quiet, smaller waters. However, white bass are schooling fish of the large impoundments and to a wide extent so are crappies. In those habitats the same cautions apply to them as to bass. Ditto for walleyes, pike, muskies, except that there are further hazards with these. Overall, the best of fishing for them is in Canada. This very often means fly-in trips, or pack-ins by various means, to backbush lakes. Don't go on these trips, guided or on your own, without maps and compass (see Chapter 5) and proper survival equipment, which will be covered in a later chapter.

**Salmon, trout, grayling.** Fishing for these handsome and most appealing fishes often leads to emergencies. Trips for Pacific salmon are not as likely to get you into trouble, because in most instances anglers are guided and fish from charter boats with reliable captains. Small craft occasionally get into serious trouble with these fish, however, for they venture offshore along the Pacific Coast in waters their craft are unsuited for. This is utterly foolhardy. Even if you ride the waves offshore, a blow can claim your life when you try to come in, on rocks or turbulent bars. Anglers unfamiliar with such big waters too often have too much confidence in their craft, which may have performed well in puny three-foot waves. Go on a charter boat!

Atlantic salmon are restricted in range and most of the good water is in eastern Canada. In far northeastern Canada you are certain to be guided and must fly in. Don't go without survival gear, compass and maps. But beware of another danger with these fish: A friend of mine barely made it several seasons back when he slipped in a Gaspé salmon stream and was carried downstream a hundred yards. An inflatable fishing vest is mandatory, and waders should be belted snugly to hold air and give buoyancy. Because of slippery rocks, an absolute must is felt-soled waders.

The Rocky Mountain region, much of Canada, and portions of Maine contain the best fishing for all trout species. Inflatable vests, easy to obtain nowadays, or the foam-type jackets that give both warmth and flotation, should be mandatory for all large-stream trout fishing. A great many western streams, even some called "creeks" there, are large rivers. They can be exceeding dangerous to inept waders, first-timers, and occasionally to incautious old hands. The power of current in such rivers—perhaps the famed Madison in and outside Yellowstone Park is the best known—is difficult for the inexperienced trout fisherman to imagine. A wading staff with thong attached for securing to shoulder or belt is also an excellent help. Some are collapsible. I am skittish of these; they could let you down.

Most important on all western streams, and in many across Canada and in the Northeast, are again waders with heavy felt attached to the soles. You may locate in some stores a felt-soled buckle-on item that attaches over the foot of regular waders. There are also heavy aluminum or steel cleats that buckle over boot feet with straps. Both types keep you from slipping on slick rocks. Felt is most popular, easiest to obtain, probably best. You can even apply it yourself.

Rocks in many streams are unbelievably slippery. Drowning is not the only danger. A fall in current means your head may strike a rock. In rivers like the Gallatin south of Bozeman, Montana, and many others, where there are large boulders both above and below water, this is a serious possibility.

The other emergencies that may occur when fishing for trout, and for grayling, which are usually in remote waters, are getting lost, or having to come out from pack-ins or fly-ins. The enormous National Forests (and some BLM lands) of the West contain the lion's share of the prime U.S. trout fishing. Wilderness portions of Canada furnish a comparable amount. And of course portions of upper New England, such as the wilderness of northern Maine, and areas of the Great Lakes States like Michigan's Upper Peninsula, all are the same. Material in later chapters refers to travel in such large forest expanses.

There is one more caution relating to salmon and trout. Today the coho and the Chinook have been stocked, as many readers know, in the Great Lakes. The lake trout is also making a comeback there after near extinction by the lamprey. The emergence of the transplanted salmons as fantastic sport fish in the Great Lakes has drawn thousands of fishermen who have never before handled a boat on waters of these proportions. The Great Lakes are among the most dangerous and unpredictable of all U.S. waters. A couple of years ago a number of salmon fishermen lost their lives and scores of boats were smashed simply because anglers were not well enough equipped or well enough schooled in boat handling. The potential for trouble is still there. Treat the Great Lakes with awe and respect, obey official warnings, and outfit properly. Nobody can tell you in a book how to get out of trouble in a Great Lakes storm you have underestimated. You probably won't! Best advice is to avoid it!

**Beaches.** There are not many lonely coasts left along our marine beaches where fishermen can lose themselves. Basic emergencies among saltwater fishermen come chiefly from three sources: using craft too small for bluewater operation; carelessness or lack of knowledge about currents and undertows when wade-fishing the surf; accidents from slipping on wet, algae-covered jetties.

About the first there is little that can be said. We can only caution boatmen against venturing into big water with small boats. Regarding the dangers of wading surf and rips, beginners should avoid getting in much past their knees, and should take the advice of, and observe, old hands past that depth. Accidents on rock jetties and other slippery surfaces have been more commonplace than most believe. The result is not nice to

Don't let yourself get knocked off balance in wading surfs and rips. To be safe, wear steel cleats or ice creepers over your footgear, and, beginners especially, avoid deep water.

describe. There are two rules: Whenever you walk on such places, wear steel cleats or regulation ice creepers over your foot gear; when wind and waves are high, stay off!

There are a few beaches where vehicle breakdowns or exhaustion might get you into trouble. The longest stretch of uninhabited marine beach in the U.S. now is the Padre Island National Seashore on the Texas coast. The island is about 115 miles long, the Seashore roughly 88 miles long. A dredged cut across the Island about halfway stops explorers from either end. It is deep and can be treacherous on moving tides. There are three rules for people in trouble on Padre or any comparable beach: Be sure someone knows where you are going and when you planned to return; in hot weather, rig whatever shelter you can for shade; stay put. Coast Guard or Park Service personnel will find you in short order.

## Birds and Animals

The roster of game birds and animals undoubtedly lures more sportsmen into emergencies than do fish. Surprising as it may seem, game birds cause hunters a lot of trouble. Part of it stems from the fact that wing-shooting seems innocuous and generally tied to well-settled locales. This should not lull the hunter. He should recognize the several potential dangers and know what to do about them.

**Waterfowl.** Of the birds tied to marsh and water habitats, geese, which feed chiefly in open fields, are the only ones that seldom mean trouble. Ducks and rails, in both freshwater and saltwater marshes, are the troublemakers.

Rails are hunted chiefly along the large salt marshes of the East Coast and the upper Gulf Coast, by two methods: wading and slogging muddy areas where deep canals may have to be forded, and by hunting from a boat with a guide poling the marshes. Invariably trouble can be laid to tides. If you walk, be sure you know tide times. You may be trapped and unable to get back to high ground. In a boat, there are occasions when a light craft can be pulled over a mud flat safely either to or from the hunting grounds. Hunting is always on the high tides, which push birds out of hiding. The safety rule here is absolutely never to leave your boat. If the bottom is especially soft, take no chances. Stay in the boat and suffer until tide change!

There are a few large marshes, especially along the upper Gulf Coast, where a duck hunter can easily become lost. When hunting such spots, map and compass are just as important as in wilderness big-game hunting. More so because there are so few major landmarks. Marsh-wading duck hunters also get into trouble. Soft spots can let you down so deep, in such thick, sucking mud that you cannot get out. You should realize that getting stuck collapses boots or waders against the legs so severely that you cannot pull your legs out of the boot as a desperate measure. Don't wade marshes you're unfamiliar with, unless you have checked with local experienced hunters about marsh conditions. Be especially wary of wading across open cuts and channels. A hard wind may lower water in these and make them wadeable, but the mud may be a dozen feet deep or bottom and once you go down, that's all. A few years ago this actually happened to a young duck hunter near Detroit, Michigan. By great good fortune he was rescued before the wind laid and water poured back in. But it took several men to extricate him.

The rule for waterfowlers hunting from boats is never to leave the boats behind. If lowering water along a seacoast puts the boat out of commission on a mudflat, stay in it until help comes or the water rises. If you have motor trouble, or some other difficulty, stay with the boat. If you have left word where you are going and about when you hope to return, you'll be found quickly. Trying to slog ashore may court disaster.

**Pheasants, Huns, quail.** Farmland game birds such as pheasants, Huns, bobwhite quail are not likely to lead you into survival situations. Desert quail, such as scaled, Gambel's, and California, might, and bobwhites might in certain regions. Desert quail, and bobwhites in the South, place a hunter in the areas of greatest concentrations of rattlesnakes. A bit about this will be found in a later chapter. But right here is a good place to note that snake leggings—aluminum or wire net with canvas covering—are readily available and provide excellent insurance.

The desert quail in the Southwest and West can lure a dedicated wingshot into losing himself, for they are great runners. Here again, map and compass are never amiss, and some knowledge of desert survival (see later chapter) is important. These quail are often found in huge expanses of arid and sparsely populated range. Don't let them beckon you into trouble when you had intended to go "just a few steps" from the vehicle!

**Grouse.** Getting lost does not require a vast expanse of solid woods. Remember that well! Scores of ruffed grouse hunters lose themselves by seeing a bird cross a backwoods trail, parking their cars and going after it. A hunter strange to dense woods may not believe that he can be no more than fifty yards in and yet not be able to look back and spot his vehicle.

The reason I emphasize ruffed grouse is that it is widespread, from the large forests of New England south into the rugged mountains of western North Carolina and west throughout much of the Rockies and the Pacific slopes. It draws a lot of hunters. Material in later chapters relative to map, compass, equipment is all pertinent and I strongly advise that ruffed grouse hunters and woodcock hunters (woodcock are found in the same coverts) take along basic survival gear in a small rucksack, even on "short" jaunts.

The mountain grouse, such as blue, spruce, and ptarmigan (presently legal in Colorado and perhaps soon in Washington), are wilderness birds that require the same "travel instructions" as the big game of the Rockies and Canada. The U.S. National Forests and the public forest lands of Canada are where most hunters will encounter these birds. These are large expanses where emergencies are common.

The prairie grouse—sage grouse, prairie chicken, sharptail—are not likely to lose anybody, except in very few instances where sharptails are found in burns and scrub willow regions of Canada. Seldo hunters purposely hunt these birds there, but you may take them as incidentals (also true of spruce and blue grouse) while hunting big game. Invariably you will, by law, have to be guided. Prairie grouse hunters within the U.S. should heed one caution: Sage grouse, and occasionally sharptails, are often hunted in early fall or late summer, and rattlesnake danger in their habitats is fairly high.

**Chukar partridge.** This introduced bird is now avidly hunted in a number of western states. It may be found in reasonably civilized regions. But not often. Its prime range is in some very tough expanses of rocky ridges and cheatgrass slopes far removed from settlement. The chukar is a runner, invariably uphill. It can lose its pursuers on occasion, and chukar hunters can easily get into injury or vehicle-breakdown difficulties.

**Small game.** Rabbits and squirrels seldom get outdoorsmen into trouble. But two varieties can. One is the snowshoe hare (rabbit) of northern cedar swamps and mountains, from Maine to Washington, most avidly hunted in forested portions of New England and the Great Lakes in winter. It dwells in winter within dense cover such as cedar and alder swamps. These are real "man losers," and at a bad time of year. If you get into trouble in snow, backtrack; don't flounder onward.

The other species is the gray squirrel, a forest squirrel nd in greatest abundance throughout the Ozarks, hern and mid-south forests, and in lesser abun- farther north. National and State Forests and large woodland expanses, often of dense big

You can lose yourself easily by chasing after gray squirrel in heavily forested areas. Have map and compass along for protection.

timber like oak, provide the chief hunting ground. Gray squirrel trouble has caught up with a number of hunters because they couldn't imagine a "little ole cat squirrel" being dangerous. Map and compass are good protection.

**Big game.** Antelope on the plains are not likely to lose anyone. But they can cause minor difficulties through vehicle breakdowns. Much depends on the state where you hunt. In New Mexico, for example, hunts are so thoroughly policed by game wardens that help is probably close by. In large expanses of Montana or Wyoming you might be a good many open-country miles from assistance. However, any nonresident hunter anywhere is usually being guided. Watch out for rattlesnakes. Stalking antelope hunters have been bitten.

Mountain sheep, mountain goats, the large northern bears, caribou and moose are wilderness creatures. But in nearly every state and province a guide must be retained in order to hunt them. Certainly there is less danger of emergencies when one is guided. The sheep and goats especially get hunters into injury situations, because of the necessity of climbing. All wilderness travel precautions apply when hunting any one of the above.

Elk are high-country animals hunted throughout much of the Rocky Mountain region. They are exceedingly wild, likely to travel long distances. A wounded elk can lead a hunter many miles. Fortunately most elk live in high mountain terrain where landmarks are numerous, even though settlement is sparse. The western National Forests are prime elk terrain. A major share of hunts are guided, or a group of hunters operates together. Injury, breakdown, fall snowstorms, getting lost are all hazards of elk country. Again, proper equipment and knowledge are mandatory.

Black bears are a prize many hunters eagerly seek. Bears are chased by hounds owned by guides, or they are baited in spring. In most bait hunts, the hunter is guided, stays by his stand, and is later picked up. Certainly if you walk in, in strange territory, you should have map and compass and other moderate equipment. Anyone who deliberately sets out to follow a black bear track—and this happens as well to deer and elk hunters in fall—is not only a bit foolhardy but generally wasting his time. Black bears ramble aimlessly, and many miles. Throughout their range, which covers most of the forested regions of the U.S. and Canada, they favor dense cover where the going for a man is rough. Black bear hunters should carry survival gear.

**Deer.** Of all the lost men and all the hunters injured each season in the woods, snowed in, broken down, and bogged down, deer, whitetails and mule deer, are responsible for most of the difficulty. In today's world many animals live on the fringes of civilization. They have adapted well. This is especially true of whitetails, abundant over almost all of the U.S. east of the Mississippi and in certain regions west of it, such as Texas, the Plains states, the east slope of the Rockies and isolated pockets elsewhere. But by and large the several million deer hunters operate in the State and National Forests, border to border and coast to coast. And in any area under forest conditions, and under mountain-forest conditions for mule deer of the West, you always run the risk of emergency.

Most deer hunters get into trouble, often serious trouble, through plain carelessness. Portions of what is to be said here apply to all other hunting or fishing endeavors.

First, a major share of deer hunters go out "just for the day," that is, a single day at a time, in territory they know, or think they know, rather well. But somehow they get turned around or they wound a deer and follow it, or they decide at the last minute to hunt in a different place than originally intended. These one-day-at-a-time hunters, even on their home ground not in a farmland community, should be equipped map and compass and basic survival gear. So should know precisely the area where the day's hunt is to be done, and the hunter should never deviate from his set plan.

Second, thousands of deer hunters camp out in the forests, usually in groups. A vast amount of trouble oc-

Taking off suddenly on a short hunt near camp is a foolhardy idea. With no survival equipment except a gun, and no one knowing where you intended to go, there won't be much help if you meet with trouble.

because certain hunters set out for just a quick
~urn in the woods near camp, and are found three
~er in bad shape some miles away. The "short
~ camp" (or vehicle) is one of the worst trouble-

makers, because invariably the hunter sets off without any equipment except his gun. Commonly he doesn't even take a jacket, or matches. He wounds a deer, or is lured on and on by flying grouse, and shortly he is lost and without survival equipment. No one knows where to look.

Remember once again that you *always* set out, even on short jaunts, as if you really planned to get lost or get into some kind of trouble. Deer hunters, because they are so numerous and because so many are really inexperienced, hunting only a few days a season, should especially heed this advice. Be sure someone knows where you are going, and always go prepared for emergency.

**Wounded game.** There are two more items that should be noted here. Each season a number of hunters are injured by wounded game. Usually they are alone, probably not expected back for some hours, and thus in serious trouble. I knew a deer hunter who shot his first deer, raced to it, set his gun against a tree, started to gut the deer. It leaped up, knocked him down, broke his leg, and escaped.

There are endless variations. A "dead" bear kills a hunter, a downed moose tosses its head and injures the carelessly eager trophy taker. Be positive a downed animal is dead. Move in slowly, gun ready. Never under any circumstances set the gun down until you are positive. Never have it slung over a shoulder. A big buck mule deer almost got me head-on a few years ago as I paced off the distance of my shot, walking with gun slung. The deer came off the ground in a vicious lunge when I was just seven paces away. It fell. If it had no certainly I could not have stopped the charge. A method suggested by some hunters is to cautiously approach the downed animal and, even though you're certain it is dead, touch its eye with the end of the gun barrel.

A number of injuries occur because a supposedly dead antlered animal jerks its head reflexively while a hunter attempts to move it for gutting or actually starts to gut it. Antlers can be very dangerous. Stay shy of them. Even when you're trying to move for gutting or draining a gutted big-game animal that is "for sure" dead, be cautious of getting hurt by the antlers.

The final item of importance is to be cautious with your knife. A few years ago a well-known outdoor writer nearly died from blood loss when he accidentally slashed his leg gutting a mule deer. A hunter is usually excited from the kill when he starts the gutting process. He is usually hurrying, impatient. Make it a rule, however, to take your time and to keep foremost in your mind that an emergency could be shaping up to ruin an otherwise enjoyable hunt!

# 4 / *What You Need for Emergencies*

NOT LONG AGO I met a young outfitter who used a cheap, skinny sleeping bag, no mattress, and just flopped. He sure went light, and he sure was young and tough, but he also got up lame, hurt almost every day, and caught cold incessantly. Meanwhile, I broke out my down pillow, the same one I use at home, crawled into my wonderful big bag, and slept on foam plastic three inches thick. The pack mule, I can assure you, never thought twice about those packages. It would have kicked just as hard if it hadn't carried anything.

I believe in being rested and as comfortable as I can get, when I am going, and there and everything is perking along okay. However, when an emergency crops up, things change. At such times you must have squirreled away the items that will do best for you under specific and sometimes lean circumstances.

## Survival and Comfort

This is when *comfort* can go hang. You must have available all of the items necessary to your *safety*, but not necessarily to your *full comfort*. My two themes are not incongruous. For example, there are many sleeping bags that can be placed one inside the other. The result is a delightful, full-comfort sleeping arrangement when all goes well. But by stripping down you can get out of an emergency light and alive. That big foam mattress is great, but I could turn my back on it in emergency because I have already prepared some sort of groundcloth or other piece of basic equipment, to make do if and when dire need arises.

We are talking about a two-in-one outfit in some far-back situations. I want comfort. But I don't believe that in an emergency it is worth even a passing thought. *Survival* and *comfort,* as modern outdoorsmen know them, are not companions.

A history of early voyageurs on the Red River of the North related how men had to line boats up the river in bitter weather. Even the toughest became ill at times. The diarist recorded: "We had two sick men with fever. But the captain said that unless they were dead in three days they were well. One died. The other two recovered, but had to continue to wade and labor in the bitter water and weather."

The ability to suffer gracefully, or at least stoically,

is one great asset for the man in emergency. Here again mental control is crucial. Bear with it. Nobody else is going to sympathize with you! The word "survival" means getting back alive. It has no relation to wallowing in lush creature comforts and having a delightful time.

## Survival Pack

Your pack for survival in any situation, therefore, is based on the most basic *attempts* at comfort. Maid service is out. What you want are the fundamentals, in as compact and light a conglomeration of gear as you can fit to the situation.

The first and most important "equipment" to take with you is the knowledge that someone outside knows where you are headed, how long you are to stay, and by what route and when you are returning. That is the easiest, probably the most important, and most often overlooked part!

What you are doing, how long you intend to be gone, how remote the territory, and your mode of transport dictates your choice of emergency kit or pack or equipment from there on. The average outdoorsman who is going fishing on a large lake, for a one-day canoe trip, into the woods after grouse, on a morning deer hunt, or hiking to a trout stream for a day should have a small rucksack that is constantly packed and ready. It need not be very heavy. It can contain scores of small items, or a very few that will be handy for comfort or necessary in emergency.

Start with this basic small pack. It can be a Boy Scout

type packsack, or a larger or even a smaller one. Most of the items to be placed in it, remember, are ones that will be needed on more extended jaunts, too. So all you have to do is think carefully about the vital items. What does *any animal* including the human need for contentment? Food, water, safety, comfort. There are varying degrees of all four. Basically the human animal needs to be able to build a fire under any weather conditions, keep reasonably dry, reasonably warm, sleep if necessary in relative comfort, eat, and quench thirst.

## First Aid Kit

First of all should come a first aid kit. There are widely varying opinions as to what this should contain. There are some very good pamphlets and booklets on first aid. There are scores of excellent first-aid kits already made up and sold in drugstores. Most good ones contain a small instruction manual, and a snakebite kit. Seldom will the snakebite kit have antivenin, however, so in snake country you must add that.

In addition, there should be a supply of band-aid plastic strips, plus butterfly-type closures for larger cuts. Gauze pads, thick ones about 4 inches square, possibly a half dozen of them, are needed for wound dressing. Wide elastic bandage, a roll of plastic adhesive, not the older cloth type, safety pins, small soap bar—these are the basics, plus merthiolate, aspirin, a tube of first-aid cream, another of burn ointment, and one or two of the modern small plastic squirt bottles for treatment of insect bites and stings. The merthiolate or comparable medicines should be replaced at intervals so they

An effective first aid kit that weighs only a few ounces includes several first aid creams, soap, merthiolate and aspirin, a variety of bandages and adhesive, safety pins, Q-tips, and snakebite kit with antivenin. In closed, waterproof bags carry a few clean handkerchiefs and a first aid instruction booklet.

do not get too old. In some latitudes sunburn cream (not oil that may spill) should be included.

Check out the various "sportsman's first aid kits" in stores and see what each contains. Some come in waterproof containers. Add a couple of clean handkerchiefs in a small, closed plastic bag. And be sure to have in your pack, not necessarily as a part of a first-aid kit, a small squeeze bottle or two of the new and highly potent cream-type insect repellent. This first-aid kit will weigh only a few ounces. You may wish to vary it somewhat, but the above should serve as a guide.

## Survival Clothing

It is difficult to suggest clothing for a small pack, because of the great range of temperatures where out-doorsmen may be. However, I made a rule long ago that regardless of what part of the country I was in, I'd always have a down jacket with me. I've seen days in Texas when the temperature dropped from 90 to 40 in a few hours. I've seen the same in Canada, and the Rockies of the U.S. West. The light jacket half of a down underwear suit is the best I know about. Worn under a wool shirt, and with a nylon outer wind-breaker, you can stay warm with it in vicious weather. It can also serve, rolled up, as a pillow when not needed for warmth.

Particularly for fall, I squeeze into a small packet a down underwear jacket, if I'm not wearing it. Let me digress here to say that on long hauls, where a large pack is made up, possibly to be carried on horseback, you should take along the full down underwear suit. It's light, can be compressed into a small space. Worn inside a light backpacker sleeping bag, the combo is like a double bag.

For the small pack we're talking about, the next clothing item is one of those little nylon windbreakers mentioned above—in red or orange or blaze orange.

Not yellow. That color can be confused with aspen or other abundant leaves in fall. Blaze orange is best. In the pack also is a rain suit of waterproofed nylon, pants and parka. If you are on horseback, you'll have a poncho tied behind your saddle. That's standard. But ponchos are heavy. The *quality* nylon rain suit is very light and packs into a small space.

In summer you may wish to delete one or another of these clothing items. But as a guide to comfort in almost any sort of emergency, these are the fundamentals.

A spare pair of warm gloves or mittens, and a spare pair of socks suitable for hiking should always be in your pack. For long trips, two pairs of socks. Also, I have long puzzled over why so few outdoorsmen who wear leather boots fail to purchase waterproof brands. There are several on the market, excellent quality, perfect for comfort, and literally waterproof. Insulated boots, incidentally, are fine even for fairly warm weather. They are also less wearing on your feet.

A notation here pertaining to water-related clothing and life-saving devices: In an earlier chapter I mentioned that fishermen wading large rivers should wear inflatable fishing vests. There are a number of these available. This is an important item for the pack of any fisherman, whether he will wade or fish from a boat or canoe. But of course he should wear it when on the water.

Another excellent product nowadays is a jacket that is worn comfortably in any hunting, fishing, or other outdoor activity, but that floats you like a life preserver if the need arises. These jackets are usually nylon on the exterior, with insulation that has thousands of built-in air cells. One of the better quality brands was tested not long ago, and after repeated immersions it still floated a man weighing over 200 pounds while he was wearing chest-high waders filled with water. These jackets can be compressed into a small space for packing, are light and very warm. For the waterfowl hunter or fisherman, this is a good choice for land-water combo wear. In addition to the above, the well known pocket-size Res-Q-Pak, the little emergency life preserver that inflates by $CO_2$ when squeezed, should be a part of every pack, large or small. It does no harm to have two. But be sure not to forget to wear it on the water.

## Special Items

Needless to say your compass and map are packed, along with a pencil for drawing necessary map lines. A small flashlight with fresh batteries is a good idea to add, plus extra batteries if there's room. I always carry, even on one-day jaunts, a few of those small paper packets of salt that restaurants or drive-ins often use. These are wrapped in plastic or placed in a small waterproof plastic container. A good knife is a must. This can be a knife worn on the belt, or a folding knife. It is a good idea to wear your belt knife but to keep a spare, a good folding knife, in your pack. There are numerous odds and ends that may come in handy: a few long leather shoe laces, for lashings in making a shelter; a spool of *heavy* fishing line; a roll of copper wire.

For emergency shelter, there are two items that can be packed in surprisingly small space compared to the amount of comfort they supply. One is a rubberized or plastic-coated nylon ground sheet or tarp. This should be about 8 x 8 feet. It folds flat in the bottom of your packsack. The other is a large sheet of heavy plastic. I have a friend who has been an innovator in winter camping. He has taken groups over the Continental

The miscellaneous section of your pack is as essential as the rest. A rubberized tarp and leather shoelaces provide emergency shelter; a good knife, rolls of heavy fishing line and copper wire, and salt packets in a waterproof container cover food possibilities. Other necessary items are a pencil, map and compass, and a flashlight with fresh and extra batteries.

Divide in dead of winter with sleeping gear consisting of a backpack sleeping bag and a big sheet of heavy plastic. They simply lay the sheet on snow, place the bag on it, wrap the plastic around and tuck it in. Such a sheet can also be used to make a lean-to or other type of shelter. The lashing material is used with either plastic or nylon tarp.

## Fire Equipment

Now to emergency fire-making equipment. You must carry matches in a completely moisture-proof container. There are several types available. Shy away from metal. It rusts and may be hard to open with cold hands. Large kitchen matches are the only kind to take. Squirrel away plenty of them. Paper matches are useless, small wooden matches not much better. But that's not the end of the fire-making apparatus.

Fire is so important that there is a full chapter devoted to it later on. But to keep items for emergency all together here, I must add that I believe in being over-prepared with the basics for fire-making. For example, there are numerous solid-state fire-starter materials on the market. A small box of these is invaluable for damp or windy conditions, especially since most persons who will really need a fire probably won't be too adept at building one under any but optimum campground conditions.

There is also the Metal Match. I believe that is a trade name, and though it is not our intent to plug brand names here, I don't happen to know of any other. The Ute Mountain Corporation in Denver is at this time the outlet for these. They really work. And, you can get a kit that contains ready-made tinder to catch the sparks. This outfit takes up such a tiny corner that I would not be without it, in addition to matches. And this brings up the fact that most fire-making instructions tell you how to collect punk or highly inflammable materials around you, from the woods. Fine. But better still, *have it ready,* in your pack, in the small packet with the fire-starter cubes.

Now add a magnifying glass about 3 inches in diameter. Though a camera lens or binocular lens or even a watch crystal may start a fire, the small glass can stay permanently in your pack. Hold it so sun shining through it focuses a small "hot spot" on the tinder or starter you already have. This glass serves a double purpose. I have spent a great deal of time in desert areas where cactus and thornbrush are abundant and can always use the small glass, and a *pair of good tweezers.* Both can be packed in your first-aid kit. The glass doubles for fire-making if needed. The tweezers remove those tiny cactus (or other) spines the glass "sees" that make life miserable but can't be removed with your nails or a knife point. Always stow in your pack, whether it is large or small, several candles. They should be those short, fat ones often called "plumbers' candles."

If you will review these odds and ends, you will discover you have fire-making equipment for almost any conceivable condition. If tinder is wet, dry it with the candle flame. You are outfitted to stay dry and warm. Even on one-day jaunts, if you take the down underwear jacket, you can sleep out with no bag in fair comfort.

### Food and Water

For short jaunts, or what are intended to be short ones, you cannot carry everything. I would not bother with a mess kit. It is easy to cook fish, or birds, or frogs, etc., on sticks over an open fire. But for long trips I certainly would have a light, basic-item mess kit in a pack: a container in which to boil water, another to cook in, a spoon. A packet of heavy foil, folded flat, has endless uses in cooking.

Halazone tablets should be in a pack, for purifying water. There are also compact water-purifying kits of several kinds, even battery-powered, on the market. Check any one of these with care before buying, however, to be positive it works as it should. On any warm-weather journey, even brief, a canteen of water is mandatory. You know best how much you require. For desert travel never be without a sizable canteen. I have convinced several friends to carry in addition an ordinary pint liquor flask full of water, for emergency use.

This leaves only food. A lot of living off the country, which we will discuss later on, can be done. But even on those short treks it is wise to have a small store of emergency grub. The amount must be matched to the terrain and its hazards. With foil and lightweight packets of freeze-dried or concentrated foods, excellent emergency meals are at hand. Wild foods supplement them. Numerous freeze-dried and concentrated foods are readily available nowadays.

A food that is to my knowledge not available commercially today, but a topnotch one we have made several times, is pemmican. I presume ours didn't taste just like old-fashioned Indian pemmican. But it keeps as theirs did, indefinitely, and it has all the emergency ingredients you need for days at a time. On many a day's hunt I have stowed a hunk of this, wrapped in foil, in my light packsack and used it and nothing else for lunch. Obviously you cannot carry great quantities of food on short journeys in a light pack. A tin or two of sardines, cocoa, raisins, nuts—these are suggestions. I would advise sportsmen such as deer hunters to *always* have along enough to "make do" for a day or so just in case.

Now then, all of the foregoing can be carried in a light packsack on short trips. At that, it may not be so light if you take along every item mentioned. But you can pick and choose according to where you are, where you are going, and balance the gear against the chances of emergency. You can make up a pack that will weigh no more than five pounds, and up to ten, that will allow you to live virtually "free and wild" in modest weather for weeks at a time, if you add to it a bit of ingenuity.

## Long Trips

For longer trips, such as by horse or plane or 4WD, some extra equipment is needed. As you select these items, think about how you can relate them to *what you will be using anyway*. In other words, this does not need to be all extra gear. It can serve both purposes. For example, you can make up a backpack outfit, an ultra-light quality one, that contains a tent of three or four pounds and a sleeping bag of like weight. By combining down underwear, as noted, with such a bag, you can get along well on any sort of trip. This outfit should be on a light packframe. It can be lashed this way, all packed, on a pack animal. It should also contain basic cooking utensils, and items previously mentioned.

Wonderfully planned backpack outfits are available nowadays, designed by people who practice the sport of backpacking weeks at a time. Check the literature on these, or look them over in stores, and figure which size will be best for you. Then if you get into a situation where you have to walk out, you are ready to go. Don't stint too much on weight. A properly put together and balanced pack of thirty-five pounds is not bad, and it will let you tote most of the ingredients for safety, shelter, warmth and food. You can cut that by ten pounds and still have a good emergency outfit.

**Gaff hook and wire.** There are some other things that might be considered. A good many years ago I was sent by a magazine to do an undercover story about some natives in Canada who had a hobby of illegally gaffing big trout during their spring spawning runs. I hiked with these people many miles into the bush, to a small stream running into Lake Superior. I had no idea of how the man heading the expedition intended to accomplish their mission. He carried a canvas pack on his back, but I saw no evidence of gaff or spear.

When we were at destination, he cut some stout, straight sticks about an inch in diameter and six feet long. He notched one end with a groove several inches long, and a cross groove in two spots. Now he hauled from his packsack several gaff hooks. Just the hook part and several inches of shaft that was flattened on the upper end. Next, out came a roll of copper wire. He lashed the gaffs to the sticks. These were used to strike big trout as they dashed up or down stream. These men were expert at it. One would make a pass at a four-pounder, the gaff would nail it, and in one motion the poacher threw gaff and all onto the bank.

I have often thought that this combo, gaff hook and wire, might come in handy in an emergency. I've never had to try, but have carried one several times. It is a good item in a pack for the far-back trip, especially during seasons when fish may be running in streams. But it could be used at other times by a careful stalker.

**Binoculars.** I never go anywhere in the forest, on horseback or otherwise, without a binocular. It has many uses besides hunting. It is a good emergency item for scanning country, seeking landmarks to get yourself oriented. I wear mine, but not flopping as most do. Shorten the strap so the glass lies fairly high on your chest. Make up a couple of tie downs (one a spare) of quarter- or half-inch elastic with hook and eye at the end, length cut to fit your chest and hold the glass snugly. You can now lift it to your eyes by stretching the elastic, let it down again where it won't flop and bounce.

**Tools.** Though a full-fledged camp on a pack trip will have a good axe, it would be foolish to carry one of full size for emergency gear. But a good sharp hatchet, in a sheath, carried in a pack or on your belt, is a must item. You may also find a kind of substitute in sporting goods stores, a head with blade and ripper that has a hole through it with heavy screw threads, into which you twist a cut stick for a handle. The good hatchet, all-steel handle, is probably best.

I also carry a saw. But I disagree with some others about what kind. The tiny wire-cable emergency saws aren't of much account. Nor are the so-called "pocket folding saws," the ten-inch saws that have a blade folding into the handle. These are toys. There is, however, a slightly larger saw of this folding type that is excellent. The blade is heavy duty, with coarse teeth, and curved exactly right to make a cut. It is a blade comparable to those used in long-handled tree-pruning saws. When folded, this saw, which costs only three or four dollars, is roughly fifteen inches long. I have cut trees six inches or more in diameter very easily with one. This often substitutes admirably for a hatchet, and in fact can more quickly do many chores that the hatchet does: cutting firewood or erecting shelters. Both, in a pack for long hauls, are sound equipment.

On wilderness hunting trips, fishing trips, or even simple hiking trips for neither purpose, I suggest some special compact fishing gear be a part of the pack. Nowadays you can buy a variety of what are called "backpack" rods. Strictly for survival purposes, the spinning or casting rod in this type will be best. These come broken down in small aluminum cases only 18 to 24 inches long, depending on the make. A light but sturdy line-filled reel for the chosen rod, stowed in a drawstring soft leather case is next. The line should be fairly heavy. Add an extra spool of line. In a small packet or plastic tube or box, put a few hooks of modest size, and a few split shot. Take line, hooks, and shot whether or not you take rod and reel.

In a flat snap-shut lure box, or better still a leather

or cloth zipper-closure pocket-type case, place a collection of metal spoons. These should be in several sizes, from three inches long down to three-fourths of an inch, and in varying colors. And here's the trick. Remove hooks from all. Outfit each spoon with a split ring. Numerous spoons can now be carried in a very small package. Leave the treble and double hooks at home. Take along in a small box some *single* hooks of various sizes, to place on the spoons as needed. A small pair of pointed-nose pliers fills out the outfit. The rod can be placed in the backpack, or lashed to it. The other gear takes up little space. Though you may not realize it, almost any species of fish found on the continent can be caught on spoons. If you don't take rod and reel, you can rig a brush-cut pole and make short casts with a spoon.

**Firearms.** A word should be said about firearms. If you are on a hunting trip, whether short or long, your survival pack should contain at least a few spare rounds of ammunition for the gun you are carrying. Many outdoorsmen nowadays have the naive idea that addition of a small sidearm will help them live off the country. Most couldn't hit the ground with it, let alone kill an animal or bird. Except for handgun experts, sidearms are more or less dude equipment. Also, you may get into trouble by shooting at large animals such as bears with it. There are small .22 rifles made that fold, or come apart easily, or that carry the barrel within the stock, etc. All these are very light, and in a pinch on a long trip by plane, boat or canoe, or even backpacking, it might be handy to have one in the pack. This is up to you.

Of great importance are signaling devices. Signaling is so important that a chapter is devoted to it later on. But to keep pack item ideas together, a few suggestions follow. These can go into the small short-hike rucksack as well as into large packs. A whistle is one, the kind that can be heard long distances. A signaling mirror is another. This is not an ordinary mirror but one designed purposely for signaling. (See chapter on Signaling.) These are generally available at such places as marine supply stores. Flares are available in a very small package that also contains the small gun for shooting them. Larger flares that burn longer are thrust into the ground. The small shooting flares are easiest to carry. Signaling smoke candles that emit yellow smoke can be obtained, too.

Try to relate the suggestions given here to your needs and your usage. You can't carry everything. But you *can* balance a survival pack, large or small, to do an efficient job. That job is to allow *you to survive* with as much comfort as is possible to pack into a small space and weight. Emphasis here is on the one-day trippers even more than on the long-haulers. Horseback, boat, 4WD and plane trips are usually planned rather well by an outfitter to begin with. Most outdoorsmen get into trouble, as we said earlier, because they are "just going to step off the road for a second" or there is a deer near camp and the cook can't resist going after it, trailing it when it is wounded, and winding up getting lost with no survival gear.

So, regardless of *where* you're going—down the big impoundment in your boat, for a fifteen-minute flight to a forest landing strip, on a one-day horseback or hiking jaunt to a trout stream or lake, or plunging into the woods when you see that bird cross the road and you park your car to go after it—take your little pack along. You know what it really is? *Home!*

# 5 / Map and Compass

A GOOD COMPASS and a map of the region where you are operating are the two most important items to carry. This does not apply only to wilderness endeavors. Even on a pheasant or quail or cottontail hunt in a well-settled countryside strange to the hunters, or on a fishing jaunt to a new lake or stream, both are very handy. An up-to-date road map helps you find the place from which you start, or locates landmarks and in some cases woodlots or state and county forests. The compass saves time in getting to and from where you want to go. Not that you are lost or are likely to become lost during such "civilized" sessions: the compass and map are simply handy. But far more important, if you get used to never being without them, and accustomed to using both at such times, you will have formed a habit that may save your life sometime in the future.

A few years ago I was hunting in the Pigeon River State Forest in northern Michigan. That Forest contains slightly less than 100,000 acres. That's around 150 square miles, and certainly ample room in which to get lost. Nevertheless it is crisscrossed by many old logging roads, trails and numerous streams. On the main sand roads there are markers at intersections. Excellent county and Forest maps notwithstanding, during my days in that region numerous outdoorsmen, both fishermen and hunters, lost themselves annually and I am sure they still do.

It is unbelievable how many outdoorsmen carry both map and compass, but don't know how to use either one. They rely on a compass to "get them out." Probably the clerk who sold it couldn't have found his way to the front door with one. And, neither map nor compass is much help if you don't know where you are to begin with, where you started from and where you want to get back to.

## The Best Compass For You

Let us therefore start from scratch. Compass first. There are several types. I don't intend to describe each, but I do intend to describe one, the best one for the average outdoorsman, tyro or expert. The extremely simple, cheap compasses so many outdoorsmen pin on a jacket lapel might be used advantageously in a pinch by an expert. They more often help only in making more confusion. The pocket-watch type is fair, but none can compare with an *orienting-type compass*.

There are several models in these. Here is a general description. This compass has a rectangular or oblong base. This base may or may not fold in the middle for compactness. In the most useful models one long and one short side of the base have ruled edges. The com-

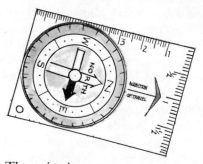

The orienting-type compass has a rectangular base and a movable housing containing the magnetic pointer. On the bottom of the transparent housing, there is a painted arrow; on the base, an arrow for sighting travel direction and ruled edges. The housing base is divided into 360°.

pass portion is affixed to the base well back toward one end, which we'll call the back end. Ahead of it there is a heavy arrow running toward the front end. This is usually an engraved, darkened arrow *to be used in sighting a travel direction*.

The compass itself is fashioned as follows: The bottom of the housing (in the models I prefer) is transparent. Across the middle of this round, transparent housing bottom there is a broad engraved, or painted, arrow. Lines run at even intervals out from this broad arrow, on either side and parallel to it. The actual compass pointer, the magnetic pointer, is affixed to this housing bottom precisely in the center of the broad arrow. The broad arrow is for orientation when you fully understand how the compass works. One end of the magnetic pointer (on the model I'm describing) is bright red. That is the end that will always point north.

Enclosing this round, transparent housing bottom and the magnetic compass pointer (needle) is the housing proper. It, too, is round, and it is also *movable*. It can be turned full circle in either direction. Its top is transparent. Around the metal edge of the top, outside the transparent disc, there are letterings: N, S, E, W. Halfway between each letter on the circle there is a heavy black line. These are read, when the compass is properly oriented, as northeast, southeast, northwest, southwest. Between each of these marks and the nearest letter there are two evenly spaced dots. These indicate gradations of an even nature, standard everywhere: NNW, which means halfway between northwest and north (sometimes read as "northwest by north"); WNW, meaning halfway between northwest and west, and so on around the circle. That is, NNE and ENE; SSE and ESE; SSW and WSW. Each of these sixteen markings—letters, lines, dots—equals a specific number of degrees when the compass is properly oriented. The marking system may differ in different brands, that is, it may have full lettering as I've given above, instead of lines and dots, but the meaning is the same.

The bottom portion of the moving, circular housing I have been describing is flanged outward and on it are numbers and lines that show *degrees* in the 360-degree circle, in 5-degree intervals. There may be deviation in design among various makes of compasses, but these are basically the parts and design of the orientation-type compass. Some of these compasses contain air, some liquid.

## Taking a Reading

Lay this compass flat on your palm now, or on a table or desk or log or stump or rock outdoors to get the hang of how it works. At first, pay no attention to the position of the movable housing. Look at the magnetic arrow. If you've made certain no metal objects are near that might deflect it (in some cases a gun barrel or knife could) it will be pointing north. Now hold the base firmly with a lefthand thumb and finger, and turn the housing until the broad arrow on the housing base (the arrow that is drawn or painted or engraved on the base) is pointing in the same direction as the compass needle. This arrow and the needle should be exactly lined up, the compass needle exactly above and within the lines of the broad base arrow.

This means that the base arrow is also pointing north. Thus all of the other directions, and every degree reading along the bottom outer flange of the movable base, are now also properly aligned, pointing toward their indicated directions. This, then, is the general plane on which the compass operates.

To use the compass to plot a travel direction, line up the painted arrow in the housing with the magnetic needle. When you place the compass flat on your palm, the needle will be pointing north. Holding the base with your left hand, turn the housing until the painted arrow also points north, identically with the needle. If, for example, you want to travel west, turn the base until the letter W lines up with the direction-of-travel arrow, and set off in that direction.

However, don't forget about that big arrow engraved or otherwise marked on the compass base, the one we said was for sighting travel direction. You now know where north and thus all the other directions are. But suppose you wish to travel due west. Hold the compass base, and turn the housing until the W is lined up exactly with the direction sighting arrow. Now turn the entire compass, base and all, until the magnetic arrow and the orientation arrow below it are once again perfectly aligned. The big sighting arrow now points the way you want to go. If you were holding the compass in your hand, with the directional sighting arrow pointing straight away from you, instead of turning the compass you should turn your *body*. When the magnetic needle and the orientation arrow below it are aligned, you are actually facing exactly in the direction you intend to go. Select a landmark—a tree or rock or sharp hill—and head toward it. Never move the compass setting now as long as you wish to keep going due west, or along whatever course in degrees you have set. From that landmark, select another toward which you are pointed and your degree setting will remain the same. These are the basics of how this compass operates.

In the field it won't always be quite that simple. Suppose you head for a big rock on a distant ridge but have to cross a valley and presently can't see it. To avoid getting off course, you can sight on intermediary landmarks in between. Start perhaps with a tree in general line with the rock, but nearby. Walk to it and take a proper bearing on another, and so on, until you *can* see your target once more.

Suppose you have parked your vehicle on a road in a State Forest. You check the road with your compass. It runs due north-south. You know by your road map in the car that another road, east-west, lies a couple of miles north, and another a couple of miles south. You want to find a trout stream about a mile to the east into the woods, and you know it flows in a generally southern direction. You take a compass sighting straight East and keep checking it occasionally. If the sun is out and the time is mid-p.m. the sun will be behind you, but it will probably not be *straight* west. Its position depends upon time of year.

However, there is no difficulty finding the trout stream by compass. It is a casual project. You decide to fish wet flies, downstream, south. You fish for a couple of hours but have not yet reached another road. All you have to do is set a west course going out and you are certain, if you check often so you don't wander, to come out on the trail your car is on, and south of it. A short hike north brings you to it. Make no mistake,

> You can use a simple road map and your compass to lead you to a trout stream nearby, a short distance to the east of where you are. When you check the road with your compass, you find it runs north-south. On the map you see that another road runs east-west, a few miles to the south. With this information, you know that you must take a compass reading straight east and follow that direction to find the stream. To return to your starting point, you would merely have to hike west, until you hit the road, then north.

however. On an overcast day many a fisherman might have wandered in circles for hours in this few square miles of forest, had he not had an assist from a compass.

**Rules for travel.** Whether by map and compass or compass alone, there are a few rules to remember. Know where you started from: camp, car, trail intersection, lake, hill. Memorize landmarks as you travel. Keep looking *back*, so you know what to look for coming out. Mark your trail here and there if you need to, by a lopped branch or some other plainly visible marker *every thirty paces*. Look back at these markers after you've passed, to make certain they are visible on return. Always be positive that someone on the "outside" knows where you are going, and if possible the point from which you started. With an orientation-type compass as described, do not reset it when you start back. Simply point the sighting arrow on the base *toward* you instead of away. It is a good idea to jot down or memorize your degree reading in case the housing is accidentally turned.

Practice with your compass in backyard or countryside or even city walks. Try on a small-scale setting a certain course, pacing off a certain number of steps, making a right-angle setting, counting a like number of steps, another right angle turn, checked on the compass, until you have covered a square. Then try triangles. Mark the starting point. You can set a course, compass properly oriented (needle and lower arrow aligned) for any number of degrees. You go a measured (by paces) distance. Now you add 120 degrees (a third of a circle) to the first reading, if the total is not over 360 degrees. Turn either way, reorient, and set a new course. You travel the same distance, add another 120 degrees and reorient again. This third leg of like distance brings you back to your starting point. Any time your addition gets you more than 360 degrees (a circle), you subtract 360 from the total to get your reading. Such practice runs get you used to the compass and how it works, and give you confidence. It is vital to your safety, and survival, that you are "compass educated" *before* you really need its help.

## Measuring Distances

Before we discuss maps, consider some facts about measuring distances. It may often be necessary to know at least fairly closely how far you have traveled or must travel. This is especially important if you are without a map, or lost. Any dedicated outdoorsman should know, and most do, the length of his *average* walking paces. Mine, on flat ground, are thirty-eight inches, two inches over a yard, from the rear heel to the forward toe. For practical purposes this means each step is a yard in average terrain. For counting, many foresters use "double paces," or the "one-two" step with the same foot each time. That would mean in my case 6 feet for each double, or a count of 880 double paces to the mile. On level ground that would be about it. Climbing or descending, rough and dense terrain will change (add to) the number somewhat. But it is still a good base figure to stow away, checked out on your own paces.

In ordinary hunting you won't be counting. But if

you are lost, you certainly had better, in order to help you know how far you have gone in any direction. Also, in locating downed game it is very handy. I killed an elk one time and had to have help getting it out. I set a compass course, counted paces to a trail, marked the spot where I emerged. Going back all we had to do was start from my mark, turn the compass around and count steps. We didn't come exactly to the animal, but by the time we were close I knew where I was and went straight to it.

In addition to counting and measuring paces, you should know how *fast* you travel. Practice, with a watch, over a known course, like half-a-mile. Try it on flat meadow or field, again climbing a rough rocky hillside, and by all means again coming down. Try it in dense brush, and in open woods. Get these figures in mind, even jotting them down in practice. Figure an all-round average. If you are going from camp to find a lake or stream, you will be trying for a straight course. Check your watch and you'll know about how far you are from camp. If you are hunting, probably you wander a lot. Still a watch check against your known general speeds will give you a good guess on how far you are from camp. Make educated guesses for terrain influence. When you are traveling a straight line with map and compass, heading for a specific point, or trying to get back to one, you will know by timing roughly how far you have gone. You'll know when you *should* have reached destination, or camp, or the vicinity. In these situations you won't be purposely wandering, as in hunting.

## North and True North

All of the foregoing compass material has one serious built-in error, purposely left until now to avoid confusion. On short hikes it won't be very important, nor will it when you are going from closely visible landmark to landmark. But when you begin using *compass and map together,* on longer hauls, you will be making seriously incorrect computations, unless you understand and compensate for it. At that time it becomes urgent. You can lose yourself with your compass if you do not make the proper adjustments.

On your map, "north" means what may be termed "True North," a straight shot toward the North Pole. However, the compass needle operates magnetically and the earth's geology affects it. There are magnetic forces that upset it. Numerous magnetic lines run through the earth, from varying angles, and these converge at what may be called the "Magnetic North Pole." This is located a long distance below the True North Pole. It is located in northern Canada. It is toward this magnetic pole that the compass needle actually points.

If you happen to be at a location along one particular magnetic line, which is considered as zero, a line that runs roughly from eastern Florida up across the U.S. about to Chicago, on up through Lake Michigan and thence straight to the True North Pole, Magnetic North and True North will be the same. Your compass will be pointing at both. But if you are east or west of that line even one degree, there will be a deviation in compass reading from True North on the map. Suppose you are 10 degrees east of the line. You are aiming for a landmark a little more than half a mile distant. You make no allowance for this phenomenon, called magnetic declination. Over that half-mile-plus, you will miss your mark by about 500 feet (over 150 yards) or about 50 feet for each degree. The rule is that if you are *east* of the line, that is, you have a declination to the east, you *subtract* from your compass course the number of *degrees east*. If you are *west,* the *degrees west are added.*

This may seem awesomely complicated. Fortunately, it isn't, because some maps, which we will discuss shortly, note the declination for the area they cover. More valuable to the traveler who takes trips in many locations is a declination chart available from the U.S. Printing Office in Washington, that gives by map the declinations, for any point in the U.S. It is essential to have this chart any time you are using a map without the declination noted on it.

Suppose you have such a map, without noted declinations. Place your compass on it, and line it up so the compass needle is parallel with one of the meridian lines that runs *map* north-south; then move the map so the needle is pointing at the number of degrees given in the declination chart for this area. The needle is now pointing True North. With the orienting compass I have described, you do not move the map but instead turn the compass housing to the proper number of degrees shown on the declination chart for this location.

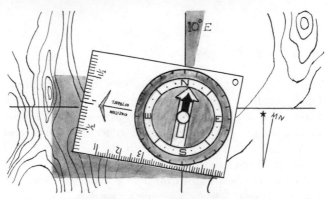

It is important to adjust your compass to allow for the magnetic declination between Magnetic North and True North. With your compass placed on the map, line up N and S on the compass with the north-south line on the map indicating True North. Next, rotate the map and compass until the needle lines up with the map's Magnetic North line. If your map does not have a Magnetic North line, use a declination chart to determine the number of degrees necessary to correct for your area, and turn the map and compass so the needle is the proper number of degrees east or west of True North.

### Reading Maps

Now to maps. For short jaunts in settled territory, ordinary road maps, if they are up-to-date, are handy enough. But they won't do for wilderness trips, or even for a day's hunt in a State Forest. Many states have excellent county maps, and most have State Forest maps. National Forest maps also are excellent. Some large Forests have detail maps showing only specified sectors. National Forest maps are obtainable from the

Forest Supervisor of a particular area, from a Regional Office, or from the Washington, D.C. Forest Service main office. State maps of counties are usually available at county seats or state capital offices. Forestry and Game and Fish Departments can furnish State Forest maps and often county maps.

Among the best maps obtainable are those from the U.S. Geological Survey, and the Canadian Department of Mines. These are the topographic maps that show specific areas in great detail. They have carefully plotted elevation contours, most useful. Once you learn to read these, you can get a good mental picture of the surrounding country, know where obstacles such as cliffs or steep mountains are, and so on. These maps utilize a standard marking code system, and you should study it so that you know what the symbols mean: a marsh, a spring, what tints are used on woodland issues to indicate types of forest and brush, what various roads and trails are like for quality.

Each of these maps has a diagram on the bottom that shows the magnetic declination for the specific map region, both in degrees and with lines indicating True and Magnetic North. These lines, projected upward across the map face, drawn in if you wish, are most useful. The maps are also *dated;* the date means that the map was made the year of the date. Be sure to get maps as up-to-date as possible. Otherwise changes since that date—new roads or trails, buildings or ranger stations, etc.—may not show on the map and will be confusing to you. If you have to use an older Geological or Geodetic Survey map, it still will get you there and back.

Just don't be too concerned if you find something that's not on the map.

These maps are made up in differing scales: an inch to a mile, an inch to 2,000 feet, an inch to several miles. In most usage the smaller the area covered by the map and the smaller the scale, that is, the smaller the distance covered by an inch, the more information it will give you. If you feel you need Geological Survey maps, you can get a list of them for the state or province in question from the Washington or Ottawa sources mentioned. Then you pick the ones you want and order them, at stipulated fees. In average instances in the U.S., outdoorsmen will be going into State or National Forests, and the standard maps from the State or the Forest Service will do very nicely. But for all the fine points, and the contours, the others are better.

## Map and Compass Together

When using any map out in the field, always take your compass reading and then lay the map out so it is turned in the *proper direction*. Then you see precisely what is where. If you aren't sure exactly what your position is, but can locate both visually and on your map two identifiable points, such as mountains, you can easily "find" yourself. Get a degree reading on one landmark, then on the other. Place your compass on the map, and orient map and compass for the first reading. Draw a line from the landmark back in the direction from which you are sighting. Repeat, using the second reading. You are at the point where the two

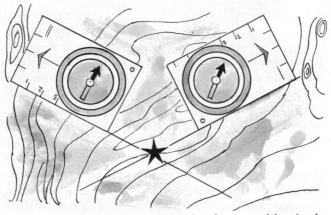

When you are uncertain of your position in the field, but you can locate visually and on your map two landmarks, you will have no trouble finding yourself. Take a degree reading for the first point, and with your compass on the map, adjust map and compass to this reading. Draw a line on the map from the landmark you just identified back in the direction from which you took the reading. Repeat the procedure for the second point. You are standing at the point where the two lines intersect on the map.

lines will cross. Now that you know precisely your position, you can forge ahead to some predetermined destination, or you can get a bearing back toward vehicle or camp. Two rules you must always follow are to *believe your compass,* and at all times *to know where you are on your map.* To be sure, compass readings in some situations are upset by metal, in the ground or in your equipment. But the chance is not great. Get away from your metals while taking readings.

In using the orienting-type compass, don't fail to work with the measuring edges on the flat base. Often you can place the base on your map so that the long measuring edge touches your *location* and *destination*. The *sighting arrow* on the base will then be pointing in your direction. If you have prepared your map ahead of time by drawing in parallel lines at intervals showing Magnetic North, all you have to do is turn the housing until the drawn-in pointing arrow on the bottom of the housing is parallel to the Magnetic North lines, and you have the degree reading for your course.

There is much more that can be learned about use of map and compass. But these are the fundamentals. Study your map thoroughly beforehand and during any trip. Use your compass often. *Memorize landmarks* and keep *looking back*.

# 6 / Travel in the Wilderness

IT IS NOT JUST when you are lost that you need a set of general rules on what to do and what not to do when traveling in the outdoors. The rules that follow will help you both to avoid certain emergencies and to extricate yourself efficiently when you do have one.

I once met a lost man in a State Forest in Michigan. When he found me he was wet from crossing a river. He had simply stumbled upon me. Had he heard me or seen me and crossed a river to reach me, his action would have been legitimate. But the fact that he crossed the stream some time earlier illustrates an error to avoid. If you are one side of a stream and have left your car, as he had, "somewhere back there," all you can possibly accomplish by crossing the stream is to get yourself more lost than ever.

The stream in this instance was a very definite boundary. Even though the man didn't have any idea where he was, he should have considered the fact that he was *somewhere between the road and the river*. This at least gave him something to tie to. Once he crossed it, though, he was "out of the pasture."

## Following Water

With map and compass and a useful *knowledge of both,* this person could not have become lost in the first place. But at times either one or all are missing. If you become lost without these, one of the *do nots* is *do not cross a stream*. A better idea is to follow it. Streams run downhill and for centuries they have been guidelines for wilderness travelers. Many have trails near them or right beside them. Streams may be crossed by trails and bridges and roads and railroads and high-lines. A stream is something to cling to.

In most instances you should not try to walk close to it. Vegetation grows densely along most streams. Swamps and bogs spread out from a stream at some locations. The stream may twist and loop and turn, making your hike much longer. Unless there is a streamside trail, it is best to parallel a stream a short distance away, and from a ridge top if there is one, where you can see it or its valley course most of the time.

Any outdoorsman worth his salt should know in which general direction a stream is flowing. Somehow misinformation got started long ago that only a very few streams flow north. This is nonsense. In the Arctic

most of them flow north, and straight away from settlement. In the northern part of Michigan's Lower Peninsula, the group of streams flows in a northerly direction. If a hunter is aware of that by map study, and
knows even a little bit about the country he is in, he
knows whether to go upstream or downstream.

In the West, where the largest expanses of wilderness are located, chiefly in National Forests, stream direction is an excellent clue to general orientation. From
atop the Continental Divide all the length of the
Rockies, streams flow downhill on the west side toward
the Pacific and downhill on the east slope toward the
Mississippi and the Gulf of Mexico. Any time you
travel downstream you know that eventually you come
to larger streams to which the one you are following is
tributary. And eventually, too, you will enter valleys
that have settlement, either farms or ranches or villages.
The hike certainly could be a long one. But on either
side of the Divide, a totally lost man should always go
downhill, downstream.

In some cases it is an oversimplification to say you
should go "west downhill" or "east downhill." There
are many individual drainages where this wouldn't
work. I think offhand of a block of the Santa Fe National Forest east of Santa Fe, New Mexico, in which
the Pecos Wilderness Area is located. The Pecos River
cuts south through these handsome mountains. Its
canyon is a main topographic landmark. Tributaries
come into it from *both sides*. Thus, if you were on the
east side of the Wilderness you would follow a creek
downstream southwest to hit the main river, and vice
versa. In other words, do know the *watershed* of the

region so you have its general pattern well fixed in your mind.

Don't make hasty decisions, lost or not. Be sure you are right. When lost, or in a situation where you have to walk out, don't rush. Conserve energy. Take it slow. If you were on a ten-day trip, make believe you still wish to spend that time. Don't compound your trouble by hurting yourself. Hunters, particularly those who get lost easily, will even find that using map and compass is a good idea. You don't need to hunt *aimlessly*, wandering. In forests from Maine to Ontario to Montana to Arizona, an old and unused log trail, a stream course, a lake shore offers just as good hunting as you find plunging off into unmarked territory that all looks alike. It may even be better because of the opening of the trail, and edge habitat. The log trail or stream or lakeshore gives you something to *tie to,* and to follow back to camp or use as a known point of orientation.

By the same token, if you are lost or having to walk out of an emergency, unless you are very sure of yourself and your ability with map and compass, don't strike out cross-country. In the woods, *there are no shortcuts!* If there is a trail, stay on it. Avoid cross-country travel unless it is absolutely necessary. An exception might be striking across an area on a ridge from which you know or can see that a stream meanders endlessly.

## Starting Out

When you set up your camp, or park your vehicle—whatever your *starting* point—don't place it at some indiscriminate spot. Have it *somewhere*. Most campers will set up at a recognized campsite—there are many in the National and State Forests—or they will camp near a stream or lake. The smart vehicle operator will park near a bridge, let's say, and hunt one side of the river. Or he will leave the car near an intersection, or a high-line or railroad crossing. In other words, such starting points give you a definite *place to come back to*.

I recall a campsite several of us had one year in the San Juan Primitive Area in Colorado. It was a lovely spot at the confluence of a tributary stream with the main river. By hunting in the morning climbing uphill, we gave ourselves the advantage of a downhill run when we were tired out later in the day. We were also hunting in a tract that was bounded on two sides by streams. We knew the main river was flowing almost straight south, the tributary east by south. If we climbed the slope on the south side of the tributary, wherever we quit we could set a course and hit one of the streams. Northeast or north would have us converging on the tributary, or straight east we'd hit one or the other. If we hit the main river, we knew we had to go upstream to find camp because it was at the confluence and we had not crossed the tributary. If we hit the tributary, we knew we had to go downstream until we got to the main river.

You won't always have it quite that neat. On a road or stream where you aren't "boxed in," finding camp can be harder than that even when you know where you are. You follow a certain compass course, let's say, hiking to a high lake to fish. But even if you follow the same one going back, probably you won't hit right on the nose. So, when you do find stream or road or trail where camp is, which way should you go on it? This is a problem you can lick by purposely taking yourself off course a bit. If, for example, you know camp should be straight south, set a course a few degrees to the east or west. This assures that you'll strike road or stream where camp or car is located a short distance from it in a *known direction*. Of course, if you have looked back often and have your landmarks well in mind, this isn't necessary.

Not only should your real camp or parking place be easy to locate, but when you make any other camp during an emergency, choose a location which is easy to find your way back to if necessary.

### When To Stay Put

We talked previously of panic. Don't. If you are lost, stop where you are the moment you realize it. Don't move again until you are calm and have done your best to puzzle out your location, and the error you made to get there. Study your map again, use your compass. If you aren't sure and it is late in the day, stay there. In the morning things will look better. Mark *this spot* well, range out after a landmark to tie to, like a stream, and make, if necessary, a permanent, come-back-to camp there.

"Staying put" is often what you should do to help yourself. If you have some difficulty in the desert, and you are by a waterhole, don't move. If you have left word, as you should have, you will be found. If you are not at a waterhole, and have a broken-down vehicle, get in the shade beside it or under it and make yourself comfortable, conserving your energy and what water you have. Stay right there until someone finds you.

There are instances when storms wipe out trails and you don't know where to point your vehicle. Park it and stay put. This is an absolute for the plane crash victim. Even if you are injured only slightly, you compound the difficulty if you try to walk out. The crashed plane is easier to spot than you will be. The same applies to boats and canoes. If you are cracked up many miles from settlement, and someone knows where you were going and when you were to be back, it is best to stay with the craft and let searchers find it, and you. There are exceptions, when you are close to settlement and know it and were to be gone a long time. You must use careful judgment The rule: if you have any doubt whatever, stay put.

## Following Trails

Some writers concerned with survival have suggested following game trails where possible for easy going. In my opinion this is precisely what *not t*o do. There are a few exceptions. A bear trail may be an easy way through a small dense thicket. A caribou trail may take you where you are going, if you know their migration routes in that area. But game isn't usually going where you are, nor for the same purposes. Get on a deer trail sometime and follow it. Many of them are as aimless as trails left by lost men. For helter-skelter try a bear trail over some distance. My advice about game trails is to utilize one when it suits *your* purpose, but never to follow one because you think it is "going somewhere."

I have mentioned sticking to the ridges in mountain or hill country. Never walk up when you can walk level. Conserve energy. At times, climbing to a ridge top is better than walking along the side of a slope because you don't fight one "short leg," and there will be less interference from down timber. Much of the down timber, in forests where it is plentiful, will be lying on a general downhill slant. Walking along a slope thus forces you constantly to climb over. It is exhausting.

Unless it is absolutely necessary, never attempt to cross unfamiliar swamps or bogs. They can compound trouble, are at best exhausting. If you have a crackup of some kind—with an airboat for example in a spot like the Everglades—stay where you are until found. Many persons get into trouble in the high country of the West with horses, because they don't realize that there are some fantastic bogholes even way up at and above timberline. These may look innocuous, but you can sink a horse to its belly in an instant if you force the mount across. Skirt all low, moist spots, even way up at the top.

## Snakes

Outdoorsmen must be continually alert against snake trouble. Rattlesnakes are the most common of the poisonous species, and most widespread. Cottonmouths are predominantly southern in range, usually found near water, and in some cases in the Southeast U.S. in large numbers. They are likely to be more aggressive

Rattlesnake

Water Moccasin

Copperhead

Coral Snake

Learn to identify the poisonous snakes in the
area you will be in, and watch out for them.
The most common species are shown at left.

than rattlesnakes. Copperheads, though smaller, range
widely and can be dangerous, especially when you are
unable to receive prompt treatment. Coral snakes are
deadly, but are burrowers and not fanged like the
others; they're chewers. It is seldom that anyone is
bitten by a coral snake except by handling it.

States where the most snakebites annually occur are:
Florida, Georgia, Alabama, Louisiana, Mississippi, Mis-
souri, Arkansas, Texas, Oklahoma, Virginia, North
Carolina, West Virginia, and California. South Carolina, Arizona, Kansas, Tennessee and Kentucky are
next. The mountain states, where so many sportsmen
visit National Forests and other public lands, all register a substantial number of snakebites annually. There
are also a few in the Dakotas, and in the Great Lakes
states. Canada has a few cases. Although surveys show
that sportsmen are by no means the most frequently
bitten group, because of the potential danger you
should always be alert to and know the basic rules for
avoiding snakes.

Never reach into holes such as animal burrows. Never
reach up when climbing to grasp a ledge, above and
past which you are unable to see. Don't put your face
near a ledge from which a snake could strike. Be extremely cautious in snake country about stepping over
a log or a rock. Step up on them. Beware of jumping
off a jutting rock under which a snake may lie. In my
home region in Texas I am extremely wary of such

places as armadillo burrows, which are often under the edge of an uptilted slab of rock. Not long ago I was walking with a friend who stepped atop just such a slab. I had seen burrow entrance dirt as I started

Don't be careless in snake country: (1) never reach into holes; (2) don't jump over a log that may hide a snake underneath; (3) avoid sitting against ledges from which a snake could strike.

around. I started to yell, "Don't step off!" But before I could do so a snake buzzed its rattles wildly. He stepped back safely. Unfortunately, not all of them give a warning.

Don't move around the corner of a shady, creviced ledge without looking at where your feet and legs will be. Always look closely before you sit down on a log, a rock, or on the gound. A high percentage of snake-bites occur from carelessness. When it is hot, in an area where snakes are common, walk in the bright places. Snakes coil in shade. Be chary of walking in tall weeds. Watch closely around abandoned buildings, caves, packrat nests. Be especially wary as dusk comes on and heat subsides. This is when snakes begin to move. Walking after dark in desert and other areas where rattlers are common is not a good idea. When gathering dead wood for fires, look before you reach. Watch those debris piles and hollow logs.

In boats or when fishing in swamps where cotton-mouths are common, it isn't just the ground that's dangerous. They love to lie on limbs. Don't push a boat in swiftly under branches without checking every-thing carefully. If you hang a lure in weeds, probe with a paddle first before reaching. One time in Florida I started to reach for a bass bug I'd hung on a water hyacinth and there lay an enormous cottonmouth. In Georgia on the Flint River I reached out to seize a limb as a partner maneuvered a boat to shore, and there was a big one on the very limb.

One of the most important "don'ts" is this: don't forget that snakes can be where you least expect them. For example, making a hands-and-knees or belly-crawl-ing stalk on an antelope in New Mexico or Wyoming can be dangerous. In some parts of Nebraska bird hunt-ers who've never seen a rattler before find some they wish they hadn't, almost every fall. The most important "do" concerning snakes: Carry a snakebit kit at all times, even on a day's outing, and study the treatment instructions included with it thoroughly beforehand. In addition, *you can carry antivenin,* and administer it to yourself if need be. A druggist can order an anti-venin kit for you if he does not carry them. In "back-in" situations such a kit can be a lifesaver.

## Horse Know-how

Outdoorsmen get themselves into difficulty with horses and mules, on pack-in trips. Nowadays so few people have contact with horses that most know little about handling them. Stay away from the "business" end, the rear. Don't even walk around the rear of horse or mule. Skirt it widely. Never come up suddenly from any angle. Be sure the animal knows you are there. Even the most docile old trail plug can come apart when startled. Never approach from the right side. Horses are trained to expect you to saddle them, put a bridle on, and mount, *from the left.* We have raised a number of horses, broken a few and ridden a good many. What you eventually find out is that you really never know *all* about what the gentlest nag may do. Just remember, neither do they!

Watch closely when you are starting on a pack-in to see how your outfitter handles the stock. Familiarize

> Handle horses carefully. Tether to a movable log whenever you must leave; stake to the ground at night to allow grazing in a limited range. Know how to hobble the horse with buckled straps or light twisted rawhide for extra protection against wandering. Never approach any horse from the rear.

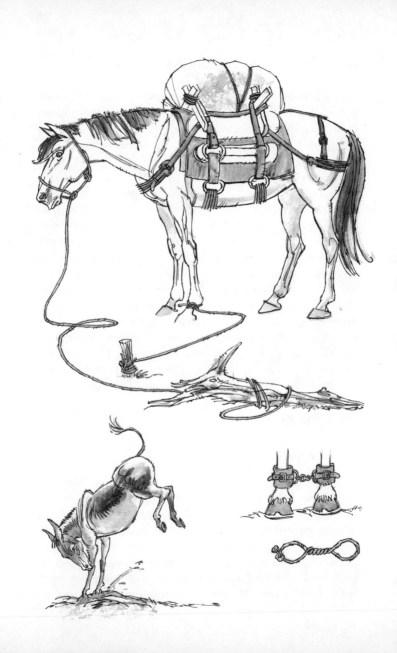

yourself with how to hobble a horse, how to stake out a "catch horse," how to lash a pack on a pack animal, how to approach a loose horse, in case in emergency you find a stray. Probably you won't ever have to do these things, but it is good knowledge to have.

When you ride and are not used to riding, get down every half hour and walk a bit. I've seen some riders literally unable to walk because they stayed in a saddle too long at a time. It's your *knees* that will give you trouble. Your rear end will just get sore but it won't cripple you. Suffer gracefully. But a bit of walking every half hour will keep you limbered up. When you are sore and stiff after the first day, go right at it again. Believe me, this is the best cure. And sit flat in your saddle. By easing your backside while sitting up on the rear flange of your saddle, or by slouching to one side for hours at a time, you can cripple your horse. You can do the same by hanging a heavy pack off the horn on one side. Keep a balanced load. The old cayuse under you is the best friend in the wilderness that you'll ever have!

## Canoe Repair

If you are to travel by canoe, you should have in your gear a repair kit for the material of which the canoe is made. They are available for fiberglass and for canvas-covered canoes. Aluminum presents some problem, but is more likely to be bent than rent. A small puncture can be filled with pine resin, or plugged by pulling a hunk of cloth through and snipping both sides fairly close. However, if you can locate any in stores, get a few tubes of what is called "liquid aluminum solder." This is soft, and is smoothed across a puncture on both sides and the hole filled with it. I once repaired a small craft I used for floating fast rivers that way, and when I sold that little floater a half-dozen years later the plug was still in place.

## Vehicular Travel

Nowadays vehicular travel in wilderness situations is popular. The 4WD vehicles can go a great many places. All vehicles, however, from short-4 to trail bike to snowmobile to the newer ATVs, are troublemakers at one time or another. I always feel far more secure on horseback. If I had a dollar an hour for all the time I've spent over the years getting "unstuck" or "un-broke-down" I could spend a few months doing nothing!

The subject of vehicular travel "back in" is vast, and there is room here only to touch a scattering of essentials. When you buy a vehicle, choose carefully. Most ATVs are more expensive playthings than rough-country transport. A pickup truck can go a lot of places, but its lack of rear-end weight handicaps it. This excepts the 4WD pickup. Trail bikes are not very comfortable or practical. Unquestionably the best rough use vehicles are the short-wheelbase four-wheel-drives.

**Breakdowns.** Most mechanical breakdown problems are with the electrical systems, fuel pumps, and belts. Carry spare parts for all—pump, belts, distributor, coil, plugs, points, etc.—and study the systems and their repair beforehand. You should have a well-selected assortment of tools, in a good waterproof box. Tires also give trouble. See that you get the best for the terrain where you'll use them most. Carry two spares, and repair tools and equipment.

The other two most common problems are getting stuck, and puncturing an oil pan on rocks. These can cause such awesome difficulties at times that I cannot imagine anyone's failing to shell out the cash to cure them. That's all it takes. If you can afford the vehicle, you can afford the cure.

**Tools.** A good winch, even though it costs two- or three-hundred dollars, is worth more than the whole vehicle when you are really bogged. There are several types of cheaper "come-alongs" that work fairly well. But a powerful winch saves hours of back-breaking labor and gets you out of snow, mud or sand when you absolutely could not get out any other way. It can also save a vehicle that has slipped off onto a steep slope from catapulting over a cliff as you try to ease back up. You can hook up to trees, boulders, even bushes.

Recently a group of us hunting near the Mexican border after a hard rain were unmercifully hung up with a 4WD pickup. When you get a 4WD stuck, you know you *are* stuck. Novices think a 4WD can go anywhere. It can't. It just sticks harder! We hauled a long length of cable off the winch, hooked to the only item in reach, a skinny clump of scrub mesquite. If you place a cable around bushes *right at ground level,* and ease on the power very gently, it is amazing what hold the roots have. We were out in no time. Be sure a winch is outfitted with plenty of cable.

To avoid oil pan trouble, and gas tank and gas line

too, all it takes is welding steel plates beneath. I have been up on rocks where the front wheels were turning in air, the front end weight sitting on a steel plate right below the oil pan. This addition is so simple and so valuable that no 4WD traveler should be without it. Most of the time, however, if outdoorsmen using vehicles would just exercise caution, and think carefully before crossing spots that look bad, they wouldn't need either winch or steel plates.

Husky jacks should be carried. You should also have an engine air pump and spark-plug wrench, and a tire gauge that reads low pressures. In sand, letting down to ten or twelve pounds tire pressure will usually get you out if you move the vehicle gingerly. Chains for all four wheels of the 4WD, a shovel, and an axe are all mandatory extras. Bailing wire, too. You can easily bridge a bad mudhole by cutting four logs, binding two pairs together and laying them across for wheel tracks. The wheels of the vehicle will creep across in the V formed where each pair of rounded logs comes together. But go slowly!

As noted earlier, don't be hasty about leaving your vehicle if it is hopelessly broken down. If you've done as you should—notified someone of your trip plans beforehand, and followed through on it—by staying with your vehicle you will be found. Also, at the vehicle you have everything you need. You can utilize various signals to assist those who will be searching for you, or to attract those who may be near and unaware of your difficulty. There is a chapter about signaling later in this book.

## Short Forages

Remember to make camps at places to which you can easily find your way back. However, a breakdown of a vehicle, a plane crash, loss of a horse, even becoming lost may suddenly place you where you have no choice about your immediate campsite. In order not to become more lost, and to avoid ranging out from a vehicle or plane till you are unable to find it again, there is a definite procedure to follow.

Suppose that you are near a stream, or on a lakeshore, or in a broad valley at the foot of a ridge, or up on the ridge itself. Any known lines—stream, shoreline, valley, ridge—give you an exact two-directional foraging area. That is, if you go up the shore and stick to it, you can come back to camp without fail. Then you can explore from camp down the shore in the opposite direction. In a broad valley, stay at the foot of the ridge and you can come back to camp (vehicle, place where you first knew you were lost) without any trouble. The same goes for ridge top or stream course.

You may need to make excursions of a half-mile to two miles, seeking food, or water, or material for shelter. When you make such excursions, stick to the *known line;* don't wander. Note landmarks, bends in a stream, pockets of vegetation, anything and everything that you will be able to identify later. Look *back* at each after passing. This is what you'll see on return. Traveling one of these *known lines* out and back—in a desert it could be a dry wash or foot of a mountain or rock wall—is the *only* jaunt you should take until you are completely familiar with the area.

When you are familiar, you can set a compass course at right angles for forage trips. That is, if you are at the foot of a ridge in a wide valley, set your course out across the valley, and return to the ridge. Walking may be such that you won't hit exactly where you had hoped

Set a compass course for short forage trips **only** when you are familiar with the natural features and landmarks of the immediate area.

to when you come back to the ridge. But because you checked out that ridge base in both directions from camp, you will know by landmarks where you are and which way to go. You are now totally oriented, at least in this vicinity. And you know something of the country around you. If lost, you might find yourself while making these side trips. If waiting for rescue, you are able to find food and other necessities. There is hardly anyplace that does not have some kind of known line to cling to.

## Choosing Ridge or Stream

I have mentioned staying on the ridges or along streams, rather than trying to travel "against the grain" by climbing up and over one ridge after another and

> In ridge and stream country, a travel line along the ridge which keeps the stream in sight provides the most helpful overall view.

crossing the valleys and streams. The given terrain will of course influence whether you choose a ridge or a stream. The stream gives you water and infinitely more opportunities to find food than the ridge top. But it may be rougher traveling unless there is a trail. Consider that climbing a ridge above a stream gives you a look at the surrounding country and better orientation. Often from a ridge top you can get a fair look at what is ahead of you downstream. Be careful when traveling a ridge, however, not to become confused by other spurs and broken ridges that come in.

If you have a binocular, glass long and carefully. You may spot a swamp filling a looping bend of the stream, or a vertical rock wall on your side, or an area of streamside brush jungle which, were you to enter it, might be difficult to get through and easy to get lost in. You may see in the distance a tributary coming into the main stream that you otherwise would have to cross. In any of these instances, the travel line should be along the ridge, but with the stream in sight. Thus you circumvent the need to cross a swamp or a patch of jungle, to climb again to get around a rock wall, or to get across a large tributary.

**Flat country.** You may be in flat country. Streams there are frequently slower than mountain streams, and seldom have falls or difficult rapids. Vegetation is usually dense near the stream. If you can keep the stream in view, or even the dense vegetation line that follows it, and travel at some distance away, you will avoid having to plow through tangles of vines, brush, weeds and forest. However, a stream of even modest size can *be* a travel route, if you can fashion some sort of raft.

**Mountain streams.** On exceeding swift, rocky mountain streams with extreme gradient, rafting attempts are simply foolhardy. If you are going into strange country, know beforehand something of stream character. Many states furnish booklets about their wilderness streams, with specifics about which stretches are good canoe water and where impassable or dangerous rapids or falls occur. If you know where you are, but are in an emergency situation where you have to get out under your own power, knowledge of the streams is invaluable. If you do not have such knowledge, forget rafting attempts on any stream of a general character that appears to you too rough or dangerous. The whole idea is to stay alive and uninjured. Your chances are better on foot.

## Building a Raft

Fortunately, on most streams where traveling via raft is feasible, materials for building one will be most common. It is along the lower-altitude meandering streams of modest current that the most vines and pliable brush stalks grow. If you intend to try rafting, don't rush your building job, and consider carefully what you use. Water-soaked logs won't float. Several varieties of wood also do not float even when dry, or else float poorly. In lumber days in Michigan, where much black walnut grew, immensely valuable booms were often lost because the heavy, high-density walnut logs would not float. If the flotation logs around them broke free, down they went.

**Logs.** For the quickest and easiest raft-building job you need dry logs, preferably of soft wood. Be sure they are not rotted or they will soak swiftly. Green logs of standing conifers can be cut, but they are heavy and difficult to handle. If you have no cutting tool, you can

> Build a rectangular raft by lashing crossbars to logs, using diagonal brace lashed to crossbars to add rigidity. Increase raft strength by lashing together the overhanging ends of two crossbars at each end of the raft.

burn standing trees by the Indian method of a fire ring at the base. But be warned, it is a slow, tedious process and not worth the effort if makeshift materials are available. You must plaster a thick ring of wet mud around the trunk several feet up from the ground. Then you build a fire around the base. The mud is kept wet, and as the trunk burns the charred portions are hacked off with sharp stones, if that is all you have, or with a hatchet. Once the tree is down, sections are burned off by building small hot fires under the trunk at intervals. I think of this entire task as a last-resort for moving an injured person. A healthy man can walk farther for the amount of energy expended than he probably would float.

**Lashings.** Don't look for huge raft logs. Use those about six inches in diameter. They're easy to handle, easier to lash together, and do not so readily break makeshift lashings. If one does break away, assuming the raft has been built to hold *more* than required weight, which it should be, the rider is still safe. Presumably you will have lashing material in your pack— rope, rawhide thongs. If not, careful work with vines, or even with selected bundles of cattails or strong grasses, or bark strips, will hold a raft together. These can also supplement what lashings you do have. Strips of green inner bark, from cedar, basswood, some of the oaks, make excellent cordage. (See Chapter 10 on making fish lines for other cordage ideas.) If these are soaked for some time in water, the fibers can be separated easily. However, most emergencies do not allow that much time. Nettles and reeds, when braided into strands, are very strong. Yucca leaves are tough as rope, although in most rafting situations—but not all—these plants would not be present.

Never try to build a square raft. Make it a long rectangle. It will handle better. Also, build it at water's edge. If it will be heavy, build it upon two slanted supporting logs down which it can be skidded for launching. Any jerry-built raft should have base logs, with crisscross smaller material atop if possible, to give the rafter a high-and-dry seat. Be sure the outer edges

A light but sturdy pushpole keeps you going through slow current, prevents obstacles from stopping travel.

of the raft have the most buoyant, largest logs. This helps stability. By all means launch in a slack pool if it is possible. Then test the raft before pushing off into current.

A pushpole is mandatory. Cut a green one, light but sturdy, of a length related to general depth of the stream. Use it for primitive guidance, for assistance in slow current, and for fending off from obstructions or bank. If you are on a broad, deep river, try for a pole ten feet long. Also take with you some sort of make-shift paddle, a square of green, heavy bark, a light, dry flat stick. This assists you if a slow, deep hole or back-eddy becalms your raft.

In warm water, you can make a small temporary raft for brief crossings or for getting around a swamp or other difficult going by lashing a tarp or backpack tent, or even clothing, over a frame of logs. There is a caution here, however. Weigh your decision to try this very carefully, as you might better go the long way around than chance losing your gear by poor lashing or a makeshift float not quite buoyant enough.

### Wading Streams

Crossing streams by wading may be necessary in numerous situations. Even on slow streams, use a staff, a *green* stick sizable enough so it will not bend with your leaning weight. You cannot wade a swift stream safely if the water is above your hips, and many streams with extreme gradients cannot be waded if water is much above your knees. If you are unused to swift water, note this well! In crossing, keep sideways to the current or nearly so, turned just enough downstream to point on a diagonal. This places the least leg or body resistance against the water and allows you to move gently with the push of the current, pushed downstream while taking diagonal steps across. Brace the staff on the downstream side.

Use a wading stick to cross a stream. In swift water, travel sideways to the current, facing your body on a diagonal downstream.

In rocky streams, be wary of holes as well as slippery rocks. If current is slow enough so you can stand quietly, probe with your staff to find good footing. Also be wary of soft deep-muck spots in slow streams. Most of these will be back-eddied into the inside of a bend. However, do not try to cross any stream of fair depth on a diagonal headed for the *outside* of a bend. This is where the deeper water will invariably be. The outside bend may also have eroded away so a vertical bank is present. This can be a trap. Try to cross on straightaway stretches, as a rule. And on a fast stream the wider stretches will usually be the shallowest.

**Swimming.** Emergencies may require swimming or floating across a stream. In such instances, equipment will get wet. And it may be all but impossible to cross with equipment. Nonetheless, you should know the basic rules for swimming various types of streams. In modest current and in case you are not a very good swimmer, shoving out a log and crossing with it as support is possible. Stay on the upstream side of the log. In swimming any stream, be exceedingly wary of cold water. It will numb you faster than you believe.

In a swift run that you are sure is deep, swim face down, headed downstream. In a shallow, swift run lie on your back and go feet first. Never fight a current; simply go with it and keep angling across. Get buoyancy assistance from your clothing. Trousers tied at the ankles, thoroughly wet in the stream then wrung gently, swung around your head to scoop in air, and then snugged at top to trap the air can form a makeshift "waterwing."

All of these ideas, however, have their hazards. It is worthwhile to know them, but remember that attempts to cross a stream that is not readily wadeable, or raftable, may only add to your problems. If at all possible, avoid such crossings. Be absolutely certain the crossing is necessary, and that no other land-based plan is possible. By no means should you take a chance on losing your most valuable possessions—gear you are carrying— in a stream crossing. If that is even a mild possibility, look for another way!

## Natural Hazards

Ice, quicksand, various bogs are all dangers to avoid by every means, even if a much longer trek results. However, if it is absolutely necessary to cross such places, here are a few suggestions. Ice may be thick and strong, but don't take chances. On streams there may

The best way to cross ice is to lie flat and crawl. A long pole stretched at right angles in front of you will give support in case the ice cracks.

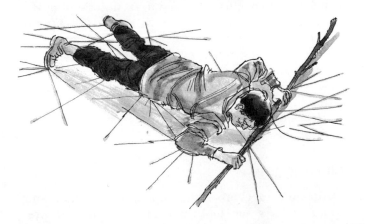

be soft pockets or open places; on lakes, springholes on bottom in shallow water may make soft spots. If you think the ice may not be well formed and of uniform thickness, don't walk. Instead crawl with a "swimming" motion, arms and legs wide to distribute weight. Better still, lie flat and carry a long pole, held in the middle and at right angles to your body. It will support you if ice cracks. In any variety of quagmire—quicksand or muck—don't try to stand up, which only keeps you sinking deeper. Get flat out on your stomach, and *swim* or crawl, through it.

The best idea is not to get into such places. Quicksand, if found along stream courses, is only localized. It will not support even small gravel-sized stones, so beware of watery-appearing sand with no stones on top. Thrust a stick into it to test it. Do likewise with muck. Most bogs or quagmires anywhere on the continent where emergencies are likely to occur are easily skirted. If you get into one in error, and it has tussocks of heavy marsh grass, plus some brush such as alders, step onto the tussocks and in the middle of the alder bushes, one step carefully at a time, test for support. Look around carefully at distant vegetation, particularly trees. These show you the closest way to high ground. Tamarack grows in bog situations. So does willow. But pine or birch or poplar, for example, grow on firm ground and indicate the edge of the bog.

## Climbing

Attempts to climb either up or down cliffs, and climbing trees for lookout sites, are two very pre-

If a rescue team lets down a rope to you along the side of a cliff, one way to secure it around your body is to make a loop at the end of the rope, large enough to stand in. Bring the loop up to your chest, and pass the rest of the rope through the chest loop.

carious undertakings when you are in an emergency situation. Avoid both if at all possible, because they may lead to injuries or compound your difficulties. Nonetheless, basic rules are a part of survival repertoire. For example, if you have been in a plane crash, you can make rope from parachute shroud lines by twisting several together. Perhaps you carried a long rope when going into mountain country. It can get you down a cliff, if that is absolutely necessary.

Select a tree or rock outcrop at the edge of the descent point. A tree must be sturdy, and a rock must be

without any question solid enough to sustain your weight. Pass the rope around this snubbing point exactly at mid-length, so the two ends, one on either side, are even. They *must* reach to destination point down below with a few feet left over. Be positive about this. Otherwise you'll wind up down over a cliff and dangling well above the valley floor!

Pass the rope, both strands, through your crotch from the front. That is, straddle it. Then bring it around across one hip, up across your chest and over the opposite shoulder. Suppose you have brought it around the left hip and up over the right shoulder. Your right hand now grasps both strands, between the snubbing point and the crotch. Where the ropes pass across the right shoulder, bring them around behind your back and let the left hand grasp them at the lower left side. Now as you descend, keeping feet against whatever holds are possible, rope is slowly paid out through the left hand, and the right hand. The friction allows a slow, secure descent. This is known in

When you must get down a cliff, use a long rope anchored safely to the descent point. For rappelling down steep areas, a double rope goes under one thigh and across the opposite shoulder. Grasp both strands with right hand if the rope is over your right shoulder. Bring the ropes behind your back, holding them at the lower left side with the left hand. Now with feet against whatever holds are possible, descend by letting rope out slowly through the left and then right hand. Make sure the rope reaches the destination point with some left over.

climbing terminology as "rappelling." You should be certain when looping the rope around the snubbing point that it will not bind. Thus, when you reach the lower elevation at cliff base, a pull on one strand retrieves the rope.

No climbing up or down should be attempted without using every precaution. Face a cliff or steep spot. Test every hold thoroughly. Watch out for any loose rock if you are going downward. Shove loose rocks off ledges, so they will not fall on you later. When traveling not necessarily on ledges and cliffs but over steep shale slides, keep your feet spaced well apart and avoid by any means starting to slide. It is better to avoid such places, even if going around means a longer hike. As we have said often, dodging possible danger is better than facing it!

**Trees.** You may find it necessary to climb a tree, such as a smooth-trunked palm. Natives do this by tying a short rope between the ankles. The hands and arms encircle the trunk, and the feet, kept apart and ankles pressed against the rope, are hunched up and braced as one climbs. You might be able to use this technique to get up a tall pine or aspen with no lower limbs. But this is a test of strength, uses an immense amount of energy, and the advantages may not equal the necessary effort. A tree with a limbless trunk too large for you to reach around is a poor bet for climbing anyway. If you must climb to get your bearings, try to select an "easy" tree, where limbs grow near the ground. Never put your weight out *on* a limb. Keep it right next to the trunk. Even a dead limb you misjudge as alive is more likely to bear your weight at the point where it joins the trunk. Select a tree with numerous limbs, for the least amount of exertion. Except in a dense, flat country where you wish to obtain some bearing or spot a landmark, there is seldom valid reason for climbing tall trees.

When traveling in the wilderness, what *to* do is certainly important, but it seems to me that the "don'ts" are even more important. Two of the highest importance, I think, are these: Whatever happens, don't panic; and, never go into wilderness situations alone. Invariably it is the loner who gets into the worst predicaments, simply because there is no one to assist!

# 7 / Where to Find Water

IN ANY CLIMATE where severe cold does not drain energy, you can live for many days without a single bite of food. The length of time depends to some extent upon how much physical energy must be expended. Starving to death is not as dangerous as finding yourself without water. Charts have been compiled showing average life expectancy without water.

Temperature is crucial here. Even in the desert, where you may encounter extreme high temperatures to well above 100 degrees, a man who remains quiet and in shade can go without water a short time. Expectancy would be from two to three days. At moderate summer temperatures in woodland latitudes, say from 50 to 75 degrees, death might not occur for ten days, but before that a man would become too sick to help himself.

Water is the most important factor in survival, regardless of where you are. It is estimated that at 110-degree temperature, an inactive person lives for 5 days if he has available 2 quarts of water per day, a total of 10 quarts. At about 75 degrees he has a chance of quadrupling his life expectancy on the same 10 quarts. But these are bare minimums and this is also a substantial quantity of water. At a moderate temperature a person even mildly active needs an average of 2 quarts of water per day. That's 3½ gallons per week. Strenuous exercise, such as hiking, will run the need higher.

## Water Supply

Obviously no one can carry that much water, except by horse or motorized transport. In any desert trip, you should know where water sources are and carry as much water as possible. If a vehicle is used, a copious supply should be stored for emergency. Then, as we have pointed out, if a breakdown occurs you should stay with the vehicle to conserve energy.

Fortunately, over the major share of the land mass of this continent where emergencies may occur, water supply is not a great problem. The large forest tracts, the vast Canadian bush all have many lakes and streams. But having *pure* water may be a problem. Even high-country rivulets may be polluted, for example, by a dead animal lying in them. The old idea that water swiftly becomes pure as it runs a few yards in sunlight over a streambed is nonsense.

Happily, on trails in many State and National Forests water has been tested at springs or other sources and signs designate whether or not it is fit for drinking. But in an emergency you cannot count on finding one of those. Thus it is best to purify all water. Once a partner of mine got off his horse, drank deeply from a clear stream, and looked up to find a dead deer a few yards above in the creek. Especially in lower elevations, or in desert country where water may stand, purification is a must.

## Purifying Water

Halazone tablets were mentioned earlier. Directions for use are given on the bottle. Iodine is also a purifier, with 2 to 4 drops per quart sufficient. Tablets used by the Armed Forces for water purification are available, too. There are other purifiers, such as chlorine, but those noted are easiest to carry and handiest for treating small amounts of water.

However, situations may arise where no chemical purification is possible—you have failed to go prepared, or have lost or used up the chemicals. Boiling water is the simple old wilderness standby. Many sources suggest boiling hard for at least five minutes. I'd suggest not being too eager. No harm is done by boiling twice as long, and even more to assure purity. Remember that altitude makes a big difference in how long it takes to bring water to a boil, and how hard it will boil with a given amount of fire.

Although water is seldom difficult to find in snow country, injury may make it necessary to stay put, or available water may be distant, and so snow must be used. If snow is plentiful, dig away the top layer, and use that underneath. It will be cleaner and more compact. A substantial amount of snow is required to melt down into a couple of quarts of water. If fuel for your fire is any problem, never fill a container brim full of packed snow and then begin to melt it. Melt a small amount and keep adding small amounts to the water formed. Melting will be faster this way. The same method applies if you must use ice. Chip it into small pieces.

Don't drink snow or ice water without boiling it. Each might be contaminated. Play it safe. It is imperative to stay well. Although boiled water will seem tasteless, some aeration occurs by pouring back and forth from one container to another. If you have foil, a second container can be fashioned from it. But emergencies are not comfort tours, and you may have only a single container. Drink the water flat and forget it.

A winter-camping, snowshoeing addict friend of mine carries a coil of small-diameter plastic tube for drinking from high-country streams when snow is deep. Granted, he takes in water that might be polluted, but under the snow mass that completely covers small creeks at high altitude the chance is slim. He uses the drinking tube because it is often very difficult to get down steep banks to the tiny open waterholes. Never eat snow or ice as a source of water unless it is absolutely necessary, and then only slowly. It may be polluted, and it chills your stomach.

## Mountains and Forests

In the mountains of the North and in forests such as those of New England, southern Canada and the upper Great Lakes region finding water is seldom any problem. If you have a map, as you should, you can easily locate water, unless you are lost. If so, canyons, valleys, gorges, any "downhill country" all lead to water almost without fail. The water table in mountain valleys or in heavily forested northern regions is

Spring or
Seepage

Look for water seepages in the cracks of hard rock areas. Water creeps along the crevices, as shown in cross-section by arrows.

generally not far below the ground surface. If you do not immediately find lake or flowing stream, it is a good idea to know where water is most likely to occur and most easily acquired.

At the foot of any steep, broken rock wall where definite cracks exist in the rocks, running out to points, there are likely to be springs or seepages. Porous and soft rocks allow water to leach out easily. Hard rocks, such as granite, turn seepage along crevices. If you locate a mountain or north-country streambed that is dry but has bluffs and rock terraces rising above it, don't assume no water is present. Check the rock strata carefully. If there are hard folds above, then a layer of limestone or even sand or clay, look for green vegetation growing along the base of this layer. The entire layer may be filled with water. A small trench dug into the edge of such strata, right along where the green vegetation grows, may attract a quick seepage of water that offers an, ample supply.

Dry mountain or northern-forest streambeds that show gravel can be deceptive, too. On occasion when you lie down and press your ear against such a gravel stretch you hear a trickle underneath. However, this

You may find water at the foot of a cliff which is broken into vertical columns. Also check around the bottom of a nearby pile of rocks.

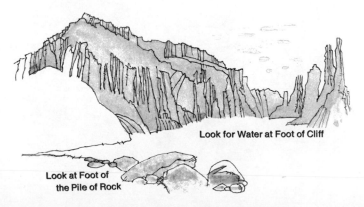

Look for Water at Foot of Cliff

Look at Foot of
the Pile of Rock

is a lucky exception and is by no means reliable. More often water is there and not heard. Dig a bit in a gravel bed, especially where the stream course is narrow. If the gravel continues on down a foot or more and is dry, better forget it. Remember that when you need water, energy spent digging deep holes is usually better spent seeking another source. However, if you strike *sand* beneath the layer of surface gravel, and it is damp, water may be nearby. Water sinks swiftly in gravel but not necessarily in sand. Damp sand may indicate that a foot or two down you will strike flowing water.

> Don't ignore a dry river bed surrounded by bluffs and rock terraces. Investigate the outside of a bend carefully; a layer of limestone or green growth along the base means water is present.

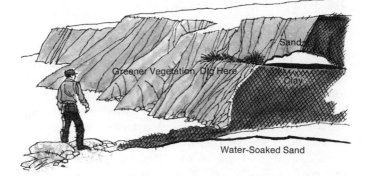

Sand

Greener Vegetation, Dig Here

Clay

Water-Soaked Sand

Because clay soil retains water, check any damp spots of vegetation on a high clay bluff. Dig around the sand at the edges of a clay area, or even in the clay soil itself.

On my own property in the Texas hill country we have a creek that flows year-round. But in hot weather long stretches of it go underground. I've had people who I've taken down there sympathizing because my stream is dry. But a few rods on downstream there is a bubbling, gurgling flow bursting out of the gravel to flow over solid rock.

Often in mountain or forest country water can be found at unexpected locations. For example, an area of clay soil atop a high bluff is a fine water source. This is because clay soils retain water. In building earthen dams engineers often use clay for a core; it holds back the water. A damp spot atop a clay bluff may indicate a reservoir of water. Look closely at the edges of the clay area for sand, or any soil with lesser water-holding properties. A hole dug here, or even in the clay, might fill with good water.

## Vegetation Clues

Vegetation growing in specific places offers excellent clues to water, in forested and mountain regions and in arid areas. A good plan, particularly if you have a binocular, is to scan the entire surrounding region, checking out both land contours and vegetation clues. Even though a water course is unseen, a line of brush that can be identified as alder or willow invariably means water. Tamaracks and balsams grow in low, wet places, and in the North cedar is associated with stream courses or lake shores.

Large willow trees always mean water, and because their root system is shallow but spreading, they commonly indicate water close to the surface. You do not need to find a stream or lake or bubbling spring. A cedar or tamarack bog or alder swamp will offer pools of water, stained from leaves and decaying vegetation but not necessarily impure. Boiling will make it potable, even though some taste—especially in cedar and tamarack swamps—may remain.

## Arid Country

In severely canyon-cut, rocky country, scan very carefully the headers of short, sharp draws or canyons. These draws may be of solid rock, but with trees growing along the edges. You often find a flat place where clay or muck has accumulated over many years on top of the rock, where heavy water-oriented grasses or sedges grow. This is true of my area of Texas, and it occurs almost anywhere throughout the continent where such canyon terrain exists. Heavy grasses indicate that water has been here over many, many years, perhaps only seasonally. However, a hole dug into the thin clay or muck below such grasses often emits a seep of water.

In numerous arid locations a rocky bluff that overhangs an apparently dry streambed has ferns clinging to it at specific spots. This indicates porous rock and sure water. I have chipped out indentations in such porous overhangs and started a drop of clean, cool water on numerous occasions. This can be a lifesaver, with an almost unlimited supply of water to which a small clump of clinging ferns in an otherwise desert situation directed you.

Throughout vast expanses of arid country, across the plains and the desert, the cottonwood tree is a sure indicator of water. It is found along stream courses. Many will be dry or at least appear so. Look for *large* cottonwoods. An ancient one of large size indicates that a consistent source of water has been here for many years. Dozens of times a pool of water will be discovered in an otherwise dry wash near a cottonwood. Or, a bit of digging in the vicinity—try upstream first—will uncover seepage. Mesquites, however, growing along a wash usually mean little chance for water. Whitebrush thickets along a wash mean, in the Southwest, that water is near.

In any arid region, glassing or searching may turn up spots of outstanding green: at the base of a rock outcrop, in a low place along a wash, even part way up a rock terraced barren mountain. Especially lush patches of different vegetation are usually indicators of water. Getting to the water may not always be easy. Conversely, there may be a spring or small oasis lower down and wide open for your use. It is surprising how water plants—even cattails—colonize a small spot in desert surroundings where water is permanent. Undoubtedly seeds were transported by birds.

## Bird and Animal Signs

Birds are very much worth watching. Flights of doves, common in U.S. deserts, all moving in the same

Flights of birds all moving in the same direction, especially in late afternoon or early evening, are likely to be headed for water.

direction toward evening or late afternoon mean a waterhole. Doves are extremely mobile, long-distance flyers, and may be going to a hole too distant for you to reach that day. Nonetheless, take a bearing on them, and watch them closely. Watch for quail, too. Some desert quails may get along fairly well for long periods without water, other than that taken from vegetation. But any desert area that *abounds* in quail will have water within 100 to 300 yards of such a concentration. Quail stay bunched up resting in shade during the middle of the day, but go to water early and late. Be particularly alert in desert situations for such birds as blackbirds, or water-oriented birds such as a few ducks in flight. Blackbirds are not desert creatures but are occasionally found in arid terrain, invariably near water. Any bird flights, regardless of species, that take a definite tack, are worth checking. They must have a water supply at flight's end.

Watch animals, too. I said earlier that following game trails when you are lost is usually a poor idea. But a game trail, or a convergence of several, may lead you to water. A very well worn mule deer trail in desert mountains, one that goes downhill, may well be a trail leading to water. Such trails are often seen from high points at great distances when you scan with a binocular. Watch desert mule deer with special concentration just prior to and at dawn. They have a habit of drinking *at dawn,* then going up into the rimrocks to bed down in shady crevices for the day. Don't expect to find a huge spring as their water source. They are desert creatures, getting along on what is available. It may be only a rocky depression that holds rainwater.

Caves or hollowed out places in rock bluffs may contain water. But be cautious about entering caves, because of snakes and the chance of getting lost. If you note a cave or hole in a rock wall, even one you cannot reach, watch it closely at evening. If swarms of bats emerge, remember that they are mammals and must have water. They will usually head for water right away. Their course may give you a clue.

## Desert Hints

Again let me caution against any vast amount of digging for water in desert terrain. The amount of energy used up may be too much, or it may be expended to better advantage in other ways. For example, following a definite, time-worn dry stream course in a desert, not just a flood wash, not only may lead in due time to a larger, live stream, but it may also bring you to small pools among rocks or in gravel and sand, even in hot weather. Evaluate carefully "sure" indications of water. For instance, in such a dry streambed, the *outside* of a bend is the place to check most meticulously. If the bank is concave, and a depression exists, water has stood here. Sandy loam should at least be probed here. If it shows any dampness, on surface or a foot down, then digging is worthwhile.

If you are outfitted with quality maps of the desert region where you are going, you should check beforehand all indications of springs and other water sources. Invariably they are shown on the maps. Then if you are not lost but have a breakdown on your hands, you can study your map and determine precisely where a water supply is located. Another type of arid-country water source nowadays is seldom mentioned. Finding it requires knowing where you are, and having its location or locations exactly pinpointed on your map. Over a number of years game management people have been building, often in remote desert expanses, what are known as "guzzlers." These are water traps, designed to catch, hold, and protect rainwater over long periods, for use by game birds and animals. Some have been built in desert bighorn sheep country, to make possible spread of range. Others are for desert quail and deer. They are designed so that these creatures can drink but cannot get into the water and thus pollute it. Contact game department personnel for locations of guzzlers in the "outback" when planning a trip as a good precaution. Mark them on your map.

## Plant Sources

Vegetation is a water source in emergency. There is hardly a place where you have much difficulty finding water across the northern half of this continent, but the arid areas are problem locations. Fortunately it is here that water-conserving plants, such as the cacti, grow most abundantly. The barrel cactus is always cited as a desert water source. It is a good one, too, but it does not grow in all desert locations. If you hack off the top of this cactus and slice and hack the pulp inside into pieces, a substantial amount of juice, mostly water, will accumulate. Prickly pear is the most common cactus and comes in great variety. The pads and fruit both contain large quantities of juice. The problem in handling cacti as a water source is the danger of getting scratches or cuts from spines,

To get water from a barrel cactus, hack off the top and crush the pulp inside to pieces until a substantial amount of water accumulates.

which quickly fester. Beware the fuzz in small clumps on prickly pear fruits or pads, or on any cactus. The various prickly pears and flat-pad cactus species are, incidentally, excellent food items as well as water sources.

With the exception of the coconut, beware of plant juices that are milky. Among desert plants, stalks of mescal, sotol, and Spanish bayonet all can be cut and drained of their juices for emergency water. In jungles, or even some shaded desert locations, varied vines are found. When you are tapping any of these for water, reach up as high as you can to cut first. Then cut the section at the bottom. The juice drains downward when the two cuts are made, but the top one must be made first to keep sap from rising. Green coconuts contain milk easy to get to. But the chances of getting into a survival situation in green-coconut country on this continent are rare.

In fact, the water-from-plants idea has been highly over-popularized. Even "cactus water" is not the bub-

> Juice drained from vines in jungle or shaded desert locations can serve as emergency water. Two cuts, at top and bottom, will start the juice flowing, but make sure to make the top cut first to keep the sap from rising.

bling fountain it is sometimes pictured to be. I have camped among prickly pear, thousands of acres of it, during dry spells when you couldn't have coaxed a quart of water from fifty pounds of pads. They contract and grow "thin" during dry times. The common grapevine is one of the most overworked plants of all in popular survival literature. Large wild grapevines are an excellent source of juice to substitute for water. Cut a length and drain the water into a container or directly into your mouth. But wild grapes seldom grow in severely arid expanses. In my travels over forty years I have *never* seen wild grapevines in any spot where I could not find water elsewhere within a short distance!

While it is important to know such sources of emergency liquids, or cordage, a false sense of security is possible. For example I read recently some advice about gathering wild grapevines to bind a raft together for a swift northern mountain stream in winter. There is just one drawback: at that latitude and in such terrain the chance of finding a wild grapevine is about as remote as finding a green coconut! Also liquid from vines—the wild grape is one—does not flow readily at all times. Summer produces best, winter not at all. In other words, know what is *possible,* but don't let cozy campfire chatter confuse the facts.

### Seacoasts

It is conceivable (though not possible in many places on this continent) that you might be caught in an emergency along a seacoast. Along all northern coasts there is little chance of being far from fresh-water sources: streams which enter the bays or oceans, near-shore ponds and lakes, or inland swamps. But you might find yourself in sand dune country. It is possible, but again not surefire, that you will be able to get fresh water by digging in sand, not deeply, during low tide just at the highwater line on the

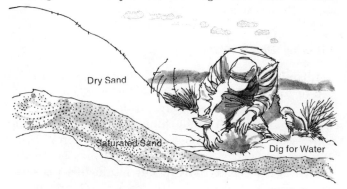

In sand dune country, look for fresh water in the first depression behind the dune closest to the sea. Dig a hole during low tide; stop digging when you hit wet sand. The first water in the hole should be fresh.

sand. In theory, the first water to come into a hole here will be fresh. It is less dense (lighter) than salt water. Or, at times you can go back among dunes and dig and locate seeping fresh water the same way. *But,* too many people accept this as a system that is *going to work,* and it may not work at all. Fresh water must be present. It's that simple. If it isn't, you don't get any.

Some distance back from the shore, perhaps among dunes but in the lowest spot, so a kind of seepage basin is formed, chances are better that if you get water at all, it will be partly fresh. It may be brackish. But a small amount of salt is not harmful. Filtering through thicknesses of cloth, or through sand, may help some. In no case should you drink saltwater. It can kill you, taken in any quantity.

### Filtering Desert Water

Inland in deserts occasionally alkali water is all that can be located. It is hardly drinkable as is, but can be made so if not too severely alkaline. First filter it through sand. Do this by filling a cloth, even your shirt, with sand and pouring the water through it. But use sub-surface sand. Surface sand may be alkaliloaded already. Next boil it, but meanwhile place in the pot some charcoal or ash from wood previously charred in your fire. If you find desert waterholes, incidentally, with no vegetation at all growing around them, at least no vegetation which is alive, beware. This water probably is not drinkable, having leached out from the soil certain minerals that have literally poisoned it.

In deserts especially, conserving the liquids in your body is almost like finding water. Conserve energy during the heat, so you perspire as little as possible. Always keep well covered—head, arms, entire body— rather than removing your clothing. This may not be comfortable, but perspiration evaporates more slowly when you are clothed, and you avoid sunburn, which raises body temperature and hastens evaporation.

## Ground Sources

In some instances dew is a source of water. In the desert, where temperature changes are wide between night and day, heavy dews may occur. A downed plane or a broken-down vehicle offers large surfaces on which dew can collect. Clean such surfaces as best you can. Prepare to mop up dew at dawn, squeezing out mop cloth into a container. A sheet of plastic, numerous

Don't let rain water get away. You can make a "run-off" from the split half of a straight pole with a V-notch gouged along the center. Use rocks to support the trough, which angles slightly downhill.

smooth rocks laid out at night, a canvas ground cloth or tarp—all can be utilized as dew collectors. Dew may even be utilized from vegetation. But small surfaces unfortunately do not furnish much. You must be up before dawn in order to collect as much as possible.

Plain mud can be a water source. Wallow absorbent material such as cloth in it, and squeeze out the saturation. Obviously this is impure liquid. It must be boiled. But a fair sized mudhole, mopped up, could save your life. Meanwhile, be ever watchful of the weather. At the least sign of rain, don't travel if you are in dire need of water. Begin immediately to arrange for catching all the rain water you can. Some ideas are as follows. Scoop a broad, shallow hole in the earth, lay your plastic sheet or tarp in it. Any small board or tree trunk or even a stick can work, in a heavy rain, as a "run-off" to direct water into any makeshift container. Make containers, in desperation, from broad leaves, or packed earth, or flat rocks.

If there is a dry wash near you that is narrow enough, you may be able before a hard rain to push sand and rocks into a makeshift dam that will hold back a flood of water long enough for you to get your share. Use every possible and available container, even to spreading your shirt, with sand spread atop it, inside a shallow depression. If a tree is near, tie a cloth around it and let a "tail" serve as a wick to drain water during a rain off into any type of container. Wring out the cloth periodically.

Palm trees are mentioned in all survival manuals. Many North Americans may be gulled into believing that they should keep an eye out for them. Palm trees are a clue to nearby, immediate, water, and to liquids from various types of palm-borne fruit. The trouble is that only far down in tropical North America are there palm trees worthy of mention in isolated situations that could possibly be helpful to persons who need them. In southern Mexico and Central America they are present. The sap from cut fronds or flower stalks might be helpful. But not within the continental United States and only in restricted areas far south of the border where these trees are *indigenous*. This popular fallacy instills confidence where it is not due. Palmettos, however, in the Southeastern low country, can give up water when fronds or stems or hearts are cut. But chances of need in this region are so few that only the fundamental knowledge is necessary. Other water is readily available, as in the Everglades, one of the few remote areas in that region.

There are many ways to filter mud and other sediment out of water. In cactus country, slash pads (as of prickly pear) and pour muddy water on them in a lined hole or container. The gelatinous moisture within the pads gathers the mud or sediment. Let muddy water stand overnight to settle out mud. Filtering through cloth, grass, a cone-shaped contrivance made from tough sedge grasses or reeds, or through sand, will help. None of these operations is especially important, *if you boil the water*. Mud is not harmful as such. Settle it out, then skim off the water and boil to purify, assuming you have no chemical treatment.

## Survival 'Still'

Among the most important water-gathering knowledge is how to build a "still" to force water from
what appears to be dry ground. Over the past few
years the still made with a plastic sheet has been
used a good many times for gathering much needed
water. This is an important reason for carrying the
plastic in the first place. Some exertion is required.
In moderate temperatures this won't matter. In high
temperature of a desert locale, wait until dusk or predawn to do the work. To make a still, dig a hole at
least one and one-half to two feet deep and a yard
or a bit more across at the top. This depression should
be bowl shaped. At the bottom, dead center, place a
container, hopefully one with a reasonably wide
mouth such as a boiling pot, or a container shaped
from foil.

Now spread the plastic sheet across the top of the
hole, and gently push down in the center so that it
becomes a large cone with the apex directly over and
within about three inches of the container. The sheet
must now be tightly sealed around the rim of the depression by piling on earth dug from the hole, or
rocks. When that is done, place a small weight such
as a stone on the bottom, center, to keep the plastic
snug and the inverted apex precisely above the container. This plastic cone, heated by the sun, will pull
from the earth any moisture that is there. It is distilled
onto the underside of the plastic and runs down to
drip into the container. This is not absolutely infallible, however. There must first be moisture present.

A survival still draws out whatever water is present in the earth. To make it, you need a sheet of plastic and any makeshift container. Dig a bowl-shaped hole, 1½ to 2 feet deep. Place the container at bottom center. Next spread the sheet across the top of the hole, making sure it is tightly sealed around the rim with piles of rocks, soil. When the plastic is lowered in the center so it takes on a cone shape, put a small rock in the center to hold the point of the sheet directly over the container. When possible, line the hole with moisture-producers, such as the chunks of cactus on the left.

Variations add to the amount of water. If cactus is plentiful, hack up chunks and line the entire bottom of the hole with pulp before spreading the plastic and sealing it. The cactus will be dehydrated and the re-sultant water distilled and dripped into the container. If you have a coil of small plastic tubing, mentioned a few paragraphs back, lay one end into the container and bring the tube up the side of the hole and from under the edge of the sheet. You are thus able to drink without disturbing your still. This can collect a quart of water a day and under optimum conditions more.

No doubt other water-gathering ideas can be concocted. However, using the foregoing as a guide, you will be basically prepared. As in every other survival endeavor, good sense, calm approaches and reasoning are of the utmost importance.

# 8 / Food for Survival

THE FOOD WE are talking about here is wild food which can sustain you through wilderness emergencies. Not long ago I read a series of recipes allegedly for survival usage. One described a stew to be made out of any wild game you could kill. The directions explained how to treat the meat and finally said, "Now add your vegetables." Just where the vegetables were to come from, the author didn't say. True, you might have in your pack, as has been suggested, some concentrated, dried or dehydrated foods suitable for making a stew. It is also possible to make a rather good stew from a rabbit, let's say, and certain "wilderness vegetables." But the chances of having all the ingredients in hand at the same time are remote.

Thus, in this chapter foods and food preparation are treated from a primitive viewpoint.

## Finding Meat

If you have a weapon, you probably can acquire meat. Almost any small animals, from rabbits and raccoons to armadillos and muskrats, and all birds, are good to eat. No person in a survival situation need worry unduly about game laws. With a .22, mentioned earlier as a survival weapon, in your pack, you can kill small animals and birds, even a deer. Shots at deer or other large game must, however, be at short range, and in the ear or head. Never waste ammunition, and never shoot at running animals. In very shallow water you can shoot and stun fish with a .22 or other rifle, at close range. Do not be fooled into trying to do this with a shotgun. It won't work once in a dozen tries!

The kill of a large animal, such as a deer or a javelina, will furnish meat for several persons or for several days if you must stay in one place. In high mountain country a deer will not spoil if skinned and hung where the dry air gets to it. If you must be on the move, you might bone out backstraps of a deer and some haunch meat and carry it with you.

An animal call stuck into a pack, whether for a one-day trip or longer, is a good little survival tool to complement the rifle or pistol. Raccoons will come to them. So will bobcats and other predators. Believe it or not, bobcat is not bad eating. I have yet to try fox or coyote, however! But a call, a small flashlight for night calling, which is most likely to be successful, and a .22 may garner some meat for you. Another weapon that will collect small game, if you practice beforehand to become proficient, is the slingshot. It is not a bad idea to have one in a pack, with a modest amount of regular ammo for it. You can also use pebbles. In case of a breakdown or crash, you may be able to scrounge material, such as elastic cord from a parachute pack and a piece of stiff cloth or rubber, and by cutting a forked stick put together a slingshot that will work at least on small creatures.

If you have no firearm, you can kill certain mammals with a long stick, club, or stone. The armadillo is not difficult to catch in your hands, or strike with a club. The porcupine is notoriously easy to approach and kill with a club. This creature has figured in many survival instructions. Porcupines are only sometimes present, however, and not easy to find. Surprising as it may seem, if you stalk javelina into the wind you can often get within mere feet of them, close enough to club and kill one with a rock.

Look for signs of raccoons, opossums, rabbits and squirrels in hollow logs, hollow trees, and stumps. It is exceedingly difficult to trap a squirrel in any fashion in a hollow. But I have caught cottontails in hollow logs by carefully blocking one end and using a long pole in the other. Long-furred animals such as the opossum and raccoon can be hauled out of hollows by use of a forked stick. The fork must be very strong, and short—one and one-half inch prongs —and the handle long enough to reach the animal. The animal must be where it can go no farther. The stick is jammed hard against it, into the fur, and twisted. Hide and fur both twist onto the fork and the animal is hauled out. This system works only under ideal circumstances. I have accomplished it several times, and failed at it also. Be ready with a club if you haul out a raccoon. These are awesomely strong, hard-fighting animals. A 'possum is dull and usually fairly docile.

Occasionally animals can be smoked out. This was long practiced by hillbilly 'coon and 'possum hunters until made illegal. You can build a smudge fire at the base of a hollow tree so the smoke is drawn into the opening. Sometimes burrowing animals can be driven out by pouring water down the burrow, and standing ready with a club as they emerge. Make certain there are not several burrow entrances and exits, and if so, plug all but the one. However, so few animals are burrowers that this is not likely to bring any vast return in meat.

Some official survival manuals suggest using fire—grasslands, for example, set afire—to drive out birds and animals. This is an exceedingly questionable practice. You might catch yourself in your own trap, or start a fire that burns out of control. From a standpoint of practicality, the odds against your killing something as it flees are awesome. To be sure, some birds or animals may be burned to death and can be located after the fire is out. But the man desperate enough to try this method of food-gathering is already too weak to profit much by it. I never recommend it. There are far better and far more efficient methods.

A *small* fire may at times be useful. For example,

pack rats commonly build huge nests in such places as cactus clumps. A fire set in such a nest has little danger of spreading and drives numerous rats out. Chances are quite good of killing one or more with a club. They are big, usually fat, and though not appealing as food, they are livesavers in some circumstances.

Snowshoe hares never hole up but live out their lives above ground. They can often be approached, especially when they are plentiful, at close range. They sit hunched in a form, thinking themselves hidden. Carry a long pole when approaching them. Move very slowly. Proper maneuvering might allow you to hit one on the head. Jack rabbits in brushy areas often have several forms scattered over a small area. Ease up to a jack and it will hop away to another form. Check exactly where these are. A jack does not want to leave its home bailiwick. There are individual differences among animals: watch closely the reaction of a single jack. If it seems less wild than others, keep following it, form to form, very cautiously, speaking quietly. I've used this technique often in photography. When after a while the jack tires of moving it will let you come within five or six feet. A rock or thrown stick will collect such an animal.

## Snares and Traps

You can take some birds without weapons. During the summer moult, when ducks are nesting, there are several weeks when they are flightless. You can run them down in marshes and catch them by hand. Nesting Canada geese often stand their ground to fight an intruder and are easily killed. The big mountain grouse of the North, the blue grouse, and also the Franklin's or spruce grouse, another northern-forest bird, are exceedingly naive. Occasionally so are ptarmigan, the grouse of the far North, and young sage grouse. You can hit them with stick or stone. In some cases ruffed grouse that have never associated with man are also just as naive.

Ruffed grouse, ptarmigan, and sage grouse are usually approached on the ground. Blue and spruce grouse are seen perching as a rule. A good many have been caught, in emergency, as follows. If you have copper wire, or nylon fishing line—anything with which to make a noose that will stay open—secure a

To catch gamebirds or small animals, tie a length of wire or string with a slip noose in it to the end of a long, slender pole.

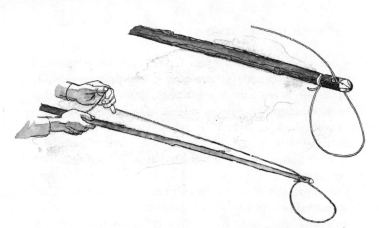

To make the more secure catchpole noose, tie a length of rope to a notch at the end of a pole. Draw the rope through a large screweye near the tip of the pole, and bring it back to your hands at the far end.

length with a slip noose tied in it to the end of a long, slender pole. Reach with extreme care and slow motion near a grouse and slip the noose over its head, then jerk.

You can make a better noose arrangment on a pole if you have ample material by arranging it like a catchpole used in handling animals. In its "domestic" form, a rope is secured to the end of a long pole, then run back through a large screweye or other similar holder set into the end of the pole, and the rope brought back along the pole to the hands. Thus the loop, slipped over the head of the animal, is jerked tight by hand at the far end of the pole, and held that way. This can be done primitively by selecting the slender pole with care, then gouging a small hole through it near the tip, or burning one through with a hot nail or whatever you have. The noose material is now tied securely to the end of the pole, preferably in a notch cut for the purpose, and then threaded back through the hole, edges of which have been smoothed. A bird can be noosed more quickly and securely this way.

The noose, in varied forms, is one of the oldest "meat-getters" known to man. If you are in a spot where you can observe shore birds, wading water birds or waterfowl resting in an exact area—a sandy point, let's say, with cattails nearby—and you have enough snare material, make several nooses and lay them out where returning birds are almost certain to step into them. Then hide immobile in the cattails and wait. When a bird is in position, yank the noose tight. Sometimes a few small sticks laid parallel with the noose atop them to keep it off the ground will get better results, noosing a bird higher on the leg.

Birds such as lakeshore scavengers, the gulls for example, are caught now and then by burying a fish-hook, or a piece of bone to which a nylon fish line has been tied at center, inside a dead fish. The gull swallows the hook, or bone gorge, as it eats. Also, a small dead fish with spiny fins can be laid out as bait to catch a gull. Simply tie the line around the middle of the fish, or around the tail. The gull will swallow the fish head first. When the line is pulled snug, the gull cannot regurgitate the fish because of the dorsal and anal fin spines. Cruel, perhaps, but forgivable in emergency.

Let me urge you not to waste time trying to catch such birds as the waders (herons), the shorebirds (curlew, snipe, yellowlegs, etc.) or the fish-eating ducks (mergansers) by putting out fish-baited hooks. Herons and mergansers take only live fish. Shorebirds take few fish at all, but subsist on a variety of small mollusks, varied aquatic worms, and small shoreside crustaceans. I have experimented, twice, under simulated survival conditions, with attempting to catch these birds in this manner. It won't work. A tethered *live* fish in a shallows, however, will catch a heron, a merganser, or a

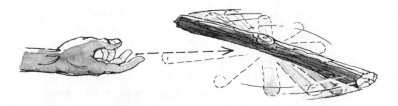

The best way to use a stick for taking birds is to hurl it with a spinning motion into the flock.

tern or gull. The best way to take shorebirds is to fashion a throwing stick at least two feet long, and make a careful sneak. They habitually consort in close-knit flocks, are rather naive, and with a bit of luck you can knock one over either on shore or in the air by throwing the spinning stick into the flock.

In the far North in summer, and in parts of Mexico in fall and winter, sandhill cranes gather by tens of thousands. These large birds are excellent eating. They roost standing in shallow lakes or ponds, gathered very compactly. If you stumble upon such a roosting site, wait until the birds come in at dusk. Mark a group well and at full dark wade very carefully out with your throwing stick. If you have a flashlight, this is easy. If not you must listen closely. The birds will "talk" most of the night. When close, hurl the spinning stick among the tight-packed flock and you may gather a fine meal.

Going back to the noose, the varied set snares utilizing it are excellent for meat-gathering attempts, for several can be placed and tended later. The easiest and most common animals for snaring are the various rabbits and hares. Well-used trails should be selected for the sets. Disturb the surroundings as little as possible, although rabbits do not shy from man scent, as most other animals will. Your repertoire of snares and makeshift traps should be small. It is better to become adept at two or three than to confuse the issue with dozens. Noose material is mandatory. Fine wire, which I have recommended for the pack, is good. Nylon fish line of heavy test is also useful. In dire emergency any cordage scrounged from clothing or a crashed plane or broken-down vehicle must serve. But be aware that at best the makeshifts are not likely to be very successful. The noose should be inconspicuous, and must slide easily.

To make the simplest of all snares, thrust two stakes down into the ground firmly, one on either side of a narrow trail such as a rabbit trail. At proper height, depending on whether jack rabbits or cottontails are likely to use the trail, bind a crosspiece to the stakes. Eighteen-inch height is a good average. If prongs from crotches are left on the stakes so the crosspiece is sup-

A simple snare across a narrow trail starts with
two stakes driven firmly into the ground. Attach
a crosspiece, supported by crotches on the stakes
when possible, and tie the noose material to
the center.

ported a bit, so much the better. The wire or other
noose material is tied to the center of the crosspiece,
with the loop dangling below at proper height so a
hare or rabbit will run its head through as it moves
along the trail. It may be necessary to keep the noose
open, if limp material, by propping a twig or two near
it. As the animal thrusts against it, the noose snugs
down; the struggle keeps it that way.

The twitch-up snare is a variation. There are many
ways to make triggers for these. The set is made as follows: Bend a springy sapling in an arc over the small
game trail, or else bring its top down near one side of
the trail. Drive a small stake, with a notch as in a tent

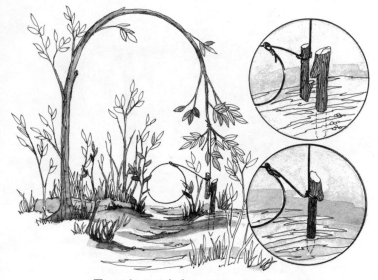

To make a twitch-up snare, bend a sapling over the trail and drive a notched stake into the ground where the top of the sapling comes down. Tie another notched stick to the top of the sapling, upside down, so when both notches are fitted together the tree remains bent. Tie the noose to the sapling end and drape it between bushes in the center of a game trail. For a simple variation, use a single forked stick (bottom insert) thrust into the ground and attached to the sapling to keep it lightly in place.

stake, into the ground exactly where the top comes down. To the end of the sapling top, tie a similar notched stick, upside down. Thus, when notch is fitted into notch, the sapling is delicately held in bent position. The noose material is tied to the sapling end and run out to be looped between small bushes at either side of the trail. Remember that a noose must be at proper height, and large enough for the head to slip through easily, but not the body. When a rabbit or other animal hits this noose, struggle instantly releases the hold of the notched triggers and the sapling yanks the animal into the air.

A much quicker, simpler method is to forget the notched trigger sticks. Use a forked stick thrust into the ground across the upper part of the bent sapling to hold it in place, but only precariously. The least struggle pulls it loose and up goes the snared creature. If the weather is severely cold, these traps may not work well, for the sapling may remain bent without spring. Incidentally, if you have wire strong enough, it is sometimes possible to snare a deer along a well-used trail. But its struggles are mighty and the snare must be very strong. It can be secured to a "drag," which is simply a hunk of log. This allows the animal to move some distance, and while it will invariably become entangled, the "give" may save a broken snare.

Noose snares can be set across the hollow of a tree base, or across a burrow mouth. However, with the exception of cottontails and prairie dogs, few animals but skunks, badgers, coyotes, foxes live in burrows. In other words, in most situations gathering mammals, and birds, without a gun is no snap, with the possible exception of rabbits. It is better to be aware of this than bitterly disappointed.

You can make an old-fashioned deadfall when no snare-making material is at hand. The classic is the ancient "Figure Four." I made many of these as a boy, trying them out on rabbits and even on mink and muskrats. The length of sticks used for the triggering mechanism depends on size of animal. For rabbits or hares, the stake that goes into the ground may be as long as eighteen inches. It must be strong. About four inches from the bottom a deep, flat-bottomed notch is cut into this stake. The stick that lies horizontally in this notch is slightly shorter than the ground stake. It is sharpened on one side. The other end has a notch deeply cut into its upper side on a slight angle (toward the stick end) so the notch has an overhanging inside lip. The trigger stick is about the same length. Its bottom is whittled flat and will fit into the above notch. At the other end of the trigger stick, two or three inches back from the end, a similar type of notch is cut.

A "figure-4" group of notched sticks holds up the log in a deadfall arrangement. The trap collapses when the animal nibbles at bait stuck on the pointed stake directly beneath the log.

Shove the stake into the ground. Place bait on the sharpened end of the horizontal stick, and lay it into the ground stake notch, with its own notch lying upward. The trigger stick now is hooked atop the ground stake and its butt fitted into the cross-piece stick. A heavy log is very delicately leaned from an acute angle and balanced atop this "Figure Four" mechanism—atop the end of the trigger stick. The log must be directly over the bait, and have the shortest possible distance to fall. When an animal nibbles the bait, the log falls to pin and crush it.

This primitive deadfall works well. The perplexing drawback in emergencies is—bait. For muskrats on a lake shore, cattail root may work. In fruit season, any wild fruit secured to the bait stick may collect anything from a rabbit to a raccoon. But often getting bait that will attract hares and rabbits is not easy. Occasionally a beaver is attracted to poplar or willow shoots tied to the trigger. If you have killed any creature, save the entrails and use them as deadfall bait for a predator.

You can build a simple box trap which is just a lidless box turned upside down and propped up on one end by a small stake, with bait under the box. Run a string or line to a hidden watcher. When quail or other birds or small animals are underneath, pull the string to jerk the stake free. In most instances, be warned, materials are not at hand to build a box, nor is it easy to find bait appealing enough to bring in the birds or animals. Also, from my many experiments with box traps and with the far better net wire traps, I can assure you that most birds and animals are extremely shy of them even when they are well-baited. Quail are not too difficult, if grain is available and you allow them to get used to feeding under the trap. But again, in a wilderness situation the grain is harder to come by than the quail and efforts may better be directed elsewhere. Desert quail are more easily snared with set nooses near waterholes or along tiny, brushy trails they utilize. If you have twine, you can weave a makeshift bird net to be draped in willow brush where ptarmigan abound, and which will also entangle quail along their runways. Again, expect failures to be numerous. If by chance you have a gill net as an emergency item in your pack, use it, draped in proper spots, to entangle birds.

## Easy Food Sources

Many animal foods are more easily collected. During nesting season for birds, all colonial nesters offer opportunity for gathering eggs and sometimes young. Eggs are not harmful even when with partial embryos. Although this may not sound appealing, food value in emergency is high. Wild pigeons and doves, such as the Mexican red-billed pigeon and the whitewing dove of the desert, offer chances for a survival meal. Once deep in the jungles of eastern Mexico, had we been forced we could have made numerous meals from fat red-billed pigeon squabs. Their nests covered acres of low thornbrush. Along seacoasts the various terns and gulls also are colonial nesters. In the far North you can gather waterfowl eggs in quantity in spring, and catch young, flightless birds.

Frogs are a fine food source, found along streams, around lakes, ponds and marshes, and even in wet wild meadows. We have often gathered them to eat. At one backwoods lake my boys and I took sixty-odd in a couple of hours, stalking them carefully and armed only with sticks. Turtles also are fairly easy to gather. Any turtle is edible. Beware of their jaws! Throughout the Southwest lizards are common, and edible. None excepting the Gila monster of New Mexico and Arizona and parts of Mexico has a poisonous bite. These big lizards, though edible, are exceedingly rare. Lizards can be killed with a stick, although it is not always easy. They're quick.

With the exception of sea snakes, all snakes are edible. I've tried them several times. A big rattlesnake, bull snake, or water snake makes an excellent meal. And the club is the only weapon you need. If you've never prepared a snake, it is easy. Tie a thong behind the head (if poisonous, be cautious) and hang from a limb. Cut skin around below thong, slit clear down the belly, and pull it off. Gut the snake, lop off head and tail. It can be fried, boiled, broiled. The meat, if you can forget aversion to it, is excellent.

Crayfish, found in streams and under large and small rocks in shallows of many lakes, are a real delicacy. Certain northern lakes and southern rivers have them by thousands. Crabs are found along seacoasts and all are edible. You can catch shallow-water crabs with a piece of meat or dead fish tied to a string. The easiest method is to patrol the surf line or shallow bays at dusk or after dark, with a torch. Scoop them up with a makeshift net made from a shirt, for example, secured to a green stick bent to form a bow and handle. Or, skewer them with a sharpened stake.

Innumerable species of edible mollusks live along saltwater coasts. Various clams of delicious varieties are common along wilderness coasts of the Northwest. Search at low tide for their siphon holes. Inlets and bay shores near the sea also support mollusks. Don't always look for large ones. The tiny coquina, about half an inch long, a bivalve that looks like a miniature clam, is found on southeastern and Gulf beaches in wet surfline sand often by millions. Gather these, boil several quarts of them, then strain the shells and sand out through cloth. The broth is excellent.

In fresh water from North to South the common mollusk is the mussel or "freshwater clam." It lives in slow streams, and in lakes and ponds. Sandy or mud bottoms are the places to look. Often you can see their shells or the trails where they have moved about. There are several varieties, all edible. In some areas terrestrial snails are abundant. They, too, can be eaten.

All crustaceans (crayfish, crabs) and all mollusks (salt, fresh, or terrestrial) should be boiled. Do not eat them raw, for they may contain parasites. Freshwater mussels or clams are invariably tough, but offer substantial food value. The tails of crayfish are the edible part. If you have never cleaned crabs, remember that the body contains more meat than the claws. It's just harder to get out.

In severe situations, don't overlook the fact that insects can be eaten. Grubs found in rotten logs or under tree bark, grasshoppers, even termites are edible. It is best not to eat any of these raw, for they too may con-

tain parasites. Frying them, if you have a speck of
grease for the job, is the most palatable way, although
they can also be boiled.

## Cooking Meat

You should know how to cook meat in a primitive
manner. Possibilities may be very limited. If you have
packed as instructed, you will have salt. You may or
may not have some dehydrated foods, but we will assume you have only meat and salt. This is no hardship.
You can even do without the salt, but it is foolish to be
without. If you have some sort of container, such as a
basic go-light mess kit, the quickest, easiest method is
to cut meat into small pieces and boil it. Use as little
water as possible, to concentrate the juices. Do not put
salt in the water. Conserve your salt supply. Boiling
meat is the best way to assure that it will be cooked all
the way through, if you give it enough time.

You can spear the pieces with your knife, or with a
sharpened stick. Salt each piece as you eat. If you are in
desperate straits for food, save the broth or cooking
water. You can drink it, salted a bit, to give you
strength. If you are not that needful, leave the broth
in the container overnight: grease will be hardened in
a layer on top the next morning. Wild meat may not
have much fat, but there may be some. Skim it off and
carry it with you, even if you must wrap it in foil or
leave it in the container. It can be used later to help
fry something, or to season a boiled wild vegetable!

Small birds or pieces of larger ones are easily broiled
on a green stick over a fire or a bed of coals. They need

plenty of attention while cooking, and you must turn them frequently. For a large bird like a grouse, run a green stick through it endwise, and lay this across crotched green sticks that have been thrust into the ground on either side of the fire. The bird must be turned; hold it in position after each turning by bracing another green stick against it. Without basting with some oil—which you undoubtedly don't have—upland birds are usually very dry, and may become hard outside, half raw inside. If you can spend the time, broil or roast them gently, high over coals for several hours. Or, wrap them in foil if you have it, double, and cook in the coals. This keeps all the juice and fats in. Waterfowl and shore birds usually have more fat. Don't skin birds; pluck them so the fat stays put.

Birds can be boiled, too. Conversely, slices of meat from a large animal can be broiled or roasted on a stick over a fire. If you must rush the cooking, make the slices thin. Where rocks, especially some flat ones, are handy, build a fire inside a ring of rocks, then lay a flat, clean one across the top. Slices of meat of any kind can be fried without grease on the rock. If you boiled meat previously and kept the grease, use it on the rock "skillet." I didn't say this is delicious, but it will sustain you!

## Fishing Gear

In most emergency situations when you are without a firearm, fish may be easier to acquire than game. Hopefully you will have line, hooks, and split shot in your pack, and will have taken my advice about spoons and perhaps about a backpack rod-and-reel outfit. In much of Canada the "jackfish" or pike is a standby in lakes and slow streams. Spoons will get you all you can eat. With a hook and a scrounged bait such as worm, beetle, or minnow caught in a rivulet by hand, you might try for a small fish, then bait a larger hook with that one and catch a pike. In trout streams, and others, crawfish and aquatic nymphs are found beneath rocks. These are prime bait. Many a tiny creek holds wonderful meals of small trout. The farther from civilization you are, the more abundant the fish are likely to be and the more naive about taking bait or small spoon.

We must assume, however, that you may not have any fishing tackle. Take stock of what metal you have available from which a hook can be made—a safety pin is ideal; a needle or straight pin can be carefully bent, although the needle is likely to break. You can fashion wire into hooks. If thorny shrubs (such as mesquite) are in the vicinity, the stiff thorns, whittled off with a piece of wood attached, can serve as a hook. You can chip shells and bone into hook shape. However, hooks made thus, as Indians made them, require long, meticulous hours of work. Any hook made from pin, thorn, etc., has no barb. Thus when a fish bites you must pull instantly and keep pressure snug or the hook will slip out.

Because in most emergencies you cannot spend tedious hours of labor making a hook, the ancient "gorge" is the best and most practical solution. It can be made for any size fish, from a whittled piece of hardwood, a piece of shell, or bone. Basically, using wood, you can make it as follows: Cut a notch around a piece of hardwood perhaps one or two inches long, exactly in the middle. Tie the line here. Sharpen each end of the piece till very fine, and taper down from the center. With line affixed, thrust this gorge inside a chunk of bait—a crawfish, a small fish, or if the gorge is very small and intended for small-mouthed species, worms. Let it down and leave the line limp. Allow a fish which takes the bait to swallow the gorge. A quick yank jerks

Makeshift fishhooks can be whittled from wood, shells, bone. From left are a straight-line gorge, a U-gorge with thorns, and a wooden hook.

the gorge crosswise and the fish cannot get rid of it. The gorge dates back hundreds of years and when properly made is most simple and effective.

Another type of gorge can be made by cutting a short length of thorny vine, or a piece of shrub with thorns. Cut a slice with two thorns on it, and bend the piece in the middle to form a U, to which the line is attached. Let the fish swallow this. A hard pull sets both thorns. When no thorns are available, a carefully, finely whittled and smoothed section taken from the slender crotch of a hardwood branch can be fashioned into a hook that has the larger side notched and bound to the line.

Two types of spears were used successfully by many Indian tribes. Each is made from a green sapling, each basically in the same manner. The wood should be hard. Cut a pole several feet long. Split one end for

A fishing spear with toothed jaws snaps shut over a trapped fish. Use a wedge to keep the wood split while you cut sharp notches; remove the wedge and tie the upper end of the split when through. Finally, insert a strong twig to hold the jaws open until the fish knocks it away.

about seven or eight inches up the shaft. Force a temporary wedge into the upper end of the split, and cut sharp teeth or notches into each flat side of the split. For a trap-type spear leave them like this. Now remove the wedge. Bark or twine or whatever cordage is at hand is used to securely bind the upper end of the split so it will not split farther. Open the "jaws" and prop them open with a twig strong enough to hold them. When you jam this trap spear down over a fish, the twig is knocked out of the way and the jaws snap shut, holding the quarry.

For more surefire variation (the trap jaws may be inhibited from closing because they strike the bottom), whittle each jaw into a hard, pointed spear, with the notches cut very keen and sharp. Insert a permanent wedge and put on the binding. The jaws are not wedged as far apart as for the trap spear. This one is strictly for impaling a fish. Indians sometimes used basswood bark for the binding and covered and secured it with pitch. Used at night with a torch while carefully wading shallows, this spear can be very effective. If it breaks, another is quickly fashioned.

If you have hooks and lines with you, a good plan is to make set lines to leave overnight. These are exactly what modern catfish enthusiasts call "tree lines." Bait hooks and attach them to a tree limb hanging over water. When a fish is on it cannot break loose for the limb bends, playing it as on a rod. This will not work with thorn hooks that have no barb. But for catfish and other rough species it may work when you use a well-turned gorge. There is practically no end to the makeshift spearing devices you can concoct. A sharp piece of bone, a sliver of flint, a shell, or a pocket knife can be lashed to a pole. An impaled fish must be pinned to the bottom, however, else it will get away. By no means take a chance on losing your knife that way!

Various hard cane and bamboo make good hooks and spears, but chances of finding these in any wilderness on this continent are rather slim. With luck you might fashion a hook and makeshift barb, by using a section cut from shrub with long thorn, and then lashing in a notch another thorn, so that it points downward and just inside the point of the other. The line is attached just above the lashed-on thorn. When a fish bites, it is impaled on the thorn used as the hook, but the one lashed on above keeps the fish from slipping off.

Bait is seldom hard to find: terrestrial insects, aquatic nymphs under stones in creeks or in mud of lakeshore bottom, crayfish, worms, a small frog or minnow trapped in shallows and scooped up in cooking container. If you must fish through the ice, cut a hole and fish *on bottom,* using very *small* baits. Fish take smaller baits in winter because their metabolism is slowed. Make a primitive ice-fishing lure used for hundreds of years as follows, if you have no bait: Use a bare fish hook, or an improvised hook of hardwood, thorn or safety pin. Try to find a small, shiny piece of shell and work a small hole through one side, to fashion a small lure. A small piece of metal will do. The makeshift lure, with a few bits of thread or streamers of bark or piece of your shirttail added, is let down to bottom and jigged up and down so it twirls and gyrates. The second a fish strikes you must keep a steady, swift pull and flop it up atop the ice, or it will get off (if your hook is barbless).

If ice is clear and fish are in exceedingly shallow water where you can see them, you might be able to stun several by hurling a heavy rock or log into the ice above them, then smashing open a hole and collecting them. The chance of success, however, is very slim. I've tried it. The fish usually take fright and leave before you get near enough or before the rock strikes. And, except in extremely shallow water, where they are unlikely to be in winter, it is impossible to exert enough force with such a blow. But in a shallow pond it may be worth a try.

Making a crude fishing line, if you have none, is possible, though it takes patience. My advice is to try first to unravel strong threads from some item of clothing, or if absolutely necessary from a tarp or groundcloth. Then braid and twist the threads together to form a line. In making any line (of bark fibers also), always start with several strands of uneven length, and keep adding as one runs out. This assures that at no point will there be a weak spot where all fibers end at once and are spliced.

You can make a line by cutting thin strips from your plastic sheet and twisting them. Bark fiber lines, though crude and large in diameter and frightening to some fish, can be turned out fairly easily. Some tree barks or rootlets make better cordage than others. It is important to know these, but you will have to make do with what is available. Linden and basswood inner bark, mulberry inner bark and roots, hickory bark, elm bark and roots, and the root fibers from hemlock, tamarack and spruce are all good. Roots, however, are not as useful in emergency because they must be dug up. Try inner bark strands first.

Weave a line by carefully separating fine bark strands. Pounding strips of bark with a rock, or soaking them will help separate the strands. Using three strands (I've mentioned unequal length) secured to some object, hold one strand in one hand, two in the other.

Twist the single strand, rolling it between thumb and forefinger, *away* from the other two, until it is twisted tight. Now bring it across and over the other two, and take the next strand in line and twist it, and so on. As the shortest strand begins to run out, lay another beside it and twist them together and continue. The result, if you stay with it, is a primitive line as long as you wish to make it. On occasion when good fibers are available, simple braiding works well. (Larger ropes and cordage for binding rafts, etc., can be made in the same manner, using larger strands. See section on making a raft Chapter 6.)

You can make a crude net from a bow and handle formed out of a limber sapling, with a piece of clothing —shirt, underwear, or whatever cloth or netting is available—secured over it. Hordes of minnows commonly gather in eddies in small streams, or along lake shores. You can scoop them up with such a primitive dip net. Use them for bait, or cook and eat them. Don't attempt to clean them. Cook entrails and all. Larger

For an improvised fishing net, bend a sapling into a loop, and tie string to the loop in overhand knots.

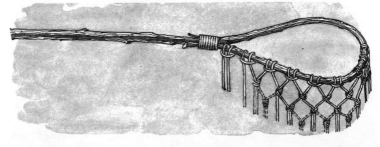

A rock-pool trap built close to bank or shore attracts fish you can scoop out with a net.

Build a more complex trap by driving stakes side-by-side into a river bottom. Fencelike walls extend out from the entrance, which is placed to let the current flow in.

fish can be flipped ashore or netted from stream pools, or tidal pools. But muddy the water first or you'll have difficulty. You must scoop blind in muddy water, but at least the fish can't see to dodge. Fish hiding in vegetation or under rocks can be driven out, if two work together, after the water is muddied. The net is held just below, downstream, and the vegetation disturbed or rocks kicked.

Under optimum conditions, trap fish or drive them into a pool that is dammed with rocks or logs or earth; then slip them out with a makeshift scoop net. It is not impossible to build, from stakes placed close together, a fish trap, and then drive fish into it. Keep in mind that this requires an immense amount of work and may not be worth energy expended.

## Cooking Fish

Primitive fish cookery is much like that for game. Cook small fish quickly as follows: Take out entrails and gills, but leave the heads on. Run a small, sharpened green stick into the mouth, on through the open body cavity, and into the tail section where the vent has been removed. Prop several such sticks with fish above coals and in five to ten minutes they are ready to eat. Assuming you have salt as I've admonished, you have a really delightful meal.

Larger fish should be split down the middle and laid open on a grill made by drawing green, limber wood such as willow switches into a kind of racquet shape, securing tip to middle with a bit of copper wire from your pack, then binding on crisscross pieces of green

To prepare fish for cooking: Clean it from the ventral side by cutting first with the point of the knife inside the mouth (1). Cut through the narrow strip of gristle joining gills to the head. Make the second cut behind the gill (2) to sever the membrane, between the bony ridge and the body, and continue the cut to the tip of the lower jaw. Do this on both sides. The third cut (3) severs the strip of gristle connecting bone and tongue. Finish by cutting from the jaw, along belly line, to the anal orifice (4). Hook your finger through the bottom of the gill cut, around the tongue, and pull sharply. The tongue, gills and intestines will come out through the belly slit. Run your thumb along the backbone to clean blood from the back vein; wash and wipe dry.

You can clean from the dorsal side by placing the knife tip ahead of the gill line until it hits bone. Cut along both sides of the dorsal fin, keeping as close to spines as possible. Spread slit with one hand to expose joinings of ribs to backbone. Make the same first three cuts as above, but don't cut along the belly. After the ribs are cut, remove gills from the slit on the back. Spread the fish to remove backbone and dorsal fin.

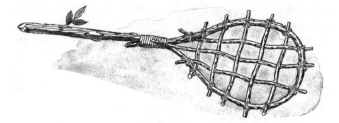

Large fish cook more easily on a simple grill. Make one by bending a switch into racquet shape, and attach green willow pieces in a crisscross design.

willow (or facsimile) to make the grid or grill. This can be propped above coals, or balanced on rocks above coals. Cross-cut steaks of a large fish, or fillets with the skin on, can be "fried" on a hot rock, fillets skin-side down. The trouts and salmons especially are oily and furnish at least enough of their own grease. Such fish wrapped in foil and cooked in or on coals will be fine for the same reason. As with game meat, a quick and efficient method for fish is to *boil* them, if you have a container.

Don't discard heads, fins or tails when boiling fish. Cut up the fish and toss it all in the pot except gills and entrails. (Save those for bait!) This is the way fish stock is made in any seafood restaurant. It is highly nourishing. If you will be staying put for several days, or even a day, the stock (any game stock, too) may be utilized as a base in which to boil various wild plants.

Some books describe gimmicky methods for cooking game and fish, such as plastering birds, feathers and all, in mud and burying them in coals. Or building a fire in a pit, wrapping and burying meat, and covering it with dirt for some hours. These work, the latter delectably. But they are tricks. During emergencies the easiest, quickest ways to nourishment are the best. They save on energy and time. Either or both may be important, depending on whether you are traveling or waiting it out, and on your physical condition.

Foil, which takes up little room, a spool of copper wire, salt, a container for boiling, and your knife are about all you need for primitive, emergency cooking of game and fish. On short treks I have even put into the rucksack a good-sized tin can. Other items can be stowed inside it to economize on room. The can becomes a coffee or tea boiling pot, a meat pot, etc. With just a tin can and a supply of salt, plus your knife, you are in the survival business in pretty good shape.

Remember that whether you are eating meat or fish or the in-betweens such as frogs, crawfish, or turtles, and adding certain wild plants to this scrounged-off-the-country diet, there may be some stomach upsets. An abrupt change to survival diet should be avoided if possible. In other words, if you do have some food supply you are used to, intermingle the "new" foods as slowly and sensibly as you can while you "taper off" from civilization.

### Edible Plants

There are literally hundreds of edible wild fruits, nuts, plants and roots. The problem with them as related to survival is their vast numbers. Most outdoorsmen know or learn to recognize a standard few, but it takes a great deal of study, both in books and in field identification to be sure of large numbers.

Recreationists should make it a point to be able to recognize the available edible vegetation in the areas they utilize most of the time. For example, a sportsman who hunts and fishes in Minnesota should certainly know the edible plants and fruits of his state that are most easily found in emergencies. He should know what time of year is best for each: young shoots, fruits, roots. In addition, the outdoorsman who is going to a new area should research the plants and fruits there. You should at least be able to identify the most abundant and common ones, which may become vital resources if you are lost or otherwise in difficulty.

There are dozens of good library volumes which contain complete material. In many states the game and fish departments or the university can help with information about wild edibles in their location. You can never amass too much knowledge, that's sure. But my approach here, a sound one for the average person, is to cover the wide variety of possibilities throughout the entire continent, and conclude with examples of species *easily recognizable* and *most abundant over large ranges.*

**Fruits.** Let us begin with fruits. Wild fruits are found in every state and province. But in any given locality most are available only at specific periods, which may not be prolonged. And fruits are usually abundant in spring and summer, with only a few in evidence in fall.

Wild red mulberry trees are found from Texas and across the South on up throughout the Ozarks and throughout New England. They are quite common in State and National Forests, especially in the South and the Ozarks. The very sweet fruit ripens in spring and early summer and falls fast. Serviceberry shrubs, in some areas spreading small trees, are called "shadbush" in the East and various names westward. They are

Red Mulberry                    Wild Raspberry

widely distributed throughout most of the U.S. and Canada. Their white blooms come in early spring, before the leaves. This is a summer fruit often abundant in wild locations, especially in old open burns or lumbered areas and along streams.

Wild blackberries, wild raspberries, wild dewberries are found over a tremendous range, one or more in any locale of the U.S. and Canada. Vast patches of wild blackberries occur, for example, in the Great Lakes forest region. Red raspberries are profuse over much of Canada and also in Alaska. Dewberries, low-growing and vinelike are predominantly southern. These are all summer fruits, with August an average ripening time in much of their range. Delicious wild strawberries range over most of temperate North America, in mountains and forests where there is shade and quite often in grassy locations. They ripen in summer.

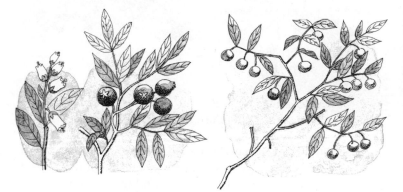

Blueberry             Huckleberry

The blueberries and their cousins the huckleberries both include several species and grow on bushes from a few inches to several feet tall. They are possibly the most abundant and important wild fruits of "emergency areas" throughout the northern states and Canada and some distance down the eastern U.S. mountains. Open woods, burns, and logged regions offer them by untold acres, usually in late summer and into very early fall.

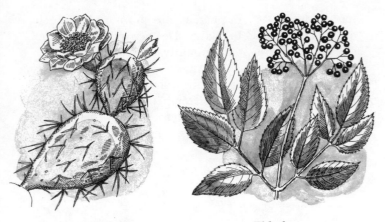

Prickly Pear                    Elderberry

The foregoing are the most widespread and abundant of the fruits. There are many others. Cactus fruits, such as prickly pear apples when ripe, are delicious and sustaining, but watch the hairlike spines. Elderberries are not especially palatable but widely distributed and worth knowing. Bearberry or kinnikinic is a mealy berry chiefly of the northern wild areas that has some food value. Wild rose hips (fruits) are most important because they are found even in winter. Wild northern gooseberries make good eating but are scattered and never plentiful. The highbush cranberry of the northern U.S. and parts of Canada is edible after frosts, though not especially desirable except in jellies. However, you should know this one, a prime ruffed grouse food. The pawpaw and persimmon are edible but not likely to be important in wilderness emergencies, although an ability to identify them can be helpful.

Bearberry

Wild Rose Hips

American Papaw

Persimmon

Wild bog cranberries and wild currants are possibles, but not very important. Wild cherries, chokecherries, pin cherries, sand cherries on low vinelike bushes, and wild black cherries on big trees are exceedingly abundant, especially across the northern U.S. The problem with them is their "puckery" taste. They contain sus-

Wild Cherry                    Chokecherry

taining sugar but may cause intestinal upsets. Wild black cherries or the rarer sand cherries are the best of the lot. Wild grapes may be locally important because they range widely across much of the U.S. and some portions of southern Canada, and especially as they sometimes hang on the vine from late summer into fall. Wild plums are an important fruit of broad range, particularly in late summer and early fall, but the majority of plum thickets are in areas close to civilization.

The major problem with wild fruits, and wild plants, is that you must also know what *not* to eat. The simple method, and listen closely, is to know a major share of the *wholly edible varieties* which are in the majority, and not be tempted by anything you can't absolutely identify. You might get a wee bit of nourishment, or

Wild Grapes                    Golden Currant

wind up defunct, by guessing. Search for *what you know*. Beware of *what you don't know*. For example, some fruits are poisonous raw but not if cooked. Others, some common, are poisonous, period. Examples: blue cohosh; bittersweet; chinaberry; mistletoe; nightshade. In many treatises on wild fruit the May apple is noted as delicious. It is, but other parts of the plant are poisonous, and even when the fruit is fully ripe it is on the "caution" list. So are wild holly berries, pokeberries, Solomon's seal. Thus, eat only berries that are commonly known, abundant and easily identified.

**Mushrooms.** All live-off-the-country experts agree that emergency people should leave mushrooms alone. Species like the spring-growing morels are delicious. But no mushrooms contain much of food value, and the chance of poisoning is too great. Our family has gathered morels for years in widely scattered parts of the U.S. But I would never recommend this as a survival measure. We happen to know the morels well. Others may not. Besides, as stated, mushrooms just taste good. They give you very little, if any, "steam."

Dandelion    Poke

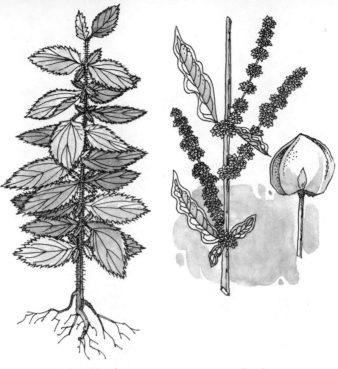

Stinging Nettle                    Dock

**Plants.** Next come edible green plants. Their numbers are vast. Many make rather tasty boiled greens. Probably the most wide-ranging of these is the dandelion. Young plants are less bitter than mature ones. A quick scalding in boiling water, then draining and final boiling, removes most of the bitterness. Various clovers, found throughout most of the U.S. and commonly in woodland openings or thin shade, are next in line as easy-to-find. Clovers may persist in sheltered locations well into frost time. The entire plant, including root, is edible. Boiling is the simplest preparation.

Other plants found over most of the temperate continent that furnish edible greens are nettles, several

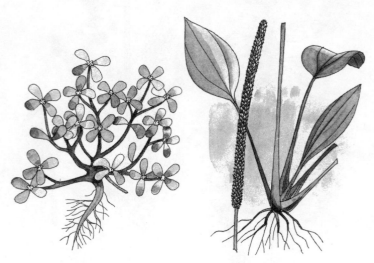

Purslane        Plantain

Burdock

varieties of dock, purslane, plantain, and even pigweed. Burdock, also common over much of the northern U.S. and southern Canada, can be used for greens. Young leaves and shoots are best. Stalks, peeled and salted, are not bad, and if you learn to identify the first-year stalks of this perennial (which lack flowers or burrs) you can peel and cook the roots. Mustard, found in great fields throughout wild lands across the northern U.S. and across into Canada, is easy to identify and makes a palatable dish. Even the flowers can be cooked.

Two favorites of mine that we often eat as a wild treat are watercress and marsh marigold. The latter we called "cowslips" when I was a youngster. Both these plants range over much of the continent. You can find them in wet openings and along streams. Since stream

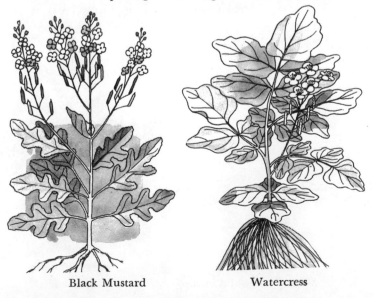

Black Mustard          Watercress

courses are highways to many outdoorsmen in emergency, these plants rate high as survival food. Neither grows in every moist terrain, but one or the other are almost certain to be seen somewhere. Spring and early summer offer the best greens from marsh marigolds, when leaves are young. The same is true of watercress, but watercress is often found quite edible all through the season until total freeze-up. It can be eaten raw and usually is. But it also makes fine greens. A piece of boiled, salted meat with watercress greens is a good wilderness meal.

Wild celery ranges widely and can be used raw or boiled. The shoots of young bracken, the large tough fern of Canadian and U.S. woodlands that often grows in profusion, make a good dish in spring when the "fiddlehead" shaped shoots are edible. Fireweed is an-

Marsh Marigold (Cowslip)                    Bracken

Lichens (Reindeer Moss)          Lichens (Rock Tripe)

other common plant found over a vast range, growing at its best in burns, logged-over areas, and other openings. The stems should be boiled.

**Cacti.** In the Southwest and some other desert areas, there is a wealth of food—and drink—in various cacti. Although these should be handled with extreme care, the pads of the abundant prickly pear when peeled and diced are excellent. Diced cactus is commonly sold in Mexico as a green vegetable to be boiled. Mexicans living far out in their deserts hack off the great blooms of the big yuccas and boil the flowers as a vegetable. Mesquite beans, green or ripe, can also be utilized for food.

The list over the continent is virtually endless. Even grass of almost any variety can serve for greens. And in the North you can boil the nutritious lichens. Know how to identify the most common edible fruits and plants. And try to study thoroughly beforehand the entire vegetation picture of a wilderness area *where you are going*.

**Roots and nuts.** There are a number of roots, tubers, nuts and grains to add to the list. Most common and far-ranging is the cattail. Young cattail shoots in spring

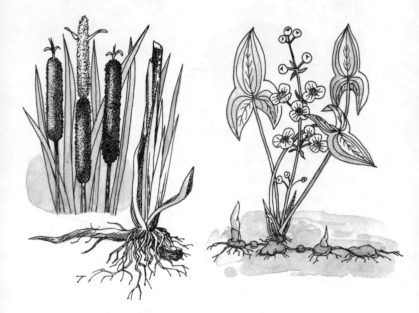

Cattail (Elephant Grass)                      Arrowhead

make a good boiled vegetable or can be salted and eaten raw. A bit later when the green flower heads appear, you can boil them and eat the outer layer. In the fall or even in winter, if you have means to keep dry wading after them or a good drying-out fire, dig the roots and boil them like potatoes. Arrowhead grows along pond and lake shores and along the edges of slow streams over most of the U.S. and portions of Canada. It has tuberous roots which can be gathered from late summer on into winter and boiled or roasted.

Spring Beauty   Jerusalem Artichoke

That common wildflower of damp woodland locations and stream courses, the spring beauty, has a small root tuber that is edible. Another that outdoorsmen should know, although its range is not as large, is the so-called Jerusalem artichoke. This tuber is available in autumn in portions of mid-Canada and the U.S. Sedges also have small, edible root tubers.

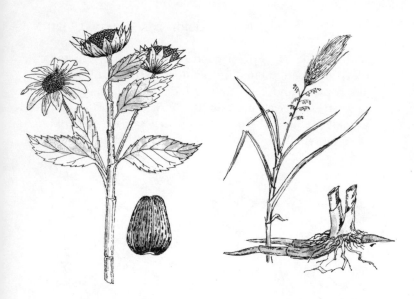

Sunflower Seeds                    Wild Rice

Wild sunflower seeds make a good energy food but are a bit difficult to husk. They are available in fall and winter. So is delicious wild rice, throughout the Great Lakes region, parts of eastern Canada and the U.S. However, a canoe or boat is all but mandatory for harvesting it. The most common nuts found over the continent are, in the Northeast beechnuts, in the South wild pecans, and in some locations both North and South, black walnuts and hickory nuts. The prime and most common nut of all in wilderness areas of the West is the piñon, the small, delicious nut found numerously in the cones of a species of pine. You can identify it easily. During some falls piñon nuts are abundant; other years there are very few. These must be rather

Beech Nut

Black Walnut

Hickory Nut

Piñon Nut

laboriously shelled, but you can gather a great many under or from a laden tree. They are most nutritious.

In dire circumstances, willow buds and shoots and even the inner bark layer, can stave off starvation. The inner layer of pine may also be cooked and eaten, or even eaten raw. Make a serious attempt to know wild foods. Try a few, using some primitive cooking methods when there is no emergency. Sometime try an overnight backpack during which you force yourself to live off the land. It is a valuable rehearsal for survival.

# 9 / *Fire and Warmth*

IF YOU HAVE OUTFITTED as suggested earlier—with water-proof matches, even with fire-starter tucked away in your pack—fires should be very little problem. Assuming you do have fire-making materials, there still are certain tips that will be helpful. For example, even if you are cold, don't be in a wild rush to get a blaze going. Whenever you build any fire, for warmth overnight or for cooking, get all the materials together in a proper place and be sure all is ready *before* the match is struck. Matches are infinitely valuable. Haste and poor preparation defeat your purpose and waste matches.

For a midday cooking fire, pick a sheltered location and make a very *small* fire. If it will be a fire for evening cooking and for overnight, plan a larger one, or

several small ones *around* you. Without fail, select a
fire site that is *safe,* where a fire cannot get away from
you and into grass, leaves, needles. For overnight, build
where it cannot set your shelter ablaze. In the latter
case, choose your sleeping site *first* and build the fire
in relation to it. Don't build under evergreen boughs,
even if they are green, and especially if they are covered with snow.

## Starting the Fire

Start any fire with patience. Plan it carefully and
one match will do. Get as much out of the wind as you
can. Lay a foundation of fine tinder such as birchbark
shredded into small pieces, or tiny dry dead twigs from
a conifer, or bits of dry willow. If necessary, whittle
shavings or cut fine shavings along the side of a stick

A fuzz stick made from dead wood makes reliable tinder. Whittle fine shavings along the
side, leaving them attached to the stick.

Arrange your firemaking material by laying a foundation of fine tinder beside a short length of stick. Lean larger twigs above the tinder, against the stick, in a pyramid. Have larger wood, 3 to 4 inches thick, ready to add once the twigs catch. Light the tinder from the bottom, on the upwind side.

but leave them on the stick. This is called a "fuzz stick." Crisscross above the fine tinder a few larger dry *twigs,* but none more than pencil size to begin. Have increasingly larger wood at hand. A good method is to lay the tinder beside a short length of stick three to six inches in diameter, lean the twigs over the tinder and against the large stick. Now when the tinder catches, the twigs go in a moment, larger ones are carefully added, and in seconds a good blaze is there.

For overnight stays, don't stint on gathering wood. But save energy by burning long pieces a bit at a time, pushing them farther into the fire as they burn, rather than chopping or sawing. Always gather standing dead wood if you can, or at least dead wood not lying on damp ground. In wet situations, and I have experi-

An Indian fire built with logs radiating outward and a small tepee of sticks in the center saves energy and fuel. Push the logs into the fire as they burn.

enced this in desert as well as northern forests, gather very small dead twigs from standing conifers or mesquite, not from the ground.

If you have a fire-starter, you have no problem. If not, shelter a tepee of these tiny twigs and hold a match diligently under it, or light and use your candle. Be ready to add more. With patience you can get a fire going even with damp twigs. Keep drying out larger sticks as the blaze grows. Always light your fire with the breeze at your *back,* and on the side nearest you, and from *below* the tinder. Once you have a big fire going, pile on damp or wet wood gingerly (not eagerly) and let the fire dry it. You must use care not to smother your blaze. Always leave space, but not too much, by crisscrossing or leaning the sticks, for air to circulate beneath to keep the fire going. Too much space lets a fire die. Almost, but not quite, contact the sticks.

When possible use wood from conifers (evergreens) for starting fires. Dry cones are great, too. The hardwoods do not blaze as readily, but fires from those last longer. You may not have time or energy to go around selecting woods. Just remember that pine, cedar, spruce, etc., will start the fire quickly and burn swiftly, and woods such as ash, oak, maple will keep it going longest yet may be more difficult to start. Aspen, poplar and birch are common firewoods in many forests. They make good cooking fires, burn hot and fairly fast. Oak, and mesquite in deserts, make marvelous coals and long lasting fires, but are hard to ignite. On sagebrush plains, you may have to gather a lot of material, but sage burns readily even if damp, and makes a very hot but fast fire. Dead cactus woods, such as cholla or saguaro, are too hard and burn hot and slowly.

## FIREWOOD RATING OF COMMON TREES

| Good | Fair | Poor |
|---|---|---|
| Ash | Beech | Willow |
| Hickory | Mulberry | Alder |
| Oak | Buckeye | Chestnut |
| Holly | Sycamore | Magnolia |
| Dogwood | Tamarack | Tulip |
| Apple | Pine | Catalpa |
| Birch | Cedar | White elm |
| Maple | Juniper | Cherry |
| Locust | Spruce | |
| Mountain mahogany | Cottonwood | |
| | Fir | |
| | Aspen | |

If tinder is a problem—it can be tremendously important—stay alert to possible sources as you travel. Pause to pocket some that looks good—a double handful of dry pine needles, a few cones from pine or other evergreen, a roll of birch bark, some dry cattail heads, a mouse or bird nest, or globs of pitch from conifers. In sparsely vegetated desert country, do the same with dry mesquite, sage twigs or bark shreds. Few North American deserts are so barren, that you will lack something to burn. In arid grazing country, dry cowdung burns well.

It is to your advantage, except under desperate circumstances, to make a small fireplace to contain your blaze. A few rocks will do it, or a small hole scooped in sand. This keeps a fire in place and assists you in cooking. If the weather is extremely cold, keep your mittens or gloves on until you are all set. Many a blaze has been fumbled because of numbed hands. A friendly, large blaze is tempting at evening, but don't overdo it. Small, controllable fires fed progressively are best and safest, even if you must arrange several around you. Stay with your fire until it burns down to a good bed of coals. If you must have an overnight fire, don't have it blazing when you turn in.

## Keeping It Going

A couple of good chunks of logs laid across the coals, with any rocks removed so the logs *touch* the coals, will hold a fire overnight. Lay them so that the rounded sides touch each other but not too snugly. The small blaze will come up between them, and heat from each keeps the other going. Properly laid, this keeps a gentle but warm, low fire all night, and by morning the logs will be barely burned in two or only partially so. Be absolutely sure, even under the strain of survival conditions, that your fire is dead-out when you leave it. I want to repeat here something mentioned earlier. From an overnight stop

When the ground is wet, lay a base of large logs and sticks, and light the fire atop them.

where you have had a good fire and found good conditions of shelter, available firewood and water, be sure you mark your next day's trail well. In case of some second difficulty, you may need to come back!

It is easy to keep a fire going when it must be built on ice, or snow, or wet ground. Melting is slow because the heat goes up. However, if you must build on snow, ice, or wet ground, if at all possible lay large logs or poles for a base and make your fire atop them.

On windy days, find a protected spot and build your fire there.

Think always in terms of using a fire to your best advantage. If a rock wall or small scoured-out indentation large enough for sleeping is present, and the wind is not blowing *toward* it, a fire laid so you will be between it and the rock makes a cozy spot. Try your best to find a fire spot, at least for overnight, out of the wind. Even small midday fires will be far more efficient, and save you much time, if built in a protected spot.

Before laying a fire, think carefully about what you have and what you need. If you need warmth all

Two green logs provide a fireplace for all-night warmth. The logs can also support a pot.

night, build a fire almost as long as you are, designed
in a rectangle, with a green or partly green log on
either side. You can build a backstop for a fire, out
of rocks, or logs, to reflect the heat. Old hands often
build a self-feeding reflecting fire if they are staying
for some time. This is done by driving stakes into the

Build a backstop of logs to reflect heat through
the night.

ground on a slant, and stacking logs one atop the
other at the outside edge of the fire against these
slanted stakes. As the bottom log begins to burn, it
slowly lets another down. A backstop can be built
simply to reflect heat into a tent or against a rock
wall. If wood for backstop is dry, drench it or throw
mud on it. However, this is a lot of work and may
not be worth the effort in your particular case.

## Cooking Fires

For a cooking fireplace, look for flat rocks to sur-
round the fire, so you can set utensils upon them.
Try to find a flat rock to reach *across,* for a skillet.
A small fireplace or pit built with rocks laid in a "V"

Rocks arranged in a keyhole design make two
fireplaces, one for warmth and one for cooking.
Start the larger, warmth-giving fire first, at the
end of the pit farthest upwind. Use coals from
this fire for cooking at the other end.

or a "U," with the open end *toward* the breeze or air
movement, will allow draft in that open end to help
keep the fire going. If too strong a wind is blowing,
reverse the open end.

An excellent technique for a fire for both warmth
and cooking is to make a long pit or fireplace of rocks
large enough to contain *two* fires. Build the large one

at the end of the pit or enclosure *farthest upwind*. Add wood progressively until a good bed of coals is formed, with an ardent blaze atop. Now coals can be raked out with a stick and piled at the other end of the pit. These are for cooking. As more wood is added to the large warming fire, more coals are always ready. Cooking is done with heat of the large fire moving *away* from the cook, and the coals do a better, gentler cooking job than the large blaze.

The most important consideration in efficient fire-building is to start with very small, exceedingly dry and flammable bits and pieces. A man who is hurrying, who makes a tepee of small round branches each, say, half an inch in diameter, is going to have to start over. The same small branches, however, split into halves or better still quarters will ignite far more quickly. Think always of starting a *tiny* fire, and of having progressively larger material to add quickly. But the first and second additions should be of small size, and no large chunk should be added until the fire is blazing well.

**Wet conditions.** In rain or snow, firemaking becomes more important, and also more difficult. Remember that preparing properly to light the fire also becomes more important now. There is nowhere that a fire cannot somehow be started in rain or snow. These times, incidentally, are when that tinder picked up along the way and stuffed into a dry pocket will be tremendously important. Break open standing dry wood, or gather small twigs of evergreens back in under spreading branches. If a sheet of birch bark, or a flat rock that can be turned up with a dry side, is available, set up a shelter, even with your jacket propped by sticks and make your try for a fire under its protection. Now the old-fashioned fuzz stick, split from inside a piece of dead wood and shaved along one edge with your knife so many small shavings curl off, comes in handy. Get just a couple of shavings or twigs going on a dry base and then gently tend it until it starts to blaze.

### Conserving Materials

Suppose your matches are at a premium. You might consider attempting to carry coals with you between stops. This was done in ancient times and is still done today in some primitive areas. For, make no mistake, starting fires without matches, though possible, is seldom quick and easy. The main caution in carrying coals is not to set fire to some of your belongings. Keep this in mind. The easiest way to carry coals is to use your cooking pot, or tin can. Coals left deep in ashes from an all-night fire will hold for hours, if little air gets to them. Place ashes in the bottom of the pot, coals on top, then more ashes. The lid cannot be placed on tightly. But with ample ashes covering coals, they will still be glowing by midday, even if in dire need you have to carry the pot in your hand as you travel. Do not use material that will blaze up. You can in a severe situation cut green bark and roll coals and ashes up in it, plugging the ends lightly with dry moss or punk (rotted wood).

## Without Matches

There is always the chance that you will be in a serious situation without matches. The chief consideration is that though fire-making is certainly not easy, it is by no means impossible. After all, Indians and other primitives lit fires daily for many centuries before matches were invented! Knowing the various methods, utilizing whatever equipment you have, and infinite *patience,* are now your allies. Are you as smart as an ancient Indian? Be prepared for failures, but don't give up. If you are caught at night and in rainy weather but weather not seriously cold, make up your mind to suffer through the night and hope that dry weather comes in the morning. It is very difficult, without a flashlight and with everything wet, to get a fire going without matches, but in daylight you can check out every possibility.

If you have had a vehicle breakdown, or have been in a plane crash, probably some fire-starting items will be at hand. But if not, remember that the electrical system of vehicle or plane, if not totally destroyed, can be used to start a fire. If gasoline is available, tie a rag or anything that will soak up gasoline tightly around a stick and soak it in the gas. Unhook a spark-plug wire. If the ignition system will work, turn on the switch and work the starter, with the gas-soaked rag between plug and end of wire. Jumping sparks will ignite it. *But,* if you are alone you'll have to jump out and be quick to grab it. Better still, get sparks from battery terminals. This is easily done by crossing a wire from one terminal and tapping it against the other. Be sure the wire is insulated, however.

If you do not have electricity to work with, but gasoline (or oil) from plane or vehicle is available, it is equally valuable. If you must leave the scene and travel, find some sort of container and take some gasoline with you, even a pint. Without matches, a few drops placed on the tinder you'll use will catch a spark quickly. Some insect repellents are highly flammable. If you have some in your pack, these may help in starting a fire much as gasoline.

Regardless of how or where you find yourself without matches in a survival situation, first thing to do is take stock of what possibilities you have. Gasoline and insect repellent are handy. If you have a firearm, you may be able to start a fire by using a cartridge or two. But before you do this, see what else is available, and save your cartridges for a last resort. Also, be forewarned that though a large caliber rifle or a shotgun works fairly well, a .22 is at best marginal, for its cartridges do not contain enough powder or enough blast from the small primer. In addition, today's powders are slow-burning and regardless of caliber or gauge, starting a fire this way is difficult. Following, however, is the procedure.

**Using a gun.** First, gather the very best tinder you can find and get it in place. Have dry twigs and tiny shavings also ready. (This is basic for any fire-starting method.) Remove the bullet from a rifle cartridge by working it loose with your knife or tapping gently around the cartridge neck with a small stone. Have a small piece of cloth ready. It can be cut from your clothing or handkerchief—anything you have—but it should be thin, and if you fray the edges it will be all the better. Pour about half to two-thirds of the powder from the cartridge into the piece of cloth. If you are using a shotgun shell, cut away the crimp, pour out the pellets and remove the wadding; then use part of the powder. Be careful now to keep the shell upright so as not to spill the rest of the powder. Stuff the cloth with its powder very *loosely* into the gun *muzzle*. Load the shell or cartridge into the chamber. Keep the gun pointed straight up into the air. Stay beside your fire site, and shoot. The cloth, if all works properly, will fly a few feet into the air and fall back either afire or glowing and smouldering. Catch it instantly and place it upon the tinder. Blow on it if necessary, but be gentle. Add tiny twigs or shavings as you get a small flame.

**Using a glass.** Probably the easiest method of fire-starting without matches is by using a glass. I suggested earlier ("What You Need For Emergencies") that a small magnifying glass, and a binocular, should be in your pack. You may have one, or both, of these. Other glasses that can be used for fire starting are a camera lens, a watch crystal, a telescope sight lens. A piece of clear ice, shaved and shaped and melted in the hand to form a makeshift lens is a possibility, although a difficult one to use successfully.

Of course, making fire with a lens requires sunlight. You might have to wait on that. Bright sun is best,

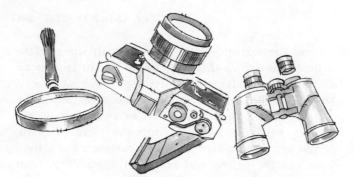

Fire without matches is possible if you have a magnifying glass, a camera, or a binocular lens. Catch a spot of sunlight on the glass, focus on the lower part of a pile of tinder laid below. To use the camera effectively, open the back, remove the film, set the shutter opening to the widest f-stop and focus sunlight through the front of the lens.

although occasionally weak sun will do the trick, given time. Lay out your tinder and other fire materials. Hold a magnifying glass a few inches from the tinder. Experiment with distance and tilt it so the bright, hot magnified spot of light is exactly on the *lower* part of the small pile of tinder. The focus here is used so that as it smoulders the heat will rise to ignite the tinder above. If the tinder is dry and highly flammable, and the sun bright, smoke should rise in no more than sixty seconds. If no flame appears, but smoke does, blow gently on the tinder, or fan it a bit, keeping the glass focused. In a few more seconds a flame should appear.

To use a camera for this, open or remove the back, take out the film, move the shutter opening to its widest f-stop, and set it so it will stay open. It can be held open by keeping the trip button depressed. Focus the sunlight through the front of the lens so that the hot spot is on the tinder. With a binocular, remove a lens and use it. Likewise with a telescope sight. A watch crystal works like a small magnifying glass. Two, with water in between, will work better, if available. If you wear glasses, the more the correction, the better a lens will work. The small magnifying glass does the best job with the least difficulty, and it should be a part of your gear, without fail.

## Flint and Steel

The most common wilderness method of fire-making when this nation was young was striking sparks with flint and steel to tinder. In an earlier chapter I mentioned the Metal Match available nowadays. However, the back of a knife blade, an axe, or any piece of metal will work. You do not need actual *flint* rock, although it is renowned as a spark-maker. Quartz, agate, various pyrites and jasper are all good spark-making rocks. If in some desperate circumstance, you find yourself without any steel or iron object, you can usually discover along a stream bed or dry wash chunks of rock, that, struck together in a severe, down-stroking manner, will themselves strike sparks. The traditional combination has been a piece of flint (or other spark-making rock) struck by the back of a jackknife blade while the knife is closed.

Think of the flint-and-steel method as comparable to the way a cigarette lighter works. There is the piece of flint and the steel flicked against it. Or, if you have traveled in a recreational vehicle using a butane refrigerator, you know that a quick twist of the steel rod strikes a spark against flint that ignites the butane gas pilot light. But these ideal conditions are made almost foolproof because the *tinder,* in each instance, is a highly inflammable gas. It is therefore easy to understand that under primitive conditions the *tinder* is the most important part of the combination. It absolutely must be capable of catching a spark and allowing it to smoulder enough so it can be coaxed into flame.

**Emergency tinder.** This requires the best of all possible materials. It is said in some survival manuals that *charred cloth* is the best tinder because it catches easily and holds a spark. Pioneers often carried charred cloth just for this purpose. But where the person in a survival situation is supposed to get his piece of charred cloth, no one ever explains. Nonetheless you can take a tip from this. Let's say your match supply is dwindling. Make it a point to ignite a piece of cloth, perhaps after your fire is lighted; then when it burns briskly, smother the flame. Put this charred cloth into a small bottle, or a piece of foil—anywhere where it will be safe and dry—and keep it against the need for starting a fire with flint and steel.

Some tinders used by early Indians were dried puff balls (watch for these as you travel), rotted wood filled with fungus growth (it must be absolutely dry), and the dried pith from inside elderberry stems. The unraveled end of a rope may serve in a pinch. Likewise the lining from bird and mouse nests or the totally shredded and pulverized bark of cedar or birch or sage. If you can kill a bird for survival, save the finest

feathers or down for tinder. An unraveled gauze bandage, if you have one, might do. Search your pockets
for lint and collect it. Or unravel cotton threads. Or
cut off some of your own hair. Lift dead bark and
scrape dust and pulverized wood where worms have
worked. If you know you will have to try making fire
with a spark, gather all such bits of tinder and carry
them with you. Guard them very carefully, keeping
them totally dry and laying them out in sun to dry
further when possible.

The spark, or shower of sparks, must fly right into
the tinder. Place the tinder in a small pile on a dry
surface, and, holding the rock and your knife above

Good materials for the flint-and-steel method
are a jackknife struck against a spark-making
rock, or steel against a piece of flint fastened to
bottom of a waterproof match case. Strike with
a sharp downward motion, cupping your hands
close over the dry tinder and driving the sparks
toward the center. When tinder starts to
smolder, blow it gently into flame and add
kindling gradually.

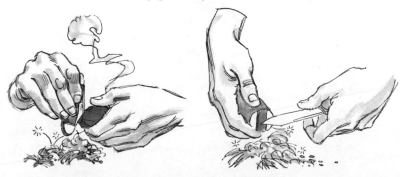

it, strike downward with the knife (or another rock) to drive the sparks home. Some experts hold the tinder in the palm of the left hand and the flint between fingers of that hand. This cups the tinder out of a draft, and when the steel strikes, the spark is sent into the tinder in the palm, where it is gently nursed and blown into flame. Then it is quickly placed in a cup of dead grass or other tiny kindling, and the fire is progressively built up. Remember that you are still far from a campfire, even though your tinder smoulders. Nurse it with all the care you can muster. But don't give up. You may try two hundred times and finally succeed. If you have carried a bit of gasoline from immobilized transport, use a bit on the tinder as an assist. Or, if you can spare a cartridge or shell, use some powder.

The basic problem for most people when they attempt to work without matches is that they are *trying for the first time*. What you should do is *practice* fire-making under the most primitive conditions right at home. The first thing you will learn is that it is extremely difficult. But you will also learn, with practice, how to do it. This assures that when you really need to make a fire in primitive fashion, you not only realize the difficulties, but also have confidence that perseverance will bring success.

## Fire Drill

The flint-and-steel method, next to the magnifying glass method, probably gets the quickest results with the least amount of effort. Indians of various tribes used the bow-and-drill method effectively. Make no mistake, fire-making this way is difficult even under optimum conditions. But you should at least know how —and again, you should *try* it until you succeed, at home, so you will be informed and practiced when the need arises.

The principle of the fire drill is friction. A pointed stick (the drill) is twirled into a notch in a fireboard, grinding off fine powder. Heat from the friction of wood against wood causes the powder to smoulder as it drops through the notch onto tinder already placed there. Some woods are much better than others for this endeavor. Willow, various elms, basswood and cottonwood, and in the desert, wood from yucca are among the best and most common. Others among the conifers are tamarack, cypress in the south, cedar, and balsam. Others will work. But any of those mentioned, if available, should be first choices. And, the drill and the fireboard, remember, are always of the *same* wood. That is basic. These are high-friction woods and one piece worked against another generates heat best.

Various Indian tribes fashioned various types of drills, but in general the *fireboard* was about the same for all. This board must be split from a branch or log. If you have an axe, that is no problem. If you have a knife, it may be possible with patience to whittle wedges and then, with a rock for a hammer, split out a fireboard. Traditionally it is about an inch in thickness, though it can be a bit more or less. Width is not especially important, but at least three to six inches is convenient. And, the board must

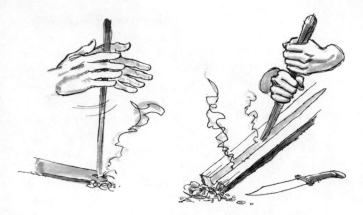

A fire drill is difficult to operate successfully, but when there are no other possibilities, it is worth a try. On the left, a tapered stick is twirled swiftly back and forth into a notch at the edge of the fireboard. The smoldering wood powder ground off drops through the hole onto the tinder below. On the right, the drill is drawn back and forth along the long V notch, driving the wood powder out at the bottom.

be long enough, at least a foot, so you can hold it down firmly by kneeling or with one foot.

If you have split out a board with bark on edges, cut it away and have one edge of the board as smooth and straight as possible. Now gouge out a hole in one side of the board, about an inch in from the edge, perhaps a bit less than that. This is the hole the drill will fit into, so first just get it placed properly and gouged possibly a quarter-inch down into the board. Now cut a V shaped notch in the edge of the board, the V pointing toward the gouged place and cutting into the edge of it. Bevel the notch so it is wider at the bottom than at the top. It is in this notch and below the edge of the drill hole that the tinder will be placed, and in which the powder, ground by friction, and ignited by the heat, will fall.

The simplest hand fire drill used by some western Indians was a slender rounded stick about one and one-half feet in length. It was smoothed as well as possible and its upper end was *tapered*. That is, the larger end fitted into the gouged hole in the board. To make one of these, keep fitting the end of the drill into the hole, forming the drill end so it fits and making the hole so that the twirling drill will rub all the way around except where the notch is in the edge of the board.

This "hand drill" is operated by kneeling on the end of the board, and placing the palms together around the upper, tapered top end of the drill. The palms then are "rubbed together," twirling the drill back and forth (reversing directions with each rub) and swiftly. Meanwhile pressure is put on by a downward thrust, and the palms quickly work downward. When near bottom the pressure is swiftly released, the palms brought back to the top, and a new start made. This requires practice to keep the operation smooth and constant. The powdered wood ground off and heated eventually sets off smouldering as it falls into the tinder, and you can nurse a blaze to life. Often a piece of bark or flat stone is set beneath the board and the tinder placed on it. Thus, when a spark catches, the tinder can be quickly removed and placed under the small twigs and more fine tinder previously laid close beside the fireboard.

Two persons can work this simple drill better than one. They should face each other. As you run your palms down the drill, your partner seizes it at the top and continues. This keeps it in constant motion and applies all possible pressure and constant friction.

**Bow-and-drill.** The bow-and-drill is more complicated, but more easily worked and perhaps more efficient. And, since pressure and speed are the essentials for creating fire by friction, this is undoubtedly the better method. The fireboard is fashioned in the same manner, the tinder placed the same. But the drill, to be most effective, is shaped somewhat differently. It can be as little as a foot long, and need not be smoothed and round. In fact, if it has several sides, six or eight, like some pencils, it will work more efficiently. The grinding end is rather bluntly tapered, to get the most friction in the hole. The upper end is more tapered, whittled down to a rather blunt but pointed end so the least friction will occur there.

The next item is the crown to hold the top of the drill. This can be a stone of palm size, rounded on top and with a hole in the bottom side, or it can be a piece of wood shaped roughly to the palm (like a tree burl) and with a hole for the top of the drill to fit into the bottom side, but not snugly. Your palm will put pressure on the drill by pressing down on this protective socket, but the drill must turn easily in it. If you have any kind of grease, or even candle wax, work it into the socket hole to help the easy twirl of the drill there.

Now the bow is made. It is simply a fairly stout piece of limb that is curved in bow shape. It should not be long enough to be unwieldy, but can be up to two feet. Try to cut the bow so there is a crotch at one end. Cut a notch around the other and attach the bow string securely there. You'll have to use whatever is available. A rawhide boot lace makes a good string. Or, if you have it, a length of nylon cord, or twine. Indians used a thong of buckskin.

The tension on the bow string must be exactly right. It can be adjusted, if you have selected a bow with a crotch at one end, simply by twisting the thong and hooking it with a loop in that end over the crotch. The idea is *not* to have the string tight. The drill is set into the fireboard hole. The bowstring is looped once around the drill about halfway down its length. A good position is to kneel, with the left foot solidly holding down the fireboard. The left hand palms the protective socket atop the drill. The bow, held in the right hand, is drawn rapidly back and forth in a sawing motion. The thong, looped around the drill, thus twirls the drill first one way and then the other. You may find it necessary to adjust tension on the thong, one way or the other.

It is obvious that the motion must be exceedingly vigorous and as fast as you can make it. Thus a stout bow and string are required, and plenty of pressure should be put on from above. To keep the drill steady, wrap your left arm around your left knee solidly. That is the foot that holds down the board. If you are lefthanded, reverse these directions.

Some Indians made more complicated drills. But any firemaker will have complications enough with those described. It is possible, though exceedingly dif-

# HOW TO BUILD A FIRE
## WITH BOW AND DRILL

**1.** Collect extremely dry tinder material.

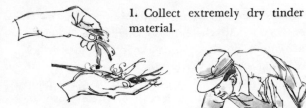

**2.** Cut sticks for the bow and drill on a granite rock.

**3.** Shape the drill to the proper size with a piece of chipped rock.

**4.** Find a knothole to steady the upper end of the drill.

**5.** Make the bow from a curved limb fitted with a makeshift lace.

**6.** Loop the slack in the lace around the drill, and place one end of the drill in the notch of a stick placed over the tinder; with the knothole atop the drill to keep it steady, saw the bow rapidly back and forth, whirling the drill in the notched stick.

**7.** Blow on the tinder to help the spark catch.

**8.** Swing the tinder in the air to give it more oxygen.

**9.** Get a real campfire going by adding tinder gradually.

ficult, to get a smouldering wood powder by propping the end of a small, very dry log of good friction wood atop another and drawing a rope underneath. A notch should be cut into the bottom of the log to hold the rope steady. Tinder is laid exactly beneath the notch and the log is barely propped above it. One holds down the log with one foot, holds one end of the rope in either hand, and saws furiously back and forth. There are two reasons for low-rating this method, as against the others. A rope may not be at hand, and if one is it may be swiftly worn in two.

**Fire saw.** A "fire saw" can be fashioned by cutting a notch in a rounded stick of high-friction wood, then sawing a V-shaped piece at right angles back and forth in the notch. If the rounded piece is split in two, and one half hollowed out below the notch so powder is dropped into tinder placed in the hollow,

A fire saw is less effective than the drill, though it works on the same principle of friction. To obtain the wood powder, saw a V-shaped stick at right angles across a notch cut in a rounded stick of high-friction wood.

a fire may be contrived. Another method used by some pioneers and occasionally by Indians utilizes a fireboard and a stick like the drill. But in this instance a slot about a foot long is gouged out in the top of the fireboard. The end of the "drill" stick is placed in the notch. Pressure is applied with both hands and the stick furiously rubbed back and forth in the notch. The powder formed is eventually ignited, and transferred to tinder. This method is by no means as effective as the drill.

### Practice

Don't wait until dire need arises to see if you can make a fire by these various methods. Try it at home! Practice makes it work smoothly. I do not want to sound too discouraging about these fire-without-matches methods, but it is unfair, and even dangerous to make it all seem very simple. It's far better to be warned that it is not. Remember, when the chips are down you won't be giving a Boy Scout demonstration with all the materials flawlessly made and every condition optimum. This may be for real!

One reason I urge you to try fire-making without matches at home is that by the time you've found out that it really can be done, you'll be so impressed with the difficulties that you'll never be caught without matches! Just remember that fire-making for comfort or cooking is easy anywhere on this continent, even fairly simple in the worst weather, if you have that finest and simplest of all fire-making friction devices—a dry match!

# 10 / *Shelter*

THERE ARE MANY varieties of emergency shelter. The type you utilize will depend upon the kind of emergency that has caught up with you, and *where* you are. In a hot desert location you will need shelter not for warmth, but for shade. In severe cold you need to get out of wind and keep as warm as possible. There are some situations in both hot and cold country where insects will be an anguish and shelter must be selected to fend them off. Insects usually mean mosquitoes.

## Insect Protection

A smudge fire, started with dry material and with green grass or boughs added intermittently, will form smoke to help against insects. But the *location* of a camp and shelter will be most important. Try for a point that runs out into a lake, on the side where an inshore breeze blows. On a seacoast the dunes just in from the surf may be swarming with mosquitoes, but dry sand immediately above high-tide line will have a breeze that will keep them away. In mountain and swampy areas of the north, get up on a ridge to make your camp; avoid the low places. If you have taken insect repellent, the kind I've suggested, you will be in fair shape. It is not possible, however, to fashion a makeshift shelter that is completely insect-proof.

If a plane crash or a broken-down vehicle is the difficulty, here are some suggestions. The interior of plane or vehicle may protect you from insects, and ordinarily in places where they swarm the climate will be neither excessively hot nor excessively cold. However, in extreme cold or extreme heat, both plane and vehicle interior (if not smashed up) may be colder, or hotter, than a shelter you can fashion outside. A great deal depends on what you have with you for warmth or shade. Shade can be improvised under a plane wing or beside or under a vehicle out in the desert. Parachutes can be utilized in many ways. But in severe cold, consider that you may be able to stay warmer in a snow shelter, or one of snow and evergreen boughs, than inside plane or vehicle. Ordinarily you will be staying by the plane or car, not traveling, for this way you will be found more quickly.

## Where To Start

The chance is very good in any of these break-downs that most of the materials you need, at least for a few days—food, etc.—will be on hand. And the chance is that you left word where you were going and will be found. Thus you can take time to make as comfortable primitive living quarters as the materials at hand will provide, improvising with chopped branches or leaned sticks through which such materials as cattails or willows are woven.

However, the man on the move, on his way out or lost and trying to get out, has an altogether different problem. In all likelihood he will use a shelter only one night at a time. He cannot take time to gather food, water, and firewood, cook food, boil water, make up his bed in a sheltered spot, and still have much time left to fashion more than the most primitive, most easily and quickly devised shelter. Next morning he is on his way again and the shelter is discarded.

Remember to stop traveling *early* enough so you can get your work done before it is dark. Base this on the type of terrain. If you must gather rocks or a lot of small switches, like willows, to make shelter, it will take longer by far than it will in dense forests of the mixed evergreen type.

Suppose you are traveling, lost or otherwise. If you have properly outfitted as suggested for a long trip, you will have shelter with you. In plane or vehicle difficulty this would be the case, in the event you deemed it necessary to walk out. If you have a full-fledged backpack outfit with a three or four-pound tent and light bag, you have no worries about shelter. Even without a pack, if a light tent and bag are in the plane or vehicle, you can contrive lashings to pack them with you, and you certainly should. Or, if you must make a choice between tent and bag, make it in relation to *where* you are. In a desert you don't need the bag but the tent would be valuable. In cold weather, you can run up makeshift shelter and the bag is more valuable.

## Tarp Shelters

Let's assume, however, that you find yourself in a situation where a plastic sheet or tarp is all you have. Or, you have one of these plus a light bag. It is invaluable to know how to fashion shelter quickly. Think in terms of very simple, primitive shelters. The beautifully planned, elaborate shelters often pictured for Boy Scout projects, for example, are really exercises in fun and games. They are of little practical value to a man in an emergency and a hurry. Only if you are *staying in one spot* should you spend long hours building elaborate shelter. In some cases it is good therapy, something to do even if unnecessary.

The tarp or sheet, plus a broken canoe or small boat—suppose you have found a canoe or small boat to use to float a river—can quickly become a crude shelter. Tilt the craft on its side, leaning at an angle so there is space beneath. It must be safely propped in this position. Secure the tarp at the rail, or by

Tarp serves as a shelter in many situations. On a canoe trip, stretch it over a tilted canoe and stay dry during the night.

A bough bed is a buffer between you and the cold. Insert branches in the ground, facing the tips in the same direction. Space the rows six inches apart and cover the top with more tips for added insulation.

rocks or a pole tied along its edge and hung behind the craft. Then pull the tarp forward and peg it down or weight it with rocks. The result is a crawl-in shelter.

Always build a shelter in cold country so the wind is broken from the interior. Also, whether in hot or cold country, never sleep directly on the ground (or snow) if you can possibly avoid it. Ground will be cold in the North, and in the desert when you are lying in shade in daytime it will be hotter at ground level than a bit above. Lay boughs or grass, anything available to make some space between your body and the ground.

**Using trees.** A second type of tarp shelter, in big-timber country, uses a large log, hopefully lying so it breaks the wind. The log must be at least a bit higher than your body will be when you lie down. The tarp or sheet is secured across the log and out from it, exactly as with a canoe, and a crawl-in shelter

A large log with a tarp secured on both sides gives protection from the wind.

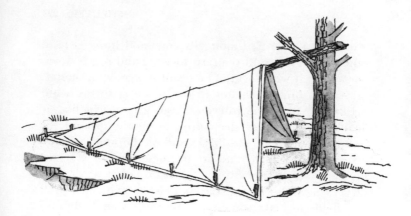

Lean a pole into the crotch of a tree branch and drape the tarp over it, staking the edges; point the rear of the pole into the wind for a draft-proof shelter.

is thus available. Numerous other quick and easy shelters can be fashioned from tarp or sheet. Cut or break a pole. Lean it in a low tree crotch or against a low, stout branch, or lash it about three feet up against a tree trunk. Lay the tarp over this pole and weight or stake the edges. The rear end of the pole that touches or is thrust into the ground, should be pointed toward the wind, if cold, and the tarp brought clear to the ground on that end and weighted, to keep draft out.

A very common and easily made triangle tent of this kind is put over a pole frame. Cut one long pole and two shorter ones. The two short ones are the "shear poles." Thrust these into the ground with the butts at least as wide apart as the tent opening will be; lash the top ends together to form an X at the

Set up a triangle tent using two shear poles lashed together in an X at the top. Lay a long ridgepole into the X and slant it back to the ground. Spread the tarp across the ridgepole, and finish by weighting the outward edges.

top. The long ridgepole is laid into this X and slanted back to the ground. The tarp or sheet goes over the ridgepole and the tent is complete, staked or weighted at the outward slanted edges.

When you cut stakes simply cut forked sticks. Sharpen the upper (long) end and thrust it into the ground inverted so the fork holds the grommet. If you have difficulty with stakes, cut a fairly heavy pole for each side, lay these on the border on either side and tie the tarp to each. If you do cut stakes, and plan to abandon this shelter to keep traveling, take the stakes along. This saves time and effort the next afternoon.

A single pole lashed between two trees can be used to make two different types of simple shelters. Lashed

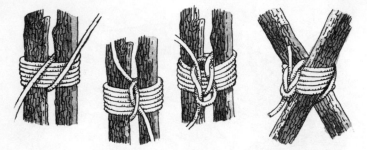

Strong lashings are essential to secure shelters. To join shear poles for erecting tents, lay two poles parrallel to each other. Make several turns around both poles, and one or two more turns of frapping between the poles and around the loops. Join the rope ends with a square knot and spread the poles apart to form the shears.

A lean-to made by lashing a pole between tree trunks and stretching the tarp to the ground leaves plenty of room for a fire out front if you need it.

at low height, the tarp is draped over it, drawn out at the bottom on each side and staked or weighted. This tent has two open ends. It is cool, keeps rain off. But if cold wind is a problem, the simple triangle shelter described above is better. The other type made with a pole lashed between two tree trunks is the simple lean-to. Lash the pole higher up, with one edge of the tarp secured to it, and the other edge pulled back on a slant and staked or weighted to the ground. A fire can be built in front of this lean-to, or in front of the other shelters, if one is needed.

**Desert shelter.** In a desert, a tarp can be laid atop several large sage bushes or other brush and tied for shade. In rocky places without trees or brush, stack up two rock piles spaced as wide as your tarp, each about two and one-half feet high. Lay a corner of the tarp atop each pile and weight it with another rock on top to hold it. Now draw the tarp back to its full length and make a lower pile of rocks for each

In the desert, a rock-and-tarp arrangement provides shade and slants downward for protection against rain.

rear corner. The corners are drawn atop these, and weighted to hold them down. Thus you have a shady shelter, slanted to keep off rain if need be. This type can be used in other than desert terrain, where rocks are the most abundant material. A pile along either side and at rear, banked with snow or dirt, also makes a fairly snug crawl-in shelter.

**Building a lean-to.** If your tarp is large enough, or you also have a sheet, or there are two or more peo-

With a large tarp or plastic sheet, you can build a comfortable lean-to with closed ends. Attach the tarp to a pole lashed between two trees. Lash another pole to each tree, slanted the same way as the tarp, and pull the tarp ends around. Make sure the tent opening is out of the wind.

ple each with tarps, a large lean-to type shelter with closed ends can be made in numerous ways. One method uses the pole lashed between two trees. You secure tarps to it, then drape the ends over other poles lashed also to the trees and slanted out in the same direction as the tarp. This three-sided lean-to, with a good fire out front reflecting heat inside, is comfortable indeed. Wind direction should be either at an angle across or from behind. If you have a rope, you can eliminate the bother of cutting poles by using a rope for a ridgepole in any of these shelters.

Incidentally, many volumes showing primitive shelter go into detail about how to make a tepee. Shy away from this. Invariably, unless much work is involved, it will leak badly down the center, and it is difficult to keep a tarp or sheet in place. Stick with the very simple designs described thus far.

## Natural Resources

Materials from forest and desert can be used to build and add to the comfort of these simple shelters. It may be that you are caught without so much as a tarp or sheet, perhaps with very little to use for lashings. You can still make suitable primitive shelters. Any lashings you can contrive from boot laces or pieces of cloth or string will be most helpful. Otherwise you will have to use twisted bark, tough grasses or reeds, or thin willow brush. Bear in mind that slabs of bark, often shown as material for roofing or siding a shelter, are extremely difficult to peel from large trees in any quantity. Unless time is no object, don't consider this.

**Evergreen shelters.** All across much of Canada, most of the northern U.S. and down the mountains of the U.S. and Mexico where emergencies are likely to occur, evergreen trees are abundant. The ones with the thickest branches, such as spruce, are best for shelter purposes, but any will do. The quickest, easiest shelter is made exactly as with the tarp, by cutting

In an area of evergreen trees, look for one with strong branches to which you can secure a pole. Lean smaller trees, ends jammed into the ground, on both sides of the pole for protection against wind and rain.

Leaning or lashing small evergreens to a ridgepole supported by two shear poles allows space
at the front for a fire.

a long pole, trimming off branches, and leaning it
into a low crotch of a tree, or lashing it, leaned,
to the trunk of a tree. If you are among evergreens,
select a small, thick one, hopefully with branches
coming close to ground. Lean the pole into its
branches and secure it. The butt of the pole that
touches the ground should point *toward* the wind if
it is cold. Now cut small thick evergreens and lean or
lash them against the pole from either side, their
butts jammed into the ground. Lash tops if necessary.
More evergreen branches cut and worked into the
spreading limbs of the small evergreens will keep out
more wind or rain.

Note that the thick spruce (if you used one) that
holds the pole gives shelter from the front. If you
want a fire out front, you cannot use this method, for

the fire would be too close under the tree. In that case, you can cut three poles: one long one, two shorter ones, as described with tarp. If the earth is soft enough, sharpen the ends of the shorter ones, the shear poles, and thrust them into the ground so that the tops form a small X, and lash this point. Lean the long pole into the crotch thus formed, cut ever-

In dense areas of small spruce, lash together the tops of several small trees for a quick shelter. Clear a sleeping place and fill in spaces between trees with branches if necessary.

greens and lean or lash against each side of the long pole. Now you have a fair shelter and can have a fire by the opening.

If you find dense stands of small spruce, maybe six to eight feet tall, you can swiftly make a shelter by pulling the tops of several together and lashing them. First clear your sleeping place by cutting off inside branches. Then pull the tops down and tie them together, cutting more branches to weave easily into the sides and between the small trees, and you can get along. In dense stands of small evergreens of many varieties you can often make do without building a shelter. Simply find the thickest place you can and crawl in. Or where large evergreens have branches coming clear to the ground, cut off a very few and fashion a kind of den against the trunk. Much depends on weather.

One of the most interesting shelters I ever saw was thrown together by a guide in spruce country in northern Canada. He cut numerous small spruce boughs to make his bed and laid these near a big blowdown. Then he cut some spreading, large spruce boughs and set them over the blowdown. With this primitive frame as a base he began cutting more boughs and propping them, then laying small ones for a roof. In half an hour he had what can best be described as a "spruce-bough igloo" with a front opening away from prevailing wind. He slept in it for ten days while we hunted.

A pole cut and lashed, or laid in crotches, horizontally between two trees, with small evergreens

Another simple shelter is made by lashing a pole between trees and leaning small evergreens on both sides. Close up one end with more trees to keep out the wind.

leaned on either side, makes another type of shelter. Fill one end with other small evergreens to break the draft.

**Treeless areas.** Though most emergencies will arise where there is plentiful timber, some won't. In treeless or nearly treeless areas, numerous materials will suffice. Plentiful cattails make a fine shelter, like a duck blind. Invariably there is some bush, log, or tree which can hold them as a starter. Dense willows are another useful material. Tie the tops of a few bushes together and cut more to heap on and weave in. Willow or other brush plus cattails or heavy grass also forms a fine combination. Cut willows and thrust into high, dry ground as if you are making a duck blind. Weave cattails and other willows among these. Slant the ones that are thrust into the earth so the top opening is *narrow;* then you can cover it with more material. If it's too wide, your roof may fall in.

Sagebrush makes a good shelter, and in open country where it grows you may need one badly. Find the thickest, largest patch you can. This will be in a

Willow, cattails and heavy grass can be woven into good shelter. Stick branches into the ground on three sides, slanting them inward so the roof opening won't be too wide. Thread cattails and grass along the edges, and cover the roof.

depression or draw, which is all the better for it will be somewhat protected from wind. If there is a heavy stand of sage that can be left standing for a frame, use it. But cut a large amount to heap around. Any makeshift shelter erected from such materials, or even from rocks, will be best if made in a V or a "rounded V" shape. Support is better this way, and the roof can be more easily covered over.

> When you can't devise other shelter, try the protected area under the lip of a bank in a deep gully.

Mountains, even desert mountains or hills of the Southwest, have untold numbers of small caves or hollows beside a rock or under a ledge where you can find good shelter. In treeless rocky country, rock shelters can be constructed, but except for the man who will be staying there until rescued, they are not often worth the effort. Usually in this country there are deep, steep gullies that have eroded for centuries. Except in very rainy weather, you can usually find a protected place over the lip of such a bank. The deeper the erosion the better, as this means a flood would have to be of major proportions to fill it. Stay as close below the lip as possible. This measure is strictly for severe emergency, such as with a blizzard coming. Otherwise it is not a good idea to hole up in dry washes: in the desert sudden rains in nearby mountains might send flash floods pouring down. A cut bank may offer a good sleeping place, but watch the weather closely. Use an undercut wash bank in the desert for daytime shade only, and travel at night. Do your heavy sleeping in the forenoon. Keep in mind that summer storms are most likely to hit nearby mountains any time from noon on, but mornings will usually be clear.

Keep an eye out for caves, even small ones, or undercut rock ledges that are in the lee. Be wary of ledges that may not be stable or have precarious overhangs above. Watch out for snakes in caves. Large boulders may provide shelter, and evergreen boughs or other materials may be incorporated with them to good advantage. Don't fashion such a shelter too close to a streambank, however. In winter this might be safe. But in summer, especially in mountains, swift rises can occur, even though there is no rain where you are. It falls higher up the mountain and comes racing down.

Even if you have a sleeping bag you will be more comfortable by fixing up a mattress beneath it, and if you have no bag you will badly need some sort of bed. Evergreen boughs make an excellent one. So do heavy grasses, dry cattails, small willows, heaps of pine needles. Size up the immediate situation and see what is most plentiful. Boughs and marsh grass can be used as a covering if you have none.

An old comfort trick used by many explorers and pioneer trappers was to carry a "stuff bag." It was a piece of cloth sewn in the form of a simple sack. Today it can be made from tough nylon or any material that is very light yet will stand hard wear. Fold it as small as a handkerchief and carry it in a pocket or a pack. It can be used if need be for gathering berries, for carrying frogs while hunting them. It can serve when wet and inflated as a water-wing, or as a tote-bag for a dozen different chores on the trail. But its chief purpose among early wilderness travelers was as a pillow. Stuffed with grass or pine needles or even spruce twigs, it works very well and is simply emptied in the morning. Comfort in sleeping is important, and the little bag is a good item to have along.

### Snow Shelters

You may be caught out in an area of deep snow. Shelters of brush and others so far described may be difficult to build. Instead of thinking of snow as your enemy, use it for the topnotch insulation it gives. Air temperature should guide your choice of shelters. For example, the lean-to is most valuable when the temperature is around zero or above. The snow cave, however, should not be built unless temperatures are relatively low, that is, below zero. This is because body heat will melt the roof when the thermometer reads between zero and twenty degrees.

Never set up shelter directly under a snow cornice

In the loosely drifted snow around a large tree, scoop out a hole around the trunk and crawl in under the branches for overnight shelter.

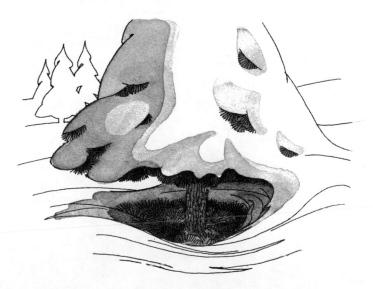

that might collapse. Look for and stay away from possible avalanche paths. Avoid locations where trees are all the same size at the edge of a steep draw. These are sure indicators of avalanche runs.

The kind of snow shelter you now build depends primarily upon the type of snow. If it is loosely

Hard snow several feet deep around a large tree provides warmer shelter. Dig down to the ground in a circle around the trunk, and use boughs for a bed at the bottom. Crawl in and curl up around the trunk for a comfortable sleep.

drifted, and you are in a forest, look for deep drifts around large trees. Crawl in under branches that are low hanging and scoop out a hole around the tree trunk. Use evergreen boughs for a bed and you will have a fairly snug den for overnight. Occasionally there will be a harder snow several feet in depth surrounding a large tree. In this case, dig down in a circle around the trunk, clear to the ground if possible. Cut boughs for the bottom for your bed, and you can curl up around the trunk. By laying other boughs for a roof, you will sleep warm and snug. If you have a candle, you can use it for a bit of warmth, or you can even build a small fire. But be sure to have ventilation through the boughs above.

One of the simplest snow shelters is a simple trench. This requires deep snow. You may find drifts deep enough and still in fairly protected places. Dig straight down, fashioning a trench long enough to lie in. The snow must be firm enough for the sides to hold. The roof, if you have tarp or sheet, is covered, and rocks, sticks, or blocks of snow weight its edges. Or you can cover the top with evergreen branches, or with poles into which grass or brush is woven. If the snow is firm, poles laid across the top with chunks of snow atop them furnish cover. In any snow shelter, however, be sure to select a location where you won't get drifted in without any ventilation. Leave an opening or keep a stick thrust up through your roof or along its edge so you can make sure there is an opening beside it.

If you find a large snow drift that is fairly firm, dig a hole into the side of the drift. Dig *toward* the wind, to keep the entrance both out of the wind and

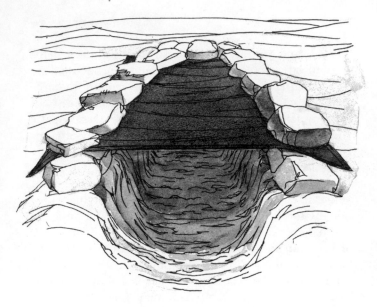

To make a snow trench, dig out an area long enough to lie in. Stretch a tarp across the top for a roof, and weight the edges with rocks or snow blocks.

from drifting full. If the drift is not large enough to make a hole allowing you to get clear back inside, at least you will have a good windbreak and insulation behind you. Place boughs or whatever you can scrounge inside for a bed. And, if possible make a pole crisscross base outside and build a small fire on it. Snow inside will not melt and you can get some warmth. If the drift doesn't have a firm crust, about two to three feet thick, and you are afraid the roof will collapse, two solutions are possible. Gather boughs

You can build a windbreak shelter by digging a hole into the side of a large, firm drift, making room for a bough bed and a fire. Keep the entrance out of the wind.

if available, and arch strong feathered ones inside. Or, remove the snow roof entirely, cover thickly with boughs and then replace snow. If you have no fire inside any snow shelter, you will have ample ventilation with all the holes well plugged. The smaller the space for you, the better your snow insulation will work. Try to avoid working so hard you perspire heavily while making the shelter, or you will chill badly later.

If you happen to find a very large drift formation where there is no avalanche danger from above but where the drift is on a slope, it may be possible to start rather low down, digging up on a slant to form an entrance tunnel. Then round out a sleeping cave in the snow above, as on a ledge. You can form a snow

Under ideal conditions, build a snow cave by digging an entrance tunnel leading to a sleeping area. Use a snow block for the entrance "door" and a stick thrust through the top of the cave for ventilation.

block to partially plug the entrance. A stick carried inside and thrust from your cave through to the outside on the slant of the drift will give a ventilation hole, and it can be kept clear by a thrust of the stick when necessary. This is a rather elaborate snow shelter. It requires *well-crusted snow*. Don't plan on being lucky enough very often to find this ideal combination of drift and packed snow.

Eskimos have made igloos of snow blocks since ancient times. This is a long, difficult process and requires far too much time and energy for the emergency situation. However, *if* the snow is hard packed and crusty, and *if* there is enough of it, you may be able to cut out blocks to form a shelter. Blocks stacked for a windbreak in a U shape or V shape will be better than nothing. It may be possible to dig a trench, then cut blocks to lay across it, on supporting poles. Rectangular blocks might be propped in inverted V shape, one leaned from either side to touch the other, forming the V apex above the trench.

While such methods are valuable to know, don't plan on being able to utilize them. Cutting blocks of hard-packed snow is not easy, and it is not likely that you will have tools to accomplish it. At a stalled vehicle or downed plane you may. Otherwise, probably your only tools will be a belt axe (which will do the job) or a knife (which may not do it without massive expenditure of energy). In any emergency, always measure possible results against the amount of work involved. Save and conserve strength at all times. Ponder the problem: is there an easier way?

A variation on the igloo calls for a trench covered by rectangular blocks propped against each other in an inverted V shape.

All of the foregoing should emphasize the good sense of having a tarp or sheet along so shelter is that much simpler to fashion. As you travel on any expedition, always watch for possible bivouacs. Remember to learn to observe. Here are two big boulders close together beside a river. A few branches staked between them equals shelter. There is a big upturned tree with roots spreading. Tie the tarp to them, or lop some branches and build a shelter with the roots as a base. There is an enormous log on the ground. The tarp, or a few branches, can make a primitive crawl-in within minutes.

I would suggest, too, that you occasionally make an overnight adventure out of actually *building* a primitive shelter and staying in it. On a deer hunt, let's say, come into camp some afternoon and make a nearby shelter for yourself out of whatever is at hand. Stay in it for a night or two. Reading instructions is fine, but there is nothing like the real experience!

# 11 / Signaling for Help

IN AN EARLIER CHAPTER ("What You Need For Emergencies"), signaling devices were briefly mentioned. It is imperative that you know how to attract help, or make your presence known. Once again, if you have filed a trip plan with someone and do not return on schedule, a search for you will undoubtedly be underway. In that event the searchers will have at least a rough idea of where to do their searching. But if you did not leave word where you were going, or deviated from your plan—both serious omissions—then searchers must work rather haphazardly. To assist them, you must do a good job of making your whereabouts known, at times making it possible for searchers to know where you have been.

Signals for help are aimed at two human senses: sight and hearing. Searchers using aircraft are for all practical purposes restricted to picking up sight signals. Ground searchers may be able to pick up both sight and sound. The chance of sound signals being heard is only fair, however, for sounds you can make travel over only very limited distances. In addition, searchers on the ground, especially in hilly or mountainous and timbered terrain, may have difficulty pinpointing exact direction of sounds. Results are amazing, for example, when you are out hunting in mountains with several companions. Ask each member of the party, when a shot is heard, precisely where he thinks it originated. Especially with whimsical breezes in rough terrain, there may be as many opinions as there are people.

## Sound Signals

Nonetheless, if you possess a firearm, and ammunition, shot signals may be helpful. However, do not be eager to fire your gun. It is useless to fire away indiscriminately, when there is no good reason to believe anyone may hear. Save the ammo. Much will depend on where you are. If you know without question that you are in an area where other hunters are certain to be, then a series of three evenly spaced shots may bring someone to your aid. It is a good plan to save your shots until you are sure that any hunters within hearing—camped, for example, or leaving the forest for the day—will be most *likely* to hear.

Just at full dark, when it is too dark to shoot game, is one of the best times.

Other hunters may not realize you have an emergency and will not be aware that your shots are asking for help. However, after dark, three evenly spaced shots may get attention. If you know searchers are out, shots may be helpful. But under today's somewhat crowded hunting conditions, and unfortunately with all too many hunters firing away indiscriminately and missing too much, shots may not be very efficient signals. In a true wilderness breakdown or crash, or when you are lost far from any outpost of civilization, it is best to horde ammunition against your need to use it in gathering food. Whatever you do, don't waste those last two or three cartridges on a wild attempt to make a hearable sound.

There could be an exception. If you actually heard searchers near you, but they missed you, then shooting is a legitimate endeavor. Or, if you hear a chain saw, let's say, or a snowmobile, or any human sound distantly, whether it is dark or daylight, wait until there is a lull in the sound (the saw stops momentarily, for example) and then fire your three evenly spaced shots.

Shouting is usually a total waste. It requires much energy. It can injure your throat if you keep at it. Worst of all, the sound of your own shouts may produce panic. If you know searchers are trying to find you and *you hear them* but you are in dense brush or perhaps injured, then by all means shout. Cup your hands and shout in the direction of the sound. If possible go toward the sound and shout. This applies if sounds you hear are not from searchers but, say, from a survey or forestry party, a group of hunters —anyone passing through.

If you have a defunct means of transport, hammering on metal with tools can send a sound message to searchers or someone passing within hearing. This sound carries much farther than a shout and because it is an *unusual* sound in the wilderness, it may draw attention that shots would not. Further, it does not require undue expenditure of energy.

The best sound signal is a whistle. Signal whistles that blow loud and are high-pitched are available in good sports stores. One packed in your gear, as suggested, could save your life. Blowing a whistle takes much less energy than shouting, and it can be heard much farther. It is also an unexpected sound in the wilderness. To someone not on a search mission, and to someone who is searching, it is a sound to home in on. Whistle from a ridge top, or out in the open, to give the sound waves the best chance to travel. I repeat, use it when you feel there is the best chance for someone to hear.

You must also keep yourself alert for *hearing* sounds. This applies to sighting a plane too. Stay as much as possible where you will be able to hear (and see) help. A snow shelter in which you may have to hole up is insulated from sound. If there are others with you, take turns standing watch, and listening.

It is even possible that by whistling to imitate the dots and dashes of the Morse Code, you can form an SOS message. Conceivably a listener would not know the Code. Nonetheless, evenly spaced "dots and

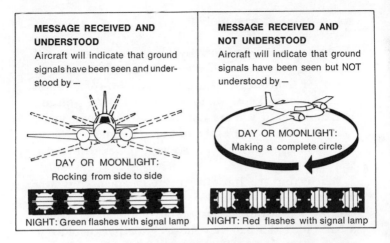

| MESSAGE RECEIVED AND UNDERSTOOD | MESSAGE RECEIVED AND NOT UNDERSTOOD |
|---|---|
| Aircraft will indicate that ground signals have been seen and understood by — | Aircraft will indicate that ground signals have been seen but NOT understood by — |
| DAY OR MOONLIGHT: Rocking from side to side | DAY OR MOONLIGHT: Making a complete circle |
| NIGHT: Green flashes with signal lamp | NIGHT: Red flashes with signal lamp |

When ground signals are seen by an airplane, there is a standard response. If your message was received and understood, the plane will rock from side to side; at night, it will flash green lights in the signal lamps. If your message was received and not understood, the plane will make a complete circle; at night, it will flash red signals.

dashes" of whistling may catch attention because of the peculiarity of the sound pattern.

## Sight Signals

Numerous sight signals can be utilized. Here we should go back to a type of sight signal more commonly associated with travel in the wilderness (see Chapter 6). I am speaking about marking a trail. The traditional method in forest country is by blazes. Suppose you have decided to leave a stranded means of transport and strike out. By blazing your trail well (assuming you have a hatchet or knife) you make it easier for someone searching for you, who comes upon the vehicle, to know where you went. Or, if you are lost, and even if you are not but must walk out, someone may cut your freshly blazed trail and catch up with you. Especially if you are lost, blazes will lead a searcher to you.

When you are initially in an emergency, if you make forays out and back as I suggested earlier, blazes can be used advantageously. You should have at least a basic idea of what they mean. Experienced oldtime woodsmen made small blazes. You should make large ones. The ordinary blaze is a spot where you have hacked a slab of bark off a tree. A single blaze, centered on the trunk in your travel direction, marks your trail. In the traditional system, this single blaze also means that you are going *away from your camp*. Now that blaze won't do you any good coming back. So, you must blaze the other side of the tree, too, making certain that you can see any blaze for some distance ahead of or behind you. On the far side of

Familiarize yourself with the basic trail blazes. A single blaze in the center of a tree indicates your travel directions away from camp. A small blaze to the right or left of the center blaze indicates a right or left turn. When it is not possible to use trees, mark your trail with rocks pointing straight ahead or to the left or right, or use logs arranged like an arrow in your travel direction. Remember to mark the far side of a blazed tree so you can read your way back.

the tree you place two blazes, one directly above the other. This marks your trail *back to camp*.

Blazes give a follower confidence that he is going in the right direction on your trail. He'll either catch up, or meet you. When you make a turn, make your regular "going away" blaze; then below and to the side of the trunk in the direction of your turn (right or left) make another blaze. When you do this, make a "going away" blaze in the new direction on a nearby tree, so that no one can miss exactly where you are headed.

Perhaps there will be no trees large enough to blaze. There are other types of trail markings, many of them used long ago by Indians and known to seasoned outdoorsmen. For example, if there is brush, break or cut sections and in plainly visible places lay them so the cut butt points in the trail direction. If you make a right or left turn, lay one that way, then break another nearby to emphasize direction. Rocks can be used, too. Small, easily visible piles mark the trail. A pile with a single rock on the right side means you turned that way, and vice versa. But make another cairn right away, again to be emphatic. Knotted marsh grass can mark a trail, and you can even indicate where you rafted across a lake or started rafting down a stream by sharpening stakes and thrusting them into earth of shore or bank, leaning in the direction of travel. When rafting a stream, pause if possible quite regularly to leave some kind of easily visible marker.

Incidentally, if you leave others, injured or otherwise, at the scene of a debacle and you start to walk out, bear on your person a written message, contrived even with charcoal if necessary, telling the situation and location of the others. If you are alone, and you can keep a brief diary as you go, do so. It will help someone who rescues you in the event you are hurt or weak, to know when and what you ate, etc.

## Flares, Candles, and Dyes

Hopefully you will have tucked away in your pack, as suggested, some signal flares and smoke candles. There are several types of flares. The large ones are thrust into the ground and ignited. Planes and vehicles, should have a supply of these. The other type, very small and compact, that can be squirreled away and carried while walking is for shooting into the air. There is a small "gun" and several small flares in the typical package. These are available in sporting goods stores, and if not a store manager can help you get them. The gun is a small tube-like gadget to be held in the hand. You fire the flare from it and the experience is about like shooting a small-caliber pistol. The flare streaks upward. You should shoot it straight up, always in the open if at all possible, and from a ridge if in hilly country. It may reach 75 to 150 feet, leaving a fiery red trail behind and a burst of red flame at the top. There is also a "bang" as the burst appears at the top of the flight. Flares can be useful in guiding both ground searchers and aircraft to you. But be advised not to shoot flares in hope. Don't waste this precious signal until you *know it can be seen.* An aircraft passing over can see it.

Ground searchers can see it. But know that they are there before you fire. Otherwise you simply waste a very precious signal.

The same applies to the commercial smoke signals. Both flares and smoke candles that emit yellow smoke, available from the same outlets, are brief signals. Each lasts only 30 seconds or so. It is foolish to waste these items unless you are trying desperately to guide a known and sighted (or heard) searcher to you. It is a good idea to carry several of these smoke candles.

Especially nowadays the primary search mission is handled by aircraft. Thus much emergency signaling is tied to aircraft in some way. Signals visible by aircraft are very common nowadays, whereas in past years they were not. Dyes to make a splash of color on water or on snow are common as standard equipment in aircraft flying into wilderness areas. Water dyes should not be used until actually needed, for they may be swept away. Dyes used on snow in severe cold, orange or other colors, will stay put. These might be available if you are in a wilderness plane emergency and the plane is not demolished. But be sure to use such dyes downwind and not over food. Don't get them onto yourself either.

## Signal Fires

Such modern methods of signaling are not always available, however. More likely you will have to build a signal fire, or mark out a message in snow, sand, or by piles of rocks. Many searchers, and others, may not know that *two* signal fires sending up smoke quite close together were the original signal that someone was lost. Today a series of *three*—sounds, light flashes, fires—is more generally recognized as a plea. Perhaps you won't be able to handle that many fires. In a total wilderness, smoke even from one fire will certainly draw attention—from anyone who is watching. In National Forests and State Forests, fire towers and patrol planes watch for smoke, even in the Primitive and Wilderness Areas. They must. Chances that smoke will be seen are good. Don't try to start a forest fire. This is a bit ridiculous. You can get caught in it, or destroy thousands of acres of forest when you don't need to.

Regardless of your situation—downed plane, stalled vehicle, lost—build your big bonfire in the *open* where it cannot start a real conflagration. The bright fire itself will be useful at night. Smoke is more useful by day. Gather your material carefully. Lay the big fire, but have green boughs or grass or green brush ready. When the blaze gets going in fine shape, smother the fire temporarily with the green material. This sends up a billow of white smoke. Oil from a plane engine also creates smoke. So will tires; this will be black smoke.

Use judgment about when to start a fire. If you are lost, there is no harm in trying to attract someone's attention with a high-rising smoke. The weather will have great bearing on your success. If you are staying in one place, waiting for rescue, the best idea is to have the fires laid and ready—even to coals always going if possible—to touch off the big blaze when a plane shows up distantly. In spruce country you could even set fire to a big lone tree out in the open. You have to prime it first by laying grass and brush in lower branches to get it started.

If fuel is easily gathered, and you are staying put, certainly there is no harm in keeping a signal fire going constantly. The more remote your position, the more attention it is certain to draw from anyone in the region. A big smoke in any National Forest, where a high percentage of lost persons and other emergencies occur, you can bet will eventually be seen and checked by some distant tower man. But it is inexcusable to take chances on destroying thousands of acres when you will undoubtedly be rescued without that. Be sure a fire is out in the open—on a ridge, a beach, a sandbar, a wide meadow—where it or its smoke can be readily seen from the ground or the air. Keep in mind, too, that a bright *blaze* in the open at night, as atop a ridge at timberline as an example, may well be more effective than attempts at smoke signals. Illustrations in books too often show that lovely smoke towering straight up for several hundred feet—but in reality it seldom does. Often the smoke hugs the ground or is dissipated by weather.

Fire and smoke are likely to be most useful and easiest to use in the amount needed when an emergency concerns a stalled vehicle or a downed plane. That is, when oil and gas are available. Consider making some sort of container, even a hole dug into sand or clay, and then igniting oil or gasoline poured over it. The earth holds the flammable liquid but causes it to burn steadily. Stand back when igniting! If no gas or oil is available you must depend on green or damp *fine* fuels—grass, cattails, feathery evergreen branches—to be laid on a good blaze to make smoke.

There is hardly a place left on this continent today where someone won't soon sight smoke, fire, or other sign that a human is in distress. In some ways this is sad, but not to the person waiting to be rescued. Another point of encouragement is that each year a few magazines print the stories of persons who got into awesome difficulty and barely got out, or sometimes didn't make it. However, the reason these stories reach print is that the incidents are so *rare*. So, be confident. Today there is almost "no place to hide."

A vehicle with a CB radio in it, or a downed plane with a radio that still works, is the best survival aid in a poor situation. Be wary of running down a battery, unless a motor can be started to charge it. Almost always someone will be listening and will pick up even the most garbled message, if the distance is not too great. A "fix" on *where* is far more important than what you may have to say. Keep it in mind. Don't pour out your anguished tale. Try to get across the message of *where*.

## The Signal Mirror

Of all signaling devices known in our air-rescue age, possibly the most useful one is the smallest, simplest one, the one least used, and carried, by the average outdoorsman. Everyone, as it is said, talks about it, or knows about it, but nobody happens to have one. This is the signaling mirror. You should have one in your pack! This is not just an ordinary mirror. It is of the type used by the armed services and you can usually buy it in surplus stores or marine supply stores. The ordinary mirror can be made to work, and you should try it if that is all you have. But sighting it properly so the flash can be seen by a plane is difficult. The signal mirror is easily and accurately sighted.

It has a hole in it. This is the sighting hole. You must keep the mirror polished brightly. Sight through the hole, holding the mirror just a few inches from your face. If you are looking in a direction that is

The first step in using a signal mirror is to sight through the hole, holding the mirror a few inches from your face, at the cockpit of the aircraft. Next, look in the mirror reflection for the spot of sunlight shining on your face through the hole. Adjust the mirror until the spot of light coincides with the hole, and you will be flashing signals directly to the plane.

If the sun and the aircraft form an obtuse angle, pick up the spot of light from the sun on your hand. Hold the mirror as before, and sight the plane through the hole. Then tilt the mirror until the spot appears on your hand. Find the spot in the mirror reflection, and line it up with the hole to flash signals. It is easier to catch the spot on your hand if you hold the mirror on the side of the sun and stretch out your other hand below it.

partially toward the sun, so that aircraft and sun are both within your view and the two of them within no more than a 90 degree arc, a spot of bright light will fall upon your face, through the hole. Note that this spot is reflected also in the rear side of the mirror, which also has a polished surface. Sight through the hole at the aircraft, or from an open ridge toward any possible rescue source, and change the angle of the mirror, while keeping sighted, until the spot of light is no longer seen. This means that it is now in perfect alignment with the sighting hole, and that flashes will be seen by the plane or distant observer.

This won't work if the sun and rescue source form, with you at the ground-based apex, an obtuse angle. This would mean the angle between sun and the point to which you wish to direct the flashes is *more* than 90 degrees. Now hold the mirror, again only a few inches from your face, and sight through the hole at the aircraft. But, you must now tilt the mirror more, to pick up reflection from the sun. You can do this most easily by holding the mirror in the hand on the side where the sun is, and holding your other palm flat and outstretched below it, to pick up the spot of light. It can't strike your face now for it will be angled too low, but it will strike upon your hand. Now, continuing to sight on the plane, adjust the mirror again until the spot disappears, that is, coincides with the hole. This operation is much harder and it is a good idea to *practice* from varied angles with a signal mirror so you know how to succeed with it.

Few persons realize how far mirror flashes will carry. For best results the air should be clear and the sun bright, of course, but surprisingly strong reflections are given on hazy days and at least weak ones on modestly overcast days. If you are really "socked in" the mirror isn't usable. It is easiest to send mirror signals into the air. A pilot at a great distance can pick them up. Thus, if you hear but cannot see an aircraft, make diligent horizon sweeps with the mirror in that direction. The flashes can be seen even when you cannot see the plane. Even when you neither see nor hear any aircraft, using the mirror in long sweeps of the horizon can do no harm and just may offer a pickup signal to someone. On a seacoast or shore of a large lake, use a mirror to signal to ships. If you are not lost, but in some difficulty, study your

map and look for locations of fire towers, Forest
Service lookouts. You may discover that one is within
several miles, so you can take a compass fix on it and
aim your mirror signal in that direction. It is a good
idea to persevere with such signaling. Keep at it!
Don't give up.

Let's presume, however, that you have no mirror.
Search your gear, or vehicle or downed plane, for a
substitute. The easiest way to make one is from the
lid of or a piece of a tin can. Punch a hole through
the center of it. If you have nothing to make a round
hole, punch it through with a knife blade in an X,
and ream it out a bit with a small stick. Don't get
it too large. Polish the lid as shiny as you can, selecting the side that shines brightest for signaling. Now

If you don't have a signal mirror, a homemade
one from the lid of a tin can works the same
way. Punch a hole, not too large, through the
center. Polish the lid as well as possible, and
use the shinier side to face the plane.

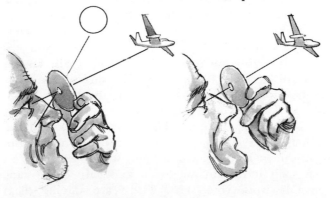

use this exactly as we have described for the signal mirror.

Lights make good signals—a flashlight, a lantern, a torch. The trouble is you are not likely to have these. Also, a flashlight beam even in full dark is not seen as far or as emphatically as the flash of a signal mirror on a bright day. Nonetheless, use lights if they are available and if the situation seems appropriate. You can flash a pine torch by holding it in the open, then obscuring it behind a branch or your jacket hung over a branch. Try such signals, with any light available, at night. But if an active search is on for you and aircraft are aloft, a big signal fire will be more valuable.

## Morse Code

This is a good place, to mention Morse Code. There are divergent opinions on whether you should memorize the Code for the entire alphabet. It is not a bad idea to have this Code and some other signals to be mentioned in a moment folded in a small waterproof packet in your duffle. Whatever your emergency, however, in signaling for help what you are doing is sending an SOS. This is so universally known as a call for "HELP" that probably you need no more Morse Code than enough to form the letters S-O-S. An S is three dots. An O is three dashes. Thus, ... --- ... spells out SOS, which anyone at all familiar with the Code will know means you need help. You can spell it out with a light, with a whistle. You can spell it out by waving a makeshift flag, made possibly from your shirt. There are waving (flag) movements that are universally standard for the Code. The S-O-S signal is made by waving three times on the right, three on the left, three on the right. It is up to you whether or not to try to learn all of the Code. My theory is that the signal described is known to almost everyone, but the complete Code and its corresponding flag movements seldom are. Keep it simple for all concerned.

## Ground Letters

In any type of terrain you can probably contrive to spell out in huge letters on the ground or snow

A pile of brush in the form of a huge letter can be seen by an airplane or other distant observer.

the fact that you need help. Keep this simple, too. You can form a single word or sign: SOS, HELP, or LOST. In an open place on a steep, high mountain this would be visible from the valley below. But most such signals will be directed at the chance of sighting from an aircraft. Bear in mind that the effectiveness of your sign depends almost entirely upon how much *contrast* you can arrange.

> Tramp out letters in the snow as deep as possible, and slant them so the sun casts shadows across for contrast.

For example, all tracks (such as animal tracks) show best when the light hits at an angle across them. This is because the side of a track then casts a shadow. Thus, if snow is deep, tromp out the letters S-O-S, or one of the other words, as deep as possible and so slanted that both morning and afternoon sun will cast shadows *across* your sign. This gives you the best chance of a sign plainly seen from above. However, if there are evergreens around, tromp out your signal, then cut branches and stuff into the letters. This makes a very dark sign upon a light background. Other dark material can be used: willow brush darker than the snow, etc.

In sand or soft earth you may have to depend entirely on shadows for contrast. At a seashore or on a broad, dry sandbar, pour water into the letters to make them darker than dry sand. If you are in rocky country, dark rocks will spell out your message on light ground. If rocks are close to the earth color, pile them up to spell a word and again depend on shadows for contrast.

In dense brush or a swamp, you have a problem in forming such a signal. But be ingenious. If you are staying at the spot, try to clear brush entirely from an area. This will make a spot to catch attention from above. Turn over sod to make letters. Cut brush to form them. Any strips of cloth can be laid out to form a signal. In fact, if you know a search is on, scatter anything of contrast that you can find. Drape rags on bushes. Climb a tree and tie a cloth that will wave in the wind. Try *anything* that may draw attention from an aircraft. Suppose you are in the North and beside a lake that is frozen over. *You* may be difficult to sight. But dark spruce limbs, any dark gear or heaps of logs laid out on the ice will show up handsomely. Spell your appeal here.

Remember that a downed plane or stalled vehicle may not be in a spot where it is easily seen. It is in fact amazing how downed planes can virtually disappear right in well-settled country. You cannot predict where the crippled transport will be. However, make every attempt to clean off upper surfaces so that they will shine or show to best advantage. Keep wiping snow off. Shine any surface that will reflect. Occasionally you can haul sections of a smashed machine out where light will be reflected from them. Again, always think in terms of *contrast*.

## Ground-To-Air Signals

Contrast is important if you use some of the signals that have come to be standard for ground to air display. Almost all airmen will know these. They are of three types, and you will find illustrations here to show the principles involved. One is the Emergency Code, Ground-to-Air that has come into wide use in search and rescue missions. These are simple *symbols*, to be formed in snow or with rocks or brush exactly as described for the SOS. Each symbol has its special meaning. Actually it is not necessary for you to know

Make the symbols of the ground-to-air emergency code shown at right from any material you have, including rocks, snow or brush.

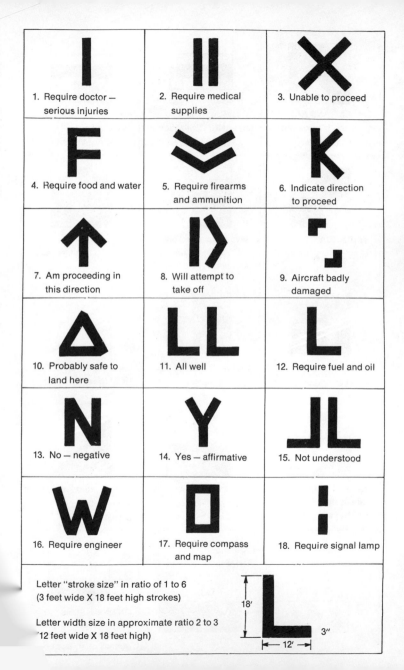

1. Require doctor — serious injuries

2. Require medical supplies

3. Unable to proceed

4. Require food and water

5. Require firearms and ammunition

6. Indicate direction to proceed

7. Am proceeding in this direction

8. Will attempt to take off

9. Aircraft badly damaged

10. Probably safe to land here

11. All well

12. Require fuel and oil

13. No — negative

14. Yes — affirmative

15. Not understood

16. Require engineer

17. Require compass and map

18. Require signal lamp

Letter "stroke size" in ratio of 1 to 6
(3 feet wide X 18 feet high strokes)

Letter width size in approximate ratio 2 to 3
12 feet wide X 18 feet high)

18'

3"

12'

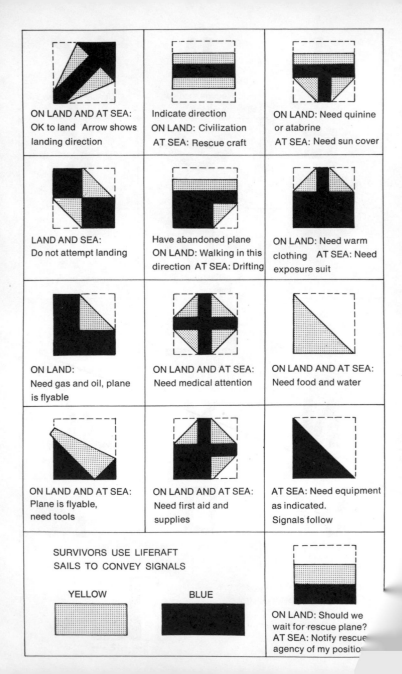

ON LAND AND AT SEA:
OK to land  Arrow shows
landing direction

Indicate direction
ON LAND: Civilization
AT SEA: Rescue craft

ON LAND: Need quinine
or atabrine
AT SEA: Need sun cover

LAND AND SEA:
Do not attempt landing

Have abandoned plane
ON LAND: Walking in this
direction  AT SEA: Drifting

ON LAND: Need warm
clothing  AT SEA: Need
exposure suit

ON LAND:
Need gas and oil, plane
is flyable

ON LAND AND AT SEA:
Need medical attention

ON LAND AND AT SEA:
Need food and water

ON LAND AND AT SEA:
Plane is flyable,
need tools

ON LAND AND AT SEA:
Need first aid and
supplies

AT SEA: Need equipment
as indicated.
Signals follow

SURVIVORS USE LIFERAFT
SAILS TO CONVEY SIGNALS

YELLOW

BLUE

ON LAND: Should we
wait for rescue plane?
AT SEA: Notify rescue
agency of my position

*all* of these. If you do carry a packet, waterproofed, with such material in it (as the Morse Code) the entire list is handy to have. But if you do not know all or have all, by all means know a few important ones. For example, one single long stroke, like a plain Figure 1, means there is serious injury and that a doctor is required. Two such strokes side by side indicate the need for medical supplies. A big X means you are unable to proceed, that is, move from where you are. A large arrow design means you are going to travel in the direction you have made it point. It could even indicate you *have* left in that direction. A large plain K is a question, asking that the aircraft indicate which way you should travel. It is possible an aircraft cannot land but can guide you out. A large F is a request for both food and water. These are the symbols you will need most, but as noted it is a valid idea to know all of them, or have them with you.

The second type of signal system is a series of designs formed by cloth panels. These are termed the Ground, Sea and Air Visual Code, Panel Emergency Signals. They were designed for armed services use, for survivors. The panels are in blue and yellow. It is obvious that most persons in the type of emergencies about which we are talking will not be equipped

The panel signals for the ground, sea and air emergency visual code shown at left can be made by a standard panel with contrasting colors on either side. If you don't have a panel, use a blanket, and cloth, earth, snow, or anything at hand to show contrast.

with such signal panels. However, without any doubt a searching pilot who saw the panel signals simply in black and white, or contrasting intermediate shades, made with earth, snow, rocks, brush or cloth if at hand, would immediately recognize them. Again, only three or four are of significance to the type of wilderness emergency we are thinking about. But the Panel Code is illustrated here nonetheless.

A code more likely to be useful is made up of *body signals*. This is termed the International Ground-Air Body Signal Code and is well known to pilots generally. Here also you would not ordinarily need to know all of the signals, but you certainly should know those of greatest importance in emergencies. Lying flat on your back with arms extended above your head indicates that medical assistance is urgently needed. This is *not* to be used indiscriminately, as for a slightly ill person. It means a matter of life and death. If an aircraft attempts to pick you up but you know it is not safe to land, stand erect and with arms extended upward wave both back and forth at same time, in same direction, across your face. If it is safe to land, squat on your heels, face landing direction, extend arms straight out in front of chest, pointing same direction as your body. If you have abandoned a vehicle or downed plane, or even a campsite, you indicate that you need urgently to be picked up by standing erect and holding both arms extended upward. There are others, as shown. These are of most importance.

Knowledge of all the signaling techniques discussed here will be of unlimited value to you in emergencies.

| | | | |
|---|---|---|---|
| Our receiver is operating | Use drop message | All OK, do not wait | Affirmative (Yes) |
| Negative (No) | Need mechanical help or parts | Pick us up, aircraft abandoned | Do not attempt to land here |
| Can proceed shortly, wait if practicable | Need Medical assistance URGENTLY | | Land here (point in direction of landing) |

Body signals are internationally known and easy to do.

But it is far better to dodge the emergency than to have to use the signals! You cannot predict where a plane may go down. But it is a fact that most of the vehicle breakdowns or bog-downs could have been avoided by caution. Getting lost, or caught without the necessaries, is invariably the result of carelessness either in preparation or on the trail!

279

# 12 / *Weather*

No TRIP-A-YEAR outdoorsman can hope to be a super-expert weather forecaster. But anyone who intends to spend a lot of time in the outdoors should store up knowledge about the weather fundamentals that apply anywhere. In addition it is wise to know in detail the weather signs and patterns of the region you visit the most.

Let me illustrate briefly. In my region of Texas I can expect the period from about mid-June to September to be extremely dry. During that time if we do get a rain, it just might be a real gully-washer. In the April-May period in normal years there will be rains, sometimes heavy ones. After the dry summer, September launches rains again. But from mid-Oc-

tober through to about Christmas we will probably
have pretty fair weather and although late afternoons
may get cloudy, there will usually be a bright hour
before sundown. That knowledge is important to me
in planning dates when I need to shoot a lot of still
or movie film.

Around Christmas and through early February we
get our cold weather; every year nobody believes it
will be as cold as it really gets. Then we'll have a
sudden respite, with too-hot weather for a few days.
This is the very general pattern. But I like to know,
and must know for photo purposes, such things as
when the leaves come out again, as well as when they
fall. Grouse hunters and deer hunters should know,
too. Trips can be planned ahead with such knowledge.

## Weather and Survival

When it comes to emergencies and survival situations, a knowledge of what "it" is going to do after
you're in trouble can be most valuable. You need to
know the general patterns for an area: When is
freeze-up generally due? Is a big snowstorm in mid-
October likely to herald full winter, or is it just a
first one that will be followed by a clear and thawing
period? From which direction are the prevailing winds
here? You must know what various weather *signs* mean
to the *immediate* future. Long range forecasting isn't
as important and can't be too accurately doped anyway.

I'd like to give you two examples. First, a general
pattern valuable to know. In the high country of the

western mountains during summer, it is common for day after day to dawn beautifully clear, crisp and cloudless. If you are not filled in on high-country summers, you might start off on a hike with no jacket, no rain-jacket, or no poncho tied behind the saddle. But the mountain-wise outdoorsman knows that he had better get his fishing or hiking or riding or picture-taking done before noon, or two p.m. at the latest.

By mid-morning fluffy white (cumulus) clouds will begin to appear. Between noon and two as a rule little showers hit the high slopes. Some of the white clouds become dark. By late afternoon the real deluges let go in spots. You may or may not quit by dusk, when there is usually a short period of sunshine, often followed by drizzle during the night. Yet the morning is almost certain to be clear again. Mountain tops, as it's said in the West, are "where weather comes from."

Relate this to an emergency situation. The well-informed person knows this pattern is almost certain to occur. He starts traveling very early, and if the weather picture begins to build as described, he gets into shelter or begins to fix shelter and get his cooking done during midday or early afternoon. What might fool you is that some of the sky may still be lovely blue, with big cumulus clouds drifting. In fact, only small showers may occur. But up a canyon a black cloud might be moving down toward where you are. They come along swiftly in the mountains and severe storms are often upon you before there's time to get a rain suit out.

Now for a second, more specific example. You are anywhere on the east slope of the Rockies, not necessarily in the mountains. You could be way down in west Texas or eastern Wyoming. It is fall. The day is almost balmy, with a small breeze from the southwest. But presently you notice the breeze is switching directions, to the west and then around to the northwest, and there are a few little clouds that old hands sometimes call "marc's tails"—little whitish skeins—in the west and northwest. They multiply. The northwestern horizon soon loses its blue. The wind rises steadily and now is definitely from the northwest and north. All these signs are yelling at you to get under cover. This could be a fake, but in fall nine times out of ten it signals a howling blizzard within a few hours. It may pass quickly, that is, after one severe day.

The weather on this east slope all the way down to the Texas and Mexico Gulf Coast originates in the Northwest and sweeps southeast. Fronts in fall are numerous and commonly move fast—furiously, too. I have seen the temperature on a still, sultry, overcast fall day drop 50 degrees in a few hours with a whistling norther in progress. This could be serious for you. But knowing the signs gives you time to make your shelter and secure it well against the blow, and probably the snow.

On either seacoast weather patterns may differ from those within the entire interior of the U.S. and Canada, because of proximity to the oceans. Most emergencies will occur in the interior simply because it is so much larger, has more outdoorsmen moving in it, and contains the major share of wilderness. If you could carry a barometer, you would have good odds on weather-forecasting anywhere. But this isn't possible. So, most of the signs you should know concern wind and clouds.

## Clouds

My feeling is that wind direction is a more accurate indicator than clouds, for the simple reason that many cloud formations are complex and confusing. But although one type blends into another as weather changes, and a lost or stranded person has enough to do to keep himself together without trying to dope out the intricacies, some cloud knowledge is certainly necessary.

We've already mentioned the big, fluffy white *cumulus* clouds. In most regions they are common in warm-to-hot weather. They build from none or few in morning to many towering ones in the afternoon, and may bring high-altitude storms from noon on. At lower altitudes they usually bring thundershowers, or at least portend them, by late p.m. to night. A darkening section of sky, in any direction, among such clouds indicates spotty or widespread storms.

If there are *nimbus* clouds, you'll know it. They are very low and without special form, in large dark masses or overcasts. Ordinarily when they are present it is already raining or snowing or will shortly. *Cirrus* clouds are wispy and white, bits of fair-weather clouds blown to feathery designs by high-altitude breezes. But

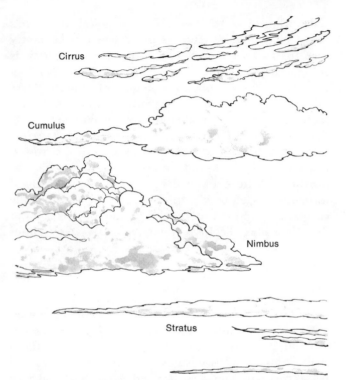

Basic cloud formations. Wispy, high-altitude cirrus clouds mean fair weather. Fluffy, white cumulus clouds may bring high-altitude storms in the afternoon, or evening thundershowers in lower altitudes. Lower, dark and stormy nimbus clouds appear in rainy or snowy weather. Long, low-altitude stratus clouds mean that rain or snow conditions are not far off.

watch these closely. They are the so-called "mare's tails," and if their numbers grow you can be pretty sure that within a few hours to a day something is going to happen, rain or snow. *Stratus* clouds look like the name sounds, long, low banks of clouds. These may not immediately bring rain or snow, but they indicate that such conditions are "making up."

Again, cloud formations are constantly changing, so that combinations such as stratocumulus, cirrostratus, etc., appear. A study of these evolutions can be puzzling. I believe a knowledge of the four basic cloud formations is enough. Otherwise, in an already difficult situation you can become more confused. *Wind direction,* plus the four cloud types, gives you about all the clues you need.

## Wind

Of course, what the barometer is doing is important: rising, falling, doing either swiftly, or slowly, or holding steady. You can't guess too accurately about that, although if you study a barometric pattern at home you will know by sky and wind "feel" what it is doing. If you know the direction from which the *prevailing* winds come, *at that time of year,* in the region where you are, you will know that most hard storms also originate from that direction.

Over most of the continent, almost without fail, a modest wind from the southwest which stays there indicates that counting *from the time it begins,* your chances are good for at least 24 hours of fair weather.

This is regardless of what the barometer is doing. But, the longer it continues, the closer you are to a change and probability of rain. Watch the clouds, and if the southwest wind direction remains constant for three days, you'd better be prepared for bad weather. Tornados generally move from southwest to northeast. This is a severe storm situation, and usually occurs in summer during "thunderstorm weather."

If the wind from the southwest begins to creep around to the west, you can be assured of clear and probably cooler weather for a time. This ordinarily occurs during the bad weather that has come from the southwest, and brings clearing. However, in many areas and at several periods during the year, a wind from the southwest without a storm that moves to the west and keeps right on going to the northwest is telling you that you may get a heavy storm. It might bring one of those early snows, or a driving rain. But a husky blow from the northwest that brings rain or snow, a wind that stays in the northwest or around toward north and whistles right along can be depended upon in most cases to spend itself in one to two days. Following it, clear weather generally appears. A steady, gentle wind from the northwest indicates stable weather for as long as no velocity or direction change occurs.

Probably the most definite sign admonishing you to watch closely and be ready to keep to cover is a wind anywhere from the *east,* anytime of year. Any eastern orientation, from southeast to northeast, invariably means the barometer is falling and that rain or snow is on the way. An east wind is usually damp. From the southeast it will bring rain quite soon. In winter an east wind will probably become higher and carry damp, heavy snow. A storm from the northeast is one of the most miserable; in winter after the storm is finished and when the wind stays there, the cold is bitter and damp.

Conversely, a winter storm from north or northwest may be severe but ordinarily is not as humid or damp, cold but bearable. My rule always is to start hunting cover on a wind from any point of the east. I am also very wary of any shift counterclockwise. This almost certainly indicates bad weather coming.

## Natural Signs

In all natural phenomena, no rules are absolute. A friend of mine, a weather hobbyist, says, "You have to remember that weather is *big*, and all over, and can get mixed up." How true!

A ring around moon or sun, for example, is the oldtimer's indication of rain, but that will not always be correct. Nonetheless, there's at least a 60-40 chance. My mother used to tell me stories about an old Irish uncle of hers who was a sailor. He, like thousands of seamen, used the rhyme: "Red sky in the morning, sailors take warning; red sky at night, sailor's delight." This refers to dawn and sunset, and it holds true most of the time.

In the mountains take great care not to misinterpret air currents. In canyons and valleys they are whimsical and do not necessarily indicate steady wind direction. Old mountaineers often say a wind is "blow-ing from every direction" except up on top. During fair spells air current drift in mountains is usually downhill or down-canyon in the forenoon, reversing toward evening. A switch is a clue that a storm may be nearing. Fog that lies low to the ground in canyons at dawn, in crisp air, will usually disappear as the sun rises. A high overcast at dawn may burn off, but keep a check on wind direction and shift. If there is fog *and* drizzle at dawn, prepare for a possible all-day of the same.

Grass wet with dew at dawn presages a pleasant day. Dawns without dew and with the air still and hot but dry, mean you should watch for a storm. Treat frost on grass the same way. If nights are still and each morning there is frost lying everywhere, you can bet the day will at least start off fair and pleasant. But if during frost-time you awake to find none, watch for storms.

Many signs can be misinterpreted. We stated earlier that stratus clouds generally mean rain or snow is shaping up. But you have to check the height of clouds, too. A general rule is that high clouds give you time to anticipate storms, low ones mean hurry up. White clouds are gentle, dark clouds can be mean. Rain clouds moving in on you whose bottoms are shaped like the bottom of an egg carton and are a dirty gray color mean hail is as likely as rain. High, thin stratus clouds commonly appear at dawn even though the previous evening has been clear. They may cover much of the sky. This is not too disturb-ing. Chances are that by nine o'clock they will have dissipated. If you have experienced a bad winter storm, and then the wind from the north or northwest suddenly dies toward sunset, and the sky becomes clear, this means clearing weather—but it may also mean a real plunge of the thermometer. Get the fire stoked.

Campfire smoke that rises straight up indicates clear weather, but smoke drifting about near the ground probably means an oncoming storm.

There are several other signs all about you in the wilderness that help in anticipating weather. One of the oldest known and checked by woodsmen is what the smoke from a campfire does. If it rises straight up, the weather will be clear. If it is a low smoke shifting helter-skelter, and blowing or drifting close to the ground, it is an almost sure sign of an oncoming storm. Old hands also observe tree leaves on the deciduous trees, during the months previous to their falling. The leaves of all trees in a given area lie naturally with surfaces upward as influenced by the prevailing winds for that region. When leaves show their undersides, you know immediately that this is not a prevailing situation and may well indicate that a storm is on the way.

These and other natural signs are probably not of such practical use to the person in emergency as they are to an outdoorsman who is not under stress. I refer to such phenomena as sounds carrying loudly and for long distances when storms are brewing. There are not very many sounds of consequence that a man lost or stranded in the wilderness is likely to hear. But you might keep in mind that during pre-storm periods, especially when the air is still, you certainly can hear sounds like traffic noises, chopping of a camp axe, a sawmill or chain saw, and others that may mean help, much more plainly than during fair, clear weather. Odors are more easily detected during pre-storm periods. Except for a possible whiff of smoke that may mean help, this too is not very important in my view, so far as survival is concerned. However, there is a bare chance that you may be able to smell game, or certain food plants better at such times.

A common indication of fair weather is the sign of myriad spider webs on grass in the morning. In general, though storms do have profound effects upon wildlife, I do not believe these really help you out of difficulty. That is, you are not likely to see enough of such effects to assist to any extent in forecasting weather.

## Animal and Bird Signs

It is interesting nonetheless to observe such signs. Deer, for example, may feed intently before a storm. The trouble is they may also feed intently at any other time. Moose feed heavily previous to a storm, but you are not likely to see any great number of moose, and if a moose is sighted feeding, who knows, it just may be hungry and not the least bit storm conscious. Don't make too much out of these signs. They can be misleading.

In western mountains where they are abundant, however, elk are good weather forecasters during that period in fall just prior to the onset of the bad early-winter storms. They seem to feel such storms on the way and head down from their high meadows toward winter range. Though many writers have touted mule deer as being as infallible a sign as elk in this regard, don't you believe it. Thousands of mule deer do spend their summers up at timberline. And all high-country mule deer do make a vertical migration to lower-altitude winter range. But they seem to have an uncanny feeling for distinguishing between a "freak" early storm and the real onset of winter. Often it takes a lot of snow already on the ground up high to launch the downward migration of mule deer. By the time they're moving, you've already had it! Don't depend on them.

Waterfowl and other migratory birds are a better indication. If in woodcock country, for example, such as New England or the northern Great Lakes region, you discover some morning that woodcock are flushing from all around you as you walk, where none had been the previous evening, be assured that they have tumbled in during the night from farther north. The ground has frozen hard up there and they can't probe with their long bills for earthworms. Cold weather is moving south. Skeins of geese heading south, even in clear weather, should warn you of approaching severe weather. Ducks are not quite as sensitive, but watch them nonetheless.

Mourning doves leave on a southern move in autumn at even the slightest cool spell or approach of storms. Bandtailed pigeons of the Rockies and western Coast Ranges are also extremely sensitive to oncoming storms and fly south in loose groups. However, remember that no wildlife forecasts weather more than a few hours in advance. None is ever as concerned about it as you have to be, and if you spend your time watching the wildlife instead of the clouds and the wind, you are concentrating on the least important matter—so far as *survival* is concerned. A bear, like the proverbial groundhog, may be out of den or going to a den too early or too late. If you tried to predict weather by its antics you'd indeed be wasting your time.

## Travel Rules

There are a few more rules concerned with weather that you must obey. When a hard storm is brewing, even if you are not certain but are suspicious, by all means stop where you are. Gather wood, build a shelter. Prepare to ride it out. In spring or summer such storms are not as troublesome or long-lasting as in fall and winter in the northern latitudes, when much snow and severe cold may arrive. Don't try to beat a storm like that. Make yourself as secure and comfortable as you can, and stay right there until the weather changes again. Convince yourself all over again that you are *not in a hurry*. Rushing in this case can kill you!

In hot desert terrain, never travel during the day. Even in searing summer weather the deserts invariably become cool in the evening. When the sun is low, begin your trek. If possible make for a specific destination, one you can reach before full dark. Then, arise in the predawn light and make for another reachable goal, hopefully, before the heat arrives. During desert travel at both times, beware of snakes. They, too, do most of their moving around in the cool periods and at night.

During severe thunderstorms when lightning is crackling nearby, stop immediately, shelter or none, and get low to the ground. Shy adamantly from shelter beneath large, lone trees, or for that matter any tall timber. Low brush or no cover is better, even if you get wet. If you are camped beneath tall trees and a hard thunderstorm rolls in, leave your axe and other metals at camp, grab tarp or rain suit and get into low, dense conifers or brush. Most severe thunderstorms occur during summer anyway, and seldom last long. You can dry out and get warm later.

Violent windstorms are quite common in summer over much of the continent. Most are brief. If you

The best lightning shelter is the lowest cover.
If you are caught in an electrical storm, don't
settle down under a large tree but look for an
open area, stay close to the ground, and still.

are in any water craft, get ashore immediately. On
a lake, keep the prow if at all possible straight into
the wind until you ground. When traveling on water
or land, get away from trees. Stay low in brush, or
beneath rock ledges or comparable cover if you can
possibly reach such a spot. The tornado and cyclone
are something else. Your chances of having to deal
with one, in most regions of this continent where survival situations occur, are not large. A cave or a cut-
bank, with opening facing toward the northwest, or

a deep gully or wash running on a northeast-southeast slant, is the best you can hope for. No one can advise you further. You just have to trust to luck.

In closing, I believe the truly important rules for survival can be summarized very simply. Be sure someone knows where you are going and when you expect to be back. Know how to use both map and compass, and treasure both as your life, which they may well be. On every jaunt, from that impetuous short trek near camp or car to a full-fledged wilderness trip, go prepared materially and mentally for trouble. Know your own country, and study beforehand the facts about strange terrain where you're going. Know your water sources, the wild foods where you'll be, the how-to of fires and shelters. On every trip, even into surrounding fields, constantly practice observation in the outdoors until you see, hear, smell and are aware of everything around you.

Then, if you meet trouble head on, don't buck the weather but bend to its will, for it's always going to do something, such as get better. And, without any question most important of all—keep your cool! Upon those three words depends the successful unraveling of all the problem threads leading to your survival!

# *Index*